LOS ALAMOS

Joseph Kanon

LOS ALAMOS

WHEELER
PUBLISHING, INC.
ROCKLAND, MA

★ AN AMERICAN COMPANY ★

Published in Large Print by arrangement with Broadway Books, a division
of Bantam Doubleday Dell Publishing Group, Inc. in the United States and
Canada.

Wheeler Large Print Book Series.

Set in 16 pt Plantin.

Library of Congress Cataloging-in-Publication Data

Kanon, Joseph.
   Los Alamos / Joseph Kanon.
      p. (large print) cm.(Wheeler large print book series)
   ISBN 1-56895-506-5 (hardcover)
   1. World War, 1939–1945—New Mexico—Los Alamos—Fiction.
2. Atomic bomb—New Mexico—Los Alamos—History—Fiction.
3. Large type books. I. Title. II. Series
[PS3561.A476L6 1997b]
813'.54—dc21
                                                   97-32438
                                                      CIP

For Robin

LOS ALAMOS

April 1945

Mrs. Rosa Ortiz found the body. She was used to getting up with the sun, but this morning she was early, too early even for mass, so she took the long way, cutting through the park along the Alameda, where mist was still rising from the old riverbed. If she had been hurrying she might have missed it, but as it happened she was walking slowly, enjoying the first light. She had not heard it rain during the night, so the moisture on the trees surprised her, and she stopped once to look at the shine on the leaves. The sky was already a sharp cloudless blue, promising heat. It was when she glanced down from the sky, temporarily blinded, that she saw the shoes.

The legs were sticking out from the bushes, and her first impulse was to hurry away and let him sleep it off. *Pobrecito,* too drunk to come in out of the rain, she thought as she passed. But it was a disgrace all the same, sleeping by the Alameda, like the Indians hunched over in the plaza, pretending to sell blankets. Then she stopped and turned around. The legs were wrong, twisted one on top of the other. No one could sleep like that. She moved closer to the bush, slowly pushed a branch aside, then gasped. In that second she took in the head, splotched red from the blood, with its mouth fixed open, still trying to draw in air. It was the only recognizable feature left in his face. But what shocked her was his body. The

1

trousers had been pulled down below the knees, exposing his genitals. Why? Mrs. Ortiz had not seen a man since her husband died and never one in public. It seemed incomprehensible to her, this exposure of flesh. She clutched her shawl and, in a gesture centuries old, crossed herself. This was what evil felt like; you could feel it around you, taste it in the air. The ground itself might be soaked with blood, spreading under her. Dizzy, she grabbed the bush to steady herself, but the branch shook its drops onto the body, spattering rain on his private parts, and she backed away. She took little gulps of air and looked around her, expecting to be attacked, as if the scene before her had just happened. But there was no one. The noise in her head was her own breathing. The Alameda itself was quiet and fresh with morning. The world had not noticed.

She hurried toward the cathedral, her mind a jumble. She knew she should tell the police, but her English was poor and what would they think? The man was Anglo, she could tell that from her shameful glance at his body, and that might mean even more trouble. Perhaps it was best to say nothing—no one had seen her, after all. Someone else was bound to find him and go to the police. But now she kept seeing the body in front of her, naked, exposed. She had not even had the decency to cover him. And of course God had seen her. So she decided, as so often in the past, to talk to the priest.

But Father Bernardo was already preparing for mass when she arrived and she couldn't interrupt that, so she knelt with the others and waited. The congregation was small, the usual group of old women draped in shawls, atoning for blameless lives. Her neighbors must have felt that she was especially devout that morning, for she prayed noisily and sometimes even seemed to sway. Surrounded by candles, the familiar words, the solid feel of her beads, she began to feel calmer, but the feeling of disquiet would not go away. She had done nothing, but now somehow she had the ache of a guilty secret. Why had she looked at him so long? This was what bothered her most. She should have turned her eyes away; there was nothing so remarkable about a man, not even one without a foreskin. But she had never seen this before, and it troubled her that in all that scene of horror, this was what she had noticed. No one would have to know that, certainly not Father Bernardo. She would not have to describe the body; it would be enough to say she saw a dead man. If she said anything at all.

So it was another hour before Mrs. Ortiz approached the priest with her story and another hour after that before he telephoned the police, in English, and a car was dispatched. By that time the dew had dried along the Alameda and the day was hot.

Sergeant O'Neill had never seen a corpse before. There had been murders in Santa Fe,

3

mostly Mexicans with knives solving domestic arguments, but he had never been assigned one. The last real murder, during a jewel robbery, had happened while he was fishing in the mountains. So the man in the park was his first official corpse, and it made him sick.

"You all right, Tom?" Chief Holliday asked him while the photographers snapped pictures. Inevitably, Holliday was "Doc."

O'Neill nodded, embarrassed. "He's a mess, all right. Where's Doc Ritter, anyway? Don't you think we should cover him up?"

Chief Holliday was crouched near the body, turning the head with a stick he'd picked up.

"Don't be so squeamish—he doesn't mind. Christ, look at this." The back of the man's head was crusted over with blood and pulp. "Here's where he got it. The face looks like decoration—maybe a few good kicks, just for the hell of it."

O'Neill was writing on his pad. "Weapon."

"A blunt instrument. What do you think?"

"Blunt instrument."

"Hammer, wrench, could have been anything. Anyway, it cracked his skull. Funny, though, there's not much blood around. You'd think to look at him he wouldn't have any left."

"It rained last night. Maybe it washed away."

"Maybe. No ID. Boys find anything further along?"

"Nothing. They've been checking up and down the Alameda. Broken bushes here where we found him, but that's it. Can't you at least shut his mouth?"

Holliday looked up and grinned. "Not now I can't. Take it easy, O'Neill. Once the doc gets here, we'll haul him off. You get used to it."

"Yeah."

"No wallet, I suppose? Keys? Anything?"

"Not a thing."

"Great. John Doe for sure."

"Doc—"

"Yeah?" Holliday said distractedly, turning the head back gently.

"What about the pants?"

"What about them?"

"I mean, what the hell is a guy doing in the park at night with his pants down?"

"What would anybody be doing? Taking a leak, probably."

"No. You don't pull your pants down below your knees to take a leak."

Holliday looked at him, amused. "You'll make detective yet, Tommy. Sounds right to me."

"Well, then—"

"Look, a guy's out at night in the park bushes. He's got his pants down and his head kicked in. What the hell do you *think* happened?"

"You mean like that guy in Albuquerque? We never had nothing like that here."

"We do now. Pretty sight, isn't it?" Holliday said, gesturing toward the man's groin. "Looks like he's been kicked there too." He moved the testicles to one side with the stick. "A little discolored, don't you think?"

"I wouldn't know."

"Well, what color are yours? Come to think of it, maybe they're blue too. Anyway, they shouldn't look like this. He's circumcised, by the way."

"I noticed."

"I mean for the report."

"Oh," O'Neill said, jotting it down. "Time of death?"

"We'd better let the doc tell us that. You got rigor, but I don't know what effect the rain would have on that. Cold too, last night."

"I can't remember that far back," O'Neill said, wiping his forehead in the unexpected heat.

"This is interesting," Holliday said, poking tentatively at the man's mouth. "He's got a full plate here. No teeth at all. Kinda young for false teeth."

O'Neill shrugged.

"Well, now at least we got a motive. Probably isn't used to them and bit down too hard on the guy's dick."

"Jesus, Doc."

By the time the coroner arrived, O'Neill had already completed the area search. "Shame about the rain. I'll get Fred to look downstream just in case anything got thrown in the river. Like his wallet."

"Yeah, if God wants to throw you a bone this week," Holliday said. "Don't figure on the wallet. Keys, though. Funny, taking his keys."

"What have you got here, Ben?" Doc Ritter said, using Holliday's real name. "Been a

6

long time since I've been called out on a murder."

"Well, you tell me. Careful of the clothes, though—I'm still hoping to get some prints."

"After the rain?"

"Well, I can hope. We sure don't have much else. John Doe with his head smashed in and his pants down."

The coroner looked at him.

"Yeah, I know. Sounds like that case down in Albuquerque. I guess the papers will be all over us, but let's try to keep them out of it until I can talk to the boys down there. We could use a head start."

"You've got the whole police force out on the Alameda in broad daylight and you're trying to keep this quiet? You've got yourself some news here, Ben, is what you've got."

"I don't know what I've got, except a corpse. Take a look at his teeth for me, will you? He's got a plate but not like one I've seen around here before. Maybe he's from back east."

"Who is he?"

"No idea. Clothes don't tell me anything. Civilian, but he could be on leave. Maybe a tourist."

"Yeah, welcome to Santa Fe, where the Old World meets the New. Not too many in April, though, usually."

"Not since the war, that's for sure. I'll check the hotels, though, just in case. It'll give them something to do."

"Maybe he's from the Hill."

7

Holliday sighed. "Don't say it."

"But he may be."

Holliday nodded. "Then we'll have the whole fucking army breathing down our necks."

"Better call post security anyhow. Maybe they've got somebody missing."

"Well, I'll tell you. Maybe post security should be checking with us, instead of telling us how top secret they are and what a bunch of assholes we are. Besides, if they've got somebody missing, we'll hear about it—not so easy to get lost up there, I wouldn't think. Place is a fort. Meanwhile, all I've got here is a John Doe with a cracked skull. A month ago some queer down in Albuquerque gets knifed and it makes all the papers, and now I've got a boy looks like he was up to the same fun and games. So before I take on the U.S. Army and all the crap we usually have to take from our secret project friends, I think I'll have a little talk with Albuquerque and see if they'd like to take this off our hands."

"Suit yourself. They find the guy who did it in Albuquerque?"

"Not yet. But maybe they haven't been looking very hard."

"So it might—"

"I don't know. But I'm going to check it out before I tell anybody on the Hill we've got a dead pansy and by the way are they looking for one. I can hear them yelling now. Just in case, though, you'd better do a good job on the autopsy. Don't want your cleaver work making us look bad up there."

Ritter laughed. "Anything else?"

"Yeah, be sure to check for any anal penetration."

O'Neill, who had been standing quietly at his side, looked up. "What do you mean?"

Holliday laughed. "Tommy, you need to have a talk with your dad someday so he can explain things." Then he looked down at the body, still twisted and pale and dead. "Poor son of a bitch. I wonder what he did to deserve this."

1

Santa Fe gave its name to a railroad, but the train itself stops twenty miles to the southeast, at Lamy, a dusty town in the high desert that seemed to have been blown in by the wind and got stuck at the tracks. Michael Connolly thought he'd arrived in the middle of nowhere. The train had been crowded, a sea of uniforms and businessmen with travel priority and women holding children in their laps, but only a few got off on the sleepy platform. Beyond the buildings and the jumble of pickup trucks that had come to meet the passengers, there was nothing to see but scrub grass and sage until the tracks finally disappeared in the direction of the mountains. The young soldier looking eagerly at each face was clearly meant for him. He looked like a high school shortstop, jug ears sticking out of his shaved head.

"Mr. Connolly?" he asked finally, when

the passengers had dwindled to an unlikely three.

"Yes."

"Sorry, sir. I was looking for a uniform."

"They haven't got me yet," Connolly said, smiling. "I'm just a liaison. Is this really Santa Fe?"

The soldier grinned. "It gets better. Help you with that?" he said, picking up Connolly's suitcase. "We're right over here." The car was a Ford, still shiny under a blanket of dust.

Connolly wiped his forehead, glancing up at the cloudless sky.

"Nothing but blue skies, huh?"

"Yes, sir. Sunny days, cool nights. They got weather here, that's for sure. Best thing about it."

"Been here long?" Connolly said, getting into the car.

"Since January. Straight from boot. Not much to do, but it beats overseas."

"Anything would, I guess."

"Not that I wouldn't like to see some action before it's all over."

"Better hurry, then."

"Naw, I figure the Japs'll hold out another year at least."

"Let's hope not." It came out quickly, a kind of scolding.

"Yes, sir," the soldier said, formal again.

"What's on the program, anyway?"

"First we'll get you checked in at Santa Fe. Mrs. McKibben will have your stuff.

10

Then my orders are to get you up to the Hill ASAP. General Groves wants to see you before he goes back to Washington tonight."

"Is "the Hill' a code name?"

The soldier looked slightly puzzled. "I don't think so. I never heard that, anyway. It's just what everybody calls it around here."

"I assume there is one—a hill, that is."

"What they call a mesa. Spanish for table," he said, a tour guide now. "That's what they looked like, I guess—flat-topped hills. Anyway, there used to be a school there, kind of a dude ranch school for rich kids, I think. Sure doesn't look like a school now."

"What does it look like?"

The soldier grinned, breezy again. "Look like? Well, if you'll pardon my French, like a fucking mess."

Santa Fe, however, was pretty. The adobes, which Connolly had never seen, seemed to draw in the sun, holding its light and color like dull penumbras of a flame. The narrow streets leading to the plaza were filled with American stores—a Woolworth's, a Rexall Drugs that had been dropped into a foreign city. The people too, dressed in cowboy hats and jeans, looked like visitors. Only the Mexican women, wrapped in shawls, and the Indians, nodding over their piles of tourist blankets, were really at home. The plaza itself was quiet, a piece of Spain drowsing in an endless siesta.

"That's the Palace of the Governors," the soldier said, pointing to the long adobe building that lined one side of the square. "Oldest

11

government office in the country, or something like that. Project office is right around the corner."

The sense of enchantment held. They walked through the quiet courtyard of a small adobe house where the only sound was the travelogue splash of a fountain. But America returned inside. A bright, cheerful woman, hair piled on top of her head, was busy on the phone as she arranged papers on the desk in front of her.

"I know space is tight, but he's just got to have it." She covered the mouthpiece and nodded to Connolly. "I'll be with you in a sec." Then, to the phone, "Edith, please see what you can do. He just won't take no for an answer. Give me a call back when you hear, okay? Yes, I know. Bye now." She smiled up at Connolly without pausing for breath. "You must be Mr. Connolly. I'm Dorothy McKibben. Welcome to Santa Fe," she said, shaking hands. "You certainly have picked a crazy day. 'Course, they're all crazy one way or another. I had to get all this together in a hurry, but I think it's all here." She handed him a manila envelope. "ID, ration card, driver's license. No names, of course, we just go by numbers up on the Hill. Local stores are used to this, so you shouldn't have any problem. Try not to get stopped for speeding, though—the police have a fit writing out a ticket to a number. You've been cleared for a white badge—that allows you into the Technical Area, so you'll be able to go anywhere. I've included the army bus schedule into Santa Fe just in case, but you'll have your own car." She raised an eyebrow. "That's pretty unusual around here, so you must be important, I guess." She made a small laugh that said she was no stranger to importance. "Security office will give you your housing assignment up top. I'm sorry we couldn't find anything at Fuller Lodge, but we've got wall-to-wall visitors for some reason, and it couldn't be helped. If any of them leave, of course, we can reassign you right away. Let's see, what else? All mail to P.O. Box 1663, Santa Fe. No other address. You should know that mail is censored. We don't like to do it, but it became a security issue. You get used to it."

"Censored here?" Connolly asked.

She smiled. "Dear me, no. I'm not *that* much of a busybody. Army censors. Off-site. Wouldn't be fair to have someone you know poking around in your mail, and of course I know everybody."

"Of course."

She blushed. "I don't mean it that way, to brag or anything. It's just what I do. That and try to find an empty seat when the general decides to fly out of Albuquerque on the spur of the moment and that means bumping somebody else, who'll be madder than a hornet."

Connolly smiled. "Well, there's a war on."

She smiled back. "You'd be surprised what little ice that cuts at the airport. I wish he'd take the train, the way he usually does. But we'll get him on somehow."

13

And of course she would. Connolly looked at her, surprised at how quickly he'd been taken in and charmed. Everything about Los Alamos seemed disjointed—the train that stopped somewhere else, this city that didn't seem to be in America, and now this good-natured, competent woman who managed émigré physicists and army generals as if they were hungry customers at a church potluck supper. He wondered how much she knew, what she made of it all. A secret project that would help win the war—was that enough? Was that all she needed? According to his briefing, there were now four thousand people at Los Alamos. Mrs. McKibben had been there from the start, settling them in, handing out numbered identities. What did she think they were doing, all these people with unpronounceable names and housing problems, working into the middle of the night on a hilltop?

"Now, if you need anything else at all, you just let me know."

"Thanks. I'm sorry to have put you to so much trouble."

"That's what we're here for." For a moment he thought he saw in her eyes the inevitable question: what are *you* here for, with your car and your wad of coupons? But if she wondered, she said nothing.

"The car. Where do I pick it up?"

"Why, you've been in it. That is, once the motor pool assigns it to you."

"Which they will."

"You bet. I signed the papers."

14

They drove for almost an hour before they got to the long twisting road up the mesa. It was graded and paved now but still had all the debris and scattered equipment of a permanent construction site. Bulldozers and backhoes perched at the edge of hairpin curves, and halfway up they passed a car awaiting rescue, one of its thinly patched tires finally done in by too many rocks and baked-over ruts. Once the road had all been dirt, a glorified mule track for pack trips up to the school, and even now it looked temporary and risky, ready at any moment to be reclaimed by scrub. It must be a hell of a drive at night, Connolly thought as he watched the soldier negotiate the curves, pulling hard at the wheel, an amusement park ride.

The landscape changed as they climbed, sagebrush and stunted junipers giving way to taller piñons and alpine trees. The air smelled fresh, as if it had been rubbed with astringent, and the bright blue sky went on forever. Connolly felt the alertness of higher altitude, awakened from Santa Fe's timeless nap. There was traffic on the road now, trucks grinding up the steep grade or jerking and halting their way back down, and everything moved quickly. The entire hill was on the march. As they approached the east gate, the activity increased. Cars waited to be passed through security, and beyond the fence Connolly could see a giant water tower and the instant city, a jerry-built ant farm of dull green army-issue buildings, Quonset huts, and barrack apartments. They were still building it. The air itself seemed obscured by dust and tangles of overhead wires, noisy with construction and running motors. Men, mostly civilians, darted through the unpaved dirt streets with the quick steps of people who had somewhere to go. Connolly's first thought was that a whole college had somehow been dropped accidentally into an army camp. While Santa Fe dreamed on below, up here in the high, cool air, everything was busy.

They passed through the tollbooth checkpoints and parked just outside the Technical Area, a group of buildings surrounded by yet another high wire-mesh fence with two strands of barbed wire running along the top. Connolly glanced up at the watchtowers, where bored MPs gazed out toward the mountains. It was an indifferent concentration camp, too cheerful to inspire any alarm. Girls in short dresses and sweaters, presumably secretaries, passed through the fence, barely flashing badges at the young guards. The two largest buildings were long barracks of offices, connected by a second-story covered passageway over the main road, which gave the town its own form of grand portal. It was late afternoon, and buses were filling with day laborers for the trip back home, down the mesa. Connolly noticed a busload of Indian women, with their stern faces and braided hair, pulling away toward the gate. In the most secret place in the world, there was maid service.

Connolly and his bags were deposited at the

security office with Lieutenant Mills, tall, pencil-thin, and prematurely balding in his twenties, who smiled nervously and kept glancing away, as if he wanted to examine his new colleague from an angle before meeting him head on.

"Look, we've got a lot to go over, but General Groves wants to see you right away, so it'll have to wait. I'll show you around afterward. Colonel Lansdale's away, as usual, so it's just us. And the staff, of course."

"How many?"

"Altogether twenty-eight military and seven civilians in G-2, but only four of us here."

"Not a lot, then."

"Well, we've never had any security problems before."

"Do you have one now?"

Mills looked at him and took the bait. "I assume that's what you're here to find out."

"But you haven't been told?"

"Me? I just run the bodyguards. They don't have to tell me anything."

"Who gets the guards?"

"All the top scientists—Oppie, Fermi, Bethe, Kistiakowsky. Anyone considered vital to the project who needs protection outside."

"Or surveillance."

This time he didn't rise to it. "Or surveillance."

"That must make you popular."

"The groom at every wedding."

Connolly laughed. "Yeah, I'll bet. Well, let's see the boss. What's he like, anyway?"

17

"Straight shooter," Mills said, leading him out of the building. "Built the Pentagon in a year. Made this place out of nothing. Does drink, doesn't smoke. Clean living. No detail too small."

"That easy, huh?"

"Actually, he's all right. This business with Bruner's got him spooked, though, so give him a little room."

"Generals are all alike."

"Just like happy families."

Connolly smiled. "You've been to school."

"Here we are. Mind your head," he said, opening the door.

Inside was a plain anteroom, barely big enough for the desk and the pink middle-aged woman who fluttered behind it.

"Mr. Connolly? Thank goodness you're here. The general's got a plane to catch, and he's been asking for you all afternoon. I'll just tell him—"

But there was no need, because the door behind her was opened by a big man in khaki who seemed to fill the entire doorframe, absorbing the space. He was not sloppy—he was tucked in as neatly as a hospital corner at inspection—but he had the pudgy flesh of an overweight businessman and his large stomach strained at his belt. There were damp patches under his arms, and Connolly imagined the Washington summers were torture for him. The overall effect was boyish, like someone who had ballooned out at puberty and couldn't, even now, pass up a jelly doughnut.

But the mustache in the middle of his round soft face was surprisingly trimmed and small, the borrowed look of a thin clerk.

"Good, you're here. Connolly, right?"

"Yes, sir."

He handed a sheaf of papers to the woman. "We haven't got much time, so let's not waste any. I've got to catch a plane in Albuquerque, and it's a heck of a drive getting there. Betty, you'll make sure the car's ready? These are all okayed and ready to go. Be sure you get copies of the first two to Dr. Oppenheimer tomorrow—he's been waiting. I'll phone you from Washington about the plumbing contracts. Connolly?"

The office was simple, about the size of a large dormitory room, with a window looking out onto the busy main street and the Tech Area fence. There was nothing personal on the walls, just a photograph of Roosevelt and a map of the country, and the desk, piled with folders and contracts and a picture of a woman with two little girls, could have been that of any bureaucrat. Only the two black telephones, a wartime luxury, suggested any importance. Connolly knew instinctively that his real office in the Pentagon was probably no different—plain, pared down, as if he were determined to remove anything that could distract him from the job. In the wastepaper basket at the side of the desk Connolly saw the incongruous shiny brown of a Hershey bar wrapper.

"Sit down," he said, gesturing to the only chair. "Please. I apologize for not seeing you in Washington, but I was out on the road, as usual. They say the war's winding down, but I don't see it. Now. You've been briefed?"

"On Karl Bruner's death, yes."

Even the sound of the name seemed to make him uncomfortable.

"Yes," he said, throwing a folder on the pile and resting his hands on the back of his chair. "First time anything like this has happened on the project. Terrible thing, any way you look at it. The question is, how do we look at it?"

"Sir?"

"I mean, is there more here than meets the eye? Less? Do we have a problem?"

"Well, you've got a dead body."

"Correction. The Santa Fe police have a dead body. What we've got is a missing security officer. That could be a heck of a lot more serious."

"Any idea how serious?"

Groves glared for a minute, then sighed. "No. Maybe we don't even have a problem. Maybe it was just—something that could happen to anyone. Maybe it doesn't have anything to do with the project or his being on the Hill. Maybe. But we need to be sure. And we're going to be." He stopped and looked straight at Connolly. "I've seen that look a million times before, so don't waste it. Groves going off the deep end again. Spies under the bed. Paranoid. In fact," he said, smiling a little, "I can almost guarantee you that's what you'll hear from my friend Dr. Oppenheimer. Says it to me all the time. But sometimes I think

20

Robert's too trusting for his own good, so where do we draw the line? I can't change the way I feel—somebody's got to worry about things. Right from the start people here treated security like a joke. They're brilliant men, I'm the first to say it, but sometimes they're like kids—irresponsible, you know, maybe even looking for a little trouble. Some of them used to play pranks with the mail—can you imagine that? Grown men? They used to cut holes in the fence just to see if they could get in and out without anybody noticing. Grown men. *Brilliant* men. So somebody's got to play principal, and I guess that's me. I don't care what anyone says so long as the project's safe."

He stopped suddenly, looking a little surprised at himself for having run on.

"I'm not a policeman," Connolly said, a question.

"I don't want a policeman. Tommy McManus tells me you're a good man and I can trust you. If Tommy says it, that's it. He doesn't know how you ended up at OWI in the first place. He also tells me you can snoop around without upsetting the horses."

"That why you wanted a civilian?"

Groves smiled. "Partly. The scientists are allergic to uniforms. It's very important to keep things running smoothly now. We're coming to the end of the project. I've got a lot of nervous types up here—sometimes I think the smarter they are, the more nervous they are. You never know what's going to set them off. I'm not going to stand for anyone running

21

around digging up dirt that doesn't mean a thing. We take care of ourselves. Do you know how many security incidents we've investigated since this project began? Over a thousand. Wives talking at cocktail parties about how brilliant their husbands are. Factory workers in Tennessee bragging about their paychecks. Newspapermen get curious, so we have to make sure they don't get too curious."

"General, I think you should know that McManus recommended me because I've spent the last two years in Washington keeping you out of the papers. That's part of my beat—the blackout on the project. Scientific journals. Everything."

"So you understand the science?" Groves asked, curious.

"Does anybody understand the science?" Groves looked at him.

"A little," Connolly said apologetically. "Enough to know what can't be said. Which is just about everything. Right down to the word atom. Anyway, I'm familiar with the operation."

"Good. Then I don't have to tell you. Over a thousand incidents, and so far, not one leak and not one day of work lost. This isn't going to be any different. You do your job right and the scientists aren't even going to know you're here. What's the matter?" he said, catching the look on Connolly's face.

"General, I'm just trying to figure out if I'm here because I don't know anything or because you don't want to. Are you trying to catch this guy or not?"

Groves raised his eyebrows. "That's an interesting question," he said finally. "I'm not sure. If somebody robbed Bruner and bopped him over the head, I hope the police catch him. But not if it means taking five minutes away from the project. It's just not worth the time. Hate to put it like that, but it's the truth. Do you have any idea how important this is, what we're doing here? I know you keep it out of the papers, but do you know what it means? We could end the war." He said this calmly, matter-of-factly, without the usual bond-drive fervor, so that Connolly took it as literal. "Right now you've got thousands of boys dying every week. You've got Curt LeMay running those B-29s over Japan like the wrath of God. We have no *idea* how many casualties. None. And the invasion will mean more and more. We can stop that if we finish the work here. So no, I don't care if they catch one killer—we can catch millions. Unless it isn't just a robbery. Unless it's about the project. That's what we've got to know."

"Okay," Connolly said, "so we want to find out if his being murdered had anything to do with the Hill, but we don't want to bother anyone on the Hill finding out."

Groves looked at him steadily. "Now you think you're being funny. I allow one wisecrack, and now you've had yours."

"Sorry. I just wonder if you're giving the police a fair shake. Or me, for that matter."

"Fair doesn't apply to you," he said evenly, "you're working for me. The police? They

23

took their own sweet time getting in touch, by which time the physical evidence—if there was physical evidence—didn't amount to much and the papers already had the story. That's the last thing we want. Luckily, it's still a John Doe to them, no connection to the Hill at all. You make sure it stays that way."

"So you put a lid on it."

"Sealed. For good. The police will cooperate. Well, I guess they have to. They're not even allowed up here."

"And they still think it might have something to do with his being homosexual?"

"Now that's just what I mean," Groves said, louder suddenly. "Where do they get that? Says who? I do *not* want allegations like that going around. We've never had anything like that up here, and once that kind of rumor starts—" He trailed off, blushing, and Connolly realized that the subject was an embarrassment for him.

"General," Connolly said calmly, "if he was homosexual, that would constitute a security risk all by itself. You know that."

Groves looked at him and sat down, a kind of body sigh.

"Yes, I know that. But do you know what it means when you start a scare like that? I've seen it happen, down in Miami. The army goes on a queer hunt and there's no end to it. You've got everybody looking over his shoulder and wondering, and that's just the kind of mess I'm trying to avoid here." He paused. "We don't know anything except Bruner got

24

caught with his pants down. Whatever that means. I want you to find out, but I don't want you turning the place upside down to do it. There's no need to smear this man's reputation. For all we know, he didn't do anything more than run into some drunk Mexican."

"General, can I be frank? It's unlikely the police are going to get anywhere—they aren't even being told the man's name. I take it you don't want to call in the FBI—"

"Are you out of your mind? You do that and you've got Washington all over it and I'll never get anything done. The FBI hasn't been allowed near this project since 1943, and I intend to keep it that way. War Department intelligence takes care of the Manhattan District of the Army Corps of Engineers. That's enough for me."

"Except Bruner *was* intelligence."

Groves peered at him. "That's the rub, isn't it? That's what we can't get past. He wasn't just anybody. He was G-2. I don't believe in coincidences. I'm paranoid, remember? I don't know what's involved here or who else is involved. I don't know whether he was a fairy or not, but if he was we had *no idea*. Now that makes me worried."

"So, an outsider," Connolly said.

"McManus said you were like a dog with a bone with a story."

"That's reporting. I haven't done that in a while. And that's still not being a policeman."

"The war makes us all into something different. I never met a reporter yet who didn't think he'd make a better cop than a cop. Besides, you're what I've got. You're educated, so you can talk to the geniuses here without getting everyone riled up. You're used to the police—Tommy said you covered the police blotter in New York before the war. If you can handle that, the police in Santa Fe should be a piece of cake. You'll be official liaison to the chief there, by the way. We don't want them to feel we're not cooperating with them. And you're already briefed on the project. Darn few have been, I might add, and nobody really knows it all except Robert."

"And yourself."

"And myself. And sometimes I wonder about that."

Connolly smiled. This was about as far as Groves was likely to go toward making a joke, and he appreciated the effort.

"Well, now at least I know what my qualifications are." In spite of himself, he was pleased. He hadn't expected to like Groves, and now he found himself wanting his respect.

"And you were available," Groves said bluntly. "There wasn't time to get anyone else up to speed. I don't know what we've got on our hands here, but we'd better find out PDQ. Any questions?"

"Not now," Connolly said, getting up. "I assume everyone in G-2 knows I report to you?"

"Mills does. Colonel Lansdale's away, so you work with Mills. As far as anyone else is concerned, you're Bruner's replacement. As far as Mills goes, you're Bruner's replacement *and* you're investigating his death. If you need to reach me in Washington, Betty will always be able to find me. And of course Dr. Oppenheimer knows everything. If for any reason I'm unavailable, consider him me."

Connolly smiled inwardly at the pairing, some odd Jack Sprat variation.

"So he's one of the trustworthy scientists. Not one of the kids."

Groves's face grew stern. "Dr. Oppenheimer is a hero." It was said utterly without irony, the highest accolade this spit-and-polish military man knew, and Connolly wondered at the intensity of his feeling. It seemed to have the brusque affection of old campaigners whose trench scars could never be shared. "He may just win this war for us. And he's got enough here on his shoulders," Groves said, standing, displaying his own capable frame, "without having to worry about some German G-2 going and getting himself killed."

"Bruner was German?" Connolly said, surprised. "I hadn't realized that."

"Well, German born," Groves said. "He's American now, of course. Or was."

"Is that usual? In G-2, I mean?"

"There's nothing in that. He was fluent in both German and Russian, which comes in handy around here. Half the people on the Hill are from somewhere over there. There's never been a question of his loyalty, if that's what you mean."

27

"Did you know him well?"

"Let's just say I knew who he was. I try to keep tabs on everybody, but it's impossible these days. The place is just too big now. Lansdale always thought highly of him. As I say, there was never a question of his loyalty."

"There was never a question of his being murdered, either."

Groves stopped, not sure how to respond, then brushed it aside. "You'd better get started. Anything else?"

"No, sir. I appreciate your confidence. One thing. Every reporter knows most murders don't get solved unless the wife or the husband did it. I don't want you to expect too much."

Groves looked at him. "I like to get started on the right foot. I think we have, so let me tell you exactly what I expect. I expect you to get this job done, no excuses, which is the same thing I expect from everybody. I expect the contractors to put up buildings in half the time they usually do. And I expect the professors here to deliver our gadget on time. So far we're on schedule. No leaks, no trouble. The only thing we can't seem to solve is getting enough water. Now, you come back and tell me I've got nothing else to worry about and I'll be the happiest man on earth. I hate to worry, it slows things down. So you go and do that. And you should know, I always get what I expect."

Connolly stared at him, not sure what to make of this vaudeville turn, but since Groves seemed perfectly genuine in the part, he saluted. "Yes, sir."

Groves saluted back, a surprisingly careless wave of the hand. "I'll be back in a few weeks. By the way," he said, a slight smile beginning on his face, "don't think my bark is worse than my bite. It isn't."

The housing office was in one of the old school cabins, dwarfed now by another huge water tank. Mills had arranged for him to have Bruner's room, and Connolly guessed this had violated the usual waiting-list order of things, because the clerk was surly as he signed the forms.

"Nothing's been done to that room," he said. "Nobody told us. You better change the sheets. Lieutenant," he said to Mills, "can you kit him out over at housekeeping? We're about to close here."

"Sure. How's my Sundt duplex coming?"

"In your dreams."

"Bathtub Row?"

The clerk didn't even bother to answer.

"Want to translate?" Connolly said as they went outside.

"Bathtub Row's for the top brass—they're the old buildings from the ranch school, which means they were actually built for people. They're the only housing on the Hill with tubs, not showers, so they're considered the top of the line. Of course, they don't get much water either, so big deal."

"Sundt?"

"Construction company that built a lot of the Hill. The housing units are named for whoever built them, so you've got Sundt units and Morgan duplexes and McKee prefabs— those are the flat-tops—and Pascos. Then you're down to trailers and huts and whatever keeps the cold out."

"I assume Bruner wasn't in a Sundt."

Mills grinned. "No, we've got a nice dormitory room for you."

Later, walking down the dusty road with piles of sheets and towels, Connolly felt more than ever that he'd gone back in time to school. The dormitory was the familiar dull green army clapboard, but the dayroom inside, with its Ping-Pong table and Remington cowboy prints, had an undergraduate look, and the rooms were the same glorified cubicles you'd find on any state campus. The polished wood floor was bare, reflecting light from the uncurtained windows, but a curtain of sorts had been hung along the frame of the indented closet area. Aside from the single bed, there was a small desk, a reading chair, a short bookcase, and a hotel-standard imitation Sheraton chest of drawers with a Bakelite radio on top. The room was almost aggressively neat, as if the slightest rearrangement of the furniture would put it hopelessly out of kilter.

"Well," Mills said, dumping the linens on the bed, "welcome to Boys' Town. It ain't much and it sure ain't home. I'm just down the hall, so I should know."

"I thought he said nobody'd touched the room."

"Nobody has."

Connolly opened the top drawer to see neatly folded handkerchiefs and pairs of shorts. "Signs of life."

"Well, I'll let you get on with it," Mills said. "Dinner's in the commissary—that's just beyond P Building, the big one with the bridge. You won't have any trouble finding it—just follow the smell of grease. Motor pool's on the other side, so don't get confused. Workday begins at oh eight hundred, but that's up to you, I guess."

Connolly continued to go through the drawer, carefully moving pieces of clothing as if reluctant to disturb the dead. "What do we do with this stuff?" he asked.

"Beats me. No next of kin, if that's what you mean. I thought you'd want to go through it before we pack it up. I'll get you a box tomorrow. I suppose we have to hold it. You know, as evidence."

It was a question, but Connolly was preoccupied.

"I suppose. What happened to the next of kin?"

"Bruner was a German Jew. His parents are still there—or not—as far as we know. We have to assume not. No other relatives in his file."

"Speaking of which, I'm going to need—"

But Mills was already pulling a manila folder from under his arm. "Bedtime reading," he said, handing it over.

Connolly looked at him and smiled. "Why do I get the feeling you're one step ahead of me?"

"Don't worry, you'll catch up. That's all there is."

Connolly glanced at the file. "Did you know him?"

"He worked in the section and he lived down the hall, so yes. But no."

"Did you like him?"

Mills hesitated. "That's some professional question. He was all right."

"That's some answer."

"He was a hard guy to like."

"How so?"

"He had an edge. He'd been through a lot and it showed. He couldn't relax. I suppose he was always waiting for the knock on the door. A lot of the Germans are like that. They can't feel safe, not after everything. You can't blame them, but it doesn't make them the life of the party, either."

"What happened to him there? Specifically."

"The Nazis thought he was a Communist and locked him up. He had a rough time."

"Was he?"

"Not according to him. He was a student who attended a few meetings. It's all in there," he said, pointing to the folder. "In the security report. Even the Nazis couldn't make it stick, so they finally let him out. This was years ago, when they were trying to deport the Jews instead of keeping them in, so they sent him to Russia."

"They took him in?"

"Uh-huh. And then arrested him as a German spy. They were even worse than the Nazis. They pulled his teeth out, one day at a time. That's why he had the plate."

"Jesus." Connolly imagined the wait every morning, the clang of the bolt in the door, the pliers and the screams and the blood. The spare, clean room suddenly seemed different, as if Bruner had tried to live as unobtrusively as possible, wanting to be passed over, out of pain.

"Yeah, I know. When they ran out of teeth they started messing up his hands, until I guess they finally decided he didn't know anything. Just one of their little mistakes. So they got rid of him too. The rest is in there. It's your standard refugee itinerary, with the usual red tape and crooks and helping hands until one day he's drinking milkshakes in God's country. And now this. Some life. You have to feel sorry for the bastard."

"But you didn't like him."

"You trying to make me feel guilty? No, I didn't like him. Maybe it wasn't his fault, but deep down he had no use for anybody. He was the kind of guy who was always looking for some angle."

"But good at his job? Loyal American and all that?"

Mills grinned. "Yeah, all that. He liked it here all right, but more because I think he hated everywhere else. Maybe it was too late for him

33

to make friends. He wasn't the kind of guy who just came by your room to have a smoke and shoot the breeze. Come to think of it, I think this is the first time I've ever been in this room. He hung out in the dayroom—he wasn't a hermit or anything—but you never felt he was really enjoying it."

"No close friends?"

"He may have. None that I knew about."

"How about his social life?"

"By which you mean?"

"What you think I mean."

"I don't know," Mills said slowly. "I always thought there might be somebody, but he never said anything. It was none of my business. It never occurred to me that it might be a man." He looked up at Connolly. "I know what the police think, but there was none of that here. Ever."

"Are you trying to tell me it's safe to use the showers?"

Mills let it pass.

"All right. What made you think he was seeing a woman? Or anyone?"

"His car. He loved his car. He was always trying to cadge extra coupons, and he used to love to show it off. You know, offer to take people into Santa Fe, things like that. And then more and more he was off by himself, so I figured he had a girlfriend somewhere."

"How did he rate a car? I thought they were—"

"Oh, it was his car. He got it in 'forty-two, when you could still get them. A Buick. And the way he took care of it, it was probably as good as the day he drove it off the lot."

Connolly looked around the room, imagining the furniture as immaculate pieces of engine. "I should probably take a look. Where is it now?"

"No idea. He took it down the Hill Saturday and neither of them came back."

Connolly thought for a minute. "And now we only know where one of them is. Hard to lose a car, though. It's bound to turn up someplace. I don't suppose you know the local black-market heavyweights?"

"Black market? Never heard of it. That's one thing we leave to the police."

"The only thing, from the sound of it. All right, I'll check it out tomorrow. I suppose it's registered to a code number like all the cars here?"

Mills nodded.

"You guys like to make things easy."

"Haven't you heard? We're the best-kept secret of the war. You might even say we don't exist."

"I know. I get paid to help keep it that way."

"So what do you do, anyway?" Mills said. He caught Connolly's look. "If I'm allowed to ask."

"Office of War Information liaison to Army Intelligence. I'm a rewrite man."

"What do you rewrite?"

"Dispatches. Speeches. News. Whatever the army thinks we should know. For a while

there we didn't have any American casualties—
only the Germans got shot—but they've been
better lately. Even they couldn't keep it up
indefinitely."

"You mean you write propaganda?" Mills
said, intrigued. "I've never met anyone who
did that."

Connolly smiled. "No. Not propaganda.
That's big lies, fake stories—the stuff Goebbels
used to do. We don't make anything up. You
couldn't, these days. We just look at it right,
make people feel better about things. So they
don't get discouraged. We don't have heavy
casualties, we meet fierce resistance. A German
advance is a last-ditch counterattack. No
body parts, dismemberment, guts hanging
out, just clean bullets. French villages are
glad to see us—I think they must be, too.
Our boys do not get the syph—or give it, for
that matter. We don't mean to bomb anybody by accident, so we never do. The army
isn't up to anything in New Mexico. There is
no Manhattan Project."

Mills stared at him, surprised by the casual cynicism of the speech.

"Just a few rewrites," Connolly said. "For
our own good."

"How do you feel," Mills said curiously,
"about doing that?"

"How would you?"

Mills looked away, suddenly embarrassed.

"So in a way it feels good to be back on the
crime beat again," Connolly said lightly.
"Except I'm not really here."

Mills picked up his mood. "Town's full of people this week who aren't really here. If you want to do some ghost spotting, though, you might check out the party tonight. I assume you're on a face-recognition basis with the world's leading physicists. Otherwise it'll be lost on you."

"Only if they look like Paul Muni."

"Now there, you've gone and done it. You're supposed to use his code name. Anyway, eight o'clock if you're interested. And all things considered, you should be."

"What's the occasion?"

"They don't need a special occasion to have a party. It's just one long bacchanal up here on the mesa. Of course, if they are celebrating something, we don't allow them to say so."

Connolly grinned. "Okay. Maybe I'll see you there later. An ordinary party might be nice."

"Well, ordinary for here."

Afterward he lay on Bruner's bed, too tired to change it, his mind drifting from the file to the expressionless room around him. Some rooms were so inhabited with personality that their occupants refused to leave; you could feel their presence like a kind of haunting. But this wasn't one of them. Bruner had never been here. But of course he had been— nobody left without a trace. Connolly's eyes moved slowly around the room. Perhaps the neatness itself was a clue, a life all tucked in, put away, leaving nothing behind to give it away.

His things had been unremarkable. A crossword puzzle book—to perfect his English or just to pass the time?—and a German-English dictionary on the desk. No mail. A photograph in the drawer of a couple dressed in the dated clothes of twenty years ago, presumably his parents. A random collection of reading books—*For Whom the Bell Tolls,* an illustrated book of Southwest Indian life, Armed Forces paperback westerns, an anthology of war correspondent dispatches. Connolly leafed through the latter, suddenly back at OWI, with burly prima donnas throwing tantrums over troop transport passes and scheming to go on bombing raids so their bylines would end up in collections just like this. There would never be a bigger story.

Suits, a few pairs of socks, and a tie rack in the closet. Connolly took out the empty suitcase to fill it with the folded, ordinary clothes in the drawers. A Dopp Kit with the usual brushes and razors, a box of prophylactics, and special denture powder. A project account book with orderly rows of regular deposits. Only when he took out the sweaters to pack them did he find anything interesting—a few pieces of Indian jewelry, silver and turquoise, hidden in one of the folded sleeves.

Now, on the bed, he held them up to the light, playing with them. A belt buckle inlaid with turquoise, a pendant (no chain), links for one of those necklaces Spanish cowboys wore around the crowns of their hats. Why jewelry? Bruner's clothes were conservative—hard to imagine him drawn to anything so flashy. A present? The same night he used the prophylactics? Anything was possible. Maybe he simply liked the stuff. The meager bookcase suggested some interest in Indians. Perhaps the turquoise was no more than a hobby collection, like FDR's stamps—Bruner's unexpected passion. Connolly imagined him taking the pieces out of the sweater at night to look at them, their glow of silver and blue-green lighting up the drab room like Silas Marner's gold. And then again, maybe not. He put them down on the bed and picked up the file instead.

What no one had mentioned was that Bruner was good-looking. Not conventionally pleasant, but striking, his high cheekbones and bush of dark hair arranged in an original angular way that drew attention to his eyes. Even in the file photo they had a frank, direct stare that still seemed alive. There was no humor in them, but a kind of hard vitality that put the rest of his face in shadow. Nothing else, not the stubble of afternoon beard covering the chin, not the hollow cheeks or surprisingly full lips, registered. What seemed at first the pale Jewish face of a hundred other photographs was now rearranged, as if the sensitivity had been stamped out to leave something hard, more determined. Connolly wondered if the extraction of the teeth had literally changed the shape of the face or simply the man who looked through it.

How could it be otherwise? The pain must have been crippling, all the worse for being repeated without end. Had Bruner counted the teeth left, wondering as his raw mouth puffed up with pain whether he could stand another day, ten? Or had the Nazis months before already beaten his face to another form? Connolly looked at the nose in the picture for the sideways slant of a break, but it was straight, and again he came back to the eyes. They were so bright that for a split second he thought he could reach through to the man, but the more he looked, the less they seemed to say. They stared without any comment at all, as if simply being alive were enough.

Connolly put the file down and covered his tired eyes with his sleeve. In the end, the pictures were always the same. File after file had crossed his desk, stories from Europe, not just the battle dispatches and the statistical pieces but the personal stories, each one terrible, each one of suffering almost unimaginable, until you were lost in the scale of it all. We would never recover from this, unless we simply stopped listening. Europe seemed to him now like a vast funhouse, dark and grotesque and claustrophobic. You were jerked along from one startling exhibit of horror to the next, rocking in alarm, squirming. Skeletons dangled, monsters leaped out, horrible mechanical screams tore the air, and you would never get out.

The stories made other stories. Something had happened to Karl Bruner, who in turn became a different person, which in turn made him do—what? Maybe nothing. But once the violence started, there was no end to it—every crime reporter knew that. It demanded vengeance, or at least some answer, an endless series of biblical begats. A gun fired never stopped, it kept cutting through the lives of everyone around it, on and on. Like some unstoppable—Connolly smiled to himself at the aptness of it—chain reaction. Until it all became part of the war.

Connolly liked the remoteness of Los Alamos, the clean, high air away from the files and reports of the world destroying itself. A simple personal crime, a police blotter item—not a war. An assignment out of the funhouse, some time in the light. But Bruner's face had thrown him back again—another European story. He wondered why it had ended on the Santa Fe river.

2

Connolly was late to the party and wouldn't have gone at all if Mills hadn't dragged him. He had needed sleep, not dinner, but Mills had gone to the trouble of getting a table at Fuller Lodge and he felt he couldn't refuse.

"Better to start off on the right foot," Mills had said. "You can eat at the commissary anytime. The lodge is as good as it gets here."

And in fact the food was good and gave him a second wind. The room itself, oversized and two stories high, with a running balcony and a massive stone fireplace at either end, looked more like the dining room of a national park lodge than the army-camp messes where most of Los Alamos ate. Every table was filled, so that the room buzzed with conversation and clinking flatware.

Connolly was surprised at how many people wore coats and ties. There was clearly no dress code—he could see occasional open shirts and even some Western-style pointed collars—but most people were in full suits, the women in bright, slightly dowdy dresses. Saturday night at the Faculty Club.

"If you want to do some scientist spotting, you might start with that table over there," Mills said, nodding his head. "Let's see how good you are."

Connolly glanced at a tall man, his apple cheeks bellowing out with the draw on his pipe. He had the white hair and gentle, puckish face of a thin Nordic Santa Claus.

"Niels Bohr," Connolly said. "I'm impressed."

"Nicholas Baker. Code names only, please. All physicists are 'engineers,' and he is Mr. Baker."

"I'll try to remember." Connolly grinned. "Who else?"

"Henry Farmer."

Connolly thought for a second. "Of the Italian Farmers?"

"You're catching on."

"Is he here too?"

42

"He's the one with Mr. Baker."

Connolly looked at the modest figure with thinning dark hair, bent over to catch the soft-spoken Baker's words. Fermi. "A penny for *their* thoughts."

"You wouldn't understand them even if you heard them. You'll get used to that too."

"How long have you been here?"

"Forever. Since 'forty-three. It was a lot smaller then. When I first got here, we only had the old school and a few buildings in the Tech Area. One telephone line. The road up the mesa was still dirt."

"The good old days?"

"Not really. For the scientists, maybe. They were gung-ho—real pioneer times for them. For the rest of us it was—" He searched for a word. "Quiet. You felt like you'd dropped right off the edge and nobody knew where you were."

"Nobody knows now."

Mills shrugged. "Like I say, you get used to it. And of course things got busier and busier so you didn't have much time to think about it. I suppose it's a little like overseas, except nobody gets killed."

"Until now."

"Yeah, until now. Not exactly a war casualty though, was he?"

"No." Connolly shifted. "What did you do before the war?"

"Lawyer."

"Is that how you ended up in security?"

"I wish I knew. Maybe they thought law

43

meant law enforcement. They aren't famous for being logical. Maybe they just thought I'd make a rotten soldier and I'd be better off pushing paper somewhere."

"Criminal law?"

"Estates and trusts. I know, boring, but you'd be surprised. Besides, it makes the firm a ton of money and everybody wants to marry you." He grinned. "They don't even notice the hair," he said, running his hand along his balding top.

"But nobody did, I take it," Connolly said, gesturing toward Mills's bare finger.

"Not yet. But wait till I make partner."

"So meanwhile, what do you do for a social life?"

"You know, you have a delicate way of asking rude questions."

"Okay." Connolly laughed. "Withdrawn."

"What the hell, I don't care. Mostly there isn't any. Just like any army base. But I suppose there's enough going on if you look for it. You don't want to go near the wives—we've had a little of that and that's always trouble. The WACs are something else again. We tried to keep the dormitories off-limits to single men for a while, and it was the WACs who screamed bloody murder, so the parties started right up again. You can't blame them. Nobody's allowed to fraternize with the locals for security reasons, so every night's prom night for the WACs. They'll never be this popular again."

"What about Santa Fe?"

"Not much. It's an old town, and the Spanish won't even look at you. Albuquerque's better. Some of the guys go on a spree there if they get a weekend pass, and sometimes we have to go get them out of the tank, but mostly they're so afraid of getting a dose that they just get drunk and end up at the movies."

"I found some prophylactics in Bruner's drawer."

"Did you?" Mills looked away. "I don't know what that means."

"It usually means he was sexually active."

"One way or the other."

"Yes, one way or the other."

"Christ," Mills said, "I don't know. Maybe he just kept them around, you know, the way some guys keep them in their wallets."

"Maybe. But we have to assume they were used sometimes."

"Look, I know what you're after, but I can't help you. I don't know anything about his sex life. Christ, I can't even *imagine* it. He never said a word. I keep trying to think of something he might have said or some look—I mean, we worked in the same office, for God's sake. All this time. How could you not notice something? I mean, what do you look for, anyway? He was here almost a year and I had no idea. Never. I still can't believe it."

"Does it bother you?"

"Of course it bothers me. Wouldn't it bother you? I mean, I don't care if he didn't like women. That's his business. He could fuck goats for all I care."

"Then why does it bother you?"

Mills paused and looked at him. "I guess because it means he was another person all along. I never knew it. I mean, what's the matter with me? Hell of a thing not to know if you're in security, don't you think?"

He felt the glow of the drinks as they walked toward Theater-2. His body was still tired but his mind was fresh now, eager to take things in. Everything was sharper in the cold air, bright in the glare of the mounted flood-lights around the Tech Area. The whole place seemed not quite real. With its dusty, unnamed streets, its wire fences and plain clapboard build-ings, it became a frontier town, but backlit, insubstantial. The strangeness of the mesa delighted him. After months in Washington, with its weighty masonry and stuffy rooms and routine, everything here was raw and new and interesting. There were still ditches in the street to catch the runoff. Even at this late hour, lights burned in the laboratory buildings and MPs walked on patrol. The night air smelled of diesel and pine.

They heard the music even before they got to the building, sawing fiddles of a Western band pouring through the open doors like the soundtrack for a movie saloon. The big room was as smoky and raucous as Connolly expected, but the cowboys were only servicemen in uniforms and bushy-haired civilians dressed up for a night on the town who had, inexplicably, wound up in a barn instead. It was one of the oddest things he had ever seen. At one end of the room, on a raised stage, a makeshift band of soldiers, country boys all, played loud accompaniment to a caller in blue jeans and a bandanna who clapped out the beat as he sang instructions to the dancers. Stamping feet echoed off the polished hardwood floor of the basketball court. There were tables of food and punch bowls and bottles along one wall and folding chairs scattered everywhere but on the dance floor itself. People talked over the music and laughed at their unfamiliarity with the steps. They all seemed to be at the wrong party, moving awkwardly but gamely through their paces, stocky middle-aged men in ties determined to be good sports and young pale men whose jeans looked as stiff and uncomfortable as a second language. Here and there someone executed steps with confident precision, but off-rhythm, as if he had mastered the dance as a matter of scientific principle. What should have been fluid was jerky and tentative, but no one gave up, and the more complicated the maneuver, the more inevitable the missteps and the better they liked them. The fun, for these engineers of perfect measurements, was not caring. Physics had come to a hoedown and seemed to be having a great time. The room hummed with high spirits.

"Quite a party," Connolly said, smiling.

"Wait till they really start drinking," Mills said.

He led Connolly toward the drinks table, where a ruddy-faced man whose hair stuck out on the sides like flaps was furiously attacking a block of ice in a zinc washtub. Chips flew out on the table as he drove the pick up and down.

"Careful, professor," Mills said.

"*Gott im Himmel*," the man said. "You would think in such a place someone would invent a *machine* for this. Here," he said, handing Mills a glass with ice. "On the rocks, yes?"

"Always. Meet Mike Connolly. Hans Weber."

"Hello, Mr. Connolly. You're new? You must be in Kisty's group. There's someone new every day. We can't get one more person, not one, and for Kistiakowsky they never stop coming."

"No, I work with Lieutenant Mills in the security office."

"Ah," he said, pausing to look at Connolly. "So. You replace poor Karl."

"Yes."

He shook his head. "A terrible thing. Terrible. So young. And for what? Some wallet? Some pocket change? How much could such a person have?"

"You knew him well?"

"No, not well. Sometimes he was my bodyguard. That's right, yes? Bodyguard?"

"We prefer 'escort,' " Mills said, smiling. Then he turned toward Connolly. "Professor Weber is one of the engineers who's always given protection off-site."

"Hah, protection," Weber said good-naturedly. "Snoops. This time it was the protector who needed the protection. What a world we are becoming. So," he said, changing tack, "you like music, Mr. Connolly?" His intonation made *mister* a literal translation of *Herr*. "Not this screeching of cats, but real music?"

"Very much."

"You play?" he asked eagerly.

"No."

"No, that would be too much luck. Our group lost a member last year," he explained, "and I keep trying to find a new one, but no. People keep coming, but no one plays. But you like to listen? We meet on Thursdays. My wife likes the visitors. You would be most welcome."

"Thank you. I'd like that very much."

"Well, we'll see. How is the saying, don't count the chicken before the hatching? We are amateurs only. But sometimes it's good."

"Oh, there's Oppie," Mills said, clearly looking for an excuse to begin pulling Connolly away. "I have to introduce Mike," he said to Weber. "You know how Oppie likes to greet the newcomers."

Weber smiled and moved his hand in a churning benediction. "Circulate, circulate."

Oppenheimer was standing with his back to them, talking animatedly to a colleague, but when he turned to be introduced, he looked at them with his full attention, as if the entire evening had been arranged for this meeting. Connolly had seen photographs, but he was unprepared for the focus of Oppenheimer's gaze, eyes that took him in so quickly that he was enveloped in an intimacy even before he spoke. Oppenheimer was thin, even frail, so that the hollow face offered no distraction from the eyes. Oddly, Connolly thought of Bruner, but those eyes had simply been intense; these were quick and curious. Behind them was a tiredness so profound that their shine seemed almost feverish. He had a cigarette in one hand and a drink in the other, so he had to bow his head in greeting, which he managed with an ironic oriental grace. His voice was low but as quick as his eyes.

"Sorry I couldn't see you earlier—there was a meeting I couldn't get out of. I hear you saw the general?"

"Yes."

"And how did you find G.G.?"

"Colorful."

Oppenheimer laughed. "Did he mention his bark and his bite?"

"Yes, as a matter of fact," Connolly said, surprised.

"Good, then you must have given him a bit of trouble," he said, drawing on his cigarette. Connolly felt the words come at him like the fast balls of a Ping-Pong match, and he saw that Oppenheimer enjoyed conversation as a form of recreational sport.

"And is it worse? His bite?"

"Oh yes, very much so. The general never lies. I don't think he knows how, actually. The most honest man I've ever met. Not an ounce of guile. How he copes with the Washington maze I don't know, but he just plunges in, full steam ahead, and before you know it, the thing's done."

Oppenheimer, with his almost feline elegance, might have been describing his opposite, and Connolly wondered again about their odd friendship. With Oppenheimer, everything must be charm and coercion and subtle juggling—it couldn't get done otherwise. Maybe his was the admiration of the master politician for the effective battering ram.

"Maybe they're so used to looking for tricks that he takes them by surprise."

Oppenheimer enjoyed the return and smiled. "Maybe so. No doubt you've experienced a good deal of that yourself in Washington. How they love intrigue. Poisonous place."

Connolly laughed. "Well, the air's better here, but offices are pretty much the same wherever you go."

Oppenheimer looked up at him, an appreciative glance. "Think you can find mine in the morning? Say, seven-thirty?"

Connolly raised an eyebrow.

"Oh, don't let this fool you," Oppenheimer said, raising his glass. "We start early here. Officially at eight, and I'm afraid I've got a meeting scheduled first thing, so we'll have to make it earlier. I do apologize—not very civilized, is it? But Janice will get you a good cup of coffee—the commissary stuff is swill—and besides, it's really the best part of the day here. Wonderful for riding. Do you ride?"

"No. Just the subways." The phrase was involuntary, a casual signaling of the distance between his New York and the Riverside Drive where Oppenheimer had grown up, busy with lessons and parties and privilege. But Oppenheimer seemed not to notice.

"That's a shame. We've still got a few horses left from the ranch school, and there's nothing like it in the mornings. Wonderful trails up the mountains, all the way to the caldera. Well, maybe someone will give you a few lessons—there's nothing to staying on."

"I doubt I'll have the time."

It might have been rude, but Oppenheimer caught it and chose to ignore it.

"No, none of us have that, do we? Less and less. But we must have some of this," he said, gesturing with his cigarette to the dancing, "or we'd all get very dull. I expect you'll be especially busy." He looked directly at Connolly. "But we'll discuss all that tomorrow. Have another drink?" He turned toward the table to find his colleague still standing there, waiting to continue the interrupted conversation. "Friedrich, I am so sorry. Let me introduce Mr. Connolly. Professor Eisler."

Connolly looked up at the tall, graying man with soft, almost liquid eyes, but after a shy nod, Eisler ignored him. "We were discussing Planck's lectures," Oppenheimer said politely. "Hardly anybody reads them anymore, which is a pity." But Eisler now had all his attention again, and Connolly saw how much of Oppenheimer's charm lay in exclusion—you were so interesting there wasn't room for anyone else. What could be more flattering than attention? Connolly wondered if the scientists fought for it like students, all of them eager for their private time with him. Even he had felt his spirit dim slightly when the light passed to someone else. And it was all done gently, with flawless courtesy. He had not been dismissed but released to drift.

He wandered slowly around the room, thinking he'd have one more drink before heading for bed. The altitude and his sudden letdown had made him lightheaded, and he worried that he had passed the point of making sense of what he saw. The whole party seemed improbable. The ordinary people stumbling out of time to country music had won Nobel prizes. The young American kid in cowboy boots might be an expert in quantum mechanics. The man in the boxy suit holding a brownie might be—what? A chemist, a metallurgist, a mathematician? The two nattily dressed gentlemen, refugees from a gossipy afternoon tea party, might be discussing critical-mass geometry or, for that matter, the real secrets of the universe. Nothing was farfetched here. People lived in air as rarefied as the altitude. And it must be just as exhilarating for them. Their ideas could leap from one mind to another, racing with the excitement of meeting none of the usual resistance of the ordinary world. The army had strung wires around them to keep the rest out, and it had worked. With all the bad water and dirt roads and inconvenience, they lived in a state of excitement. Everybody was intelligent; everything was possible. Something as ordinary as a murder victim seemed almost vulgar, an unfair intrusion.

The band played a few foxtrots and even one faltering lindy, but they were lining up another square dance when Connolly got his drink. Warm from the liquor, he stood against the wall not far from the punch bowl, trying to catch a breeze from the open doors at the end of the room. The vanished Mills had reappeared on the dance floor, linking arms with an attractive young girl and dancing with surprising ease. She was looking up at him as if, his prediction right, she wanted to marry him. Next to her a formally dressed, swarthy man with luxuriant eyebrows scowled in concentration. Connolly became fixated on the eyebrows; they arched over the man's eyes like dormers, tufts spilling out on top and then running off in unexpected corkscrews on the side. His partner, a pleasant-looking woman in a print dress and sensible shoes, never looked at him but stared straight ahead, a smile fixed on her face. Connolly began making up stories for them. Given another drink, he could do this all night.

"Lovely, isn't it?" she said. "Norman bloody Rockwell."

The scorn in the voice seemed so strong it must have been designed to provoke. If she had been a man, he would have heard the scrappy challenge of someone looking to pick a fight, but she was looking straight ahead, not really talking to him at all. Her voice was English, throaty and full-bodied with drink. She was dressed in riding boots and jodhpurs topped with a white blouse, and he thought she was the first woman he'd ever seen who looked right in them. The trousers seemed to bend and follow the lines of her slim hips, not expand them. Her clothes were dusty, as if she had really come in from riding, not dressed up in costume for the party. Her hair was piled up on her head like a factory worker's, minus the kerchief. She wore glasses and, as far as he could tell, no makeup at all, but her carelessness, her indifference to what anyone thought, had the effect of drawing him to the features that mattered—her luxurious skin, the tight lines of her body. And there was the voice. As he looked at her, she swayed slightly, and he guessed the sharp insolence had come from too much drink. But the voice, he sensed, would never slur. It would never flutter or pipe or somehow go wrong. It would get more and more controlled, not belligerent but impatient, as if things had become so clear she couldn't understand why they weren't clear to everyone else.

"You don't like square dancing," he said, not knowing what else to say.

She looked at him for the first time. "Do you?"

"Not much."

"Well, then, have a drink and let's start again. Not much of a line, was it? Square dancing. You might as well have Morris

55

dancers bouncing up and down with their bloody bells."

"You're English," he said.

"Christ, that's not much better," she said and laughed. "Of course I'm English. So what? And yes, I come here often. Too often, really. No, we haven't met before. And yes, I like the pictures but I'm not sure I want to go sometime. And—well, what else? What else do you say to break the ice? I like to hear all the lines."

"Is that what I'm doing? Breaking the ice?"

"Aren't you?"

"No."

"Well, perhaps you're not," she said, drinking. "Sorry. I get confused. So you're not. Would you like to?"

"Yes."

She smiled. "Thanks, but better not. I'm a happily married woman."

"Well, that's disappointing. And I was just getting to know you."

"Better not do that either. I'm mad, bad, and the other thing—what was it? Ask anybody. You're new. Who are you, anyway?"

"Michael Connolly," he said, offering his hand. "And not dangerous to know." He caught her expression. "The other thing," he explained.

"Oh. Says you. Everybody's dangerous, once you get to know them." She looked at her glass, as if what she had said had just slipped out and she needed a minute to think it over.

"Not here," he said, nodding to the dance. "Looks pretty wholesome to me."

She laughed and stared at the dancers. "Yes, isn't it just? Your typical all-American city. We ought to be in the bloody *Saturday Evening Post*. We've got everything you could possibly want. Girl Scouts, Boy Scouts, chess club, baseball, Little Theater group—quite a little treat they are, by the way—and the victory garden ladies, and—" She stopped. "Sorry. I'm ranting again, aren't I? I'm supposed to watch myself. Anyway, we're a hive of activity here. Something for everyone, to help pass the time. Well, for the ladies, that is."

"And what do you do?"

"You mean when I'm not running up quilts and making jam and not asking any questions? Not much. They encourage the wives to do some sort of job. Afraid we'll go starkers, probably. A lot of us work in the admin offices or teach, but I'm not allowed to do that— no aliens, please. Americans only in the school."

"But so many of the children must be—"

"Foreign. Yes, funny, isn't it? I suppose it's our *values* or something. Such as they are. Awfully corrupting, I don't doubt. And so the days fly by. Actually, I don't mind. I don't want to teach in their bloody school anyway. What I do want, though, is another drink," she said, pouring one from the punch bowl. "Oh, don't worry, I'm not a lush. I'd hold it better if I were. You needn't look like that, I know I'm tight. I'm not a bit proud of it, if that makes you feel any better."

"I don't care. It's your head in the morning."

"It's my head now, if you want to know the truth. God, I hate getting tight. I knew I would, too. These little town hall meetings always bring out the worst."

"You're doing all right."

"Oh, we're all doing all right. Considering what we're doing here. What do you do, anyway? Or am I not supposed to ask? My husband works with Bethe—I shouldn't even say that, should I?—and that's *all* I bloody know. You can imagine what it does for dinner conversation."

"I'm with the security office."

She looked up at him as if someone had shaken her by the shoulders. "Oh." She put down her drink. "You might have told me. You'll think I'm always like this."

"Don't worry," he said, "I'm not on duty."

"There's no such thing. The enemy never sleeps. Or so they say." But her voice had lost its bite.

"That's just something we put around to keep you on your toes. Your secret's safe with me. I don't know Bethe and I can't stand Little Theater either. I don't even know your name. You keep not telling it to me, remember?"

"Oh God, he's going to be nice. Please don't do that. I particularly wanted not to be nice tonight. Emma Pawlowski." She noted his surprise. "Née Harris, as they say in the *Tatler*."

"Why particularly tonight?"

"I don't know. Bad day or something. Let's just leave it at that. Oh, the hell with it," she said, picking up the drink and tossing it back.

"Do you really dislike it here so much?"

"Actually, I love it here. The place, I mean. I just hate all the Andy Hardy business," she said, pointing to the party.

"Why come, then?"

"Daniel wouldn't miss it. I can't think why. Maybe he thinks it's part of the citizenship course. Like the bloody Founding Fathers."

He smiled at her. "You're feeling better again."

"Actually, I feel like hell." And in fact she looked pale, her skin shining with sweat. "Let me have a cigarette, will you, and I'll just toddle along home before I say anything indiscreet. We'll save that for next time."

"I hope so," he said, lighting her cigarette.

She coughed a little as she blew the smoke out. "I didn't mean anything by that," she said.

"I know."

"I mean, it's been swell, but as far as I'm concerned, if we never—" She stopped, looking shaky.

"You all right?"

"Oh God," she said, stubbing out the cigarette and searching the room for the door. "I hate to drink and run. Do give my apologies to the rest of the guests." She moved unsteadily away from the table.

"Are you all right?" he said, following her. But now she bolted for the door, and by the time he caught up with her, they were outside and she was doubled over by the side of the building, retching.

"Don't watch, for God's sake," she said sharply, choking. He looked away, up toward the wonderful night sky, not knowing what to do. It seemed wrong to stay and impolite to walk away. He took out a handkerchief as he heard her heave. Finally, when it was quiet again, he turned and held the handkerchief out to her. She took it without looking up.

"God, how embarrassing," she said, gulping now for air. "I've never been sick before. You didn't have to *stay.*"

"Sorry," he said, moving away. "Sure you're all right now?"

"Of course I'm not all right. Oh," she said, clutching her stomach.

"It's the altitude."

"It's not the altitude. It's the bloody drink." She held up her head and took in a deep breath. "Well, this is awfully intimate, isn't it?" she said, laughing at herself. "Or is it just part of the security service?"

"Do you want me to find your husband?"

"No, let him dance. Wot larks. I'm perfectly capable of—" She started to move unsteadily, then stopped, swaying. "Christ. Look, as long as you're here, do you have an arm that goes with that handkerchief? I'm just down that way."

He took her arm and felt her lean against him

60

as they walked slowly down the dirt road. Her body was warm, and it trembled slightly, either from the chill or from the aftereffects of being sick. She said nothing, as if she had to use all her concentration just to walk, and in the quiet he felt more aware of her than he had before. But why was everything confused up here? As she leaned into him, holding on to his arm, they might have been a couple walking home from a dance, eager to touch each other, slightly tipsy from drink and the promise of sex. But they weren't that. She was someone else's wife, and in the morning, with her headache, she wouldn't even remember who he was.

"This is it. My Sundt palace. Thanks. I'm sorry."

"No, don't be."

She smiled wryly. "I've got a feeling I'm going to be even sorrier. Well. You've been a gentleman. Now if you're really a gentleman, you'll forget all about this. Mum's the word, just like the loose-lips posters." She was trying to rally, but her earlier high spirits had wilted with the evening. "Just forget you ever met me."

"No, I don't want to do that."

She looked up at him. "Thanks. Do it, though, will you?"

"Do you have your key?"

"What?" she said, looking puzzled, then remembered the walking-home ritual. "Oh. No, it's not locked. We never lock doors here." She gestured around her to the isolated dark, implying the fences, the guards. "It's the safest place in the world."

3

Oppenheimer was as alert as he'd promised, and the coffee just as good. His office was not much bigger than Groves's, but it was filled with the nesting memorabilia of someone who had come to stay. Connolly glanced around the room, taking in the ashtrays, the piece of Indian pottery, the files piled everywhere. He wanted to linger over the photographs on the walls—colleagues from Berkeley? student days in Göttingen?—but it was impossible to look at anything else while Oppenheimer was in the room. He sat there smoking, so animated and intense that the rest receded to the flatness of a still life.

"I suppose you'll want to talk to the police first," he said. "I'd appreciate your reporting back to me on that. All I know is what Lieutenant Mills tells me, so now I'll have to rely on you." He looked at Connolly mischievously. "He is not, I trust, under suspicion himself?"

"You haven't talked to the police?" Connolly asked.

Oppenheimer smiled. "You forget. Officially, I don't exist. None of us do. You're among ghosts now." And with the smoke floating around his gaunt face, he did, for a minute, look like one.

"Right. My mistake."

"Never mind. We forget it ourselves from time to time—it's difficult, not existing. No doubt the good general has already given you his security speech, so I won't bore you by repeating it. Nothing must compromise the security of the project. As far as that's concerned, you'll have our full cooperation. Having said that, I should also say that I don't want this incident to compromise the *work* of the project."

"That's just what General Groves said."

"You surprise me. I felt sure he'd use this as an excuse to turn the place inside out. The general's a great one for looking under mattresses and peeking through keyholes and all the rest of it. He seems to feel safest when no one knows anything at all."

"He said you'd say that too."

Oppenheimer smiled again, thinly, and put out his cigarette.

"Well, the general and I have been down this road many times before. We walk a very fine line here. On the one hand, the project is secret—everyone understands that—but on the other hand, its success depends on the free exchange of ideas. G.G.'s original plan was to compartmentalize everything. The production centers would be scattered around the country, and even here the units would work on parallel but separate tracks. Impossible, of course. Scientists can't work with blinders on—you'd never get anywhere. So we worked out one of our Solomonic compromises. The department heads meet once a week to discuss where we are and keep everyone in the picture."

"And what did the general get in the bargain?"

He smiled again and took out another cigarette. "Oh, I suppose that we still don't communicate outside. You remember, of course, that in the Solomon story they never did divide the baby."

"But everyone saved face."

Oppenheimer nodded. "Anyway, we do what we can to keep security the way the general likes it. Something like this, however—" He trailed off to light the cigarette. "I don't want it used as an excuse. After all, the poor man wasn't killed here. General Groves may not like the idea of homosexuals in his army—actually, I doubt very much that he believes they exist anywhere; the general's an innocent in his own way. But that's no reason to ignore the obvious and launch a full security investigation because you'd prefer it to be something else."

"Is it obvious?"

"I was told it was," Oppenheimer said, somewhat surprised. "Isn't it?"

"I don't know. Maybe."

He sighed and pinched the bridge of his nose, and Connolly saw that behind the intensity he was already tired.

"Well, certainly it would be convenient. Embarrassing for your office—and to think, of all the departments—" He picked up the thought again. "But convenient. Not the end of the world."

"It was the end for him," Connolly said, thinking of the photograph back in his room.

"Yes. It was that. You think me unsympathetic. I hope I'm not." He continued rubbing the bridge of his nose, closing his eyes for a moment to ease the strain. "We keep losing the individual—it's become so easy." His talk drifted, almost to reverie, and Connolly was fascinated; it was like watching someone think. "You grow callous just to get through it." He sat up, pointing to one of the piles on his desk. "How do you separate out what's important? There's algae in the water again—some of the women are complaining. Important? It is to them. Conant's sending a delegation from Washington tomorrow and they'll want a summary, which isn't ready, and then a tour, which is disruptive, but it's important to give them both somehow. Dr. Teller wants to see me and of course that's always important, even when it isn't, because if I don't see him he'll sulk and not work and *that* will be important. It's all important, and sometimes you forget, just to get it all done. But a life— yes, you're right, that's something else again. I'd like to help you any way I can. I don't want you to think otherwise. It's just there's so little time to go around."

"I appreciate that, Dr. Oppenheimer. I don't want to take any more than I have to."

"Do you know how far along the Germans are with their gadget?"

"No," Connolly said, unsure where he was heading.

"Neither do I. No idea. We do know they have Heisenberg and some of the finest scientific minds in the world. We have to assume they're working on it. After all, the same information is available to everyone. Was, anyway, before the war—" He paused for effect. "Compartmentalized us all. Now we don't know. But what if we're running out of time?"

"Right now it looks like the Germans are running out of everything."

"A year ago they said London wouldn't be bombed again, and then the V-2s came. Nobody knows anything. You were briefed about the gadget in Washington, I know, but I wonder if you appreciate how very powerful it will be. If the Germans develop one first, they could take England out of the war."

Connolly raised his eyebrows skeptically.

"You think not?" Oppenheimer said. "I think so. It's a gamble we can't afford to make. We have to get there first. So sometimes individual things—get lost. On the one hand, every little detail is important; on the other hand, nothing is important except the project. You have to bargain one against the other all the time. But a murder can't get lost, can it? So. What sort of bargain do you want me to make with you?"

Connolly looked at him for a minute, surprised to be so abruptly brought back to business. Or was this where Oppenheimer had been going all along?

"I want unrestricted access to all security files. I want to be able to talk to anyone I think might be useful without having to clear it first. My being Bruner's replacement makes this easy; it's the most natural thing in the world to talk about. I want more background on the scientific details of the project—if there is a connection, I need to know where to look. And I want to be able to appropriate any personnel—all of G-2 if necessary—if I need them."

"Done," Oppenheimer said, looking at him thoughtfully. "But surely you already have all this from General Groves."

"I'd like it from you."

Oppenheimer nodded. "I see. All right. Anything else?"

"What's the gossip? What have people been told—what story's been given out and what do they think of it? You can't have a murder in a small community without some sort of explanation."

Oppenheimer brooded for a minute. "No, I don't suppose so. But there's been remarkably little talk, now that you ask. I'm not sure why. Possibly because he really wasn't part of the community, not the work community anyway. They know that he was attacked and robbed. Shocking, especially in a town like Santa Fe, but then you have to move on. It's not as if it were one of the scientists." He paused. "Don't disapprove, I'm just trying to be truthful. If it had been Kisty or Enrico—"

"Do they know why?"

"You mean, were they told he was homosexual? No, there was no reason for that. I'm sure it never occurred to them—it certainly never occurred to me. At the time, I think there was a feeling that it would be, well, disrespectful. The poor man was already dead—no need to rake his life over the coals. Hold him up to ridicule."

"Or the army."

Oppenheimer frowned. "I don't think that entered into it. We may have our moral failings, but I hope we're not hypocrites. It was my decision—I never even considered the army's feelings in the matter. I don't care what his sex life was, but some people do. Is it a sin? What's a sin? But since Bruner never said anything, I felt we should respect that."

"Maybe he never said anything because it would have meant dishonorable discharge."

"That's irrelevant," Oppenheimer snapped. "He was dead."

"But he may have had associates, just as vulnerable, just as—" A sharp rap was followed by the secretary's head, disembodied, poking around the doorjamb.

"You've got an eight o'clock in five minutes," she said.

"Right." Oppenheimer glanced at his watch and stood. "Where this time?"

"B Building. You'll need the Critical Assemblies notes."

"Walk with me, would you?" Oppenheimer said to Connolly, an apologetic command, putting the cigarette in his mouth to pick up a thick folder from the desk. And then he was out the door, leaving Connolly to trail after him.

"I don't like where this is going," Oppenheimer said as they walked through the Tech Area, nodding to people in a kind of civilian salute. "And I suggest you leave the poor man in peace. And his friends—if he had any, which I doubt. You keep forgetting he was forty miles away when this happened. That's not exactly slipping out behind the bushes here for a little refreshment. Maybe he felt he needed the distance. Maybe there *were* no opportunities here. I don't know."

"But you admit that it would be useful to find someone who does, who *could* tell us about his life."

"Yes," he said reluctantly. "Of course I see that. But how do you propose to do that? Go through the library cards to see who checks out André Gide?"

Connolly smiled involuntarly at the Berkeley view of the world. In B Building they stopped in front of an open door. Over Oppenheimer's shoulder, Connolly could see the scientists already assembled, canvas director's chairs forming an impromptu circle around a portable blackboard. Half the board was filled with a chalk diagram, a ring of pointed arches surrounding a core, like a flower folded inward. A short man in a rumpled double-breasted jacket was filling the other half with the hieroglyphics of higher mathematics, numbers and squiggles as meaningless to Connolly as a lost language. No one turned around. Most of the men were wearing jackets and ties, but a few in open-necked shirts sat back in the chairs, legs draped casually over the arm,

69

chins resting on pointed fingers in concentration. The rowdy hospitality of the dance was gone, replaced by an intense quiet, as if they were straining to hear, not read, the chalk scratching across the board. Connolly didn't know what he had expected—lab coats and Bunsen burners and tubes—but instead he felt himself back at Fordham, eager and attentive, waiting for Father Healy to begin the day's assignment. They were making war in a classroom. But what were they actually saying inside? The room seemed as closed to him as Karl's life.

"I found some prophylactics in his room. He must have been having sex with someone."

Oppenheimer sighed. "Oh, how I wish this had never happened. Well, do what you have to. Could I simply ask that you start at the scene of the crime, as they say, before you leap to conclusions and start interviewing everyone on the Hill? The work *has* to come first," he said, indicating the sounds of the room behind him.

"I intend to. The likelihood is he was so afraid of his secret that he went as far away as he could go before he could trust anyone with it."

"Yes, that's possible. Except for his being afraid. Bruner was never afraid of anything." He drew on his cigarette, thinking. "It was probably the deviousness of it that appealed to him. Not a very trusting sort, Bruner. Well, what did he have to be trusting about? Of course, I suppose that came in handy in his job."

"You found him devious?"

70

"I hardly knew him," he said. "Devious may be unfair. He was a survivor. Quite literally. I think we're always a bit surprised to find survivors often aren't very nice. Goes against the grain, doesn't it? We'd like to think it's the noble spirit that pulls us through, when so often— Well. I sometimes think there isn't any moral quality to it at all. A purely neutral act. Like the insects. But then, who are we to say? Don't you often wonder what you would do to survive? I don't know how Bruner got through it, all those terrible things, but it didn't make him any nicer. I know it's unkind of me, after all that suffering, but he always struck me as something of a shit."

The drive down from the mesa was spectacular. The morning was beautiful, and under the cloudless blue sky the land stretched out for miles, waves of pink and brown earth dotted with clumps of piñons rolling all the way to the Sangre de Cristo Mountains in the far distance. After the busy claustrophobia of the base, the country felt even larger, and Connolly's spirits rose to meet it the minute he passed through the gate. The fences and sentry boxes were behind, ahead only the bright freedom of the high desert. Mills had told him that Oppenheimer had selected the site—he'd had a vacation ranch in the area, about sixty miles away—and Connolly wondered if this was another of those paradoxes he relished, working with the smallest particles of matter in one of the most open landscapes in the world.

The Rio Grande was swollen and brown, muddy with spring runoff, and Connolly could see in its long valley the cottonwood groves and new green fields that had drawn the first settlers in from the desert. He had never been to the West before, and the sheer size of it overwhelmed him. But it was exhilarating, not lonely—you expanded to its scale. His mind had been cluttered with a hundred questions, but the sight of the country emptied it. There was no brooding in this clearheaded sky.

The road was no better than the day before, however, and he lurched and bounced, afraid for his new tires, all the way to the outskirts of Santa Fe. He drove around the cathedral, lost in the unfamiliar streets, until he found the police station in a large adobe building that resembled a Western movie jail. Inside, however, everything was up-to-date and all business.

"You can call me Doc," Holliday said. "Everyone does, sooner or later, and I've got no time for the suspense. Now if you're going to start by dumping all over us and telling us how top secret and important you all are, you can save your breath, 'cause I've heard it all before. I don't suppose you've come to tell me just who our John Doe is."

"His name is—was—Karl Bruner."

"Well, I'll be damned. First time a liaison man ever told me anything. Usually the way we liaise around here is kind of one-way—you don't tell me anything and I get to like it. A German?"

"By birth. American citizen. Army. Also a cop."

Holliday stared at him. "You don't say. What kind of cop?"

"Security officer."

Holliday continued staring at him, as if he needed time to take this in. Finally he said, "Do I keep going, or is this where you cut me off with all the classified horseshit?"

"I'm new. They usually give you a hard time?"

"They don't tell me much."

"They don't tell me much either. Maybe there's not much to tell. But that's who he was. And now that you know, you'll have to forget it again. Officially, he's still a John Doe. Now you know most of what I know. What's important to me is what you know."

"You're not trying to flatter me by any chance, are you?"

"Would it work?"

Holliday grinned. "Never fails. I don't suppose while you're in the mood you'd like to tell me what you boys are doing up there?"

"Doc."

"Well, a try. Actually, I don't give a good goddamn. The only reason anybody wants to know is you won't tell him. You got explosions going off up there at five o'clock in the morning you can hear clear across the valley, but nobody's supposed to hear them. The

73

smart money says it's rockets, some kind of new V-2. I just hope you don't aim them over here. One goes off and there'd be a hell of a time explaining that away."

"At the moment all we've got is a body."

"Yeah. If he was security, are you telling me the army's taking this over? Just put my feet up and have a cup of coffee and politely butt out. You want some, by the way?" he said, nodding toward the hot plate behind him. "It's cowboy coffee, just boiled in the pot and tastes like shit, but since we're such great friends—"

"I'm okay, thanks. You still have a case. To tell you the truth, nobody thinks it's connected to the Hill anyway, so you might have the only case."

"But without a name, rank, and serial number."

"Let's go over what you do have. Who found the body?"

"Mexican woman. Just about had a heart attack and been gibbering ever since. None of it means a thing, or maybe my Spanish isn't what it used to be. Priest says she's practically living in the church now to get over the shock. Nothing there. She found him in the morning, but he'd obviously been out all night."

"How obviously?"

"Rigor. Plus he got rained on a lot. Coroner estimates time of death anywhere the evening before and won't budge on getting more detailed. I tried. I've been assuming he was killed sometime after eleven—earlier than that and you figure someone would have seen something. After that, it gets pretty quiet here, even on the Alameda."

"State of the body consistent with that time?"

"Coroner says so. You've seen his report, haven't you?"

"Not very specific, is it?"

"Well, let's just say Ritter's a careful kind of guy. You can't hold him to much."

"Let's just say he's incompetent. What's your guess?"

"Figure midnight, one o'clock at the outside."

"No witnesses, no signs of struggle, nothing that tells us anything?"

"Right. Rain did a good job on the site. Some broken branches on the bushes, but that could be from falling down. From the looks of it, though, I'd say he was dragged in."

"Why?"

"There wouldn't have been room for two of them there where we found him. You know, if they'd been together. So I have to assume he was put there. We did find footprints, partial ones anyway."

"That's interesting."

"No it isn't. No special marks, just a standard workboot. All the Mexicans around here wear them."

"Just the Mexicans?"

"No, I didn't mean that. Anybody. Any working man."

Connolly frowned. "Hmm. Does that seem right to you?"

"They've got dicks too."

Connolly looked up, surprised at the sharpness of it. "Okay, let's get down to it. I read about the pants. Any evidence of anal penetration?"

"No."

"Semen?"

"No."

"What about the park? Is it one of the meeting places?"

"I don't know."

"You must. You're chief of police."

"Well, you know, this is a quiet town. I'm not saying we're Dogpatch—we know what it is. You go up to Taos, where all the artists are, or down to Albuquerque, and I guess you'd find plenty of what you're looking for. We've got a few antique dealers and sandalmakers—well, one look, you can see they're covered in fairy dust, but they don't bother anybody. We've never had this kind of trouble. Honest to God, I don't even know where to look."

"You mean you haven't checked the bars or anywhere someone's likely to have heard something?"

"Well, I'll make you a deal. You find out where they are and I'll check them out for you."

"I'll make you a deal. You get your men to talk to their snitches and get *them* to tell you where people go at night. Then check it out and talk to people nice so they talk back to you and see what you can see. You do that and I'll forget you haven't even got around to basic police work. You're putting it out this guy was

76

homosexual and then you turn around and say you haven't got any here. Who do you think killed him, then?"

Holliday stared at him, offended. "You tell me. What I'm telling you is we've got no problem in that park. Take it or leave it."

"All right," Connolly said, "let's leave it for now. But check about the bars, will you?"

"I'll do that. Now suppose we both get down off our high horses and look at what we do have."

"Such as?"

"Such as another case down in Albuquerque just three weeks ago."

"Same MO?"

"Close enough. Parking lot behind one of those bars I guess you're talking about. Another guy caught with his pants down. Stabbed this time. They found him behind his car."

"Who was he?"

"Local businessman. Ran some laundries down there, which is a good business since the war got going. Seems he met somebody in the bar and they went outside to have themselves a conversation. Must have been about money, since he didn't have any left in his wallet when they found him."

"All this according to—?"

"The bartender. He's the one found him."

"Any idea who?"

"No. Boys there think it was a Mexican, on account of the knife, but they always think it's a Mexican, so you probably can't count on that."

"They get a description from the bartender?"

"Yeah, I'll get you the file on it. I'd say it was a little on the vague side, though. Medium height, medium build, medium nothing. 'Course, his memory isn't the best. He doesn't remember anyone else being there. I guess they don't have any regulars. They sure haven't had any since—nobody's been near the place."

"He might have to close it."

"The police had that idea too."

"What about the victim—any signs of sexual activity?"

"Plenty. At least this one got his money's worth."

Connolly frowned and got up to pour some coffee, pacing and looking up at the ceiling as he talked, as if he were thinking aloud.

"Okay, so what do we have here? Let's reconstruct."

"Shit."

"Well, let's try it. A guy goes into a bar, meets another guy, and they go out to the parking lot to get friendly. Either because they took a shine to each other or because one of them's paying. Now what do they do?"

"For Christ's sake, Connolly."

"No, follow me for a minute. What do we think happened? What's the lab report?"

"You mean the semen? Everywhere. In his mouth, some on his face."

"But nothing behind?"

"No."

"So they got to know each other real well.

Then one stabs the other and takes his money. So we have to assume it's not a lover's quarrel, not with the money gone. How old was the victim, by the way?"

"Forty-one."

"Right. How old did the bartender say the other one was?"

Holliday turned over a folder cover and glanced at a sheet. "Twenty something. Not under drinking age, of course. He wouldn't allow that. Not him. I don't think you can go by any of this," he said, closing the folder with disgust.

"No. But not middle-aged, either. Clothes?"

"Jeans. Blue shirt. Like I said, anybody."

"Even a working man. Bar cater to that?"

"I don't know. From the sound of it, I'd say it was a fairly democratic place. I don't think they care about your job."

"Okay, so let's take this same guy—you assume it's the same guy, don't you?—let's take him and put him in our case. What do you think happened?"

"You're going to make me do this, aren't you? I think they met somewhere, maybe one of those bars I don't know about that you think the town's full of. Maybe just sitting in the plaza. Anyway, they meet and go down to the park and do whatever they do in the bushes. Then one smashes the other on the head, pulls him further into the bushes, takes his wallet, and gets away."

"So what's wrong with this?"

"I don't know, what?"

"I don't know either, but there's something. Let's take our boy from Albuquerque—let's say he's young, let's say he's still in jeans and workboots, and let's say he lets guys give him blow jobs. Probably for money. In Albuquerque something goes wrong. Maybe the guy won't pay, or maybe our boy's ashamed or— So he meets Bruner, or Bruner meets him, and they strike a deal. But why should Bruner pay? He's young too. Good-looking."

"There's nothing in that. Why do guys go to hookers?"

"Okay. So let's say he likes the convenience. Or even just likes the idea. They go to the park. They have sex, but before they even finish our guy kills Bruner, takes his money, keys, everything, steals his car. Is this the same guy? Why not finish? Who stops in the middle of a blow job?"

Holliday followed Connolly around the room as if he were watching a court performance, caught up in the story. "Well, I sure as hell never did. From a woman, I mean. Unless I was going to—"

"Move on to something else. Right. But they never did."

"They didn't in Albuquerque either, remember?"

"Yes, but our guy'd already finished. Maybe the other one was still hoping. So why stop this time? There's something we're not getting here. Why take everything? You just have to get rid of the wallet somewhere else. Why even bother?"

"Maybe he's not real bright."

"And the car. That's just looking for trouble. It's not so easy to lose a car."

"Well, that's where I disagree with you. Everybody wants a car these days—when's the last time you saw one for sale? So we put a trace on the license, which it won't have anymore, and check out the used lots and the black market—yeah, we do have that—but I'll bet it's already gone. You just drive down the road to Mexico and first thing you know you've got money in your pocket and keep the change. Hell, they don't care down there. If it's got wheels, you can grab yourself a stack of pesos."

"But he didn't do it before and he was in a goddamn *parking* lot."

Holliday was quiet. "Well, maybe it's like you say," he said finally. "But you know what that means?"

Connolly nodded. "Somebody else did it."

"And where does that leave us? We got a victim we don't know anything about and a killer we know even less. No victim, no suspect. Fact is, the Albuquerque case is *all* we've got. Without that, we might as well hang it up."

Connolly leaned on the back of the chair. "But it doesn't fit."

"And here I was having all this fun, just like a big-city detective." Holliday grinned at Connolly. "You spend your life handing out parking tickets and then you get a real live murder and the next thing you know you're up a creek without a paddle. Guy says nothing fits. Might as well go take a vacation. But it's got to fit somehow. Look, we're making this too hard. It could have happened just the way we said it did in the first place, couldn't it?" He looked up calmly. "Couldn't it?"

Connolly shrugged. "I guess so."

"In fact, you might even say there's no reason—no real reason, anyway—to think it didn't happen that way. So he took the car. So what? Maybe he needed a way home. We don't know where they met. Maybe your man drove him all the way from Albuquerque and he didn't want to hitch back. You might even say it's *likely* that it happened the way we said."

Connolly nodded. "But I can't picture it."

"Oh. Is that some of that professional police work you were telling me about earlier? The kind we don't do?"

Connolly smiled. "All right. But I can't. Why the pants?"

"What do you mean?"

"Why would he have his pants down? Why would he need to?"

"Maybe they were taking turns."

"Maybe. But that doesn't sound like your parking-lot guy."

"Maybe he was playing with himself. It's possible."

Connolly nodded. "Okay. Then why don't I believe it? Why can't I picture Bruner doing that?"

"Maybe you need to be—you know, to imagine it."

"I'm not, if that's what you're asking."

"I wasn't," Holliday said firmly, then grinned. "Might have come in handy, though, all things considered. We're flying blind here."

"Okay, let's go with your story. What else?"

"You want to tell me about his car?"

" 'Forty-two Buick. Probably in great condition—he loved the car, apparently. Liked to go for drives. I'll get you all the numbers. Any point in sending the info across the border, in case you're right about that?"

"To the *policía*? We'd just be spinning our wheels. Well, hell."

But Connolly was smiling. "Okay, so we stay home. Then we need to get the Albuquerque police to lean on that bartender. They listen to you, or do you want me to pull in big guns? I'd rather they didn't know we're involved in any way."

"I've been saving up a favor or two."

"Let's use them, then. I'll bet the bartender can be persuaded, upstanding citizen that he is."

"Any idea what else your man may have had on him?"

"Other than the wallet? No. Probably kept all his keys on one ring. He was that kind of guy."

"What kind is that?"

"Neat." Connolly paused. "Obsessively neat, in fact."

"You mean the kind who wouldn't want to get his knees dirty on the grass?" Holliday said.

"My mind is that easy, huh?"

"No. Just one track. But I'll tell you something, I wondered about that too. Why take all his stuff? It doesn't fit that kind of crime. I thought maybe somebody didn't want us to know who he was."

"And you didn't."

"Not for a while, anyway. Now we know everything," Holliday said wryly. "By the way, who wants the body? Any family?"

"The army, I guess." Connolly got up. "You'll let me know about Albuquerque. And the bars?"

"Everything. No secrets here."

"Doc, so far we've got nothing to be secret about. How did the papers cover this?"

Holliday took a clipping from his desk. "One-day sensation. Your people tried to pull the plug, but it was too late. Tourist killing, unknown assailant. Police following up leads. This kind of thing we could spin out for weeks around here, but they got closed down after the first day. If you want to do *me* a favor, you could square it with the paper so they'll talk to me again."

"I can't. Not yet. Any connection made to the Albuquerque case?"

"Not directly. Just the rise in crime. Things going to hell all over. You know. They got a good week's run out of Albuquerque, so you can't really blame them. They even had pictures of the bar. No wonder business fell off. But people here didn't have time to get nervous. We put a patrol car on the Alameda

84

for a few nights and that was it. The smart money's on it being a drifter who passed through town."

"And right out again."

"Headed north when the smart money last spotted him."

"Doc, it's nice doing business with you," Connolly said, shaking hands and turning to go.

"Any time. Store's always open."

"That reminds me," Connolly said, turning back. "Do you know anyone who sells Indian jewelry around here?"

"Are you crazy? *Everyone* sells Indian jewelry around here. What kind do you have in mind?"

Connolly took a handkerchief from his pocket and carefully unfolded it to display the turquoise pieces. "I don't want to buy any. I want to get these appraised. You know anything about turquoise?"

"Only that most of it looks like crap. You're not supposed to say that here, so don't quote me, but it always seems a little clunky and cheap to me. What do you want to know?"

"What it's worth."

"Better take it over to Sonny Chalmers on San Francisco Street. Most of the new places have gone out to Canyon Road, but Sonny can't be bothered to move. Anyway, he's your man. Chalmers of Santa Fe. Around the corner and two blocks down. How'd you happen to come by the pieces? Belong to anyone we know?"

"Doc."

Holliday dismissed him with a wave.

Sonny Chalmers had been a boy in the last century and even now he had the slight, boyish look of the perennially young, something Connolly guessed he had managed by conserving energy. San Francisco Street was quiet, only a few people passing in the morning light, but the inside of his shop was utterly still, and he scarcely looked up when the soft ping of the entrance bell broke the silence. He stood behind one of the glass jewelry cases, leafing through the morning paper. Half the store was given over to conventional jewelry, the usual display of engagement rings and charm necklaces, the other half to local turquoise, several cases of elaborate belt buckles and bolla ties for tourists.

"Can I help you?" he said, still not looking up.

"I hope so. I wondered if you could tell me about these pieces," Connolly said, unwrapping the handkerchief and laying them out.

Chalmers moved the paper aside. "You wish to sell them?"

"No. Just have them appraised."

Chalmers's glasses hung from a chain around his neck. He raised them now and peered at the turquoise. "Oh, yes. Very nice, aren't they? Navajo. You see how fine the settings are—only the Navajos work silver like this. The stones are good, but of course it's the silver that gives them value. The *dine* use sand-stone molds. You can always tell."

"Can you tell me how much they're worth?"

"Oh, exactly. I sold them, you see."

Connolly looked at him, surprised at his luck. "These pieces? You sold these pieces?"

"Oh, yes. I'm not likely to forget them. Might I ask you how you came by them? I'd be curious to know what you paid."

"They're not mine. Chief Holliday said you might be able to help me appraise them."

"Are you a policeman?"

"Not exactly. I'm helping them."

"Well, that sounds mysterious. May I ask how?" Chalmers said, looking directly at him over his glasses.

"It's about the man who bought them. Do you remember him?"

"I don't know his name, if that's what you mean."

Connolly took out Bruner's photograph. "Is this him?"

Chalmers nodded at the photograph. "Yes. What has he done?"

"He's dead."

"Ah."

Connolly paused, waiting for Chalmers to offer more. "Do you remember how much he paid?"

"Two hundred dollars. Each time."

"They're worth two hundred dollars?" Connolly said, surprised.

"Well, that's what he paid for them,"

Chalmers said. "The original price was higher, but he was a man who liked to bargain. Yes, he liked that. He took *great* pleasure in that."

"But they're worth more?"

"I didn't say that. I said that's what he paid for them. It was the same each time. He'd pick a piece—always one of the better ones—and in the end he'd say, "I'll give you two hundred for it.' "

"And you took it?"

"Well, you don't turn down two hundred dollars lightly. Not since the war. The tourist trade—well, you see," he said, indicating the quiet shop. "One has to make a living."

"But you didn't sell at a loss?"

"Oh, I'd never do that. No indeed. But they're fine pieces. He got a good price."

"Did he know anything about jewelry?"

"Not a thing. He bought strictly by the price tag. I don't think he cared about the pieces at all. Of course, the most expensive pieces are the best, so he did very well. He wasn't cheated. He did come back, you know."

"But if he didn't care about them, why was he buying them?"

Chalmers looked at him quizzically. "I assumed they were gifts for a lady."

"They're women's pieces?"

"Oh, yes. You see the fineness of the settings? Not at all appropriate for a man. The *concha*—I suppose you could stretch a point there, but the other two are definitely ladies'. But I gather he kept them?"

"Yes. Do people ever buy these as an investment?"

"These, yes. Ordinarily, no. Turquoise isn't a fine gemstone. There's a lot of it around, and I have to say, the tourist trade has devalued it. The Indians just stamp these out now, and who can blame them? No one seems to know the difference. But a piece like this—" He held one up. "Look at the workmanship. You're not likely to see this sort of thing again. There'll always be a market for this."

"But why not diamonds or rubies or something?" Connolly said, half to himself.

"Perhaps it was his price range," Chalmers said, trying to help. "You can't get really first-class stones, not really first-class, for two hundred dollars. Turquoise is something else. These are top of the line."

"How long ago did he buy them?"

"The first? Last fall sometime. Before Christmas, anyway, because he came in again at Christmas."

"And the last?"

"A little after that. I can tell you exactly if you give me a few minutes."

"Please."

Chalmers brought out a black account book and leafed through the pages. "Yes, here's one. I'll jot down the dates for you, if it's important," he said, taking out a piece of paper. "November. Well, I wasn't far off." He made a note. "Was he the poor boy who was killed in the park?" he said, not looking up.

Connolly said nothing.

"A terrible thing. So young. And you think it might have something to do with the jewelry?" he asked gently.

"Frankly, no. But we need to check everything. It's a lot of money."

"Yes, I wondered about that too. He had all that money, and yet he didn't seem the type. Of course, since the war—"

"He paid in cash?"

"Yes, always in cash."

"Is that usual?"

"Usual? At that price? In Santa Fe? No, indeed. Still, I must say it was a convenience, not having to wait for a check to clear."

"But you didn't think there was anything wrong?"

Chalmers looked up at him.

"Wrong? There is never anything wrong with cash, my friend. Where he got it was his business, not mine. He wasn't a gangster, not that I could see. Maybe he gambled. Maybe he sold tires on the black market. Maybe he just preferred cash—some people do. I don't ask customers for bank references when they're handing me cash. I didn't know he would be killed."

"I didn't say he was."

"No, you didn't. But who else could it be? Maybe that explains it, carrying all that cash. And to think of such things in Santa Fe— robberies in broad daylight—"

"We assume it happened at night," Connolly said. "We don't know it was robbery. He may have been meeting a friend." He held the jeweler's gaze. The store was now very quiet.

Chalmers stared back at him, then spoke slowly and distinctly, as if he were using a code he did not want Connolly to misunderstand. "Perhaps. But I've never heard of such meetings. Not there. In Santa Fe, friends see each other in their houses. In private. It would be a shame to have anything disturb that. People get along because they keep to themselves. You wouldn't want to disturb that peace. Not here."

4

At first he didn't recognize her. She was walking toward him across the plaza, still dressed in the blouse and riding pants of the night before but with her hair down now, swaying lazily behind her, and her face partially hidden by sunglasses. She was carrying a few books under one arm, leaving the other to keep time with her long stride, and stopped short when she saw him on the curb.

"Oh God, it's you," she said. "Now I don't even have time to think what to say. I just hoped—you know, a few days and you'd forget." He looked at her, not saying anything, and she took off her sunglasses, as if he needed to complete the identification. "Don't tell me you *have* forgotten. Hard to think which would be worse. Emma."

He smiled. "Yes, I know. How are you feeling?"

"Not too bad, considering. Look, I am sorry. I don't know what got into me. You must think—well, I don't know what you must think. Quite an introduction, being sick all over you."

"No, you kept your distance. Don't worry about it."

"That's something, anyway. How *does* one apologize? Do I send round flowers or something? Believe it or not, I've never done that before."

"You could have lunch with me."

"A bit early. Or is that a line?"

"No, it's an invitation. I hate eating alone."

She looked at him for a minute. "All right. I could do with some eggs. Been to La Fonda yet? Oh, I forgot, you've just arrived. Better see it, then. Come on," she said, turning to her left, "it's just up the street. They say it's the best hotel in town. Which wouldn't be hard. They also say the barman's a spy—you know, one of your lot. FBI or whatever you're calling yourselves these days."

"Is he a good bartender, at least?"

"I suppose so. Actually, he's probably just some nice little man. Everybody looking and pointing and putting their hands over their mouths—probably doesn't have the faintest idea. Almost worth it to stick around after the war to see if he *does* go back to Washington or just keeps wiping down the bar."

They had huevos rancheros at a table near the window, flooded with sun.

"Where will you go after the war?" Connolly said.

"You mean, where's home? London, I suppose. It really depends on Daniel—my husband. Maybe he'll stay here, assuming there's anything to stay for. I don't know. He could go back to the Cavendish, but perish that."

"Why? It's the best lab in England."

"Yes, and think of all those lovely Sunday lunches on the Maddingly Road. Dreary old dons and watery sprouts and one glass of bad sherry. Sounds like I'm obsessed with drink, doesn't it?"

"Sounds like you'd need it there."

"You're right. Not Blighty, then. Where?"

"But your husband's not English."

"He is now. By marriage, anyway. You mean the name. He was Polish. A Polish Jew. That's twice nothing now, so he'll have to be English, won't he?"

"Where did you meet?"

"In Berlin. He was at the KWI." She answered his unspoken question. "Sorry. I forgot you're not an "engineer.' Kaiser Wilhelm Institute. He worked with Lise Meitner."

Connolly raised his eyebrows appreciatively.

"Yes, he's quite a boy," she said. "Look, did you ask me to lunch to talk about my husband? I'm not fishing, but I could think of a hundred more flattering things."

"Such as?"

"Well, you could say you wish I didn't have one, for a start."

"Does it matter?"

"Yes," she said evenly.

He looked back at her. "At least we have that established."

"Deftly, too, I hope you noticed."

"I don't miss much."

"Then don't miss that."

"I suppose that's by way of letting me down gently?"

She smiled. "Is there such a thing? Look, I'm a hopeless flirt. I can't help it, I was brought up that way. We all were, in my set. Here I am now, being *blinded* by this light and still hung over, and I wouldn't dream of picking up these sunglasses. It wouldn't be polite to the man, you see. But you'll have to settle for the charm. It doesn't go any further."

"Got it. It's just eggs, you know," he said, gesturing to the plate.

"It's never just eggs. Now, tell me about you."

"That's not even subtle," he said, smiling.

"Tell me anyway. What did you do before the war?"

"Newspaperman. In New York."

"Real news or agony aunt or what?"

"I guess you could call it real news. City desk. Police blotter. Nothing very special."

"And after the war? You just take up where you left off?"

Finished with the eggs, he lit a cigarette. "Sure. But where's that? You spend most of the war wanting to get back before you realize it won't be there anymore. It'll be something else. But you don't know what, so you just wait it out."

She looked at him thoughtfully, lighting her own cigarette. "They don't think that on the Hill," she said finally. "They're having the time of their lives up there."

"And that bothers you?"

"No, I envy them. They're not filling in time and wondering what's next. You've got that right. They've no idea how boring it is for the rest of us while they beaver away." Then she brightened. "Still, they're happy. Daniel's happy."

"So you're jealous of the project?"

"Bloody stupid, isn't it? No, I'm glad for him—it's what he was meant to do. They're making history. Oppie keeps saying so, anyway. You can't ask more than that. I just wish I knew what I was meant to do." She stubbed out the cigarette with some of her old fierceness.

"So what do you do, while you're waiting for the call?"

She looked at him, then laughed. "I'll have to watch you. You catch me out, making a fool of myself, and I don't mind. Why is that, do you think?"

"Maybe I don't scare easily."

"Oh, scare. That's what it is, then. I've always wondered. I thought it was my charm that sent them all packing. But not you."

"No, I'll stick around."

"I give you that. After last night I thought I'd seen the last of you."

"Don't apologize again. We've done that."

"So we have. What's next, then?"

"I wish you weren't married."

"We've done that too. Look, I'd better go. Let's get the bill."

"Now I'm scaring you. I'm sorry. I was just being cute. Don't run off—here, look, I'll stay on my side of the table."

"I still have to go."

"I thought you were going to show me Santa Fe."

She laughed. "You've seen it." She stopped and looked at him, as if trying to make up her mind about something. "I tell you what, though. If you really want to see something— the country, I mean—I was just on my way to a friend's ranch. Out past Tesuque. You could come along. Would that interest you?"

"Yes." He paused. "If I ask you something, will you answer me honestly?"

"No."

"Would it interest you?"

"Honestly? Well, if memory serves, darling, you boys in G-2 are rolling in coupons and I'm always running out. It was your car I had in mind. Honestly."

They drove north on the Tesuque road, past old adobes settled in cottonwood groves, shady and cool, but when the outskirts of town were behind them, the landscape opened up again, miles of country stretching off to the Jemez Mountains on their left. He stared straight ahead, concentrating on the road, but he could feel her next to him, one leg pulled up away from him on the seat as she blew smoke out the window. She was leaning back, her sunglasses on against the glare of the day. He couldn't tell whether she had her eyes open, but he imagined them closed, so he could take her in with quick side glances without her knowing. He could smell her skin.

"I thought you weren't allowed to fraternize with the locals," he said.

"Oh, Hannah's different. The project used her ranch before they built all the housing. They had us stashed all over the place in the early days. Before the fences went up."

"So she was your landlady?"

Emma laughed. "Well, a landlady. I never thought of her in that way. You'll see what I mean when you meet her."

"A local character?"

"Hm, but not local. She lives in Los Angeles. Something or other in the movies—sets. Here she's an artist. Quite a good one too, actually. Daniel and I kipped in her studio—the others were in the main house. So I spent my first few weeks here surrounded by corn."

"Corn? The vegetable?"

She laughed again. "Yes, maize. Giant ears of it on these whacking great canvases. She calls it her corn series. Says she spent two years *living* in corn. I can well imagine. Anyway, so did we, at least for a few weeks. In some ways, it was my favorite time here. I think that's when I really fell in love with the place. All this space.

She lent us her horses, and you could ride for hours and not see a soul. I thought it was about as far from England as you could get."

"And that's what you wanted?"

"Oh, no one wants to get away like the English. Unless you're one of those who don't want to go anywhere at all. I couldn't wait to get away. And this," she said, opening her hand to the view. "You can breathe here."

"But your family's still in England?"

"Yes. I couldn't wait to get away from them either. Still, I suppose it's a bit hard on them—I mean, they haven't a clue. Box 1663, Santa Fe. That's all they know. It can't possibly mean anything to them. We're not supposed to make any reference to the place or the work or anything, really."

"So what do they think you're doing here?"

"Haven't the faintest. They know I go riding and they know Daniel's a scientist, but since that doesn't make sense, they've probably given it up as a puzzle. Of course, Mother's been puzzled for years. She just rattles around this barn of a house while my father drills the locals in some awful Home Guard practice, and everybody's happy in their own dotty way. God, it's lovely to be here."

"Brothers or sisters?"

"You can read my file, you know. Yes, two sisters. Thoroughly satisfactory. Deb balls, good marriages, dogs—the lot."

"Which leaves you."

"Yes. I'm not satisfactory at all."

"You're delighted to say."

She glanced over at him and nodded. "I'm delighted to say."

"Anything else I should know?"

"Better save something for another day. You can peel me away, like an onion."

He grinned at her.

"It's a turn of phrase, dear," she said. "Nothing more."

After a few more miles they took a right, up a dirt road that paralleled the base of the Sangre de Cristo Mountains.

"How big is this place?"

"Not very. Hannah's got horses, but it's not a working ranch. You need thousands of acres for that. She started with just the adobe and then added the studio and the stables when she could put the money together. She's been here on and off for ten years or so."

"How did she end up in Hollywood?"

"Well, actually, she ended up *here*. She started there. She left Germany early, in 'thirty-four—there was a whole group that went straight from UFA to California. I don't know how she got here. You could ask her."

"Is everyone around here foreign?"

"Careful."

"I didn't mean you."

"I know. Sometimes it does seem that way, doesn't it? Packing us all away here. Odd they should have picked a place that doesn't look American, though, don't you think? I mean, you've got all these expats thinking America's like—"

"Spain."

"No, not Spain," she said, slowing down. "I've been there. It's nothing like that. Awful place. Of course, there was a war on, which didn't help."

"What were you doing there? Driving an ambulance or something?"

"Mostly just sitting around hating the place. Lots of little men strutting about like stout Cortez. You can't imagine the dreariness of it. Not like here at all."

"Why Spain?"

"Oh, I don't know. It was the thing to do, like some finishing school for English girls. The unsatisfactory ones, anyway. All sorts of us went out—you know, fight the good fight against fascism. And take a Spanish lover into the bargain."

He looked at her, interested. "But not you."

"I didn't say that. I just said they weren't my cup of tea. Maybe it's the mustaches—too silly."

"I'm glad I shaved."

"You'd have made a hit with Hannah. She loves a big mustache. Well"—she giggled—"big everything. Wait till you see Hector."

"Her husband?"

"Her foreman. Hand. Lover, according to everybody."

"He's big?"

"Hm. They should have called him Ajax. I love the way the Mexicans use these classical names. Anyway, he's strong as an ox—he can move anything. He's got a construction job on the Hill now that she's closing the ranch, and Hannah claims she's heartbroken. She dotes on him, but he won't go to Los Angeles. I don't know, maybe it suits them both. Hannah says he's an Aztec god, but then she treats him like a servant. I can't imagine what they talk about. Maybe they don't. I'm fond of Hannah, but every time I see them together I have to laugh. They look like one of those adverts for sex clubs in Berlin."

"The things you know," Connolly said.

But in fact she was right—the odd pairing was almost comically sexual. Hannah turned out to be a slim, pétite woman still wearing the short-cropped bangs of the 1920s, as if she had just stepped off Pabst's set. Next to her, bending over a tub of mud, was a large Mexican, stripped to the waist, his back rippling as he stirred the wet earth with a paddle. When he stood up at the sound of the car and wiped his forehead, his frame seemed a wall of muscle. Ladders had been placed on the side of the house, and two Indian women, entirely covered in long skirts, were applying the wet mud to the walls, smoothing it over with their hands in long, regular strokes. They moved with a sure, unbroken rhythm, practiced for centuries. Against this backgrund, Hector seemed even more a primitive figure, a builder of ancient cities.

"Emma!" the woman shouted happily, extending her arms. "You came!"

Her voice was German, deep and thickened by years of smoke but not at all heavy. It seemed to float instead with an ironic playfulness.

"Just in time for the last coat. You see my *enjaradoras*?" she said, pointing to the Indian women. "Hector found them at Ácoma. Aren't they wonderful? So smooth, look at the walls—like new."

"Hello, Hannah," Emma said, embracing her quickly. "I've brought a friend. Actually, he brought me. Michael Connolly, Hannah Beckman."

Hannah held up her muddy hands and bowed in greeting. "Forgive me," she said, smiling at him. "Today I'm a worker. I couldn't resist—the feel of the earth on your hands is something wonderful. I wanted to build my own house, just like the three little pigs, yes?"

She wiped her hands on a cloth. Neither Hector nor the Indian women paid any attention. They continued plastering the wall, their faces grave and impassive. Hannah took a cigarette out of her jacket pocket.

"But I am so glad you came. I thought I would not see you before I left. How is Daniel—he's well?"

"Busy."

"Ah. That's good, yes?"

"Well, it's good for him."

"Then it's good for you, my darling. So," she said, glancing at Emma's pants, "you came to ride and I've sent all the horses away. Now you'll be disappointed."

"No, I came to see you. We can't stay long. Isn't it early to be plastering?"

"What could I do? Next month is better, but

I have this week. Pray for me. Appease the gods." She looked up. "No rain, please, so Hannah's house can dry."

But the day was hot and clear and she spoke as if she knew luck was running her way. The house was a large square adobe with a hacienda-style overhanging porch decorated with long *ristras* of dried chiles. In the bright sun, the old tan walls had faded to the color of buckskin, accented by the traditional sky-blue paint around the door frame and windows. The wet mud would dry smoothly, without a crack.

"But why go to the bother if you're shutting up the house?" Emma said. "Can't it wait till you come back?"

"And when is that? No, you see the cracks from the winter? If you protect the bricks, they last forever. If not—" She left the consequences to their imaginations. "It must be done before the storms come in July, so better now. While Hector will still come. You're filling his pockets with gold up there. Maybe he'll never come back."

She spoke as if he were not there in front of them.

"Come. We'll have some tea, but first come watch my *enjaradoras*. You see how they measure the layer? Their hands tell them. Not too thin, but not too thick or it will fall off. They *feel* the mud and they know. They're great sculptors, these women, and everything they make is from the earth. Think of it—earth and water and straw, that's all. Buildings of earth.

Paintings of sand. Ah, but you disapprove, Mr. Connolly, I can tell." She turned to Emma. "He thinks I'm being a romantic."

"Not at all," Connolly said. "I was wondering how often this needs to be done—the walls."

Hannah laughed. "You see, I was right. A pragmatist. Every few years," she said to him, "depending on the severity of the winters."

"So not so very different from painting an ordinary house."

"But think what it means. You take the earth and build it all over again—your work is in the house. Not some cosmetic, not a Max Factor."

Connolly smiled. "Except for the blue eye shadow," he said, nodding to the window frames.

"Yes. The blue keeps the evil spirits away. Everyone knows that," she said lightly.

"Why blue? Because of turquoise?"

"It's odd you should say that," Hannah said. "The Navajos believe that turquoise keeps evil spirits away. But these doorways—these came from the Moors. They brought the custom with them when they took Spain. So it's nothing to do with the Indians at all. But blue—the same in both cases. It's odd, yes?"

"Maybe it has an appeal for desert people," he said. "A feel for the sky, something like that."

Hannah beamed. "Well, a romantic after all. Quite a catch, Emma."

It needn't have meant anything—a turn of phrase with nothing implied—but Connolly was pleased that Emma let it stand uncorrected. It was only a moment, but he took in it the furtive pleasure of conspiracy.

"Hector, I must give our guests some tea," she said, taking Emma by the arm. "Shall I make some for you?"

"Later. I need to finish up the flashings on the *canales*," he said in flat, unaccented English that slid into quickly inflected Spanish. He nodded to Emma and Connolly, his only greeting, and returned to his work.

"As you wish," Hannah said, her arm still linked in Emma's as they walked toward the house. "You see," she said, leaning her head toward Emma, "he's angry with me. Should I be pleased? I don't think so."

"But you've gone away before," Emma said.

"Yes, but this is different. The straw on the camel."

"Nonsense, he'll be here when you come back. He always is."

"Well, always," Hannah said dubiously. "Nothing is forever, my darling. Just the bricks. People have to move on. I think, you know, this will be the end of Hector."

"Why go, then?" Emma said as they entered the house.

"My new master. They don't like these long vacations at Fox. On the lot every day. What can I do? No more freelance. Mr. Zanuck says I have *responsibilities* now. Yes, sir." She raised her hand in a mock salute. "So I obey. The good soldier."

"You?" Emma said. "He doesn't know what he's letting himself in for."

The wide center hall, with two rooms off each side, was cool and dim, but it led to a large open room in the back that ran the entire length of the house, bordering the patio. It was an artificial room, clearly made by combining several smaller ones, and its whitewashed walls were Hannah's art gallery, filled with large, vivid canvases. She painted in closeup. Over the fireplace, Connolly noticed two paintings from the corn series, massive abstract ears of multi-colored kernels, but there were other subjects as well—desert landscapes, still lifes of chiles, an adobe wall lined with morning glories, so like the actual courtyard wall outside that it made a trompe l'oeil effect in the room. There were large terra-cotta jars on the tile floor and the geometric colors of Indian rugs. Single low-lying shelves held found objects—a rusty farm tool, little piles of pink rocks. Nothing was out of place. It was one of those rooms entirely arranged to serve an aesthetic.

The tea was ready so quickly that Connolly guessed she kept a kettle always near the boil. It was served, incongruously, in pretty Meissen cups, floral and delicate in the severe Southwestern room, like some gap in taste she could not leave behind.

"It was different before, of course," Hannah said. "At Paramount they didn't care. Well, maybe they did, but they didn't say. When Mr. da Silva was there—Buddy da Silva," she said, rolling his name. "So appropriate, you know. My Buddy." She lowered her voice to imitate the song and laughed. "You could come and go there. They appreciated the artists at Paramount. From the first. Think of Von Sternberg, what they put up with from him. Such behavior. But now it's a mess. Nobody knows anything. Before it was Marlene. Now Betty Hutton. It was time to go."

"Hannah, you've been complaining about Hollywood for as long as I've known you," Emma said.

"Yes? Well, that's not so long, is it? No, it *was* different before. I was different, perhaps. So now I go to design musicals. Boost morale. Make Mr. Zanuck happy," she said, smiling.

"And will that be any better?"

"But, my darling," Hannah said, laughing, "think of the *money*. They have so much money now. Why not take some? If I stay on the lot and keep everyone happy, I can come back here for good. Just paint and paint and paint and let them tap-dance until they fall over."

"You won't," Emma said. "You love it there."

"No," Hannah said seriously, "now I love the money. Besides, it's finished for me there. Europe is finished. They used to call me for the 'European touch.' They would say it just like that. "Hannah, give it the 'European touch.'" What is that now? A bomb shelter? Rubble? No, no more Europe here, I think. It's too serious now. This is a country of children." She glanced at Connolly. "Oh, my country too.

But now it's for children. Mr. Zanuck and his polo friends. I don't think he wants that European touch."

"What does he want?" Emma said.

"Now?" Hannah replied, her mood light again. "Havana nightclubs. Palm trees. Girls. More girls. So now we go to Havana for a while and have fun. And then I come home to paint."

"You're really going there?" Emma said.

"No, no," Hannah said. "They don't want to *go* to Havana, just the nightclubs. It's always the same nightclub. I went to Ciro's. They have a long staircase there. You stop at the top when you enter, you stop at the top on your way out—*two* appearances, you see. All the producers go there. So they see my set and they say, yes, *this* is a nightclub. Wonderful. Hannah's done it again. Maybe now I'll have the Ciro's touch."

Connolly watched them as they smoked and talked, a quicksilver flow of gossip, and saw that for Emma it was like leafing through some colorful magazine of the outside world. Selznick's divorce. The mad sets Dali designed for *Spellbound,* which Selznick was making because of his own psychoanalysis. Brecht, who never washed. Thomas Mann, who had recreated his Berlin apartment in Santa Monica. The difficulty of photographing Veronica Lake without making her look foreshortened. All messages from that world far from the mesa, where no one worked behind barbed wire and worried about algae in the water, where you could talk about anything. But what did she make of it? And as he watched her he realized, with a start, that she was watching him and that Hannah was aware of them both. They talked around him—he didn't have to say a word—but Emma would glance over at him secretly, to see what he thought, his expression conversation enough. He became in some curious way their audience, without either of them addressing him directly. The talk was as ephemeral as column filler, and after a while he felt that neither of them was really paying attention, Emma because she was caught up in some disturbance he caused, Hannah because she was watching a drama play out. He felt like someone brought home to dinner on approval and wondered if Emma regretted bringing him, now that it was his approval she seemed to care about. When he lit a cigarette, she was alert to the sound of the match, and when he looked at her through the smoke, she flinched involuntarily, as if she felt him touching her. It was Hannah who rescued them.

"But enough of this foolishness," she said, standing. "You must think I'm selfish, Mr. Connolly, talking only of myself like this. I'm afraid Emma's to blame—she likes to listen to me, and you know, I can't resist that. I don't see many people. Now you must tell me about you."

"He works up on the Hill," Emma said protectively, before Connolly could answer. "Here, let me help you with the washing-up."

"Ah, then I mustn't ask any more. So all my

chattering, it's just as well. I know the rules. Emma told you maybe that some of your colleagues lived here at the beginning? With the scientists, no questions."

Emma was collecting teacups and made no move to correct her, so Connolly said, "That must have been frustrating."

"For me? Not at all," Hannah said gaily. "I love secrets. And everyone was so charming. How is Professor Weissmann? Does he still play chess with Dr. Eisler? And that funny boy from New Jersey with the nice wife?"

"I never see them anymore," Emma said. "Everyone's scattered. Busy. I never see *you* anymore, come to that. It's like people you meet on holiday and then lose touch."

"Not you, my darling. Here you are, coming to see me off to Havana. And now you want to play *hausfrau*. Very well, here's mine too. You wash up and go be nice to Hector, say nice things about me, and I'll show your friend the ranch and say nice things about you."

Emma glanced at her, disconcerted. "That won't take long," she said.

"That depends on how much he wants to know. You see that I'm a terrible gossip," she said to Connolly. "Would you like that?"

"Very much," he said, smiling.

Emma, holding a cup in each hand, gave a helpless shrug. "Do be back for supper."

Surprisingly, Hannah leaned on his arm as they walked slowly toward the corral, not saying anything, an old couple. Even the silence seemed an unearned intimacy.

"She wants me to like you," she said finally. They had reached the corral and stood at the fence, looking west toward the mountains.

"Do you?"

"Me? It doesn't matter. She likes you."

"Look, I don't want you to think—"

"Ssh." She put her finger to her lips. "It's all right. Sometimes, you know, it's easier to say something to a stranger. Do you mind if I say something to you?"

He looked at her expectantly.

"Be careful with her. I've been worried lately. I knew something was troubling her—now I see it was you."

"You're mistaken."

"No. We can be honest with each other. Like strangers. I can see that you're—well, "in love,' what's that? Something for the night-clubs, a fantasy, yes? Something for the children. No. Involved with her. That's something too, you know. You can't help it either, I see. You watch her all the time."

"Do I?" Connolly said, trapped now in her premise, wanting to see where it would go.

She smiled. "Of course. That's why I'm saying this to you. I think you can be good for her. At first I thought it was the boredom, something to do. The same way she studies those Indians. But now I see it's more. With Emma, it's always something more, you know? She can't be casual. So you cannot be casual either, my friend. Don't hurt her. She deserves to be happy."

"Everyone deserves to be happy."

"Do you think so? Such an American idea. No, not everyone. But this time, yes." She patted his arm. "So make her happy."

"She's in love with her husband."

"Ach," she said, waving her hand dismissively. "Don't be foolish. She's in love with her own heroism. She got him out, that's why she married him."

"Out of Germany?"

"Yes, out of Germany, where else? She didn't tell you? It was the only way he could leave—become a British citizen. She married him to save his life."

"They're still married."

"Yes, it's as I say. Never casual. She had an impulse, she does a wonderful thing for him. A favor. A political act, even. Except with Emma, everything is personal, not political. So then? Does she live with that for the rest of her life? Evidently. She follows him to America, to this camp. She plays *hausfrau* while he goes to the laboratory. She studies her Indians. Anasazi." She pronounced each syllable of the word, a foreign-language joke. "Is that a life for her? So stubborn. This marriage—what is it? Some duty? I used to ask myself this. Now maybe you'll give us the answer."

He felt as if he had been pulled down a rabbit hole between past and future, his leg held in the grasp of her internal logic. To contradict her now seemed itself illogical. Like Alice, he began to doubt his own sense of things, and let go to follow his curiosity. She

112

didn't know what she was talking about; she might be right.

He must have been staring at her, because now she patted his arm again and said, "Yes, but not today, eh? Enough from this busybody, you think. But you don't say. You are polite. Not angry, I hope?"

"Neither. I just don't know what to say."

She sighed. "Then that is the best answer." They began to walk back toward the house. "You are right, of course. How can we know anything? We can only meet our destiny and then we know."

"Do you really believe that?" he said, eager to change the subject.

"Oh yes, of course. I'm a great believer in destiny. All Germans are. Maybe that will make it easier for them when their destiny arrives, now that those idiots have destroyed them."

"They don't seem finished yet."

"A death rattle, my friend. They are destroyed. There will be no Germany left at the end. Nothing. At least it will be the end of the gangsters too." She tossed her head, as if to shake off her somber mood. "But that is what we've been working for, yes? You with your work, me with my palm trees. The end of the gangsters."

"But if that was their destiny all along?" he said, sparring.

She smiled at him. "That is what makes destiny so interesting. Sometimes it needs a little push."

Emma was waiting for them at the house, visibly anxious to be off. Hector was now on the roof, and she stood alone by the new wet wall, which glistened in the drying sun.

"I'm glad you came to see my land," Hannah said to Connolly. "This is my whole country now."

"But you have to leave it," Emma said, joining them.

"I'll come back. I have nowhere else to go. Hollywood is not a place—you can't live there. This is a place."

"Can't you find someone to live here?" Emma said. "Then at least you wouldn't have to send the horses away."

"No, it's better this way. I don't want other people here. You come once in a while and be my caretaker. You always know where the key is," she said, looking directly at Emma. "Anytime. Then I won't worry."

Emma, flustered, simply nodded her head.

"I don't mind friends," Hannah said to Connolly. "It's the idea of strangers I don't like."

"But you had people here before," Connolly said.

Hannah looked at him, puzzled at his interest. "Well, I couldn't refuse then. Robert asked me."

"Robert Oppenheimer?"

"Yes. Robert asked all the old-timers. We all knew him, you see. What could we do? Some army man said it was our patriotic duty— you know, they talk like that—but Robert, he was clever. He just said he needed a favor, and, you know, he's charming, no one could refuse him."

"I'd forgotten he had a ranch here," Connolly said, backing off.

"Yes, in the mountains. For years. He loved to ride in those days. Does he still?"

"You haven't seen him?"

"No one has. He never comes here. Is he still up on the Hill, or is that one of your classified questions?"

Connolly shrugged.

"Well, then, I don't ask. But if you do see him somewhere, give him my regards. He should take care of his health, that one. And tell him that we're still waiting to hear what it was all about. Making history, he said. Oo la, that sounds important, but what kind of history, eh? Anyway, never mind about history, my darling," she said to Emma, giving her a goodbye kiss on her cheek. "Be happy." She shook Connolly's hand. "And you. Good luck with your destiny."

"And yours," he said, smiling.

"Oh, don't worry about me," she said, "I have the Ciro's touch."

Emma asked to drive back to Santa Fe, and he was surprised to find her inexperienced, coming up fast on curves and then jerking the clutch at the last minute as if she were pulling on reins. He was by now so used to her self-assurance that this inadequacy behind the wheel seemed touching, an opening. She held the wheel tightly, afraid the car would bolt.

"Sorry," she said after an audible moan from the gears. "I haven't got the hang of this one yet." She spoke straight ahead to the road, unable to switch her concentration.

"It's all right. It's stiff."

"No, it's not. But thanks. How did you like Hannah?"

"She seemed to think we'd known each other for some time."

"Did she? I wonder why. What did you say to her?"

"I didn't get a word in edgewise."

Emma grinned. "Yes. She can be like that. I wish she'd listen to Hector, though. There's something wrong there. He was positively churlish. He's usually rather sweet, in a way."

"I don't believe it."

"No, really. But he seemed all on edge. Something's happened."

"The bust-up?"

"Maybe. Oh, don't laugh. I know they're an odd couple. Still, it's sad to see any couple come to an end. They suited each other in a way."

He felt for an instant that now they were a couple, falling aimlessly into a postmortem after dinner with friends. "What way?"

"Now you're going to be impossible. I don't know—the way people *do*. There's no explaining it."

"No."

She glanced over at him quickly, then looked back to the road.

"She said you married your husband to get him out of Germany."

"Did she?" Emma said nervously. "I married him. He got out of Germany. They're not necessarily connected."

"Not necessarily."

She was quiet for a minute, avoiding the conversation. "Anyway, what does Hannah know about it?" she said, concluding an argument.

"I thought maybe you'd told her."

"I didn't. It's her imagination."

"Maybe she's intuitive."

"Maybe you're not a very good intelligence officer. Do you always believe the first thing you hear?"

"When I want to."

"Well, don't." She downshifted, flustered. "What else did she have to say?"

"Not much. This and that and Germany and destiny."

"Quite a chat."

"Very gloomy and Wagnerian."

"Hannah?" She laughed. "You must bring out something in her. She doesn't usually get much further than Louella Parsons. Louella *O.* Parsons. What do you think the O stands for?"

"Are you trying to change the subject?"

"Trying."

"All right. How about banks?"

"What do you mean?"

"Is there a bank in Santa Fe everyone uses? Where do you go, for instance?"

She laughed. "That's certainly changing it. I don't go anywhere. We're not allowed to have accounts off-site."

"What do you do? Keep it in a sock under the bed?"

"There's not very much to keep, for a start. What there is we keep in a post account. I suppose everyone does. Why do you want to know?"

"So if you made a large cash purchase, you'd have to withdraw the money from this account? I mean, you wouldn't write a check?"

"No. Cash. I suppose if it were a lot, you'd get a money order from the post office. Except I never do. It always just goes somehow."

Connolly was quiet for a minute, thinking.

"Now may I ask why?" she said.

"I was just wondering why anybody would carry a lot of cash, when a check is so much easier."

"Not anybody. You mean Karl, don't you?" she said, her voice suddenly tight. "They said he was robbed. Is that why? He was carrying a lot of money?"

"I don't know."

"Are you—" She hesitated. "The police?"

"No," he said easily, "but naturally we're curious too."

"Naturally."

"I didn't realize you knew him."

"Everybody knew him. He was security. There's no escaping you."

"Did you like him?"

She seemed surprised by the question, at a loss. "He was all right, I suppose," she said finally.

"So you weren't tempted by his coupons?"

"What?"

"You said before that G-2 had lots of coupons."

"Did I? Quite the elephant, aren't you? No, I wasn't tempted by his bloody coupons."

"Just mine."

She sat back in the seat, smiling involuntarily. "Just yours."

"Well, that's something, anyway. Maybe next time it'll be for the pleasure of my company."

"Is there going to be a next time?"

"Isn't there?" he said quietly.

She turned to look at him. "I don't know," she said seriously. "Don't ask me, okay? I don't know."

When she changed cars in Santa Fe, she shook his hand nervously and tried a casual good-bye, but since they were both heading back to the Hill, she didn't leave him after all. He followed her car up to the Parajito Plateau, watching her glance into the rearview mirror as she spurted ahead, then waited for him to catch up, darting along the empty desert road like birds from the mesa in a courtship flight. She drove fast, carelessly ignoring the speed limit, but he trailed smoothly in her wake, close enough to keep eye contact in the mirror, until finally she laughed and waved and, allowing herself to be pursued, they drove together.

5

Mills was uncharacteristically official about
getting Bruner's account records.
"We'd need some kind of order," he
said. "They have the same legal protection as
real bank records would. We can't just—"

"How long would it take to get them?"

Mills sighed. "About an hour."

But Bruner's account was no different from
his passbook, as orderly as his room had been.
Connolly scanned the even columns, month
after month of regular deposits, with no significant withdrawals. When he compared
them to the payroll records, he found himself
staring at an unrevealing window into Bruner's
life. Once he deducted the subsidized rent from
his salary, he was left with the account deposit
and the same amount of pocket money each
time.

"Look at this," he said to Mills. "Did he have
any expenses?"

"Well, Karl was close with a dollar. He
never grabbed a check if he could help it."

"But this goes all the way back to 'forty-four.
At the most, a ten-dollar variance here and
there."

"Clothes, probably," Mills said.

"What about his car? That can get pretty
extravagant these days."

"He fiddled that."

"How fiddled?"

"Whenever he needed gas, he'd sign up for

escort duty—you know, taking the scientists around—and he'd top up from the motor pool supply. Repairs, same thing. He was like that. What exactly are you looking for, anyway?"

"Three two-hundred-dollar withdrawals in the last six months."

Mills whistled. "You're kidding. Where did Karl get that kind of money?"

"That's what I want to know. According to these, he saved everything. So where did he get the extra money? He hasn't touched this account in over a year."

"Maybe he had it from before."

"Maybe. Then why not bank it?"

"The Europeans are funny that way. Some of them don't trust banks at all. They just stash the money or put it into gold or something they can carry. You know, refugee stuff. Maybe he brought something over with him and then sold it."

"No. Why do that and turn around and buy something else?"

"What did he buy?"

"Turquoise jewelry."

"Karl?"

"That's what I thought."

Mills was quiet for a minute. "Then he must have been trying to hide it."

"How do you mean?"

"Keep it off the books. Put it somewhere you couldn't trace it. You know, sew it in your jacket lining to cross the border, that kind of stuff."

"You've been seeing too many movies," Connolly said.

"Maybe, but they did it. They weren't allowed to take anything out. Professor Weber's wife had her earrings ripped out on the train."

Connolly winced. Another European story.

"Okay, but where did he get it? He didn't deposit it, but somebody must have taken it out. Tell you what, let's have a look at all the records."

"Are you kidding? Do you know how many people we have up here?"

"Over four thousand. But not all of them have accounts, and we can eliminate the crews and the enlisted men—in fact, anyone making less than two thousand dollars a year. They wouldn't have that kind of money lying around. That ought to bring it down to a few hundred at most."

"This will take weeks."

"Then the sooner you get started, the better."

"I get started?"

"We both get started. Six hundred bucks shouldn't be too hard to find."

"Assuming it's someone with an account. Assuming they took the money out. Assuming it's someone up here."

"Assuming all that."

"I didn't know we were assuming it was someone on the Hill," Mills said pointedly.

"We're not. We're looking for six hundred dollars, and this is somewhere to start. You can eliminate all the women, too."

Mills looked up at him. "So that's where you're going. You think Karl would do that?"

"What would have happened to him if he'd been exposed as homosexual?"

"He'd have been discharged."

"So he'd want to keep it very quiet then, wouldn't he? Anyone like him would. He'd understand that. He knew what that felt like. What if he wasn't the only one up here who needed to keep things quiet? What if he thought that might be—well, an opportunity. Is that so farfetched?"

Mills nodded. "Not very nice, but not farfetched, I guess. So you think Karl was putting the bite on someone?"

"Let's just say he sounds capable of it. For all I know, the money was a present. Maybe he had a boyfriend. Maybe there's no connection at all. But we have a general who'd rather not know, a director who doesn't want to know, and a police force that wouldn't know if you showed them 'cause they're too busy pretending everyone's Buster Crabbe. So we'd better start somewhere. You want to get the records?"

"You're going to need Oppie's okay on this. Getting Karl's account is one thing, but my friend Eddie over there isn't going to turn the whole goddamn project over. That's pretty personal stuff you're talking about. People aren't going to like us sniffing around their money. Hell, *I* don't like it."

"Don't tell them, then. You don't make enough to be so touchy," Connolly said, smiling.

"I just mean it's personal, that's all."

Suddenly the windows shook as the sound of a blast came up from the west.

"What the hell was that?"

"Kisty's group. Explosives. They use some of the lower canyons around the plateau for testing." He grinned as another blast sounded in the distance. "You get used to it."

"How do you keep bombs a secret when you keep shooting them off?"

"These are just the triggers. And how do you test them if you don't explode them? They used to do it at night, but everybody complained. No sleep as far away as Santa Fe, or so they said. I don't know who we think we're fooling."

"All of the people all of the time."

"Yeah." Another explosion went off as Mills turned to go. "Now for the quiet life of a bank examiner."

The records, when they finally arrived with Oppie's warning to keep the audit secret, proved more absorbing than Connolly expected. He had imagined tracing tedious columns of numbers, but instead the whole complexity of daily life at Los Alamos seemed to lie there undeciphered, spread across their desks like messages in code. To understand the savings, he needed Mills to explain the expenses. Paychecks were cashed at the commissary, supplies purchased at the PX. Some expenses were fixed: rents pegged to annual salaries—

$29 a month at $2100, $34 at $3400, etc.; utilities to space—$9.65 for a three-room McKee. But beyond that, there was the sheer variety of financial lives—the thrifty savers, the spenders borrowing down, the hoarders who must have kept their cash, since none of it appeared in the books. He wondered why auditors were considered boring. Maybe they were simply hypnotized by the stories behind their numbers. He was surprised, though, to see how low the amounts were. They might be making history on the Hill, but no one was making much money. Two hundred dollars should leap off the page. But so far it hadn't.

The problem with the decoding process, for all its fascination, was that it could take weeks. They needed a smaller test group, like scientists who worked down the table of elements to narrow the possibilities. It was Mills who came up with the morning tagging system, and for the next few days they followed the same routine. Connolly would telephone Holliday to see if the police were any further along, exchanging disappointment over coffee, then sit down with Mills for the quick first pass. Files with regular deposits were immediately put on the return pile. Variations under a hundred dollars were given a quick glance, then returned as well. Anything else was tagged for the afternoon, when they could piece together the file with more care, no longer as overwhelmed by the size of the pile to come. Now it was the exception pile that grew instead, so that they were working out of alphabetical sequence, the names often not even noticed as they looked at the number patterns. A choice few, where the numbers seemed puzzling, went on to the small pile for further investigation. But the Hill's privacy, thought Connolly, was safe. The names were meaningless to him.

It was only when he examined Emma's husband's account that he felt Mills might have been right—this was personal. He felt prurient, like a burglar going through drawers. There was nothing odd about the account—erratic deposits, but marginal amounts—yet he stared at the paper as if he were staring into the marriage itself. Did Emma handle the money? Or did he dole out allowances? Why no deposit one month—a celebration dinner? A weekend in Albuquerque? Did they fight? Did she use up her clothes coupons or wait until she had enough for a splurge? But the paper, typed numbers on army buff, in the end told him nothing. He touched it as if he could coax it to reveal something, but the numbers were simply numbers and the lives were somewhere else. The audit suddenly seemed foolish. What did he expect any of these accounts to reveal? He was looking at the financial life of the Hill, but the people were as unknown as ever. The numbers kept their secrets. Why expect a connection to Bruner anywhere? Here was a file to which he could attach a face, and it told him nothing that mattered. How often did they sleep together? What was it like? Why, for that matter, should he care?

"Got something?" Mills said, looking up.

"No," Connolly said. "My mind was just drifting." He put the file on the stack of discards before Mills could see the name and lit a cigarette. "You know, maybe we're looking at this the wrong way."

"I told you that two days ago."

"No, I mean, it's not what's in here that's interesting, it's what isn't here."

Mills looked at him oddly.

Connolly smiled. "I guess I'm not making much sense."

"No, I was just thinking. Bruner used to say that. "It's what isn't here.' Just like that. I remember him saying it."

Connolly stared at him, disconcerted. They couldn't possibly have been talking about the same thing. What had Bruner meant?

"When?" he asked.

Mills thought for a minute. "Well, that's the funny thing. It was just like this, when he was going through the files."

"These?"

"No, security clearance. Karl liked to go through the files. Of course, it was part of his job, but he said it was a great way to get to know people. So he'd go over them. And when I'd say, "You must know everything in there,' he'd say, "It's what isn't here.' Just the way you did."

Connolly was silent. "Where do you keep them?" he said finally.

127

"In a safe over in T-1. Oh, no."

"But he removed them. So there must be a log?"

Mills nodded.

"Let's see who he checked out over the past six months—no, nine months."

"Why not a year, just to play it safe?"

"Okay."

"I was being funny."

"Be convenient if we found something that matched up with one of our exception files here, wouldn't it?" Connolly said, patting them.

"A miracle."

"Anyway, it's something."

"Mike, it's a *phrase*. It was just something to say. This isn't getting us anywhere."

"Maybe. But he was interested in them. The least we can do is look at what interested him. Maybe it'll tell us something about him."

"Want me to get a forklift or bring them over one by one?"

"How about just the log for now? Let's see if he wanted to get to know anybody real well."

But Bruner had often been assigned to do vetting—he was one of several security officers who interviewed new employees and did updates on the others—so his initials were all over the log. Even using the same process of elimination they'd fixed on for the bank accounts, they were facing a long list.

"Let's focus on the repeats," Connolly said.

"Anyone he was particularly interested in. There has to be something." He looked up to find Mills staring at him. "What?"

"Nothing," Mills said, looking away. "What if he didn't log them out?"

"Could he do that?"

"He was security. He was supposed to take files. Nobody's going to check on him."

Connolly considered for a minute. "No, that's not like him."

"How do you know? You never knew him."

"I live in his room. He'd log out."

"In other words, he'd commit a criminal act, but he'd never break the rules."

"You'd be surprised. I've known guys run somebody through with a knife and then wipe it clean because they're naturally neat."

"He wasn't like that," Mills said quietly, scraping his chair as he stood up.

"Something bothering you?"

"Let's get some air. I can't think straight, and I know you're not."

Surprised, Connolly followed him out, waiting until they were on the dusty street before he said anything. Mills leaned against a rough utility pole, the bald spot on his head shining in the afternoon light.

"So?"

"Look, I'm just a lawyer, not some hotshot reporter. Maybe this is just going too fast for me. First I'm thinking you don't know what you're looking for. Now you already know what you want to find. Is there something I'm missing here?"

"Relax. You're ahead of me."

"Am I? A few days ago, Karl was the *victim*. Then he's queer and now he's blackmailing somebody. And you're all hot to get the story. It's not—right. Look, I worked with this guy. He wasn't my favorite drinking buddy, but he was all right. What are we trying to prove, anyway? That there's a murderer walking around up here?" He gestured toward the street, the usual mix of trucks and jeeps churning dust, technicians walking between buildings.

"Stranger things have happened."

"I don't believe it. The police don't believe it. So what makes you so sure?"

"Not a goddamn thing. But there's something wrong with the police story. They've got Karl wrong."

"How do you mean?"

"It's careless. Did he strike you as the kind of guy who'd go in for pickups? In workboots?"

Mills looked at him, puzzled. "Why workboots?"

"Police found prints. That seem right to you? Wouldn't you say he was more the fastidious type?"

"I guess." Mills frowned, then looked away toward the old school buildings as if he'd pick some answer out of the air. "I might have said that once. Now? I don't know." He shrugged. "All that time, and it turns out I didn't know the first thing about him. All that time. He was someone else all along."

"Tell me about him, then. Help me with this,

Mills—don't fold on me. I need to know what he was like."

"I thought you'd already decided that."

"Does it make sense to you that someone who survived two prison camps would be careless with strangers?"

"Well, you know what they say—a stiff prick has a mind of its own."

Connolly ignored him. "Does it make sense?"

"No, but none of it does. Okay, so he wasn't the pickup type. He didn't *seem* to be. But he was there. He wasn't alone. So who was it?"

"I think he met somebody."

Mills stared at him again. "You mean somebody from up here."

"Maybe."

"Then why go to Santa Fe?"

"I don't know." Connolly thought for a minute. "You said he liked surveillance detail. Was he covering someone that day?"

"No."

"You sure?"

"Sure. It was his day off. You can check the sign-up sheet. I remember because we were shorthanded that weekend and I asked him, but he begged off."

"What happens when you're shorthanded?"

Mills shrugged.

"They go without cover?"

"Not the priority list. Oppenheimer, Fermi— there's a group that always have a bodyguard or they don't leave the project. The others, we

131

do spot covers. The whole point is that they don't know when they're covered, so they have to assume they are. It works all right. Nobody's been kidnapped yet."

"Congratulations."

"Or had any trouble. They're not the kind. They go on *hikes*, you know? Picnics. Family stuff. Once in a while a dinner at La Fonda. You don't seriously think it was one of the scientists."

"Why not? That would explain the money. They're the only ones here making more than six grand a year. Two hundred bucks would be a big piece of change for anyone else."

"No," Mills said, shaking his head. "It's ridiculous. They're professors. Pointy-heads. Half the time they're up there somewhere in the clouds anyway, not down here with the rest of us. They're not—" He searched for a word. "Violent. I mean, that's the last thing they are."

Connolly smiled. "They're making a bomb."

"They're not, though. They're solving a problem. That's how they see it."

"That's some trick," Connolly said. "Okay, so they don't go around knocking people over the head. But we don't know why he was hit. People do some unlikely things when they're upset. You admit at least that it's possible he had a friend up here?"

"Anything's possible."

"He met somebody. Why not a friend?"

"Then we're back where we started. Why go to Santa Fe?"

"Maybe they were discreet. Maybe they liked to meet off the Hill."

Mills shook his head. "God, I hate this. Pretty soon you'll have me thinking just like you do, walking around here thinking "Is he one?' Suspecting everybody. This isn't New York, you know."

"Don't go small-town on me now," Connolly said. "You're a big boy."

"But this is a small town—that's just what it is. Do you know how much trouble we've had since the project started? None. A few kids sneaking through the fence. A little hanky-panky in the women's dormitory. A fight now and then over in the hutments. That's it. It sounds crazy, but this is the nicest place I've ever lived."

"Except it has one dead guy in it."

"Who was killed forty miles away. But that doesn't feel right to you, so now we've got a killer on the loose up here. And we're going to catch him by going through his bankbook. Aw," Mills said, waving his hand in disgust, "we're not thinking straight."

"You can't get away from the money. Where did he get the money?"

"If his friend is so rich, why was he wearing boots?"

"You got me. Maybe they're not connected."

Mills looked up to answer him and then stopped, his attention drawn away. They had walked back toward the Tech Area and now stood beside the fence, sidestepping a jeep. A girl in heels, her white badge flapping against her sweater, brushed past the MP guard, her face covered in tears. Outside the gate, she squinted into the late afternoon sun, then, blinded by the light, walked unsteadily past them, nearly knocking into Mills as she went.

"What was that?" Mills said.

"Trouble in paradise," Connolly said lightly. "The boss yelled. The boyfriend took a hike. Maybe it's—"

"No, look," Mills said, stopping him with a hand on his shoulder. "Something's happened."

Suddenly the street began to fill with people coming out of the buildings, then standing around aimlessly, unsure what to do, as if an explosion had gone off inside. Some of the women hugged each other. Others began to move in haphazard groups toward the open area in front of the Admin Building, anxious and listless at the same time.

Mills went up to the guard. "What's going on?"

"It's the President—Roosevelt's dead," he said, not looking at them.

Nobody said a word. Connolly felt winded, caught by an unexpected punch. He was surprised by how much he minded. Only the war was supposed to end, not the foundation of things. Now what? He imagined himself back in Washington—bells tolling, people stupefied in their maze of offices, the humming of gossip about a new order that was beginning before its time. Most of the people he knew there had come to Washington for Roosevelt, measuring their lives by his successes. They never expected to know anything else. Now the others would begin scurrying to make the town over—it wasn't too soon, even now. For the first time since he'd come to Los Alamos, Connolly missed it, that nervous feeling of being at the center of things, where telephones rang and everything mattered. He felt suddenly marooned on a cool, bright plateau, looking at an inconsequential crime while the rest of the world skipped a beat.

They joined the others drifting toward the Admin Building, drawn home like children after dark. It was only when he saw Oppenheimer appear on the steps that he realized why they had come. There was a different White House here, and the plain army-green building was as central and reassuring as the one across from Lafayette Square. There were no loudspeakers and Oppenheimer barely raised his voice, so that Connolly missed most of what he said. There would be a service on Sunday. He knew everyone must be shocked. He knew they would carry on the President's ideals. The words faded even as he spoke them. But no one looked anywhere else. His face visibly troubled, Oppenheimer held them all with the force of his caring. In Washington there had been the rakish glint of Roosevelt's eyes, his generous celebration of worldliness, but here the center was held by Oppie's almost luminous intelligence. It was his town. When something went wrong—the water supply, a death in the larger family—they didn't have to hear what he said. It was enough to have him here.

Connolly looked around the crowd of his new town. Scientists in jeans. Nurses and WACs and young typists with vivid red nails. MPs. Fresh-faced graduate students in sweater vests and ties—you could almost see them raising their hands in class, eager to impress. Some were openly weeping, but most people simply stood there, sober after a party. And then Oppenheimer was finished, coming down the few steps to join the crowd, and people began drifting back, not wanting to burden him further.

Connolly couldn't stop watching him, and Oppenheimer, glancing up, caught his stare and looked puzzled for a moment, until he placed him. He was walking toward them, and Connolly felt oddly pleased to be singled out, then embarrassed when he saw that Oppie had been headed for Professor Weber all along.

"Well, Hans," he said, placing a hand on his shoulder, "a sad day."

Weber, always in motion, now seemed to bubble over. "Terrible, terrible. A gift to the Nazis. A gift."

Oppenheimer looked at his watch. "It's already tomorrow there. Friday the thirteenth. Dr. Goebbels won't even have to consult his astrologer. For once, a clear sign, eh?"

"But Robert, the music. What should we do? Should we cancel this evening? It seems not respectful."

"No, by all means let's have the music," Oppenheimer said softly. "Let the Nazis look

136

at their entrails—we'll take our signs from the music."

Weber nodded. Oppenheimer, in a gesture of remembering his manners, turned to include Connolly. "You know Mr. Connolly?"

"Yes, forgive me. I didn't see you. We met at the dancing."

"How are you getting on?" Oppenheimer said.

"All right, I guess."

"Good. You must invite him to your evening, Hans." Then, to Connolly, "All work and no play—it can be a disease here. They're really quite good."

"But I have invited him. Yes? You remember? So come."

"I'm planning on it. If there's room."

"Oh, there's always room," Oppenheimer said. "And the cakes are even better than the music."

"*Vays mir*," Weber said, putting his hand to his head. "Johanna. You'll excuse me, please?" But he went off before anyone could answer.

Oppenheimer lit a cigarette and sucked the smoke deeply, like opium. "He likes to help. *Schnecken*. Seed cake. I think the music is an excuse. How *are* you getting on?"

"Slowly. Thanks for running interference on the files."

"I hope they're worth it. They say bad things run in threes—maybe you'll find something yet."

"Would that make three? Has something else happened?"

"No, I'm anticipating. It's been just the

opposite. Today Otto Frisch finished the critical assembly experiments with metallic U-235." He paused, looking at Connolly. "You haven't the faintest idea what I'm talking about, have you? Well, so much the better. I probably shouldn't be talking about it in any case. Suffice it to say, it's a significant step—best news in a week. And now this. No doubt there's some philosophical message in it all, but I'm damned if I see it."

"Did you know him well?"

"The President? No, not very well. I've met him, of course, but I can't say I knew him. He was charming. But that's beside the point."

"Which is?"

"It was his project. He okayed it. Now it's anybody's guess—"

"Truman opposed it?"

"He doesn't know about it."

"What?"

Oppenheimer smiled. "You know, I'm constantly surprised at security's being surprised when something secret is kept secret. No, he doesn't know. Nobody there knew except Roosevelt and the committee. And I expect he'll be furious when Stimson tells him what he didn't know."

"Touchy, anyway," Connolly agreed. "But he's not going to pull the plug at this point."

"How well do you really know Washington? This project has cost nearly two billion dollars." He watched Connolly's eyes widen. "None of the men you sent to Washington to spend your money knows a thing about it."

138

"That's a lot of money to hide," Connolly said, thinking about his own paltry search.

"Only Roosevelt could have ordered it," Oppenheimer said. "It had to come from the top. Still does."

"So you're off to Washington, hat in hand?"

"No," Oppenheimer said, "nothing that drastic. General Groves will take care of it—he knows his way around those land mines better than anybody. But it's—" He hesitated, grinding out his cigarette. "A complication. We were always racing against time, and now it's worse. It's a bad time to get a new boss."

"It always is."

"This is a par*tic*ularly bad time."

"Can I ask you a question? What if it doesn't work?"

"I never ask myself that. It will."

"Because it has to?"

"Because the science is there. It will work. The question now is what happens after that. The generals will want to own it. We'll need a whole new kind of civilian control. Otherwise, all our work here—" He looked away, rehearsing some talk with himself. "Otherwise, it will be a tragedy. Roosevelt saw that. Now we have—who? Some politician nobody ever heard of. How can he be expected to make such a decision? For all I know, he'll think it's just a giant hand grenade." He stopped, catching himself. "Well, let's hope for the best," he said, looking back at Connolly. "A little music for the soul. Seven o'clock. Weber's on Bathtub Row—just ask anyone. By the way, I hope you're not looking too closely at my bank account. It feels like someone's going through my laundry."

When Connolly got back to the office, there was a message to call Holliday.

"I have something for you," he said, not even bothering to mention Roosevelt. Most people on the Hill had taken an unofficial holiday and left early. "We found out where your boy went that night. Or at least where his car went."

"You found the bar?"

"He wasn't drinking. He went to church."

"Church?"

"San Isidro, out on the Cerrillos Road. A Mex place."

"What would he be doing in church? He was a Jew."

"I didn't say he was praying. I just said his car was parked there. An alley next to the church. Not a parking lot, exactly, but people park there."

"What's around?"

"Houses. A gas station. No bars. Quiet."

"And one of the neighbors saw him?"

"No. Actually, one of my men. You were right, put out the word and you always haul something in. The night of the killing, he was driving past on his way to some complaint and noticed the car there. Didn't think anything of it until I put out the description of the car."

"What made him notice it?"

"A 'forty-two Buick? In a Mexican neighborhood?"

"But he didn't stop?"

"There's nothing illegal about parking there. Figured it must be somebody visiting."

"The church was open?"

"Not for mass. They don't lock churches around here. This one pulls in a tourist now and then. They've got an old *reredos* there that's supposed to be something special."

"At that time of night? What time was it, anyway?"

"Nine maybe, more or less. He's a little fuzzy about that. If you ask me, he was taking his own sweet time about answering the complaint and didn't want to say so."

"Where's the church in relation to where Bruner was found?"

"Well, it's out a ways, but you go straight down Cerrillos over the bridge and you're on the Alameda."

"So it's the first park?"

"In that direction, yes."

"Okay. So he saw Bruner?"

"No, just the car. He thought it was funny, a car like that, but like I said, he figured it was somebody visiting. You know, some Anglo with a girlfriend down there."

"Is there a lot of that?"

"All over the world."

"Very funny. So if he didn't see him, we don't know for sure he was actually there."

"Oh, we know. We found his blood."

He imagined Holliday's face as he said it, the jaws clamping shut in satisfaction. He listened to the silence for a minute. "Want to tell me about it?"

"There's a patch of ground near the church, right under where the tile sticks out. Seems it never rains there, so we got some dry ground with some blood on it."

"And it's Bruner's."

"O negative. I figure it's a safe assumption."

"So Bruner gets hit next to some Spanish church and his body winds up in the park and his car disappears."

"That's what it looks like."

"I wish I could say any of it made sense."

"Well, I wish you could too. And while you're at it, try making some sense of his pants now. Kinda changes things, don't you think? Doesn't fit, that kind of activity at a church. Would they do that there? Then driving him all over with his pants down. No sense to it. Could be we're sniffing around the wrong tree here. You know, maybe he wasn't that way at all."

"It was your idea."

"Well, I've been known to be wrong. Once or twice."

"Then how do you explain the pants?"

"I can't. Yet. I'm just saying it's a hell of a place to have sex."

"Well, for that matter, it's a hell of a place to kill somebody. But why move him?"

"The thought that occurred to me was that

they didn't want him found so easy. He'd stick out like a sore thumb at the church, but he could have been days in the park. Well, one."

"Then why not just take him out to the country and bury him?"

"Well, if you get a better idea, let me know."

"You talk to the neighbors?"

"Sure. *Nada.* Amazing how the Spanish mind their business when the police come around. I never knew a people for going to bed so early."

"But why move him? That's what I don't get."

"I don't know. But I tell you one thing, it sure wasn't out of respect for the church."

6

P erhaps people needed to be together after a death in the family, or perhaps Professor Weber's evenings were always better attended than he liked to think, but his house was crowded. A cluster of music stands had been set in one corner of the living room, and people spilled out in groups down the hallway in a line to the kitchen, where the coffee and trays of cakes were arranged on a crocheted tablecloth. The air was warm and close with cigarette smoke and the overpowering scent of butter, sugar, and cinnamon. Connolly felt wrapped in the cozy sweetness of a prewar bakery and wondered for a minute where all the coupons had come from; did the bachelors trade Frau Weber their ration books for these once-a-week memories of home? The coffee smelled rich and strong, but as many people held glasses as coffee cups, and the hum of conversation rose and fell in the familiar lapping waves of a cocktail party. Pregnant women occupied the few upholstered easy chairs, with friends draped on the broad arms, balancing plates. Oppenheimer was there, a martini glass in one hand, his hair so short that without his hat his head seemed almost shaved. He barely acknowledged Connolly with a nod. His wife, Kitty, sat near him, her legs curled beneath her on a sofa, an ashtray in her lap, but paid no attention to her husband as she stared through her smoke, preoccupied with some interior conversation. She had clearly ceded all hostess duties to Johanna Weber, who bubbled all around her, directing people to food and making introductions.

"Mr. Connolly, yes, my husband has told me about you. I'm so glad you could come. Do you know Mrs. Oppenheimer? Kitty, Mr. Connolly." Kitty glanced up, but Johanna Weber had already moved him along, introducing everyone in their immediate vicinity. "Mr. Connolly, Professor Weissmann, his wife, Frieda. Mr. Connolly. Dr. Carpenter. Dr. Carpenter is visiting us this week—" And so it went, a party trick, one name following another without pause and without forgetting. Connolly thought she was wasted on the Hill. In Washington she could have run one of the great houses in Rock Creek, her mind a vast photographic file of names and connections.

"And this is Emma Pawlowski." She hurried on, scarcely noticing that Emma's back was turned to her. "Her husband, Daniel."

Connolly stopped and nodded, hopelessly curious, but Pawlowski was a pleasant-looking young man, eager to be polite, who had obviously never heard of him and wanted only to resume his conversation with Carpenter. His skin was a scholar's pale white, with what seemed to be a permanent five-o'clock shadow.

"Yes, we've met," Connolly said as Emma turned around. She looked oddly festive, her nails and mouth vivid red, her eyes shining. Connolly realized it was the first time he had seen her in a skirt, so that she seemed overdressed, as if she had put on heels and makeup for another party and landed here instead.

"Again and again," she said. "You seem to be everywhere." And then to her husband, who looked mildly puzzled, "Darling, this is Mr. Connolly I told you about. Or did I? Anyway, he very kindly drove me to Hannah's, so you must be especially nice. He's new on the Hill."

"Welcome," Pawlowski said in the flat, monotonal accent of one who had learned too many languages. Connolly wondered fleetingly if Conrad had sounded like this, both Polish and English squeezed of all inflection. "Whose unit are you with?"

"Oh darling, he's not a scientist. He's with *security* or something. It is security, isn't it?" she said, all innocence.

145

Connolly nodded.

"But you like music," Pawlowski finally said, at a loss to explain him, and not sure it was worth the effort.

"No, he's come to spy on us," Emma said playfully. "Absolutely tone-deaf. Can't hear a note."

Pawlowski looked at her, then smiled gently, a lover's indulgence for what he didn't understand. It seemed enough that she was lovely and spirited; he didn't have to keep up to admire her for it.

"Then I will have to play more loudly," he said, missing the joke. The effect was to make him seem younger than he was, a boy making his way. Connolly looked at his polite face and thought about the unreliability of language. He had studied with Meitner, a man of importance at the KWI, but faced with idle chat he became an awkward teenager. Like so many others on the Hill, he would have to retreat to the language of science to find his maturity.

Johanna Weber was there again, a tugboat still steering him through the harbor. "As loudly as you like, Daniel. Never a wrong note. Not like Hans. But come, some coffee, Mr. Connolly?"

"Or perhaps you'd like a drink," Emma said, holding up her glass. For an instant, Connolly wondered if that explained the shine in her eyes.

"Coffee would be fine," he said, and Johanna Weber beamed, clearly pleased, and took him in tow to the tall urn. Emma gave him a weak, ironic salute with her glass.

"Here," Johanna Weber said, handing him a cup. "Shall I get you some cake?" But she was distracted by a new arrival, and Connolly watched the party game begin all over again, one accurate name following another.

The day had been somber—these were some of the same faces he had seen drawn and grieving in front of the Admin Building—but the party had taken on a life of its own, and as each voice rose to be heard above the others, the small house hummed with a kind of decorous gaiety. The Webers' rooms were small but, unlike other interiors on the Hill, had the settled look of lives accumulated bit by bit. The heavy furniture, the antimacassars, the shelves of porcelain knickknacks, seemed to have come out of a time machine launched when the world was solid, weighted down and explained by things. There were no cactuses or Indian throws or anything else to suggest they had all gathered on a cool night somewhere on the Parajito Plateau. Warmed by the lamps and the yeast cakes and the smell of furniture polish, they were back in old Heidelberg. The Webers were at home.

"Don't be noble," Emma said, coming up to him at the urn and handing him a drink instead. "You'll want two of these in you before they start playing."

He took the drink and smiled. "Past experience?"

"Years of it."

"What was that all about?" he said, gesturing to where they had talked before. "Jealous husband?"

"Daniel? No, he wouldn't dream of it. That was about Johanna. Always on the qui vive. She gives me the pip."

"A gossip?"

"Terrible, and she doesn't have much to go on. She already thinks I'm disreputable."

"Why?" he said, biting into a cake.

"Consorting with the lower orders, I suppose. She's a fearful snob."

"Lower orders meaning me?"

"Well, let's just say you're not a scientist. There's always a pecking order, even here."

"Who else do you consort with?"

She looked up at him, then took a sip before she answered. "You'll do for now."

"Your husband seemed nice."

"Don't."

"What?"

"Just don't. God, here she comes again."

"Ah, Mr. Connolly," Johanna Weber said, as if saying his name aloud sealed it in memory. "You're meeting people, good. Emma's an anthropologist, did she tell you?"

"Yes, we were just talking about the Anasazi," Connolly said.

Johanna Weber hesitated, clearly surprised. "Fascinating, isn't it?" she said, recovering. "Emma's become quite an expert on the subject." She looked at Emma to contradict her.

"In an amateur sort of a way," Emma said smoothly. And then Frau Weber was being embraced by a new arrival and they were alone again.

"You've got a pretty good memory yourself," Emma said. "However did you remember the poor old Anasazi? Most people can't even pronounce it."

"Anthropologist?" he said playfully.

"Pompous old trout. Everybody has to be something grand. Her maid is probably an Indian princess. And you—"

"Dick Tracy?"

"No, darling, Hoover at the very least. What's the J stand for anyway, in J. Edgar?"

Connolly shrugged. "Maybe it's like the O in Louella O. Parsons. Maybe they're the same person."

She laughed. "That's a thought. Do you take anything seriously?"

"Everything. Freud tells us there are no jokes."

"Does he really?"

"Uh-huh. Of course, he meant something else, but I doubt he had much of a sense of humor anyway."

"How do you know things like that? Who are you, anyway?"

"You pick up things in the paper."

She looked at him appraisingly. "I don't think so."

"But then, you're an anthropologist," he said easily.

149

"Quite. Maybe you'll be my next project. The mysterious Mr. Connolly."

"Don't drop the Anasazi yet. That would be fickle."

She was quiet for a minute, studying him over the rim of her glass. "Tell me about yourself," she said softly.

"Such as?"

"Well, who are your people, as they used to say at garden parties."

"My people? My mother's dead. My father works at an insurance company and spent his life doing crossword puzzles in ten minutes and resenting the fact that he worked for people who couldn't. He saved everything to send me to school."

"Then what happened?"

"I went to work for the same people and now he resents me for the education he wanted himself. It's a very American story."

"You like him."

"I feel sorry for him. Not quite the same thing." He paused. "Yes, I like him."

"And you—are you good at crosswords too?"

He nodded. "I used to be. In the genes, maybe. I like figuring things out, watching them fall into place."

"And have they?"

"No. Only in puzzles."

She stopped, still staring at him. When she spoke again her words seemed almost unconscious, drawn out of her in a trance. "What are you working out now?"

"Now? I don't know. Why I'm here in a room full of pinheads eating cake instead of getting shot on Okinawa. Why anybody's on Okinawa in the first place. What the Jap pilots think about when they crash into the ships. Why somebody got killed in a park. What are we going to do after the war." He stopped, looking at her. "Why I'm pretending I'm thinking about any of this. All I'm really trying to figure out is how I can go to bed with you."

She looked at him as if nothing had been said, but the longer she was silent, the more real the words became, hanging between them like visible shapes. For an instant he thought he had frightened her, but he held her eyes without apology, determined to play the hand through. Then, still saying nothing, she took a drink and walked away from him into the room.

He stared after her, unable to read any expression in her movement, not sure what he had done. Then people closed around her in the crowded room and she was gone. Someone at the table jostled his arm, and finally distracted, he looked at the rest of the room. People were still eating and talking. In the music corner, one of the players began tuning his viola.

"Now where is Hans," Johanna Weber said to nobody in particular, busy now with a new hostess assignment. Connolly decided to look for the bathroom before the music began. The room had become even warmer, and despite the chill someone had opened the door to let in the fresh night air. He brushed past some smokers lining the narrow hallway and went through a half-open door to the bedroom. The bed was heaped with jackets and coats, and in the corner, under a desk lamp, Professor Weber and another man were leafing through pages. The room itself seemed oddly solemn, a refuge from the conversation just steps away, and Connolly realized that the effect came from the men themselves, wordlessly and gravely turning the pages of a magazine. He had clearly interrupted them, but Weber, glancing over his shoulder, nodded with an automatic courtesy.

"The bathroom?" Connolly said.

"Through there," Weber said, pointing to a door. And then, still courteous, "This is Friedrich Eisler. Friedrich, Mr. Connolly."

Connolly nodded, but both men returned to the magazine as if he had gone. "Oh, Friedrich," Weber said, a plaintive sound of such quiet distress that Connolly stopped, alarmed. The room suddenly was no longer solemn but filled with the disturbance of something gone wrong. Connolly looked toward the open magazine—*Life,* or something like it—and stopped, shaken.

He had seen combat pictures before, and pictures of rubble and bodies crushed in suffering, but this was something new. Skeletons covered with a thin layer of skin looked out at the camera through a wire fence, their eyes utterly without expression. Some wore the black-and-white stripes of dirty prison camp uniforms. Behind them bodies lay on the ground, one so thin that a thighbone seemed to puncture the skin. In another, bodies were heaped in piles, limbs at unnatural angles, mouths wide open to the air. Connolly looked at them, paralyzed. Children. The men at the fence seemed to hang there, as if they needed to hold the wire to remain upright. In another picture, a vast open pit was filled to overflowing with shaved heads and naked bodies. Everyone was dead, even the ones pretending to be alive at the fence. Their eyes burned straight through the camera. Connolly wondered who had taken the pictures, who had recorded not just lifeless bodies but death itself. Only a mechanical box should see this. He imagined his finger trembling on the shutter, refusing to look. His eyes swam. He darted from picture to picture, trying to make any sense of it, but the world had tilted slightly on its axis, rearranging everything, and it was impossible to understand anything so new. Another picture: a ragged group of Nazi guards, their eyes dead too. A camp entrance. More piles of bodies. People lying in bunks, a bony arm jutting out for help. But all too late. Even those with open eyes were already dead. He could hear, outside, the rasp of the viola tuning and people talking, and he realized that in the bedroom they had almost stopped breathing.

There was a shame in seeing this—the act of witnessing made one a part of it. And there was the shame of failed hopes. The past few weeks had been filled with exultant news from Germany. The Rhine crossed. A city taken. Berlin within reach. Refugees marching to a somber future, richly deserved. Since the offensive of the winter, the war had taken on the pace and excitement of a long sporting match finally about to be won. The world was beginning to make sense again. Now he saw it was too late for that too.

"So many," Eisler said, a low intoning.

"We knew, but we didn't know." They were still oblivious to Connolly, but looking at the photographs had drawn him into their circle. "Friedrich," Weber said, "they killed everybody."

Eisler put his hand on Weber's shoulder, glancing up at Connolly. Connolly took him in for the first time—a tall, scrawny man with the pallor of laboratory duty about his face. His neck stretched unnaturally high, with a prominent, bobbing Adam's apple and the slight discoloration of a birth defect to the right of his chin. Connolly noticed his long fingers, delicate and tapering, as if they had been formed, or trained, for precision work. His hair was uncombed, landing wherever it fell over his gentle face.

"They've won," Weber said, almost to himself.

"No. What are you saying?"

"They killed everybody. It's too late, don't you see? All this work. We're too late now." He shrugged in resignation just as his wife came to the door to summon him.

"*Liebchen,* come start, please. It's getting late," she said, barely sticking her head in, unaware that she had trivialized the moment.

Dutifully, Weber got up and shuffled out of the room, leaving Connolly and Eisler in uncomfortable silence. Still holding the magazine, Eisler sat heavily on the bed, cushioned by the heap of coats. Connolly stared down again at the pictures. Personalize the crime, an old journalist's trick. Focus on one person—that man looking through the fence—to construct the story. But as he stared at the picture, everyone became disembodied. There were no people left, just those rows of blank eyes. Then Eisler let the magazine slide shut and he was staring at the bright color of a Chesterfield ad on the back.

"What did he mean, we're too late?" Connolly said quietly.

For a moment he thought Eisler hadn't heard, but when he finally spoke, his soft voice was precise, as if he had been carefully considering his answer. "We came here to defeat the Nazis. Soldiers, you see?" He smiled weakly. "This was our way of fighting. With our slide rules. Our tests." His voice had only a trace of accent. "We were the little boys wearing glasses, not the big ones with the boots and the armbands. But we had the intelligence. We could fight with this." He tapped the side of his head. "We would build a bomb to kill all the Nazis. A terrible thing, yes. But with the Nazis, anything was permissible. Even the bomb. They wanted to kill everybody. And now, you see, they have. What are we going to do now?"

"The war isn't over yet."

Eisler looked up at him, surprised at the sound of his voice, and Connolly realized he'd been thinking aloud, not talking to him at all.

"It is for them," Eisler said, rising slowly and handing Connolly the magazine. "It will be over for the rest of us very soon. You think perhaps they have a secret weapon? A new rocket for London? Well, it's an idea. Convenient, certainly."

"Convenient?"

He took off his glasses and rubbed them slowly with a handkerchief. "If there are Nazis, we don't have these inconvenient moral questions. But what shall we do with this bomb if there are no Nazis?"

"I don't know," Connolly said, at a loss.

"No," he said, smiling. "None of us do. Sometimes I wonder what we have been thinking. Maybe the Nazis did that to us too. But you must excuse me. You came to hear the music, not to discuss—well, what do we call it?"

Outside, the music had begun, the precise lilting phrase of a Bach partita.

"German music," Eisler said ironically. "Such beautiful music. You must admit, we are an extraordinary people. Or were."

Connolly felt again that he was eavesdropping on someone else's conversation.

Eisler might have been talking to Weber, not a stranger holding a magazine. His shy face seemed to be looking elsewhere, at some invisible sadness.

"Something always survives," Connolly said, not even sure what he meant.

"Yes, we survive," Eisler said gently, opening his hand to indicate the house. "Americans now. Oh, I can see you think I'm being sentimental. You're right, of course. That's very German too. But our culture is over. Perhaps it had to end this way—killing ourselves. Very German. The end of the world. But now it is really over. There won't be any more music, you know. It's finished. Only this bomb is left—our last gift. I wonder what you will do with it. Perhaps you'll become Germans too. Everybody can become monsters now."

Connolly felt claustrophobic, as if he had stepped into Eisler's self-absorption and couldn't find his way out. Los Alamos had struck him as some overgrown international campus, everybody's project, but that seemed irrelevant now. To Eisler, the Americans, the Hungarians, the Italians, the whole polyglot community were simply spectators to some violent national drama.

"If someone has to have it, I'm glad it's us," he said finally.

The blunt pragmatism of the answer roused Eisler, and his faraway milky eyes gleamed with attention. "Why? Because we're not monsters? I say *we*. I'm American now too. But perhaps I don't trust us quite so much. Once, perhaps. Not now. We have all learned to be monsters in this war. I wonder, are those lessons we forget? I don't think so."

"Nobody ever won a war being nice."

"Fire with fire. Shall I tell you something? I am from Hamburg originally. You read about the firebombing there. The number of houses. The docks. Even the casualties. But what was it like? Most people don't want to read that. The fire so high that it sucked in all the oxygen. For miles. You can do the calculations with slide rules. So you step out of the house and your lungs collapse. No escape. You jump into a canal and you are boiled alive. They found people trying to cross the street. Their feet were stuck in the melting asphalt, so they just stood there—screaming, I imagine—until they burned to death. Thousands. What difference, the numbers? Everybody."

Eisler glared at him as if he knew Connolly had rewritten those first dispatches, headlining the statistics of victory. A payback for London.

"We didn't start the war," Connolly said stupidly, a reflex.

"Mr. Connolly, neither did my friends in Hamburg."

"That was an English raid, you know."

"Now you are splitting hairs with a vengeance. Tokyo was all yours. That was even worse, if there is such a thing. What do we do now, argue over degrees of terror? You think there is a hierarchy of suffering?"

158

Connolly was quiet. "I don't know what point you're trying to make."

Eisler sighed, his shoulders slumping in a kind of apology. "Forgive me, please. I'm not myself." And he seemed then physically to return to his earlier manner, his face growing gentle and sensitive, a young boy too polite to offend. When he spoke, he was distracted, as if he were examining his own outburst. "My point. What was my point? I'm sorry, my point was not to disturb you. I suppose only this—be very careful when you fight monsters. Be careful what you become."

Connolly held out the magazine. "We've never done this."

"No." Eisler's voice sank in defeat. "Not that. So," he said reflectively, "they make it possible for us to make the bomb. Now what else will they allow us to do?" He hung his head.

For the first time since he had come to Los Alamos, Connolly felt himself an intruder. He had expected the science to be over his head; what went on in those barrack laboratories was some new form of alchemy, too mysterious to be reduced to a set of formulas. Now everything that surrounded it seemed equally complicated and incomprehensible, a series of questions to which there were no answers. They folded back on themselves, contradictory, insistent, then got lost in vagueness, their scale as measureless as theology. Connolly liked a problem with a solution. He liked the crossword filled in, a murder explained. But what

159

was happening here left him finally over-whelmed, and out of place. All of them—the gentle émigré scientists, the eager American kids—were living in a state of abstraction as high and remote as the plateau itself. He turned toward the door and the audible sounds of the music, something real.

People were listening politely, some of them with their eyes closed, nodding to the familiar notes. The group was amateur but com-petent. They approached the music with a hes-itant respect, but at least they didn't plow through it, and the music rewarded them, carrying them through difficult patches with the logical force of its own structure. The music leaped; the notes joined each other and rose with the lamplight to brighten the room. Connolly realized with some surprise that everyone already knew the piece—it was as familiar to them as a jukebox hit—and he felt again oddly out of place, the little boy with his face pressed against the glass. But the music itself was welcoming, racing along now, simple at its heart, and no one in the room was excluded.

At his cello Professor Weber, usually bubbly, was sight-reading with determination, so fixed on the page that he seemed unaware of anything around him. Next to him a young American in a busy V-neck sweater played with confidence, glancing up from his instrument to take the audience in when the notes began to answer each other. Daniel, Emma's Daniel, looked only at his violin, his eyes sometimes closed in concentration, his movements sure and accomplished. Connolly imagined him as a boy in Poland—what was that like?—practicing on a rainy afternoon. A good boy, responsible. Or had he been chased home by bullies, his case flapping as he ran from the tram? Connolly's imagination bounced with the staccato notes, but the fact was, he didn't want to imagine Daniel at all. A decent man, a gifted scientist. Why go further? As he brought down his bow across the strings, there was a surgeon's accuracy—the strength was in knowing where things went, not in being forceful. But what did that mean? That he was self-possessed, or merely that he'd been trained properly all those rainy afternoons? He had seemed diffident before, but now Connolly wondered if he had misread him. And then suddenly his eyes opened and Connolly had to look away, embarrassed by his reverie. He didn't want to know him. It was safer to speculate about the others; there were no consequences to that. The fourth member of the quartet, for instance, with his bulky double-breasted suit, Slavic cheekbones, and pudgy fingers that grasped the bow like a lance. But he couldn't imagine anything about him.

Aside from the occasional rattle of coffee cups, the room was quiet and attentive. Still standing against the wall, Connolly found himself lulled by the music. The sharp rising notes had played themselves out, followed now by the deep bass of a cello bridge. In the slow, moody interlude, Connolly's mind went back to the magazine and then, like a succession of snapshots, to Eisler's wistful face, the cocktail chat in the hall, Johanna Weber's name-remembering trick, Emma walking away. He looked around the room, trying to match faces to the faceless columns of the savings accounts. They'd be offended if they knew; he wished he could tell them it hadn't meant anything. He wondered how many had seen the magazine. The room didn't seem to be in mourning, not even for the President who had brought them all here. It was instead a kind of time-out, an evening of friends and yeast cakes and music from before the war, an evening from that culture Eisler claimed had already disappeared. Had it? In this room on Bathtub Row it still glowed.

He was so used to the placid, almost dreamy faces in the room that he noticed instantly Johanna Weber's look of quiet alarm. He followed her eyes to the musicians. Hans Weber was still staring at the sheet music but was now obviously not reading—perhaps he had never needed to. As he played, he was listening to his own music, a passage of such beautiful sadness that everything else in the room had stopped. Involuntary tears rolled down each of his cheeks, as if the music itself were squeezing him in pain. He never stopped playing. His face was impassive, not scrunched with emotion, so that the tears seemed to come from somewhere else, a sorrow so secret that he was not even aware of revealing it. Connolly couldn't look away. A few others in the audience had now noticed and looked around in dismay. The

162

music never stopped—it seemed to grow even lovelier—and the tears rolled quietly, unwilled. What did they imagine was wrong? Did Weber, bubbly sentimentalist, frequently get carried away by the music? But no one looked as if this were normal. Something had happened. What was the protocol? Offer assistance? Pretend nothing was the matter? No one moved, and no one, Connolly saw, realized this was a larger mourning, beyond all courtesies. They hadn't seen the magazine. They didn't know he was playing for the dead.

The room, cozy and warm, now seemed stifling, and Connolly fought the urge to bolt. He didn't want to be in Europe, all knickknacks and solid furniture and mistakes past repairing. Soon they would all choke on tears and he would suffocate. Then Weber, sensing their discomfort, paused briefly, wiped his face, and joined in again on the next stanza, right on the beat. To those who had not noticed, he might have been wiping away perspiration. Connolly saw the others relax. Oppenheimer, across the room, stared at Weber in astonishment, frankly curious about something he didn't understand. Eisler, his hands at his side, bowed his head. Only Johanna Weber, her eyes shining with held-back tears, understood that something remarkable had occurred. Out of either blind loyalty or a shared distress, her face reached out to Weber across the room, ignoring the others, and Connolly saw that he had got her wrong, so eager to notice her manners that he had missed the woman. He thought suddenly that he didn't understand anyone here, their sorcerers' jobs and their terrible stories. How many in those camps had the Webers known? And wouldn't it be the same if they hadn't known any? The room was too close, and he didn't belong here. Quietly he slipped through the door, unnoticed, with the music following him out into the night.

He gulped in some raw fresh air, surprised at its chilly bite, and looked up at the sky. The stars were always wonderful in the high air of Los Alamos, but tonight they seemed spectacularly abundant, masses of them, laid out for the music.

She was standing near the end of the building, smoking a cigarette, huddled in a cardigan, her arms folded across her chest to keep in the warmth. The weak yellow light from the window kept her face in shadow. She glanced over quickly when she heard him, then turned back again, unsurprised. For once there seemed to be no movement on the mesa, no truck exhaust and grinding gears, so that the music poured out of the house as if it were being played in the open air. She shivered from the cold and inhaled, making the end of her cigarette burn a flicker of orange.

"It might snow this weekend," she said, her voice low but distinct, not a whisper.

"Don't you like the music?"

"I love the music. I just don't like to watch. They're so—intense. I can't bear it."

"Won't he notice?"

"No."

As his eyes adjusted to the dim light, her face became clearer, and he saw that she was looking directly at him, the conversation a pretext for this other contact. She dropped her cigarette to the ground.

"Fire hazard," she said, running it out with her shoe. "Bloody fire hazard. What about you?" She moved her head to indicate the house. "Bored so soon?"

"No. Just restless."

She looked at him again, interested.

"I don't know," he said. "It's all over my head."

"You seemed sure of yourself a while ago. That's a hell of a thing to say to anybody."

"I didn't say it to anybody. I said it to you."

She was quiet, just studied his face until the silence between them became a conversation. Finally she leaned back against the building and let him come closer.

"What are we going to do about this?" she said.

"What do you want to do?" he said, his face close now. He could feel her breath on his cold cheek.

"I don't know," she said simply, her honesty a kind of provocation.

He leaned forward and moved her arms down to her side, and when she stood there, unresisting, he kissed her, gently pressing her against the wall, tasting her.

"Don't," she said, but not moving away, letting him kiss her again.

"Why not?" he said, his words kisses of breath now as he moved against the hollow of her neck.

"No good will come of it," she said, a catchphrase to ward off a spell.

"Yes it will," he said, still kissing her neck.

"Yes." Then she opened her mouth to him, kissing him back, moving her tongue with his, her arms now behind him, pulling him closer.

"Oh God," she said, whispering. "It won't, though. No good at all."

"How do you know?" he said, pressing against her, excited.

"It never does." She buried her face in his chest. "Never."

But he wasn't listening; the words were a kind of chant, just a rhythm. Instead he kissed her harder, pulling her body next to his so that she could feel him. "It will," he insisted, the words some code for sex. He could sense her own excitement as she twisted against him. But she was pulling away, catching her breath, shaking herself awake.

"No," she whispered, moving away from the wall, and for a moment he thought he had lost her, frightened her away. He grabbed at her arm, moving her back into the embrace, but when he saw her eyes, angry at his force, he took his hand away and instead moved it gently down the side of her face. He touched her hair as he stroked her, and, shivering, she moved her face into his hand, bending her neck, calmer.

"I want to make love to you," he said.

She nodded.

He leaned forward and kissed her again, gently this time. "Since the first night."

She nodded again. "Not here. Not on the Hill. I won't, here," she said finally.

"Where?"

"I don't know. I'll think of something," she said quickly, a conspirator.

"I'll drive you someplace," he said softly, kissing her again. "With my coupons." But when he looked up, her eyes seemed stricken, as if she had already been found guilty of some terrible crime.

"Yes," she said, catching his look. "You can drive me someplace."

"Anywhere you like."

"Anywhere I like. We'll go away."

He kissed her, a reassurance.

"But go home now, okay?" she said. "No more. I can't."

"Okay," he said quietly, and turned to go, moving away from the house to the darkened street. He heard the music again. Suddenly she caught his arm and fell against him, bringing his face down.

"You'll make it all right, won't you?"

He looked at her and nodded. "You think you're taking an awful chance with me. Don't you?"

She didn't say anything.

"Maybe I'm better than you think I am."

"I don't care," she said.

Mills was waiting for him when he got home, stretched out on Karl's narrow bed with his hands behind his head, staring at nothing.

"Make yourself at home," Connolly said, surprised to see him.

"Thanks. You sure haven't done much to it, have you?" he said, getting up and looking around the spare room. "It's like old Karl never left."

"I wasn't planning on a long stay."

"None of us do."

"Something on your mind, or is this just a social call?"

"Take a look," Mills said, taking a sheet of paper out of his jacket. "I went over to the office before. The movie stank—Lee Tracy and Nancy Kelly. Jap spies and the Panama Canal. I mean, a little late for the canal, don't you think? You wonder who thinks them up."

Connolly glanced at him, cutting him short.

"So I went back to the office to go through a few more files, and this caught my eye. Probably nothing, but you said you wanted to see anything interesting."

Connolly was looking at the figures. "Two withdrawals of five hundred dollars. That's a lot of money. Who is it?"

"That's the funny part. Oppenheimer."

Connolly glanced at the paper again, then handed it back. "Better keep looking."

"That's what I thought you'd say."

"Meaning?"

168

"Nothing. I just think you're under the spell. I know all the signs."

"What spell?"

"Our great leader. Those blue eyes. That lightning mind. I've seen it all before."

"Mills, have you been drinking?"

"I have, as a matter of fact. But not that much. Hell, I don't think it's him either—I don't think it's *any* of them. I was just hoping we'd stop all this bank business. But out of curiosity, are you going to ask him about it?"

"Yes."

"He'll love that. You've got guts, I'll say that for you. Questioning Caesar's wife."

"Except he's Caesar."

"That's something worth thinking about," Mills said.

It did snow over the weekend, and the ground was covered with the dry, powdery snow of the high desert when they met for the memorial service on Sunday. Despite the cold, the April sun was bright, reflecting off the snow, filling the morning with an unnatural glamour. The flag in front of Fuller Lodge was at half mast, and Oppenheimer spoke in the theater, his voice no longer filled with the hastily assembled emotion of Thursday but with a more public eloquence. All of Los Alamos, it seemed, had turned out for this final salute, and Connolly felt himself looking at them again as if they were in a lineup. It was absurd. All these bright, well-meaning faces—he doubted there was even a traffic violation among them. He looked at the men, in formal overcoats and shiny shoes, dressed for a winter Sunday's outing in Vienna. Some of the women wore hats. There were children, looking solemn. Oppenheimer quoted from the *Bhagavad Gita*: "Man is a creature whose substance is faith. What his faith is, he is." Roosevelt's faith, the faith they all shared, was a belief in a better world. His voice was simple and unaffected. The room was hushed.

Could Oppenheimer really be involved? Wouldn't Caesar sacrifice anything to win? But what could make Karl so important to him? The answer was, he wasn't. Perhaps Mills was right—once you started, you tainted everything with suspicion until no one was truly innocent. There was always something, even something that didn't matter, that was only about itself. They were chasing shadows.

While Oppenheimer spoke, Connolly's eyes drifted elsewhere. She was sitting on the aisle three rows away, her head tilted toward the stage in attention. Her hair was down, and it caught the sheen of the snow glare through the windows. Her shoulders were straight, and he imagined holding them, warm to the touch, and feeling them go slack when they moved their bodies together. Her skin would be cream. Even while he listened to the meaning of leadership, the search for a better world, he saw the messed bed, her body barely covered by a tangled sheet, her skin slick with perspiration, all that fierceness dissolving in his hands, wet for him.

170

And then, as if she had read his thoughts, she turned her head and looked at him, a direct glance, an intimacy that said they were already lovers. It was the last thing he had expected to happen, and for one quick instant he wanted to get away before it was too late, just run back to Washington, leaving them to stew in their own unsolvable murder and impossible moral questions and affairs from which—of course she was right—no good could come. But he felt the pulse of his erection and he knew he would never leave now. The murder would solve itself somehow and the moral questions would drift to that limbo where they always went and he would have her. Again and again. It was as clear and simple as that.

When they all stood to leave, he realized with embarrassment that he was still hard, and folded his coat in front of him. People filed out quietly. When she passed by him, her husband at her side, they exchanged a glance. In all this somber crowd, did anyone else see that her eyes were shining? But no one noticed at all, and he saw that the secret itself was part of the excitement for her.

Outside they stood in small groups, like people after church, and to avoid looking at her again, Connolly found himself talking to Pawlowski instead.

"I never got a chance to tell you how much I enjoyed the music," he said. "Are you playing again this week?"

"Not me, I'm afraid," Pawlowski said politely.

171

"But you were very good."

"No, it's not that," Emma said, cutting in. "Daniel won't be here. He has to go off-site."

Connolly felt a prick of excitement, as if she had touched him, declared herself.

"Emma, you're not supposed to—"

"Oh, darling, I'm sorry. But he is security. Surely it's all right?" she said to Connolly easily. And while her husband said something polite about the other players doing well without him, Connolly looked at her for the first time. *Do you really want this?* her glance said. This is what it will mean. The code words. Sex would be the beginning. While he imagined those afternoons, she had already seen what would come, all the complications, furtive and tricky and maybe even doomed, like the movie Japanese risking everything for worthless plans of the Panama Canal. *Yes, I want it,* he thought.

7

B ut it wasn't Emma he got to drive that week, it was Oppenheimer.

"Any idea why he requested me?" he asked, annoyed at this complication.

Mills shrugged. "Maybe he likes your conversation. Maybe he doesn't like mine. Anyway, you'll have to wear this," he said, holding out a gun.

Connolly took it hesitantly. He had handled guns before, always with the sensation that they

172

were about to go off. "Christ, am I actually expected to use this?"

"I thought you were a tough-guy reporter."

"That's Winchell. I just go to press conferences and lock my door at night."

"You know how to use it, don't you? I mean, you don't need a lesson or anything."

"I'll manage."

"Just remember about the safety. Of course, you're supposed to catch the other guy's bullet first, so what the hell."

"Catch how?"

"By dying, mostly. Put your body in front of Oppie and do your bit for the war effort."

"Can't we send someone else?"

"You have something better to do?"

Connolly looked at him, wondering for a minute whether Mills suspected anything. Did it show, this heat? Like some priapic blush? But Mills was only being sarcastic. "Just finish the accounts, okay? You might give Holliday a buzz. He'll let things slide if you don't goose him now and then. Where am I going, by the way?"

"South. To the test site."

"I didn't know there was one."

"They built it in December. Must be getting ready to do something, 'cause there's been quite a little traffic back and forth lately. Try to avoid lunch if you can."

"Why?"

"It's antelope. Enlisted men have nothing to do down there except shoot rattlesnakes and antelope and roast them—the antelope, that is. They say it tastes like beef, but that's only because they've had their brains bleached out in the sun. It tastes like antelope."

"How far is this place, anyway?"

"About two hundred miles."

"Christ, that's all day."

Mills grinned and handed him a test site pass stamped with a large T. "Don't forget to ask about the money."

In fact, it was the first thing they discussed.

"I hope you don't mind," Oppenheimer said as Connolly started down the switchback road in the morning sunlight. He was sitting in front, at his request, and was clearly expecting to talk. "This will give us a chance to catch up. Any progress? Suspects?"

"Only you."

"I beg your pardon?" He twisted in the passenger seat, his eyebrows raised, anticipating a joke.

"Why did you withdraw a thousand dollars over three months this winter?"

Oppenheimer was quiet, then lit a cigarette. "None of your damned business."

"If you say so."

"I do."

"Then I'll take your word for it."

Oppenheimer looked out the passenger window and smoked. Finally he said, "You needn't do that. It's personal, but not, I suppose, secret. I'm not allowed secrets anymore."

"I'm sorry. I didn't mean to—"

"No, you're just doing your job," Oppenheimer said. "Go ahead, do it."

"What did you do with the money?"

"Put it into two postal orders and sent them to an old friend who needed it."

"Why?"

"She's been under psychiatric care, if you must know. She's broke. We call it a loan."

"No, I mean why a postal order?"

"How else? We don't have checks up here. You know that."

"Do you still have the receipts?"

"Yes."

"Does your wife know?"

"Yes." He was silent again. "You've got a hell of a nerve, you know that?"

"You authorized the search."

Oppenheimer sighed. "So. No good deed goes unpunished. I never imagined you wanted to look at mine. More fool me. Of course you would. I'm the obvious person to beat someone up in the park. Do you ever feel embarrassed doing this?"

Connolly downshifted. "I don't feel great now, if that's what you mean."

Oppenheimer sighed again. "No, of course you don't. And now I should apologize for being rude, which somehow makes it all my fault, when you were the one asking the questions. Interesting how we tie ourselves up in knots, isn't it?"

"Well, don't do it on my account. Look, I'm eliminating any loose end I can. I didn't mean to intrude on your personal life. Let's just forget it."

"But what did you *think* it meant? What are

175

you looking for? What's the point of it all?"

"Bruner came into some money before he died. He may have been blackmailing somebody. He may not. I want to find out where he got it."

"And you thought he was blackmailing me? What on earth about? Do you think there's a single thing about me the government doesn't already know? Maybe you should see what it feels like to be on the other side of a security check. Your left-wing friends. Your right-wing friends—well, such as they are. Your old girlfriends. Your Jewish friends. Your students. An ambulance for Spain? Was that politically motivated? What did you study in Germany? How much do you drink? Do you ever feel conflicted loyalties? My God, does one ever not?"

"I said, let's forget it."

"Bruner didn't know anything about the project."

"I wasn't thinking of that."

"What, then?"

"He was homosexual. That gets to be a pretty sensitive issue."

"Oh," Oppenheimer said, then laughed. "Well, I have to hand it to you—that's one question they never asked. Are you writing this up for my file? Am I supposed to formally deny it?"

"I'm not writing anything."

"It would almost be worth it to see the look on G. G.'s face," he said, still amused.

"I thought you might be sensitive on someone else's behalf. A friend. Someone who needed the money."

Oppenheimer looked over at him. "Only the once," he said, ending it.

Connolly drove for a while in silence. The air was warmer down in the valley. They had passed through the slopes of piñon and juniper to the sage desert. Oppenheimer had lifted some papers from a briefcase and was working through them on his lap, tapping his cigarette out the open window. Ordinarily Connolly would have turned on the radio, but he was too interested in Oppenheimer to think of it. Everyone else got fifteen minutes, and he had hours to go.

"What did you mean when you said he didn't know anything about the project?" he asked.

Oppenheimer looked up from the papers. "Anything that would put it in jeopardy," he said deliberately. "He couldn't. Only a scientist would know that."

"The way I hear it, he liked to nose around. Maybe he knew more than you think."

"He wouldn't know how to separate what was important. The basic principles were perfectly clear before the war, you know—any physicist worth his salt understands the principles. Someone like Heisenberg would know a lot more than that. It's the mechanics of it that matter now. A layman wouldn't be able to differentiate. He simply wouldn't know what to look for. In that sense, the complexity of the project is its own security."

"If you don't know what to look for, you look at everything."

"Rather like you and your project."

The quickness of the answer took Connolly by surprise. "That's some connection."

"That's how science works. You guess, you make connections, then if it fits you prove what you guessed in the first place. Isn't that what you're doing?"

"I haven't guessed yet."

"But you've guessed *where* to look," he said, his voice playful. "Where would you start looking to find out about the gadget?"

The question had the effect of a chess piece put into place. Connolly, alert to the game, moved his own. "Where would I start? Your briefcase."

Oppenheimer looked at him appreciatively, then smiled. "You might be disappointed. The only thing you'd learn in here," he said, casually holding up a sheaf of papers, "is how utterly fouled up our bureaucracy is."

"Fucked up," Connolly corrected him.

"As you say," Oppenheimer said, enjoying himself. "Why bother with the euphemism? What would you make of this, for example?" He took up a sheet. "This one's from Bainbridge—a good man, in charge of Trinity."

"Which is?"

"Where we're going. The test site. He wants it officially designated Project T. It turns out the business office calls it A and Mitchell over in procurement calls it T but ships to S-45 and last week it was made Project J, to prevent any confusion with Building T or Site T, but people call it T anyway since the passes are marked T, so he wants to go with T."

"And do you?"

"Oh yes. Whatever Ken wants. Here's another. Procurement wants to create a new series of ratings. We've got X, A, B, and C, X being priority. Now they want to break X out to XX, X1, and X2."

"What's XX? Special delivery?"

"Virtually. Goes right to the War Production Board to dispatch a cargo plane anywhere in the country."

"And will you approve it?"

"Certainly. We can't afford to wait for matériel while the services squabble over priority." And there it was again, the unexpected steel, the arrogant willingness to override. "Of course, it's easy to make fun of all this alphabet soup. The problem is, it's important, really. Every detail. It's all important to somebody."

"How much matériel are we talking about?"

Oppenheimer sighed and lit another cigarette. "We handle about thirty-five tons a day at the warehouse. Maybe five of that is going down to the site."

"Five tons a day?" Connolly was staggered.

"Yes," Oppenheimer said, "more or less. Everything from beer to—well, everything."

"But it must be huge. How do you hide something that big? I never heard of it before today."

"Yes," Oppenheimer said, smiling, "and

179

you're in security. Special security, anyway. I often wonder myself. You know, when we set up the site we needed our own wavelength for the ground shortwave system, and what we got, by accident, was the one they use in the San Antonio freightyards. They could hear us, but I doubt they knew what we were talking about. We routed the phones through Albuquerque and Denver so nobody outside would make a connection to the Hill. Elaborate security precautions. But we still have to ship the stuff off the Hill—no way around that. So we send out trucks every night after it gets dark, ten of them sometimes, and you know, I don't think anyone's noticed? It's as I said, you have to know what you're looking for." He smiled, as if he had just demonstrated the neatness of a formula.

"Maybe," Connolly said. "On the other hand, sometimes you come up lucky. I've just collected information about the scale of the project, the code names, the exact telephone connections, and the personnel in charge, and I haven't even been through your brief-case."

"So you have," Oppenheimer said quietly. "Maybe you're more dangerous than I thought."

"Only if I have to use this." He nodded down at the gun. "One more question?"

"Could I stop you?"

"*Is* there anything in the briefcase you wouldn't want the Germans to see?"

Oppenheimer considered. "Yes."

"But you brought it out anyway?"

"I doubt we're going to be attacked by the Nazis on the road to Albuquerque. It's a long drive, and I've got a lot of paperwork to do. It seemed worth the risk."

"But strictly speaking, it's against regulations? Do the other bodyguards know this?"

Oppenheimer smiled a checkmate grin. "Of course. Why do you think I requested you?"

They had lunch at Roy's in Belen, a designated project stop, and Connolly found himself sweating under the punishing sun. After the cold air of Los Alamos, the desert here was a furnace, hot and almost empty all the way to Mexico. Even the stunted piñons of the rolling high plateau had now given way to cactus and scorpions. In his gray suit and porkpie hat, Oppenheimer seemed unnaturally cool, dabbing the back of his neck with a handkerchief while Connolly dripped large patches of sweat through his shirt. But afterward, as the dust blew through the windows on a constant wind, scratchy and irritating, he gave up too, abandoning his work and staring listlessly at the wavy glare that stretched for miles.

"Yes, Virginia, there is a hell and we're in it," he said to the air. "All this to win the war." He pulled his hat to shield his eyes and slumped down in the seat, pretending to sleep but continuing to talk. "The Spaniards called it the Jornada del Muerto, and for once they weren't exaggerating. If your wagon broke down here, there wasn't much you could do but bring out the rosary beads."

"Then let's hope we don't run out of gas. We're pretty low."

"That's poor planning, I must say. There's a station up ahead in San Antonio. Keep an eye out—if you blink, you'll miss it. There's a bar there too. We're not supposed to stop, but everyone does, and you've already broken all the rules."

Incredibly, the bar was crowded. Connolly wondered where, in all this barren emptiness, they could have come from. The room was dark—he had to squint when he walked through the door—and one wall at the end was entirely lined with bottles, a trophy wall to past conviviality. When his eyes adjusted to the gloom, he saw that at least part of the crowd had come from the Hill. They made an elaborate show of pretending not to notice Oppenheimer, as if one security violation could be redeemed by obeying another, but Oppenheimer ignored the charade and went over to talk to them. Connolly saw Eisler and Pawlowski, and he smiled to himself at the irony of discovering Pawlowski's destination after all. It was a small world in the middle of the desert. While Emma sat alone, both the men who wanted her faced each other over beer in a Mexican bar. It was an irony Oppenheimer would appreciate, Connolly thought, absurd and elegant at the same time. A young Mexican bartender went busily back and forth, popping caps off beer bottles, his eyes shining at what must have been unexpected traffic. Eisler, his pale skin gleaming in the half-light, managed to look formal even with his short-sleeved cowboy shirt and Coca-Cola, like someone who had stepped into the wrong advertisement.

But Oppenheimer didn't want to stay—they had miles to go—and his leaving broke up the party for all of them.

"So this is what you meant by off-site," Connolly said to Pawlowski as they left together.

"We're not supposed to say," he said simply. He glanced at Connolly's gun, confused, as if he were still trying to place him. "I didn't know you were coming here."

"I'm driving Oppenheimer. Is there someone with you?"

He smiled shyly. "No, I'm not that important. The only danger to me is from Friedrich's driving."

"We haven't done so badly so far," Eisler said pleasantly. Connolly noticed that one of his forearms was sunburned, bright pink against the short sleeve, and he imagined him driving with it hanging rakishly out the window, his fingers light on the wheel, an old schoolmaster free on the open road. He wondered what they talked about and knew instinctively it would be serious, the arcane mechanics of the gadget that Oppenheimer believed constituted its own security. "Shall we follow you? It's a comfort to have another car. In case of a breakdown, you know."

And so, with a third car Connolly hadn't seen before, they set out in caravan across the flat desert. Oppenheimer resumed his slumped-down position, angling his hat to avoid the blazing afternoon sun.

"You could nap in the back," Connolly offered.

"I could nap in the front if it were quiet," Oppenheimer said. He sighed and took out a cigarette. "Which somehow I feel it won't be. What else is on your mind?"

Connolly grinned. "Nothing. What's Pawlowski like?"

"Don't tell me you suspect him too?"

"No, idle curiosity. It passes the time."

"Hmm. Like the radio." He exhaled, thinking. "Hardworking—enjoys working. Bethe thinks the world of him. Determined, even stubborn," he said, playing with it now, as if he were composing an applicant's recommendation. "Wonderful mind, but interior. I've always thought that physics became a substitute world for him, but that's just a guess. Actually, it's not so unusual here—we're all a little interior. No patience with showboating. He can be a little—what does Herr Goebbels call us? Stiff-necked. Thinks Teller's an ass, for instance, and wouldn't work for him. Not a homosexual either, by the way."

"No. I've met his wife."

"Emma? Yes. She's quite a girl."

"Meaning?"

"Meaning she's quite a girl. English. Most beautiful rider I've ever seen. You have to be brought up with it to ride that well."

"Unusual marriage."

"Is it? I wouldn't know. I think all marriages are unusual unless you happen to be in them."

"No, I mean coming from such different backgrounds."

He laughed. "Don't be such a snob. You obviously don't know the English. Least conventional people in the world—once you get to the gentry level, anyway. She fought in Spain, you know, so there must be a wild streak somewhere. You should watch her ride. You can tell everything about an Englishwoman by the way she rides." He took a drag on his cigarette. "On the other hand, what could it possibly matter to you?"

He dropped it lightly, like an ash on the seat, and for a minute Connolly didn't know what to say.

"It doesn't."

"Just looking at everything," Oppenheimer said. "I had no idea you were casting your net quite this wide." He paused, waiting for Connolly to respond. "She's an attractive woman."

"Yes, she is," Connolly said flatly. He felt, talking to Oppenheimer, that he was always moving a piece into place. But the game was unfair—it didn't matter to Oppenheimer, so he didn't have to play carefully. "I was wondering. The way science works? If you guess wrong, there won't be any connections to make, will there?"

"No, not if you guess wrong."

Connolly let it drop. Then, annoyed at himself for having somehow started it in the first place, he grew even more annoyed at not knowing whether Oppenheimer had meant anything or not. It was a reporter's instinct to hide behind a one-way mirror, not revealing anything himself. Now he felt he was too close to the surface, unreliable, as if the slightest poke would show his hand.

"Dr. Eisler said something interesting the other night."

"That's unusual," Oppenheimer said, bored. "Friedrich doesn't usually say anything. Maybe you have a gift for drawing people out."

"What if the Germans give up before you finish the project?"

"Friedrich said that?" Oppenheimer said, drawing his neck up, turtlelike.

"Not exactly. He said the Nazis, the fact of them, gave us permission to make the gadget, so what would we do without them?"

Oppenheimer took off his hat and rubbed his temple. Connolly saw that his face had grown taut with disapproval.

"We haven't made it yet," he said finally. "His qualms are premature. He may be premature about the Nazis as well."

"But if he isn't?"

"That's something devoutly to be hoped for. Every minute this war goes on."

"But would you keep building it?"

"Of course," Oppenheimer said simply. "Do you think we've come this far not to build it?"

"But if we didn't need it to win the war?"

"Then we'd need it to end the war. The

Germans aren't the only ones fighting. Sometimes our European friends forget that, but that's understandable. How many more casualties are acceptable in the Pacific? Another year? Less? I don't know how anyone makes that determination. I certainly can't."

"No," Connolly said quietly.

"Mooning about "permission' when there's so much at stake."

"But you can see what he means. That's why they wanted to build it."

"We wanted to build it because it was going to be built. By someone. We wanted it to be us, all of us here wanted that. Does that shock you? Sometimes it shocks me. Where do our egos come from? We are trying to release the energy of matter itself—literally transform the composition of things. What physicist would resist that? Would you? The science is there. It doesn't ask for permission. It asks to be revealed. But so difficult. Expensive. The price was the military—how else could we have done it?"

The sun was still high when they passed the test site perimeter guards and exchanged their passes at the security office. The base camp, another instant city of hutments and army buildings wrapped in miles of overhead wires, baked unprotected in the glare. Most of the men were shirtless, a few even down to skivvies, but despite the heat they moved quickly, full of purpose, like stagehands making last-minute adjustments before an early curtain. The only shade lay in the slim patches next to

187

the east side of the buildings. At noon there would have been none at all.

Connolly was struck yet again by the sheer scale of the project. On the Hill, with buildings sheltered by trees and water tanks or tucked away in nearby canyons, it was easier to imagine it a familiar city in the grip of a construction boom. There were wives and clotheslines and musical evenings. The land rolled away to calendar mountains. There were ranches. But here, on the endless stark desert, the site was undisguised in all its strangeness, a bleached oasis willed into existence overnight. Connolly knew the Manhattan Project had factories elsewhere in the country, huge plants created just to make the gadget's fuel, but it was at Trinity that he finally grasped the enormous ambition of it all, because nothing belonged here, and when the test was finished nothing would remain. A whole city—all those millions of tons of matériel—had gone up for a single moment in time.

Oppenheimer had one inspection to make— a bunker almost completed, about six miles away to the south—and then a series of meetings back at the camp, so Connolly was left to his own devices, as smoothly dismissed as a family servant. Despite a creaky air cooler, the mess was stifling. He took a cold Coke and went outside to sit in the dusty wind. The beads of condensation on the glass evaporated instantly in the hot air. He leaned against the side of the building in a sliver of shade and watched men stringing more wires overhead, working in bulky gloves to prevent scorching, their eyes covered by goggles against the blowing sand. Jeeps went back and forth, throwing up dust, but each time they passed they left silence. There were no birds. Only men ventured aboveground; the rest of the desert burrowed in, waiting for night.

The camp lay in a hollow bowl whose far sides, the Oscura Mountains, were too distant to be much more than hazy frames. Connolly had never seen so much space. If you walked into it, stepped beyond the plywood shacks and telephone poles, you would be lost. He had spent most of his life trying to find enough room—the cramped pull-out couch in his boyhood living room, the cubicle at the newspaper, where there never seemed any surface to put down a cup of coffee—and now, unexpectedly, he had found it. This was as far away as you could go.

Everything here seemed remote—the war, the office in Washington, all the life of the past. The desert erased it away. He stared at the landscape blankly. It was impossible to think here—the sun burned through the connections, allowing only stray thoughts to float out like the little eddies of dust, meaningless. He drained his Coke, and the thick bottom reminded him of Manny Wonder's glasses, smeared from constant wiping so that Connolly thought he barely saw at all. Manny was the paper's columnist, a short, perpetually sweaty man who turned every morning to page 10 of the *Mirror* to see what Winchell had done, then spent the rest of the day sifting through the reams of press-agent tips to make a column out of what was left. An assistant cut up releases and sorted them in piles for him: Wonders of the City, Seven Wonders, Wonderfuls. He never took his jacket off in the newsroom, as if he might have to leave any minute for El Morocco, and treated the copyboys with elaborate courtesy, his thin voice barely audible above the typewriters. In his column debutantes did the rumba, idle women got divorced, actresses sacrificed their careers to war bond drives, and the country saw Manny with them, up all night on the town, but in the newsroom he was a sweaty little man with the manners of an accountant. He had had four wives. Connolly smiled. What was his real name? He had never asked, and now he would never know, because Manny too drifted away, just another ghost on the desert who might never have existed at all.

He wasn't going to return to the paper. He had loved it then—the handlers at City Hall, the cops on their free lunch—but he didn't care anymore. He was tired of those stories too. The war had taken him away and parked him finally here at the end of an army lifeline down Route 85 on the edge of something new. It was what gave the project its exhilaration—not the high mesa air, not ending the war, but this feeling that they might be the only people in the world who were not still sorting out its past. Everything here was brand-new—the raw wood, the calculations, the profound mystery of what it would be. Maybe that's what

Oppenheimer had meant. They were staring at a blank piece of paper, like this endless white sheet of desert. Nobody knew what would be on it.

He heard a roar overhead and saw three bombers flying toward him from Alamogordo. Getting ready. But what was he doing here? Everyone else was busy preparing for something. Maybe this is what sunstroke was like, a weightless dreaming. It wasn't his project— he didn't even understand it. If he were still a reporter he'd be taking notes, amazed at his luck in being in the middle of a story that dwarfed anything on the metro desk. But he had given that up. He was here only to solve a crime everyone else was too busy to care about, nothing more than an interruption in their lives. And, oddly, he didn't mind. He felt grateful to the project for letting him imagine a future. The war made everyone live day to day, never promising anything beyond its own ending. Now he felt the urge to get on— it didn't matter where. All that was left was to put things in order so he could pack up. But now that he'd come here, he really didn't want to go anywhere else. The future was here.

He lit a cigarette and wondered whether Bruner had ever come here, felt the new freedom of the desert space. Probably not. Connolly guessed that it would have terrified him. He had lived in too many cells to feel comfortable without walls. And yet he liked to go driving. Why? Where did he go? Maybe, a new patriot, he wanted to see this movie Western land-scape come to real life. Connolly tried to imagine him gazing out to the horizon, hand shielding his eyes, but the picture wouldn't come. His face in the file photo was pale, a stranger to the sun. His life had been formed in the furtive corners of rooms, bargaining for food, tapping on walls—but this was non-sense. There was no way of knowing. He could try the Oppenheimer method and start with a guess, but no connections seemed to follow. If you had been a victim, you could believe in conspiracy. Now what? If you believed in conspiracy, you believed in the value of knowing about it. How else to be safe? The world was organized in a series of invis-ible networks—in prison, where survival depended on it; in a secret community, where sex flourished more freely the more it was hidden. When everything important is invis-ible, do you begin to take pleasure simply in discovering it? It wasn't just keeping your eyes open, that wasn't enough. It became, finally, a love of knowing for its own sake. An advantage.

So Karl read files. Whose? Yes, he could pic-ture that, Karl sitting under a lamp at night, absorbed in a folder, looking for a date that didn't match, anything. Or something specific. It's what isn't there, he had said. But then why the car? Why take time away from the hunt pre-tending to be an indifferent tourist, unless this was playing cat and mouse too. Unless you were tracking somebody. Unless you were *with* somebody. Until curiosity killed the cat. And now Connolly, as always, ran out of connections. There had to be someone else. It's not possible to live without a trace. Karl, neat as a monk, had left prophylactics in his drawer. There had to be someone. Even, though he still could not believe it, a pickup.

"You got a light?"

After days of modulated European accents, the thick American twang of the voice surprised him. Texas, probably, or Oklahoma. He looked like someone who had played football in high school, broad and muscular, with an unshaven chin that jutted out in jock confidence. He was stripped to the waist, his chest covered in an alkali film, so that the bandanna facemask now pulled down around his neck flapped like the collar to a shirt that wasn't there. Young jug ears stuck out beneath the fatigue hat. Connolly handed him the lighter.

"You new on the site?" He was one of those people whose most innocent question came out like a challenge, as if he hadn't learned to mask some fundamental belligerence. Connolly imagined him starting a bar fight, a redneck quick to take offense.

"Just down for the day. Guard duty."

"No shit. Join the club." He grinned, easier now that Connolly had explained himself. He flashed a security badge to establish club contact. "Who'd you draw?"

"Oppenheimer."

He grunted. "You're lucky. He never stays

over. You don't want to stay here. No fucking way."

"You been down here long?"

"Twenty-eight days. Twenty-eight fucking days. They moved a bunch of us down last month. Let me tell you, this is about the hardest time there is."

Connolly looked at him with interest. He thought he'd already talked to everybody in the intelligence unit. No one had mentioned transfers to Trinity. "Yeah, it's hot."

"It ain't the heat. We got heat in East Texas. It's the Mickey Mouse. They got this tighter than a rat's ass. Nobody goes out. There ain't nothing to do but shoot rattlers. The well water's got all this shit in it so's you can't drink it—gypsum and stuff—but you wash in it so everybody gets the runs anyway. You got to stamp on scorpions in the latrine. Said they wanted only the best for Trinity duty, so naturally we all thought it was something special. It is."

"So what do you guard?"

"Them Gila lizards mostly. There ain't nothing *down* here to guard. Worst problem they got is all the antelope tripping over the sensor wires they got running everywhere."

"That's why they shoot them?"

"Yeah, that's the excitement. Just the shooting. Nothing to eat and nothing to fuck. At least they got women on the Hill. Once some of the WACs came down to keep us company, but they don't put out, never, so what the fuck?"

Connolly put out his cigarette. "Well, it won't be much longer."

"According to who?"

Connolly shrugged. "What do they tell you?"

"You kidding me? Brother, they don't tell us nothing. We're not supposed to know. They told us when Roosevelt died—that's it. For all I know, the war's over."

"It's not," Connolly said.

The kid took off his hat to wipe his forehead, the skin now turned permanently red under the short blond hair. "Well, I got to get going. I was just on my break. Nice talking to you."

Connolly looked at him to see if he was joking, but the face was earnest.

"Watch out for the centipedes, they sting like hell."

"I'll do that. Mind if I ask you a question?"

The kid, about to move away, turned toward him, his eyes suddenly wary. Connolly had seen the look before, the automatic reaction of someone used to the police, the legacy of too many Saturday night brawls that had got out of hand. He waited.

"When you were on the Hill, did you know a guy called Karl Bruner?"

"Karl?" he said, looking puzzled. "Sure. He was G-2. Everybody knew him. Why?"

"He's dead."

"Karl?" He was genuinely surprised. So not even gossip had penetrated the news blackout. Or maybe nobody had cared.

"He was killed."

"No shit. How?"

"He was murdered."

The kid stared at him. "You kidding me?" he said quietly.

"No. He was found in the river park in Santa Fe, off the Alameda. You hadn't heard?"

"I told you, we don't hear nothing down here. Who did it?"

"That's what we're trying to find out."

"You're a cop," he said, an accusation, as if Connolly should have declared himself earlier.

"No. Army Intelligence. We're looking into it on our own."

"I don't understand. What happened?"

Connolly watched his reaction as he answered. "We don't know. The police think it might have been a homosexual murder."

It was a surprise punch. The kid caught his breath with a nervous laugh of disbelief. "That's fucking crazy."

"Why?"

"Why? Karl wasn't any fruit."

"How do you know?"

He sputtered. "How do I know? He just wasn't, that's all. Christ Almighty. Karl?"

"Did you know him well?"

"He was just a guy in the office. He used to give me duty assignments after I came off the mounteds."

"So you don't know who his friends were? Whether he was seeing anybody?"

"No."

"Okay. I just thought you might have noticed something. He talk to you much?"

"Some."

"What about?"

"Nothing. Stuff. You know."

"What kind of stuff?"

He hesitated for a minute, and Connolly could see him debating with himself, embarrassed.

"Did he ask about your girlfriends?" Connolly said, steering him.

"Like whether I was getting any? Yeah, he asked that."

"And you liked to tell him."

"Go fuck yourself," he said, angry now.

"No, it's important. Did you get the sense that he was interested or just making conversation to make you *think* he was interested?"

But this was too complicated for him, and he looked at Connolly blankly. "He was interested. He liked to know where you could go, things like that."

"And who?"

"Sometimes."

"And did you tell him?"

He darted his eyes away, searching for a way out, wondering how they had got here. "Sometimes."

"But he was just curious? He didn't want the names for himself?"

"No," he said, seeing the implication, "but

not because he was a fruit. He was already fucking somebody."

Connolly was quiet, unsure where to go with this. It was possible that in the Texan's mind, bored and adolescent, somebody always had to be fucking somebody. It was possible that Bruner had used this as a cover, a lure for a braggart's gossip. But it was just possible that it was true, the missing link.

"What makes you think so?"

"I don't know—things he said, I guess. You know, like he'd say he had a date."

"Those exact words? He had a date?"

"Something like that. Yeah, exact, I guess. I didn't pay much attention."

"He mention a name? How did you know it was a woman?"

The Texan flushed. "Well, what else? Jesus Christ. I mean, why would he want to hear about what I was doing if he was a fruit?"

"That's a good question."

"What do you mean by that?" It was at once hostile and uncertain, as if the situation were so foreign to him that he wasn't sure he should resent it.

"Did he ever ask for any sexual details? You know—"

"No. You don't talk about stuff like that."

"So it was just "I had a good time last night,' or "Boy oh boy, you should see—' "

"Yeah. Like that. Nothing dirty. Look, he asked. What was I supposed to say?"

"Maybe your reputation preceded you. Maybe he was looking for pointers."

"Is that supposed to be funny?"

"So how often did you guys compare notes?"

"For two cents I'd push your face in. You got a right to ask all this, I suppose?"

"All the way up to Groves himself."

"Shit," he said, disgusted. "Look, you're making a big deal out of this. It's just the way guys talk. You know. Every once in a while."

"I thought you were scoring all the time."

"Hey, more than you, I'll bet," he said, sullen, childlike.

"You'd win that one," Connolly said, smiling. "Listen, I don't care if you fuck around. More power to you. I just want to know what you said about it to a murder victim."

"I don't know nothing about that. The guy liked to kid around once in a while, that's all. We didn't compare notes. He had something going all by himself. And then they broke it up, I think. Anyway, he didn't say anything much lately, so that's what I figured. And then I came down here. I was just kidding around, you know? Not some federal case. He liked to listen. He was that kind of guy. And he wasn't no fruit." He said this with emphasis, as if it were important to him that Connolly agree.

"I wonder how you can be so sure."

"I'd *know*. I'd just know." He drew himself up, almost physically taking a stand.

"You got a lot of them down in East Texas, huh?"

"Not alive."

There were four other security guards who'd been reassigned from the Hill, and by dusk Connolly had interviewed them all without learning anything he didn't already know. Oppenheimer still hadn't returned as he lined up with the others for dinner, so preoccupied that he barely noticed the food filling his tray. He sat with a group of machinists who were working on protective aluminum goggles to keep off the alkali dust. It was cooler now in the mess and he lingered over coffee, even after the men at his table had filed out for an open-air movie. He smiled at the idea of one of Hannah's nightclubs lighting up a patch of the nighttime desert. Even here, in the Jornada del Muerto, people danced. He stirred the coffee and absentmindedly played with the spoon, lifting it out of the cup, then lowering it to watch the coffee rise.

"Displacement theory," Eisler said, interrupting his thoughts. "You see how scientific principles never change. First Archimedes in his bath, now a coffee spoon. May I join you?"

Connolly smiled and opened his hand to the empty chair. "Did he really run through the streets naked, shouting 'Eureka'?"

"I hope so," Eisler said. "It makes a lovely story. But perhaps only after he'd written his report to the scientific committee."

"In duplicate. With copies for the file."

"Yes." He smiled. "In duplicate." His soft eyes were tired, his skin pink from the sun. He leaned forward over the tray as he ate, his shoulders slumped in the same concession to weariness Connolly had noticed in Oppenheimer. While he had been looking at the desert and toying with an overgrown teenager, they had been working hard.

"Where's Pawlowski?" Connolly said.

"Oh, he won't be coming back with us tonight. He's here for the week, poor devil."

Connolly felt a surge of happiness, so sudden and unexpected that he was afraid it would show. A week.

"I hope you had some rest," Eisler was saying. "Oppie doesn't like to drive, and it's difficult for me to see at night. Such a long drive. It would be better, you know, to stay the night."

"No, we need to get back," Connolly said, now eager to start.

Eisler misinterpreted him and smiled again. "Yes, it's not the Adlon here, I agree. Think of Daniel. All day at Station South. Every step you have to watch."

"Snakes?"

Eisler shuddered. "Or scorpions. Who knows? I confess, I am a coward in the desert."

"What's he doing here?"

"Am I allowed to tell you? Is this a security test?"

Connolly shrugged. "I'm pretty safe. I won't understand it anyway."

"The instruments to measure the radioactivity. Not the actual, of course. Simulated, at low level."

"The test isn't the real thing?" Connolly asked, surprised.

Eisler smiled. "This is for the test before the test. Only this time, TNT, one hundred tons, to study blast effects. Actually, to test our instruments. So we put one thousand curies of fission products in the pile to simulate the radioactive material. I'm sorry, do you understand this?"

"I understand one hundred tons of TNT. My God."

Eisler smiled weakly. "That's the trial run only. The gadget will produce more, as many as— well, nobody really knows. They have a pool to guess. A game, you see." His sad voice trailed off in thought. "How many tons of TNT blast can we produce with one gadget? A hundred? Five thousand? More? We cannot know yet."

"How many tons did you bet?"

"Me? I don't bet, Mr. Connolly. It's not a lottery."

"But think?"

"Twenty thousand tons," Eisler said matter-of-factly.

Connolly stared at him, appalled. "Twenty thousand," he repeated flatly, as if he were trying to confirm the figure.

"My friend," Eisler said softly, "what do you think we are doing here? Why do you think we call it a gadget? Security code? I don't think so. Maybe we don't want to remind ourselves what it is we are making. Yes, twenty thousand tons. My calculations are quite precise. I would bet on it." He smiled ironically. "Of course, we can't yet calculate the dispersion. There are no good formulas for radioactivity. Even our Daniel recognizes that."

Connolly felt stunned by the figures. They were calmly talking in a makeshift mess hall in the desert; the rest was beyond imagining. He could only fall back on the details of what was real, like a terminal patient still interested in medical procedure.

"Is that what you do too?" he asked. "Measure radioactivity?"

"Partly. We are not allowed to say, you know."

"You work with Frisch in G Division, Critical Assemblies Group."

Eisler flinched, surprised. "How do you know that?" Connolly didn't say anything. "I see. Another test. So if you know, why do you ask?"

"I know where you work. I don't know what it means."

"So. Do you know fast neutrons? Do you know critical mass? How can I explain?" His eyes looked around the table, searching for props. "How much uranium do we need for the gadget—that's the problem. We know it theoretically, but how to test the theory?" He moved Connolly's coffee cup to the space between them. "Suppose this coffee were U-235. If we took enough, if we reached critical mass, there would be a chain reaction and, of course, the explosion. But when does that happen? So we take the coffee we think

we need but we keep a hole in the middle—
you must use your imagination here, I'm
afraid—so the neutrons can escape. No reaction. The spoon will be the coffee we took out."
He held it over the cup. "If we lower it, like
this, the neutron bombardment increases,
the chain reaction accelerates. You have then
the conditions for an atomic explosion."

"But not the explosion."

"We cheat a little—we use uranium hydride
so it reacts more slowly. And we drop the
slug very quickly. But yes, when we pass
through the core," he said, letting the spoon
fall in, "we momentarily form a critical mass.
It's as close as we can come to an atomic
explosion without having one. Of course, you
can also produce this effect by simply stacking cubes of U-235 in a tamper of beryllium
blocks. A critical assembly. But the other is
more sophisticated. Perhaps also a little safer."

Connolly stared at the coffee, then looked
up at Eisler as if he were someone else. The
last thing he had ever imagined him to be
was daring. "You must have nerves of steel,"
he said finally. "That's like playing chick-
en."

"Dragon," Eisler corrected him.

"What?"

"We call it the Dragon Experiment—tickling the tail of the sleeping dragon."

"And you don't worry you'll blow the place
up?"

"No. We can control that. It's the radiation
that's dangerous."

"Well, better you than me."

"Mr. Connolly, please don't be so impressed. It's a scientific experiment, no more. I think sometimes we're all tickling the dragon, just a little. Testing how far we can go. Don't you feel that? It's only—" he searched, "the radiation we don't expect."

"I guess," Connolly said, feeling that Eisler was really talking to himself.

"And now may I ask you something?" Eisler said politely. "What do you do? You're not a driver." He anticipated Connolly's protest with a dismissive wave of his hand. "Please. I know. Drivers don't go to Weber's for the music. Oppie wants to drive with you alone. That's very unusual, you know. We notice things like that. You have my dossier. I assume others as well. What exactly are you doing here? Am I permitted to know? A government agent of some sort, I think. So there must be something wrong. What dragon are you tickling?"

Connolly was struck again by how different the émigrés were. Their first assumptions were still those of the police state.

"No," he said, "nothing like that. I'm just helping to investigate a murder."

"Oh? Whose?" His voice was so controlled and deliberate that Connolly took it for indifference.

"A security officer named Bruner."

Eisler sipped his coffee, saying nothing.

"Did you know him?"

"No. That is, I knew who he was. We are still a small community on the project. I was sorry

205

to hear about it. I didn't realize it was a security matter," he said, the last an uninflected question.

"It may not be."

Eisler raised his eyebrows in another question, but Connolly didn't elaborate.

"But you don't know who killed him?"

"Not yet."

"I see," he said slowly, pushing aside his tray. "So you will be our sword of justice. Well, I wish you success in your hunt. To think of catching even one. So many dead these days, and never any killers."

"I'm only looking for one in particular."

"Yes, of course. Forgive me. I seem always to argue philosophy when you have work to do."

"Are you married?"

Eisler looked at him dumbfounded, the subject swerving so abruptly that he'd been caught in its whiplash. Connolly could see him sorting through explanations and failing, until he sputtered a sort of laugh. "Why do you ask? Is it the investigation? Place of birth, school, married—"

"No, just curious."

Eisler looked at him thoughtfully now. "I think you are never just curious, Mr. Connolly." He sipped his coffee. "I was married. She's dead."

"I'm sorry."

"No, it was a long time ago. Many years now. Trude. She was killed—no, not like your friend. There was no killer. A street fight in

Berlin. We used to have so many in those days. The Freikorps and the GPD and— Who remembers them now? What could have been so important? But riots, you know, real blood in the streets. If you happened to pass by, you could get caught. Just taking the wrong street. Like a traffic accident. So."

"You never knew who killed her?"

"Who? Who?" he said, his gentle voice impatient now. "History killed her. There's no one to hunt. Like a disease." He shrugged.

"I'm sorry. You must still miss her."

"No, Mr. Connolly. I'm not a romantic. She's dead. I put the past behind me. The old world. Isn't that the American idea? Start fresh, leave everything behind?" Connolly thought of the white empty stretch of desert, his own impulse for something new. "No more history. You don't believe in history here. Yet. Sometimes I think we don't believe in anything else. So. We'll see who was right."

"And what would you bet?"

Eisler smiled. "Twenty thousand tons. For the rest, I don't know. It's hard to leave everything behind. It's always there somewhere. You think—but then it surprises you. A little like the dragon's tail, eh?"

"What is?" said Oppenheimer, putting his coffee on the table as he took a chair. He seemed jumpy and annoyed.

"History and philosophy," Eisler said. "Such matters."

Oppenheimer shot Connolly a glance. "Another seminar? How about finding us

207

some gas instead? We need to start back or we'll be up all night."

"You're not eating, Robert?" Eisler said.

"No, just coffee." He scratched one of his hands.

"You should eat something," Eisler said kindly.

"Not now," he snapped. It seemed to Connolly he was living on nerves. "What a god-forsaken place," he said, rubbing his hand again. "You wash and the water's so hard you're covered with magnesium oxide. Now I'll be scratching all night."

Connolly smiled at the scientific exactness of the complaint. It was, he realized, the first time he had ever heard Oppenheimer complain about anything. He had seen him buried under work, exasperated, worried, but that all seemed part of what he liked. Other people complained, leaned on his endless optimism to keep them going. If he felt things were all right, then the problems were just sandflies. Now, however, he was irritated and fretful, finally done in by an itch.

"We have five trunk lines here. You'd think they could manage to keep one open. G.G. throws a fit when he's cut off. Now we have to sit around and wait for them to get the connection back. Waste of time."

"In that case," Eisler said, "have a little something. You'll get sick. A roll, even."

"Friedrich, stop *hovering*. I'm fine. I heard something today that might interest you, by the way."

208

"Yes, Robert?" he said, chastened.

"The army took Stassfurt." He paused, waiting for a response, then plunged in. "The Germans had the uranium ore there. Over a thousand tons, most of the original Belgian supply. They can't have much anywhere else, so I think we can rule out the possibility of a German gadget."

It seemed to Connolly he was taunting Eisler, getting back at him for having raised any qualms at all, and Connolly was surprised by the sharp cruelty of it. No more Nazis to give permission. He was daring him to question the project again.

But Eisler refused to be drawn. "That's everything we hoped for," he said carefully.

"Yes. Now there's only the Japanese."

Eisler's face clouded for only a moment, but what Connolly saw there was terrible, a resignation so profound it looked fated, as if a long-awaited punishment had finally been handed out. And then it cleared and he was composed again. "Yes," he said.

Was Oppenheimer aware of what he was doing? Connolly looked again at Eisler, so easily troubled, so alert to contradiction, and he wondered if what Oppenheimer saw was some part of himself he needed to override. How else to become a general, to see things through, but to put everything else aside? The prize no longer allowed him any doubts, not in any part of himself.

"Phone call, sir." The GI had barely reached the table when Oppenheimer leaped up. "No, sir, sorry, not for you. For Mr. Connolly."

Oppenheimer was too surprised to be angry. Since he was already standing, he made an "After you" sweep of his hand. But the unexpectedness of it restored his good spirits, and he laughed at himself.

"Don't tie up the line. You'll keep the general waiting. And by the way, tell your mother or whoever it is that it's illegal to call here."

Connolly shrugged his shoulders. "Be right back."

"You'd better hope this is important."

It was Mills, sounding elated. "I thought you'd want to know—they got him."

"What?"

"The killer. Holliday called. Albuquerque police nailed him. Both crimes. Looks like you can start heading back to the bright lights."

But Connolly realized with a sharp pang that it was the last thing he wanted.

"You still there?" Mills said, louder now, as if he feared a bad line.

"It doesn't make sense."

"Brother, you don't give up, do you? They closed the case. *Fermata,* as we say in the Rio Grande. He's Mex, by the way. Just like they thought."

"I want to see him."

Mills paused. "Holliday said, if you asked, to tell you that the Albuquerque police want you both to politely butt out. They'll send a copy of the report, but—"

"Tell him I'll be there tomorrow. I have to get Oppenheimer back tonight."

"He said they're pretty firm about it. Probably got some bug up their ass about the army coming in—"

"You listening? Tell Holliday I'll be in Albuquerque tomorrow and I'll interview the suspect then. If I'm not interviewing the suspect tomorrow, I'll be on the phone to General Groves and he'll be talking to the governor of New Mexico and *he*'ll be dealing with a severe manpower shortage on the Albuquerque police force. Clear?"

"Could you really do that?"

"Probably. I don't know, but it's a risk he's not going to want to take."

"All right, calm down. I'll see what I can do. You don't sound very happy. I thought you'd be pleased as hell."

"I don't believe it."

"What do you mean?"

"I just don't believe it. He's not the guy."

"Mike, you'd better believe it," Mills said calmly. "He confessed."

8

They drove through the night, Eisler asleep in the back seat, Oppenheimer hunched down in front in a counterfeit of sleep, restless but quiet. The road was completely deserted, their headlights the only points of light in miles of darkness, but Connolly was alert, rubbed by the tension beside him,

Oppenheimer wanting to ask about the call and Connolly not telling him.

He wasn't sure why. Oppenheimer had a right to know. What could be more conclusive than a confession? It was useless to pretend he could offer any reason to doubt it. The rest of the story wrote itself now: Oppenheimer's wry thanks and a ticket back to Washington; his billet in the house on L Street, shared bathroom down the hall; another year or so of shuffling paper, until the war came to its end; his discharge to a life that wasn't there anymore. But it wasn't finished yet, not the case, not anything about Los Alamos. He wasn't ready to go. The truth was that he felt alive here, somehow on active service at last, a part of the project. He understood for the first time how the scientists felt, unwilling to think about anything else until the main point was reached, until it went off. There would be time later, but there wasn't any now. They were so close. And as long as he had his case, his peripheral investigation, he could still be part of it. Didn't he owe it to Bruner to follow this through to the end?

But even he could see that he was building an absurd house of cards. You can talk yourself into anything if you try. It wasn't his project. He didn't owe Bruner anything except an apology for trying to use his death to do something interesting with his own life. A Mexican pickup, a senseless crime. Life was like that. Maybe his refusal to accept it had a simpler reason: if he left the project, he'd be leaving her. He glanced over at Oppenheimer. He deserved to know. Connolly's silence bordered on military insubordination. Dereliction of duty. All because it might interfere with his urge for a woman? Was that really what it came down to? Still, Oppenheimer didn't care, and what did it matter? He wasn't asking for a lot of time—just enough to be sure, before he gave it all up.

They were still south of Santa Fe when first light streamed over the Sangre de Cristo Mountains, lifting mist off the sage and the juniper trees. It was going to be another spectacular morning, erasing all the uneasiness of the night, clear and uncomplicated. Oppenheimer, exhausted finally from whatever worries had preoccupied him in the dark, now fell sound asleep. Eisler, who confronted demons and then offered a roll, was snoring softly in the back. The car felt safe and ordinary again. Why was the night always filled with ultimatums? Go one step at a time. In the new light, he would see what he would see.

He dropped both men, groggy, at the entrance to the Tech Area, then returned the car to the pool, eager now for a shower and a fresh start. But Los Alamos was still asleep, glistening and empty. Mills wouldn't be ready for hours, and Albuquerque would be hours after that. Only a few trucks disturbed the peace. He could have coffee, check in at the office. He could take a walk, shake the drowsiness off by strolling around Ashley Pond. Instead, he stood at the edge of the dirt road, not doing anything. He started toward his dormitory, then hesitated. He turned toward the Admin Building, then stopped a second time. He was a teenager again, nervously looking for excuses in the street, when he knew what he had to do was go up on the porch and ring the bell.

He rapped softly on the door in the Sundt complex, afraid to wake the neighbors, but she must have been up early, because the door opened at once. Her hair was down, uncombed, and she was wrapped in a robe, a clinging pre-war silk that draped slightly at her breasts. He felt the warmth she still carried with her from bed.

"Are you mad?" she said quietly. "You can't come here." Her eyes looked quickly to each side.

"Come out, then," he said.

"Sssh. Someone will hear. Do you know what time it is?"

He nodded, but didn't move.

She glanced around again, then swung the door open further. "Come on," she said, drawing him in, then closing it behind her. "What is it? You look like hell."

He had turned to face her, unconsciously pinning her back against the door, and stared at her for a minute, his face close to hers, as if the distance would lower the sound of their voices. "You don't," he said, moving his eyes over her face.

She gave a half-smile. "I asked for that, didn't I?" she said softly. "At six in the bloody morning."

214

"I need to talk to you."

"Not here."

"He won't be back till Friday."

"It isn't that. We can't—not here." But she didn't move, and he could feel her in front of him, warm, their faces almost touching.

"I need to tell you. I may have to leave."

She looked at him. "Will you?"

"I may. They found someone. I may have to leave."

"Why are you telling me?" she said, her eyes still on him.

"I can't promise you anything. You should know that."

"I know."

"It may be important to you. I don't want to be unfair to you."

She placed her hand along his cheek. "But you're not fair," she said, drawing him closer. "There's nothing fair about you." She kissed him. "You're here," she said, kissing him again, lightly, as if she were drawing a breath between words, "and then you're not. It's not fair. You're warning me. What else?"

"I don't want to leave," he said, kissing her back.

"Then stay for a while. Now."

"Are you sure?" he said, still kissing her.

"Yes."

"I don't want to hurt you."

"This is a funny love affair. Apologies at the beginning, not the end. It's not fair."

"No."

"Let's pretend we're at the beginning."

He kissed her hard then, pinning her against the door, his hands behind her, drawing her closer. He could feel the heat of her skin through the silk as his hands moved down her back, pulling her toward him so that their bodies ground together. Then her robe fell open and he moved his hands inside, feeling the skin itself, hot, alive to his touch. She held the back of his head, her mouth everywhere on his face.

"Come to bed," he whispered.

"No." She was gulping air. "Not there."

And as his hand rounded her, moving toward the back of her thigh, she brought her leg up beside him, as if he were taking her right there, standing up, and his prick jumped with excitement. He rubbed his hand under her thigh until he felt her hair graze his fingertips, already moist, and the wetness made his erection pulse again, almost painful now in his pants. His fingers moved up along the moist lips, slick, back and forth, so that she began to ride them, her mouth making stifled noises behind the kiss. Then he turned his hand so that his open palm held her, the heel of it grinding against the front of her as the wet finger still slid back and forth, and she pulled her mouth off his to gasp for air, her lower body still moving against him. But he couldn't stop now—the fierceness of it, the hurry, was outside them. He could feel her breath, ragged, in his ear. He covered her mouth again, their tongues slippery, as he moved his hand away to unzip his pants, fast, so that when it sprang out it moved toward her at once to replace the hand, sliding along the wet part of her until it slipped inside and he thrust up, filling her, and she gasped, dropping her head on his shoulder. He thought for an instant he would come then, still, her heat wrapped around him. There was nothing but feeling now, so complete he was afraid to disturb it. But then he felt the walls of her vagina grip him, making gentle spasms, and they were moving again. "Oh," she said, a low sound from her throat, her head back against the door, and the sound of it excited him more, and he put his mouth back on hers, kissing her as he gripped her below, pounding into her with her thigh still drawn up beside him. He could hear them thudding against the door, oblivious as animals, and then a sharp sound from her as he felt her grip him again inside, and he knew she had come, so that he was released now too and after a few more jabbing thrusts it spurted out of him, everything in him shooting out, taking his breath with it.

They stood there for a few minutes, still locked together, gulping air, and he knew they must look absurd, their mouths smeared with saliva, standing against the wall like dogs, his pants down below his knees. But her face glowed, and when he looked at her he felt an immense gratitude. It had been so quick, but she had let him, not protesting, giving herself to it. He had wanted to make love, not just fuck, but they had already waited too long to take their time. Now he kissed her gently and lifted her up, still hard inside her, and moved haltingly toward the couch, his pants wadded foolishly around his calves. But the point was not to leave her. It didn't matter how they looked, messy and awkward, so long as he remained inside her. When he laid her down on the couch, still inside, she smiled at him, and this time they kept a different rhythm, moving smoothly in and out, and the sensation in him spread outward so that his whole body was making love, every piece of skin sensitive. This time his hands felt all of her, drawing along her breasts, kissing the side of her neck, until they both began racing and she wrapped her legs around him, urging him, waiting for him to come so that they could finish together, shuddering in the same jolt of pleasure.

They lay quietly for a while until, calm now, he sensed his weight on her and slipped out, his penis finally soft, and moved to the side, still holding her. He saw her face moist with tears.

"Don't," he said softly, brushing them lightly off her face.

"No, I'm all right," she said, turning on her side to face him. She held the side of his head, looking at him. "What will it be like, do you think?"

"I don't know."

"No. Never mind."

"Like this, maybe."

"Maybe," she said, tracing the shape of his ear.

"Why do we ever think anything else matters?"

She smiled. "That's sex talking."

"I guess."

"I've never done it standing up."

He grinned. "What do you think?"

"Not sure yet."

They would have gone on like this, he knew, comfortable, idly touching each other, but there was a rap on the door.

"Oh God," she whispered, sitting up, pointing him quickly toward the bedroom. "Bloody hell."

What had seemed smooth before, no more than another stroke of lovemaking, was clumsy now, and he almost tripped as he staggered toward the door, holding his pants.

"Coming," she said out loud, belting the robe around her and running her fingers through her hair. She waited until he had closed the bedroom door. Inside, he flopped on the bed, too exhausted to dress and afraid of making a sound.

"Emma," he heard a woman's voice say through the door, "thank God you're up. Do you have *any* coffee? I don't know how I ran out, but Larry'll be a *bear* if he doesn't have his coffee. I'll pay you back."

"I was just making some. This enough?" she said over the rattling of a tin.

"Hmm. You're perspiring."

"It's this damn central heating. You'd think I'd be used to it by now, wouldn't you?"

"Thanks," the woman said, obviously taking the coffee. "Sorry to bother you so early. Where's Daniel? I thought I heard somebody."

"No, just me. He's off-site. Awful, talking to yourself, isn't it? If I'm not careful they'll put me away."

There was more as she lingered at the door, but Connolly stopped listening. He lay there instead, looking up at the ceiling, still drifting in a haze of sex. Now there was the sound of water running, the rattle of a pot being put on to boil, the scrape of a match. Everything seemed to him erotic. He imagined her measuring out the coffee, her robe half open so that her flushed breasts stood out, the nipple firm against the silk. He imagined lying here every morning, listening to her being busy in the kitchen as the stickiness of sex dried on his skin. When she opened the door, her finger to her lips in warning, she giggled at the sight of him.

"Look at you," she whispered. "Do you think you might put your trousers on, or do you just want to stay like that all day?"

"All day," he said. "Come to bed."

But she shook her head. "No, I told you. I won't do that to him. Come and have some coffee," she said, leaving the room.

He got up, pulled his pants on, and followed her out. "Funny scruples you have," he said teasingly.

But she came up to him and held him. "Don't scold. I won't, that's all."

"Sorry," he said, kissing her. "Do you want me to go?"

"No. Let's not waste the coffee, now that I've made it. Bloody cow next door. She's probably put her ear to a glass at the wall."

He sat at the little kitchen table near the window, smoking, watching her as she poured the coffee and brought it to the table. Every movement seemed interesting—the way she smoothed the back of her robe under her as she sat down, blew gently on the coffee, reached for a match.

"What?" she said self-consciously.

"Just looking," he said. "I can't get enough of you."

"Well, you've only just started," she said dryly, lighting a cigarette.

"No. Weeks. From the start."

"That's nice," she said, taking a sip of coffee, playing. "It must have been the sight of me doubled over sick that made you decide. Was that it?"

"No. The ride back from the ranch," he said seriously.

"Really?" she said, interested.

"Uh-huh. There was that moment."

"What moment?"

"There's always a moment between a man and a woman when you know something can happen. It doesn't have to—it can just pass right on by. But it can never happen without that moment. You know, when you feel it's possible."

She laughed. "You've got cheek."

"Didn't you feel it too?"

"It's different for a woman."

"I don't believe it. Not that part."

She shrugged and looked toward the window, at the shaft of sunlight pouring between them on the table. "What was all that about your going away?"

"I may. I don't know. But we can see each other. He's not back all week."

"How do you know that?"

"I've just come from the test site. I saw him there."

"That must have been cozy. Look, if anything's going to happen, you've got to leave him out of it. I mean it."

"He's not in it. I'm talking about us. You and me. You can make whatever rules you want."

"All right," she said softly, "but not here. No one's ever come here."

"Where did you go with the others?"

She looked at him. "Don't pretend you're jealous. You've no right. I never said there were others. I just said no one's ever come here. You can see what it's like." She tilted her head toward the neighboring apartment.

He followed her gesture, taking in the room for the first time, a blur of terra-cotta pots and Navajo rugs draped over simple government-issue furniture. He reached across the table for her hand. "We can meet somewhere."

"Yes."

"I'll find a place."

"There's the ranch. We could go there."

"She left you a key," he said, a statement.

222

Emma nodded. "She thought I might need it."

"That day," he said. "Before the drive. You thought about this before the drive."

"No. A suspicion. I didn't know."

He smiled. "But you thought it might. You were ahead of me. Come here."

She shook her head, but he gripped her hand, pulling it gently, and she followed the pull, getting up and moving to where he sat, her robe falling open as she straddled him. His face was level with her breasts and he began kissing them, barely touching them at first, then, as he felt the nipples harden, moving over them in a steady rhythm, pressing, so that she anticipated each stroke of his mouth. She closed her eyes. His mouth opened to lick the nipple, tasting her, still salty with sweat. He pressed his face into her, and her head, no longer flung back, now dropped down next to his. "No," she gasped, "you'll break the chair," a last vestige of practicality. He carried her again to the couch, his mouth still on her, tasting all of her this time, slowly, making love to every part of her, teasing her sex until she held his head there, shuddering as she came under his tongue, so that when he entered her again she lay open, already his.

Mills was waiting in his room, lying again on the bed.

"You going to make a habit of breaking in?" Connolly said.

"That was hours ago, when I thought you'd need a ride. Then I just got fascinated wondering where you were. After being so anxious and all."

"Well, I'm here now. Everything set?"

"Holliday will meet us there. Threatening to call the governor did the trick, just like you said. He's not happy about it, though. Said you put his ass on the line and he doesn't like it there. Christ, you're a mess."

"We drove all night."

"Right."

"What the hell does that mean?"

Mills grinned. "I haven't seen a look like that since college. Larry Rosen, the pussy king. Just like Larry. Out all night and then he'd come back too shagged out to go to class. Except he'd want to tell us about it. You have fun?"

"Don't be an asshole."

"Hey, I didn't say a thing. Better grab yourself a shower, though. The memory lingers on. Those cons down there get a whiff and they'll start tearing the place apart."

"Mills—"

"All right, all right. I'm just jealous, that's all. I have to hand it to you—I've been here a *year* and I still can't get laid."

"How about just getting the car? I'll be right with you," Connolly said, stripping off his clothes.

"Okay. You sure you don't want to get some sleep instead? This can wait, you know.

They've got a signed confession and a witness."

"Who?"

"The bartender in Albuquerque. Turns out he recognized him after all."

"Was this before or after they took his liquor license away?"

"There were others. The guy was a regular. It's *him*, Mike."

"I just want to get a look at him."

Mills shrugged. "Suit yourself. If it was me, after a big night, I'd get some sleep."

"Well, that's you. I don't feel sleepy at all."

But he slept all the way to Albuquerque, his eyes drooping as soon as they left the Hill and Mills's cheerful voice faded into a background hum. By the time they reached the familiar highway he was out, not even disturbed by the sun on his face. They were in Albuquerque before he surfaced again, slightly groggy, and saw Holliday's grim face.

The Albuquerque jail had none of the adobe pretense of Santa Fe; it was a streamlined modern government building in the post office pork-barrel style, official and utilitarian. Chief Hendron, on the other hand, was a throwback to the frontier one-room jail with a big key ring. He had the authority of height and carried himself with the swagger of one who was never far from his six-shooter. He was clearly put out about the interview, his natural belligerence hemmed in only by the threat of a higher authority, an even bigger bully.

"Holliday here says you got some special

interest in this prisoner, is that right? You mind telling me what that might be?"

"It's a government matter."

"Shit, what isn't?" He looked at Connolly's ID and snorted. "Army Corps of Engineers is taking an interest in all *kinds* of things these days, aren't they? I suppose we got to wait for the war to be over before you tell us what the hell you're all doing here."

"You'll be the first to know."

The chief looked at him. "Don't go fresh on me," he snapped. "Don't you do it. I'm still the law around here, and I won't have it." He handed back the ID. "If Holliday vouches for you, I guess that's that. But I'm not going to have you messing with my prisoner. You want to talk to him, you've got to have one of my boys with you. We got a self-confessed murderer back there and I *still* don't know what business that is of yours."

"The other victim was one of our men."

"One of your *men*? That's a good one. Now just what would one of you army engineers be wanting with old Ramon back there?"

"That's what I'd like to know."

"Helluva thing, that kind of shit going on in the army. If it was my outfit, I'd be ashamed."

"If it was your outfit, so would I," Connolly said and then quickly, before Hendron could reply, "Can I see him now? I'll have Chief Holliday with me—that should satisfy your concerns about being alone. Has he got a lawyer?"

Hendron glared at him, ready to pounce, then backed down.

226

"He will have. You got one hour with him, that's it. You just find out what you need to find out and don't come back. You interfere with this case and the governor himself won't keep me off your ass."

"I appreciate your cooperation."

Hendron stared at him again. "You do that. Holliday, I'm counting on you to make sure nothing goes wrong here. We're going for a conviction on this one."

"I understand you have witnesses?" Connolly said.

"Bartender saw them leave together. Some of the other, uh, patrons'll verify that. Turns out old Ramon worked that parking lot before. No question he did it. We got a signed confession, you know."

"So I heard."

"Yeah, well, Arnold here will show you the way. You be nice and easy with him, now. Old Ramon come to a little grief the other night, so he's probably not feeling his best."

"What kind of grief?"

He smirked. "The kind they got in jail when you're not too popular. Seems they don't go for Ramon's type back there. I guess he did better with the army engineers."

They were left to wait in a room down the corridor from Hendron's office.

"You're not making any friends here," Holliday said, handing him a copy of the statement.

"I wish I knew what the big deal was. What does Hendron care, anyway?"

"You ever step on a snake by accident? You didn't mean to and he doesn't want to, but he's just got to bite. It's the surprise of it."

"Then what? He crawls back under a rock?"

"If you let him alone."

Connolly read through the statement. "Kelly? I thought you said he was Mex."

"His mother. Father probably worked on the railroad. We get a lot of that here. Mostly they don't hang around long enough to leave a name, though."

"Maybe it was love," Connolly said absently, still reading through the transcript. "Christ, fifty dollars? He stuck a knife in somebody for fifty dollars?"

"That's a lot of money to some folks. Anyway, it was just a fight. You know how accidents happen in a fight."

Connolly looked up at him. "Manslaughter?" he said, a larger question.

"Murder second degree would be more my guess."

"And you don't hang for second degree."

"Not in this state."

"He have a fight with Bruner too?"

"No. He was defending his manhood," he said flatly, not willing to meet Connolly's eyes. But Connolly refused to look away. "That's what it says."

"You believe this?"

"No reason not to believe it. He said it, didn't he? Machismo's a big thing with these people." He paused. "It's something any jury here would understand."

228

Connolly turned back to the paper, not wanting to press him. "How much did he say he got off Bruner?"

"He didn't."

"Well, it wouldn't be fifty dollars. Karl would never carry that much."

"He says it wasn't about money."

"That's right, I forgot. He was protecting his honor. So he smashes Karl's skull in. Messes up his face."

Holliday sighed. "Just didn't know his own strength, I guess."

But when Kelly was led in, he seemed to have no visible strength at all. He shuffled in, careful of the guard, and stood before the table, quiet and sullen, a schoolboy brought up before the principal. He was slight but wiry, his shoulders hunched as if the handcuffs were weighing him down. His face was like a map of his mixed ancestry, the copper skin and Aztec slant of his cheekbones set off by the surprising blue of his eyes, now half lost in the swelling on one side and the deep purple bruises. A thin scraggly mustache was pushed up by the cracked puffiness of his upper lip. There was no disguising the meanness of his face, however. The discolored skin stretched across a hard mask of defiant wariness, the look of someone who'd never known a favor in his life.

"Thank you," Connolly said to the guard. "He need these?" He pointed to the handcuffs. The guard looked at Holliday, who nodded, and reluctantly unlocked the cuffs. Kelly rubbed his thin wrists, surprised and suspicious at the same time.

"I'll be right outside," the guard said. "Ramon here give you any trouble, you just holler."

"Sit down," Connolly said, ignoring the guard and offering a cigarette. Kelly winced slightly as his cracked lip curled around it, then let it dangle from the side of his mouth, his eyes closed against the rising smoke.

"I work for the government and I need to ask you a few questions," Connolly began.

"I don't know anything about that."

"About what?"

"About no government. What's this have to do with the government? Nobody told me about that."

"One of the men you killed worked for the government."

For the first time Kelly looked alarmed, his bruised face furrowed in concern. "I don't know nothing about that. I didn't kill nobody. It was an accident."

"And with"—he searched the paper—"Jack Duncan, that's the man in Albuquerque—that was an accident too?"

"No. Jack was different. That was a fight."

"What was the fight about?"

He shrugged. "You know. A fight."

"You knew Duncan?"

"I seen him around."

"Did you have sex with him?"

He took the cigarette out of his mouth. "Hey. I don't do that. He had sex with *me*."

Connolly looked at him, surprised at the distinction. "What did he do?"

"What, are you kidding me? He blew me, what do you think? He liked doing that."

"Did he pay you?"

"Nah. It was for, you know, the fun of it. I let guys do me once in a while. When I can't get it any other way. What's the difference?"

"But you had fifty dollars."

"He give me that. It was a loan, like."

"So even though he gave you fifty dollars, you two had a fight."

He shrugged again, stubbing out the cigarette.

"That where you got those bruises?"

He stared at both men as if it were a trick question.

"The fight was a while ago," Connolly said. "Those look pretty fresh."

"I fell."

"Where? Here?"

"Yeah, here. I fell." He looked away.

"What about the man in Santa Fe, did you know him?"

"No."

"Where did you meet?"

"In a bar."

"Which one?"

"I don't know. Some bar near the plaza."

"What were you doing in Santa Fe?"

He shrugged. "I was just there, that's all."

"Then what happened?"

"We went for a walk. Then he—look, I already told all this stuff. Why are you asking me again?" He took another cigarette, more confident now.

"I just want to be sure I got it right. So you went for a walk. Not a ride?"

"No. A walk."

Connolly felt Holliday stir beside him, shifting in his seat, but he didn't say anything. "Down to the river," Connolly prompted.

"Yeah."

"Then what happened?"

Kelly smirked. "He come on to me."

"Did that surprise you?"

The question seemed to catch him off-guard.

"You just thought he wanted to talk."

"I don't know. Maybe. Okay, I thought maybe he wanted to do me. It crossed my mind."

"Did he talk about himself? His work?"

Kelly looked puzzled. "No."

"So what did you talk about?"

"Nothing. I don't remember."

"He was a pretty big guy," Connolly said evenly. "Did that worry you?" Again he felt Holliday stir.

"I can take care of myself."

Connolly looked at the thin, sinewy arms, the bloated face, and wondered how often he had said this before, how often the posturing had protected him. "I can see that."

"Hey," Kelly said, offended. "I told you. I fell."

"So you went for a walk and you ended up hitting him. Why?"

"He got out of hand. I told you."

"He didn't want to have sex with you?"

"He wanted me to do *him*. I don't do that."

"You tell him this?"

"Sure, but he don't want to listen, you know? And then he's all over me, so—"

"So you hit him. With what, by the way?"

"With what?" Connolly could see his face working, sorting through answers.

"Yes. Did you just use your fists, or did you have something?"

"A branch," he said quickly. "It was lying there right on the ground. Hey, what do you want to know all this for?"

"And you threw it away afterward?"

"Yeah, I guess. I don't remember too well."

"But you do remember hitting him."

"Yeah, I *said* I did. I didn't know he was dead, I just thought he was out, you know."

Holliday got up then and walked over to the window.

"You must have been pretty angry," Connolly said smoothly.

"I was surprised, you know? I just did the first thing that came into my head. I wasn't trying to kill him."

"What surprised you? The sex?"

"Yeah."

"You didn't expect it from him? Was that because he was Mexican too?"

He could feel Holliday turn to them from the window, watching Kelly's confused face. Kelly hesitated for a minute, then said, "No. It was just the surprise, you know."

"Ramon, have you ever been to San Isidro?"

"What's that? A church?"

"Yes. Ever hear of it?"

"I don't understand."

"It's a church in Santa Fe. You ever go there?"

"I don't go to church much." Then, suspicious, "What do you ask that for?"

"The man you killed—the man you hit—used to go there. I just wondered if you'd ever gone there with him."

"I told you, I only saw him the one time. No, I didn't go to no church with him. What do you think?"

Holliday sat down again. When he spoke, his voice was surprisingly gentle. "You know, Ramon, the police really appreciate cooperation."

"Yeah," he said, not looking at Holliday. Connolly came from somewhere else; this was the devil he knew.

"Makes our job a lot easier, so we appreciate that. When you make it easier for us, then we're more inclined to—well, make it easier for you."

"Yeah."

"When we understand something, we got a much better idea what the charge should be. Like here, for instance. Somebody might think first off this is nothing but a murder one, you know, but when they understand it, when they know all the facts, they might think it's not so bad. We don't want you to hang for something you didn't do."

Connolly sat back, watching him work.

"That's right," Kelly said. "That Jack Duncan. That wasn't no *murder*, that was just a fight, you know?"

"That's what it sounds like to me. The boys down here understand that? They explain that to you?"

Ramon looked up at him. "Yeah, they explained it."

"Good. You know, it's a funny thing, boy in your position. Sometimes the police are the best friends you got."

Ramon absentmindedly rubbed his cheek. "Yeah."

"So you'd just want to go right on cooperating with them, wouldn't you?"

"Sure."

"I mean, we got two dead bodies here, so we got some kind of trouble, but that don't have to be murder trouble, does it? Not the worst kind. I mean, two counts of second ain't nowhere near as serious as even one first. You still got your life. They explain that to you?"

"Yeah."

"Well, good. Now I got one more question. After you hit the guy, you go through his pockets some?"

Kelly hesitated for a minute, suspecting a trap, then went ahead. "Yeah, okay, I did. What the hell—I figured he owed me something."

"Uh-huh. You find much?"

"I don't remember. Some. Not much."

"You throw the wallet away too?"

"Yeah, I guess."

"What about the car?"

"I don't know nothing about a car."

"Oh, well, maybe he didn't have one. You didn't find any keys, huh? Just the wallet."

"Yeah, that's right. Just a wallet."

Holliday turned to Connolly. "Anything else you want to know?"

"No. I guess that's it," Connolly said. "Better get the guard."

"You got another cigarette?" Ramon said.

"Sure. Anything else we can do for you?"

Kelly stood up, the cigarette tucked behind his ear. "I'd sure like to get out of solitary. Think you could do something about that? I mean, it's not like they're accusing me of being a murderer or something."

Afterward they stood on the steps of the building, caught in the glare of the afternoon sun. Holliday lit a cigarette, ignoring Connolly, looking deliberately at the street. Only a few cars broke the quiet.

"Well, that explains the warm welcome," Connolly finally said.

Holliday just continued smoking.

"How do you want to play this?" Connolly said.

"I don't know what you mean," Holliday said, his voice low.

"Yes you do. They can't railroad a confession like this. Who the hell do they think they are, anyway?"

"I don't know that one either."

"Is this just some more Wild West stuff? What do they think's going to happen when he talks to a lawyer?"

Holliday sighed. "Well, that's a funny thing, isn't it? Lawyer gets him to change his statement and he'll hang for sure."

"But he didn't do it."

"He did the first one all right."

"Then let him take the rap for that."

"Well, aren't you the hanging judge. I don't know as I'd recommend that if I was his lawyer."

"They're going to hang him anyway."

"Maybe. But we don't know that. Maybe he thinks it's worth the chance."

"This is what they're doing in Germany, for Christ's sake."

"In New York City too, I hear."

"We don't beat phony confessions out of people just to make the police look good."

"No? Well, then I stand corrected."

"You're not going to do anything about this, are you?"

Holliday turned to face him, his expression more weary than angry. "Just what did you have in mind?"

"It's not right."

"I didn't say it was. But it's done. Kelly's a little punk who's probably going to get better than he deserves. The boys here are going to take credit for solving crimes they probably couldn't ever have solved anyway. Nothing worse than a murder hanging over you. People don't like it, makes them feel uneasy. So now

everybody can just go about his business.
Until the next guy goes out in the parking lot—
but at least he won't have Kelly getting his rocks
off and playing with knives. So maybe everybody's better off all around."

"Except us. We've still got a murder to
solve."

Holliday didn't say anything.

"You're keeping the case open, aren't you?
You know he didn't kill Bruner."

"I can't, Mike," Holliday said quietly.
"He'll have my badge. I can't go against him
like that."

"Don't, then. Just don't close the case."

"It's closed."

"Doc, you've always been straight with me.
At least I think you have."

"Then don't ask me to do something I can't
do," he said, his voice resigned.

Connolly stared at him. "You know I can't
let this go."

"Maybe. But as a police matter, it's closed.
What you get to up there on the Hill is your
business."

"I still need your help."

He looked at the street, deciding. "What,
exactly? I can't hold every drifter who passes through town."

"And I can't go talking to everybody who
lives around San Isidro. Only the police can
do that."

"Why San Isidro?"

"Because Bruner was killed there. Somebody

must have seen something. There's always somebody."

Holliday raised his eyebrows. "Then why move him?"

"I don't know. Maybe they didn't want you snooping around, just in case somebody *did* see something. No crime, no questions. People don't volunteer, do they?"

"Not much."

"And they didn't want him found."

"So they move him to the center of town."

Connolly sighed. "Yes."

"Damnedest thing, isn't it? You roll a guy, and instead of running away you take *him* away. All right. You don't want him found—put a little distance between you and the law. So you've got all of God's country around here, you can just drop him off somewhere in the woods and let the coyotes have him. But you don't. You take him right back into town, where you *know* he's going to be found. And then you take his ID, everything, so he's not exactly found. Nobody knows who he is. Sounds like you can't make up your mind one way or the other."

"Go on," Connolly said quietly, watching him.

"Now you take Mr. Kelly here. That's a whole lot of trouble for him to go to. He's more what I'd call the careless type. Love 'em and leave 'em. Don't think he'd bother much about covering his tracks. He'd just get the hell out."

"We know it's not him," Connolly said impatiently.

"And it's not anybody *like* him either."

Connolly looked up at him. "Meaning?"

"Meaning I don't think he was rolled. I think it was somebody he knew. Or anyway who knew him."

"That's what I've been saying all along."

Holliday grinned. "I never said you were dumb. Just an arrogant son of a bitch."

"So why would whoever it was want him to be found?"

"Well, he was going to be, wasn't he? You don't just lose a security officer in a top secret government base. They'd be all over the place. In fact, you were."

"So we're back to square one. Why move him?"

Holliday lit another cigarette, taking his time. "Well, I've been giving that a little thought. And what occurs to me is *how* he was found. See, we don't know him from Adam—all we got is a victim. You find a body in the desert, you got a real mystery on your hands. San Isidro? Well, what would he be doing there? But the way we did find him, there was no mystery about that. You get the picture right away. What you got there is kind of an embarrassment. You don't want to look into that too closely—you never know what you're going to find when you turn that rock over. You just want to clean it up. The army wouldn't want to go looking for pretty boys. They'd be squeamish about that. He just thought they'd sweep it away."

"And now they will."

Holliday shrugged. "I have to say, I'll bet he never figured on old Ramon. That's just another example of how the Good Lord looks after his sinners."

"So where do we go from here?"

"Like I said, this case is closed. I can give you the benefit of my wisdom—that just comes from being in the business. But Hendron finds out I'm conducting an illegal investigation and he'll have my ass. He can do it, too."

"Not if you blow the whistle on him first."

"Forget it," Holliday said. "Not me. Not you either. He's got a signed confession, and you don't have much more than a theory about a parking lot and a few pieces of goddamn turquoise. That's not just sticking your neck out, that's handing him the ax. So right now it's his show and there's not a damn thing we can do about it. Hendron's the kind of guy, if we were in combat you wouldn't be surprised if he got shot in the back. One bullet and out and nobody'd look twice. To save themselves, you know. But we don't do that here yet. Maybe you ought to use some of your contacts in Washington and get the bastard drafted. Let him go push the Japs around." He ground out his cigarette, finished with the conversation. "But I guess he's too valuable keeping the peace at home. Something for our boys to come back to."

Connolly was silent for a minute. "What about the car?"

"The car?" Holliday said, looking up, intrigued.

"You still need to find the car."

Holliday smiled. "Well, you know, a missing vehicle is another story. Strictly speaking, it's not part of this case at all."

"Unless you find it."

"Well, we have to find it first. Plenty of time to worry about that."

"Thanks, Doc."

Holliday looked at him. "This isn't anything. Just a missing car."

"Thanks anyway. You'll sleep better. I guarantee it."

"Don't go giving me too much credit. I sleep pretty good now."

"You'd think they'd want to know," Connolly said, shaking his head. "I mean, don't they care that whoever killed Bruner is still out there somewhere?"

"Well, you know, they probably should, but to them it's just some fairy fight. Don't matter. The thing is, nobody's ever really cared about this except you."

"I can't now," Oppenheimer said, coming out of the building. "I'm already late. I'm flying to Washington. Can't it wait?"

"No."

"Ride with me to Albuquerque if you like,"

he said, nodding to the driver, who held the door for him.

"I've just come from Albuquerque. Two minutes."

"Then ride with me to the gate. I really am late. Just like the White Rabbit." He smiled, climbing into the car as if it were the hole in the tree. Connolly followed.

"Bad news?" Oppenheimer said as they passed the Tech Area.

"That depends on how you look at it. I thought you should know. The police in Albuquerque have arrested someone."

"Splendid. Anybody we know?"

"No. Some kid who knifed a guy down there a few weeks ago. They got him to confess to both crimes."

"Poor Bruner," Oppenheimer said indifferently, his mind clearly elsewhere. "Well, it's a relief in a way, isn't it? One less thing to worry about." He looked up when Connolly didn't answer. "Isn't it?"

Connolly shook his head and nodded toward the driver, a slight fair-haired soldier, but Oppenheimer waved his hand.

"He's the wrong man."

"Do you know that?"

"Yes."

"Do they?"

"Maybe. They don't care."

"I don't understand."

"He killed their man. He didn't kill Karl. But it suits them to wrap it all up, I guess. Neat and tidy. Anyway, they're doing it."

"You said they had a confession?"

"He's lying. It wouldn't hold up for five minutes in court."

Oppenheimer looked at him, frankly puzzled.

"But no one's going to challenge it. The police want to believe it, and Kelly—that's the guy—wants them to believe it. He thinks he's making a deal."

Oppenheimer took this in. "What are you going to do?"

"Nothing. There's nothing we can do. But I wanted you to know. It'll be in the papers. Are you seeing Groves? He'll want to know. He'll want to believe it."

They had reached the gate, and Oppenheimer asked the driver to pull over. "What exactly do you want me to tell him?"

"That I'm continuing our investigation and you support it."

"Do I?"

"Yes, if you want to get to the bottom of this. Of course, you can go along with the police and send me back to Washington."

Oppenheimer smiled. "Oh, I'm in no hurry to do that. I rather like playing Dr. Watson." He hesitated. "Do I understand that you're seriously suggesting there's a miscarriage of justice—"

"It wouldn't be the first time."

"And we're not going to do a thing about it?"

"Not now. What do we get by that? Officially,

Karl was rolled in the park having sex with a street thug. Case closed. Theirs, anyway."

Oppenheimer looked out the window. "It's a hell of an epitaph, isn't it? That's how Karl's going to be remembered."

"That's what the papers will say anyway. We don't get to write our own obituaries."

"No, we don't," Oppenheimer said. "So. The expedient thing. What do you want me to do?"

"Agree with them. Case closed. I'll just go about my business in my own way. Officially, you're relieved it's over."

"I'll be relieved when it's really over."

"Yes," Connolly said, opening the door to get out, "but imagine how relieved the real killer is right now."

But having cleared things with Oppenheimer, he now found himself at loose ends, tired, unsure where to begin again. At the office he talked with Mills, now sheepish after hearing about Kelly's interview, and leafed absent-mindedly through the savings files. He thought about Holliday's reconstruction of the night of the crime. But why San Isidro in the first place? It was an unlikely rendezvous—there was always the chance of tourists or parishioners. He made a note to check the schedule of services, but more out of thoroughness than conviction—he couldn't imagine Bruner meeting someone at mass. In fact, he couldn't imagine Bruner meeting someone at all. And yet he must have. He must have arranged it somehow,

y

245

without telephones, from a city so secret it didn't exist, just a post office number in the high desert.

He was thinking about Los Alamos, the communications procedures, when Emma came into the office. She nodded to him but dealt with Mills, filling out a req for an overnight off-site pass.

"Do you need the whole route? I'm going to Chaco. I've been before, so you've probably got it all somewhere."

"Purpose of visit?" Mills said, bored.

"See the bloody ruins. What do you think? There's nothing else there."

"Archaeology?" he said, pencil still poised to write.

Emma laughed. "No. Hiking, put "hiking' down. That covers everything."

"Tourism," Mills said, writing.

Connolly shuffled papers, not trusting himself to look at her, but when he did he found her staring directly at him, her eyes shining.

"Number where you can be reached?"

"Not for miles and miles. That's the point. You ought to get out once in a while," she said to Mills. "You'll get pasty in here. Ever see the Anasazi sites?"

"Not yet," Mills said, completing the form.

"You really ought to. Get some proper hiking shoes and start with Bandelier. It's closer. Chaco's a bit remote. You have to leave here at six to have any time there at all, but it's worth it."

Mills handed her the pass. "Don't talk to strangers," he said, smiling.

"That's what my father used to say."

And then she smiled at both of them and was gone. Connolly stared back at the desk, afraid to watch her out the door, and realized it had all been arranged. The time. The plan. What he'd need to take. A clandestine meeting, all fixed in the security office itself. That easy. Why had he ever imagined Bruner couldn't do it? Everything that mattered was secret, arranged under the thin cover of the visible world.

He had dinner with Mills in the commissary, then walked over to the movie. He couldn't go home. He'd lie there on Bruner's chaste bed, thinking about tomorrow, tempted to slink over to the Sundt apartments in the dark. Instead he sat on a folding chair in the crowded auditorium, dazzled by color. It was a musical, bright and glossy. There was a nightclub. There was a misunderstanding. There was a spot with Carmen Miranda. Afterward, he couldn't remember anything about it. People filed out, complaining about the night chill, and drifted away in pairs, just the way they did on Main Street. He was too tired to go back with Mills for a beer, so he found himself alone, the street suddenly empty, smelling of woodsmoke and resin.

"Excuse me." The voice startled him, coming from behind. "Could I speak to you for a minute?"

Connolly turned and tried to make out the face in the dim light, eyes blinking nervously under short blond hair.

"You're the driver. Today."

"That's right. I couldn't help overhearing. I mean, I—" He faltered.

"What?"

He took a breath. "I wasn't going to say anything. I mean, I'm not saying anything *now*. It's just you seem like an all-right guy." It was a question.

"What is it?"

"It's just that—Look, you're making a mistake."

"About Kelly?"

"No, not about Ramon."

Connolly was surprised. "You know him?"

The soldier shrugged. "Lots of people know him. He gets around."

"So do you, huh?"

He stiffened. "No, not like that. Ramon's just one of those guys who's around, you know?"

"In the bar."

"Yeah, in the bar. But Karl wasn't. That's what I'm trying to tell you. You're looking at this wrong. He wasn't—"

Connolly waited for him to finish, but he had stopped, whatever courage had prompted him now gone. "How do you know?" Connolly said finally.

"I'd know, that's all."

"You were a friend of Karl's?"

"No, just from the office."

248

"That's right, you're a driver. So you'd be attached to the office."

The soldier bit his lip.

"Don't worry, I'm not going to say anything. I don't even want to know who you are."

"What's the difference? You could find out in a minute."

"Why say anything, then?"

"You're right, maybe I'm crazy. It's just I can see where this is all going. I've seen it before. They start looking at everything. I hear you're going through our savings accounts." He smiled at Connolly's expression. "I have a friend over in admin," he explained. "Things get around. Everybody gets along fine here. Nobody bothers anybody. But now you think it's a sex crime. Wait and see. All hell will break loose. I was on a base once where they started—"

"I'm not looking for that."

"No? And what if you find it? All the sudden they've got *records* on people, stuff they never bothered about before, and then you've got trouble. I've seen it. That's bad enough, but this time there's no *point*. It all starts because of Karl and he wasn't like that."

Connolly was quiet. "So you said before. How do you know?"

"I'd know," he said again.

"You guys have a secret handshake or something? Like the Masons?"

The soldier wrinkled his nose in disgust. "Okay, forget it. I knew I was crazy to do this."

"I think it took a lot of guts."

"You do, huh?"

"Yes, I do. But what do you expect me to do with this? Ignore everything because it might be inconvenient for you? You didn't even know the guy. All we can go on is what we know, and what we know here is we've got a guy dead in the park with his pants down."

The soldier looked at him. "I could pull your pants down right here and what would that make you?"

The quiet hung between them. "If you killed me, I guess it would make me Karl."

The soldier nodded, then turned to walk away.

"I'll make you a deal," Connolly said after him, watching him turn back with suspicion. "What if you look for me?"

"What do you mean?"

"Maybe you're right. But what if you're not? What if Karl was so secretive that even you couldn't spot it?"

"And?"

"It's important that we know for sure, know who his friends were. Know who he was seeing. We need to talk to other people who might know."

"You've got the wrong guy."

"I'll take your word for it. That's the deal. You're telling me there are things going on up here I don't know anything about and I'm going to make a mess trying to find out. Okay, I won't. No mess. You do it for me. Talk to people— don't tell me who, just tell me if you find out anything about Karl. I'll look somewhere else. If you're right, fine. I'll take your word for it. But make sure. That's your part of the deal."

"No tricks?"

"No tricks. You'd be doing me a favor. And your friends. Nobody wants to turn the place upside down."

The soldier stuck out his hand and took Connolly's. "Christ, I don't believe I'm doing this. What does this make me, an undercover cop?"

Connolly smiled. "Well, you've got the handshake down."

"Nobody knows about this, promise?"

Connolly nodded. "By the way, what's your name? So I don't have to look it up."

"Batchelor." He grinned. "Yeah, I know. Some joke. Maybe it was in the stars. Okay, I'll let you know if I come up with anything. But don't get your hopes up. I'm right about this."

"Just out of curiosity, do you always know?"

"Well, sometimes you hope. It would be nice to be wrong about you, for instance."

Connolly was shocked, then laughed, caught off-guard. "Am I supposed to be flattered?"

"No, I think that about lots of people," he said, waving his hand in a mock salute as he left.

Connolly watched him for a minute, then turned toward the dormitory. He felt cheered by the meeting, as if a road sign had been replaced, finally sending him on his way

251

instead of around in circles. But now there was the deflation of having to begin over. Los Alamos began with a secret and now it seemed it lived on them, one layer wrapped around another. He wished for a minute to be back at the movie, where everything was before you, a shining self-contained surface that stopped at the edge of the screen, hiding nothing.

9

The car was still covered in early morning dew, a film of rime catching the pale light, but she came out in hiking shorts, her long legs shivering in the cold. She threw her knapsack in the back as she motioned him to the passenger seat.

"Are you trying to be provocative?" he said.

"Come on," she said quietly. "It's bloody freezing. I want to get the heater going."

"Next time you could wear nothing at all."

"You'd like that, would you?" she said, pulling the car away and heading west. "You'd be surprised how fast it heats up here. It'll be boiling in a few hours. Any trouble getting away?"

"Not when you write your own passes."

She grinned at him and he saw that she was excited, as if they were children ducking out of school and the day an adventure.

"Where are you going? The gate's that way." He pointed behind them.

"West gate. We'll take the back road—it's faster."

"Oh."

"What's wrong?"

"Nothing," he said, thinking about the investigation. "I just forgot there was another gate. I've never been there."

"You haven't missed much."

In fact it was much smaller than the east entrance, with a single sleepy MP at the barrier, stifling a yawn as he checked the passes and waved them through.

"There's tea in the Thermos. Hope you don't mind, but I hate drinking coffee all day."

"As long as it's hot."

They turned right onto Route 4 and climbed higher into the mountains, the mist burning away from dense green forests of pine and aspen. The heater blasted at their feet, a cocoon of warmth, and tiny streams of condensation streaked off the hood of the car.

"You brought coupons?" she asked.

"Isn't that what I'm here for?"

"It'll do for a start."

"How far is this place, anyway, or are we just going to a hotel?"

"Miles and miles. It'll take the morning, so just sit back and relax. Oh, but wait till you see it. It's marvelous—nothing like it anywhere."

He watched her drive, remembering the trip back from Tesuque, when he first thought it would be possible. They kept climbing, the sun rising with them, so that when they finally reached the high ridge the land was flooded with light. Aside from one rusty pickup truck with goats in the back, headed toward Santa Fe, theirs was the only car on the road. Connolly rolled down the window, breathing in a rush of fresh air, and looked out across an immense valley of grass. A handful of cattle were grazing, dotting the rippling fields like miniatures in a diorama, the grass arranged in folds of green velvet. A series of peaks surrounded the bowl. It was a world away from the Rio Grande Valley, with its low, twisted conifers and dry riverbeds.

"That's the Valle Grande," she said, nodding to the right. "Except it isn't. It's really a caldera—you know, the top of a volcano. It stretches for miles back there, beyond those hills. It just kept bubbling and falling in until you had this great lake of lava. And now this. It's wonderful riding. Oppie likes to come here—you can really let the horses out. Down the other side you're always running into arroyos, but up here, well—"

She trailed off, letting him watch the view.

"You spend much time with Oppenheimer?"

"A little. Not lately. Last year it was easier, things weren't quite so tense."

"Like him?"

She considered. "Yes. Oh, it can be a bit much, all that man-of-destiny business, but I suppose he *is*, really."

"He's difficult to read."

"Everyone's difficult."

254

"Are you?"

She laughed. "Ask anybody."

They were in the high mountains now, the trees close, with patches of alpine wildflowers dotting the clearings by the road. She was driving fast, putting distance between them and the Hill as if they were racing horses across the caldera. The car throbbed a little as they climbed, then galloped across the open stretches.

"Do you still have to go away?" she said.

"No. They made a mistake. I'm back to square one."

She took her eyes off the road for a second to look over at him. "Is that such a bad place to be?"

"Not at the moment," he said, smiling. "Trouble is, you can't stay there."

"No," she said. "But maybe for a little while."

She put her hand on his thigh, nothing more than a comforting pat, but it jumped at the touch, an involuntary spasm. The reaction made her laugh. "My," she said, withdrawing her hand.

Connolly felt teased, embarrassed to be so sensitive to her. "You can put it back if you like."

"Mmm. Maybe later," she said. "You'll need your strength for the hike. Where'd you get the boots, by the way?"

"Borrowed." He was going to tell her about Bruner's closet, the disconcerting moment when the boots fit, as if he had learned something new about him, but Karl had been left behind at Los Alamos. There wasn't room for anyone else in the car.

"How do you manage this?" he said. "Being away. With your neighbors, I mean."

"Eileen? Oh, she doesn't think anything of it. I'm always going off. It's my project, you see. That's the great thing about the Hill—everyone's trained not to ask. So they don't."

"What does she think you're doing?"

"What I am doing—studying Indians. Whatever that means. Actually, I don't think she cares, really. She just swans around in blissful ignorance."

"Listening at walls."

She giggled. "Well, that's something different, isn't it?"

"What about your husband?"

"I left him a note," she said quickly, not wanting to talk about it. "In case he's back early." Then, as if shifting into second, "God, it's good to get away, isn't it? Look at this morning."

So he let it go, glancing out the window at the shafts of light through the trees, thinking about Los Alamos. Everything was secure, so nothing was noticed. Then Los Alamos faded away too, left behind in a rush of miles and the bright, sharp air. They were heading west, where the day, even the landscape, was new.

They drove for a long time without talking, as comfortable with the silence as an old couple, and then he sensed the gradual beginning of the descent. The dips seemed longer now, the road twisting to skirt the uneven hills.

The speed they'd kept on the high ridge began to seem faster, hurtling them toward curves so that Emma was forced to brake to check the pull of gravity down the other slope. They raced up the sides of hills, unable to see over the top, pausing carefully before the downward plunge. The views were closed in, a series of hollows and bends. It reminded him of mountain roads in the East, up and down waves of hills.

When they reached Jemez Springs, a cluster of buildings stretched a few blocks along the road, they had already slowed to thirty, so he was startled to hear the short whoop of a siren behind them. A police car, its roof light now shining in the morning sun, had slid out of its hiding place to follow them, motioning the car over to the side. "Oh God," Emma said, pulling to the curb in front of a white clapboard hotel with the wide rocking-chair porch of an old Adirondack resort. The policeman, in full uniform, took his time getting out of the car. On this sleepy street in a notch of mountains, there was never a reason to hurry.

"Ma'am," he said in a cowboy drawl, "we got a twenty-mile speed limit in this town. It's clearly posted. Can I see your license?"

Connolly could see Emma about to rise to the bait, could already hear her sharp answer, but her shoulders shrank in resignation and wordlessly she handed the cop her wallet.

"Oh, another one of these," he said, glancing at the anonymous project license. "Well, I reckon we can write a ticket to a number just as well as a name." He pulled out his ticket pad. "You from up that ranch school, huh? Funny thing, all you people with no names. Enough to make a person wonder. But that's wartime—that's what they tell me, anyways. You ought to slow down, though. Live longer." Connolly recognized the tone, the mix of folksiness and swagger, as familiar as a blue uniform.

"How much is it?" Emma said.

"Ten dollars."

"You're joking."

He looked at her sharply. "Well, no, ma'am. We don't consider putting our children at risk a laughing matter." The road was deserted.

"But ten dollars," she repeated, injustice rising in her voice.

He smiled. "Well, you can mail it in. Lots of folks like to do that. Be sure you do, though. We'll yank that license sure as shooting, name or no name." He handed her the ticket, bending down to peer into the car. "You ought to get your wife here to slow down. Buy her a new dress. Cost you less in the long run."

"I'll do that," he said, automatically polite. He was struck by the smooth assumption of it. How easy it was to become someone else. The policeman would probably swear to it.

"Bloody thieves," she said after the cop had left.

Connolly smiled. "It's what we call a speed trap. It's how they make their living."

She had begun driving out of town with exaggerated slowness, creeping along the street.

258

"That's one word for it."

"Anyway, now we've been arrested together. You said this would be an adventure." He noticed that she was trembling, clutching the wheel to hold herself steady. "You all right?"

"It just gave me a turn, that's all. I must be mad to do this. I run off with a man and I've got the police onto me before I'm even down the mountain."

He laughed.

"I suppose it is funny. But it's not. The police. What if—?"

"Do you want me to drive?"

"It's not the driving."

"What, then?"

"I don't know. Maybe I don't like being married off so fast. Maybe I'm not very good at this."

"Don't worry. I'm not going to buy you a dress."

She smiled. "No, you wouldn't." She drove quietly for a minute. "I just don't want anybody to get hurt," she said softly.

"Nobody's going to get hurt."

"Yes they are," she said, her voice distant. "We're all going to get hurt."

He waited, afraid now of easy reassurance. "Does it make any difference?" he said finally.

She didn't answer, then slowly shook her head. "No. That's what's so awful. It doesn't make any difference." She shifted. "Oh, to hell with it," she said suddenly, stepping

259

on the gas. The car shot forward. "You never get two tickets in one day, do you? We might as well do as we like."

The road continued twisting downward, its curves even narrower, bordered only by a margin of soft shoulder. Emma hugged the center line, letting the sloping grade make its own speed, trusting the road. Connolly felt his ears pop. Here and there he saw signs of settlement, the surprise of a few fruit trees blossoming after so many miles of dark pine. The views began to open out to a wider sky, until finally they were near the bottom and the hills disappeared entirely, like curtains pulled back to show an immense panorama of red sandstone buttes and mesas, a sky beyond measuring. It was the most spectacular landscape Connolly had ever seen.

On 44 they drove on a highway river, entering sandstone canyons dotted with slides of red rock and juniper whose walls grew higher and higher around them until they were completely surrounded by rock and then, a bend in the road, opening out again to a blue tent of sky. This was the West he had always imagined and never seen, not the cactus emptiness of the desert at Trinity, not even the greasewood and sage arroyo country of the Rio Grande, but land that seemed to exist at the beginning of time, monumental, so resistant to man that it found its beauty in geology, as if vegetation were a hapless afterthought. The mountains to the right seemed the border of the known world. Before them, the giant mesas rose up like islands from an old ocean floor, the distances between them whole seas of sandy earth. The walls were striated, discrete sediment layers of white and yellow and maroon and red, a color map of time, with slabs of rock broken or withered into shapes, statues of what might have been gods.

He felt her smiling beside him, enjoying his reaction. When they finally left the twists of canyon walls and headed straight across the empty flat plateau, the promised heat arrived in a bright glare that flooded the open country with light. They rolled down the windows now to catch the dry air, baked with dust and sage. Clouds were everywhere, darting back and forth making shadows, so that the tawny grass would turn gray for an instant, then gleam yellow again when they passed. He saw chollo cactus and thin bushes whose names he didn't know, survivors. The sun burned through the windshield. They were alone on the road, nothing around them for miles but a desolate landscape alive with clouds and shadows and hot wind.

When they entered Chaco wash, they left the highway and bounced along a narrow dirt road, trailing dust behind them like smoke. Emma slowed down, dodging ruts and dry potholes with only a trace of moisture on their cracked muddy bottoms.

"You said it was remote," Connolly said. "How much more of this?"

"Twenty miles or so." She grinned. "It discourages the fainthearted."

"God. Let's not break down."

"Think of the Anasazi. They walked."

He looked out at the desert again, trying to imagine it filled with people. "Why here?"

"No one knows. Presumably it was wetter then, but not much. They've found logs that must have been carried over forty miles—so why not build where the trees were? But they didn't. It's one of the mysteries."

"What are the others?"

"Mainly what happened to them. They disappeared about eight hundred years ago. Just like that. It all just stopped. There were settlements everywhere—there's a big one near the Hill, in Frijoles Canyon—and then nothing."

"They all died?"

"Well, the archaeological record did. Probably they became the Hopis. Pueblo architecture's much the same—block dwelling, kivas, the lot. But no one really knows. It's difficult without writing. Imagine the Egyptians without hieroglyphics."

"Then how do we know their name?"

"We don't know what they called themselves. Anasazi's our name for them. Navajo. Park Service says it means 'the ancient ones,' but I read somewhere that it actually means 'ancestors of my enemies.' Quite a difference. Of course, that fits perfectly with the Hopi theory—they're *still* fighting the Navajos. Here we are. Watch out for the park ranger. Nobody comes here anymore, since gas rationing, and he'll talk your head off if you let him."

They were entering a broad open canyon formed by a long mesa along the north and two smaller ones on the south that opened like gates to the desert beyond. Connolly could see clumps of stone ruins backed against the walls of the canyon, small villages placed up and down the valley. A dusty official pickup truck was parked next to the building at the southeast end of the canyon road. The park ranger, an incongruous uniform in the emptiness, stared casually at her legs as he warned them to take water on the trail. But Emma seemed not to notice his interest, as if she had left all that behind in the miles of desert that separated them from the world. In fifteen minutes they were back on their own, the ranger another shadow, as they ate sandwiches on the kiva wall of the Bonito ruin, their faces lifted to the sun. With his eyes closed, he could hear the faint movement of insects. When he opened them, the sound retreated back into the stillness of the canyon. He looked over at her, at the line of her raised throat running into the now blazing white of her blouse, and marveled at their being here, away from everything.

She guided him through the site, pointing out the masonry patterns, the low chamber entrances, the arrangement of the rooms, so that what had been an inexplicable maze of stones now became real, filled with imagined life. People had lived here, moving from ceremonial kiva to irrigated field to storage room. The valley floor had hummed with noise. As they walked from room to room, the place began to make sense, there was an order to things, and he wondered suddenly if years from now people would walk like this on the Hill, picking their way through its buildings and rituals and puzzles until they arranged themselves in the simple pattern of a town. Maybe it would keep its mysteries too, and maybe they would seem just as inconsequential.

"But why here?" he asked again. "It can't have been easy to farm here."

"No," Emma said. "Frijoles makes sense—there's a river there. And Mesa Verde—I haven't been, but presumably it's green. Of course, they liked difficult places, they were always building on cliff faces and overhangs. But I agree it's a problem. The archaeologists think there were as many as five thousand people here at the peak, so it may have been an administrative center of some sort. Perhaps religious. I think it's more likely it was geographic—you'll see what I mean at the top. It's pretty much in the middle of their territory, so they may have picked it for just that reason. You know, an artificial capital. Like Canberra or Ottawa."

"Or Washington."

"Or Washington. What are you looking at?"

He took her hand. "I'm just looking."

She was flustered but pleased. "You haven't listened to a thing I've said."

"Yes I have. They built in the middle of

nowhere because it was the middle. Keep the bureaucrats away from the fleshpots."

He leaned over and kissed her, a soft, long kiss because now there was so much more time.

"That's never a bad idea, is it?" she said, her face still close to his.

"I don't know. Maybe they need it more than anybody." He kissed her again, but then she drew away.

"He'll see," she said, nodding her head toward the park station.

Connolly laughed. "All this way and it's still the neighbors. Is there anywhere we can go?" he asked playfully, taking in the vast stretch of land.

"Later," she said, pushing him away. "Are you always so anxious?"

"No, I'm shy. I just hate to pass up an opportunity. We could always go behind that wall."

"No we couldn't. If you think I'm going to lie down on a kiva for you, you're very much mistaken." But she had come closer to him.

"Afraid of disturbing the spirits?"

"Maybe. Maybe I just don't fancy a stone floor."

"You can be on top."

"Later," she said again, laughing at him. "Come on. You could do with the exercise."

But the moment had made the emptiness around them sensual. He was aware of her skin in front of him as they climbed up the mesa trail, her leg stretching to a rock footing, flexing as it pulled the rest of her upward. The heat was tangible now, his body suddenly damp with sweat, and the air was busy with the crunch of their boots on the rocks and the sound of breathing. They climbed through a chimney between tall boulders, the path cluttered with loose rocks and sand and the tough root of a broken bush. When they cleared the top, on a shelf of slickrock, he found himself slightly winded, his heart beating faster. Except for the hint of a little breeze, everything around them still lay inert, but the torpor of the valley heat was gone. He felt alive with movement, his leg muscles straining as they went up another steep stretch. She looked behind her and laughed, leaping goatlike to another rock, daring him to follow. The canteen tied to her belt slapped against her hip. A trickle of sweat ran into his eye. The trail switched back, following a series of cairns he imagined the ranger had made, then rose steadily on packed earth until the great ledges of slickrock began, like sidewalks running around the rim of the mesa.

She waited for him on top, her blouse sticking to her, shading her eyes with her hand as she looked south to the valley floor. From here the ruins below took on the cellular shapes of a blueprint, circles and squares spreading out flat with only their dimensions to suggest buildings. She handed him the canteen. In the landscape nothing moved but shimmering heatwaves rising lazily off the desert. They were the only things alive in the world.

They followed the slickrock around the edge, steps away from steep drops into canyons, but the path was level and broad and they could walk together, moving quickly from the view of one site to another. The strain had left his legs and he was unaware of his steps now, buoyant, sometimes not even sensing the cairn markers. When she stopped suddenly, sticking her hand out in front of him, he almost pitched forward, carried by the unconscious momentum. She stood motionless, not breathing, so that the quiet was its own alarm. He darted his eyes around, not seeing anything on the barren slickrock until she extended a finger, pointing silently toward the edge. Ahead of them, on a ledge a few steps below, he saw the gray gnarled twist of an old juniper branch, nothing more, and then his eyes focused and the branch, sharper now, took on markings of gray and brown in a thick unnatural coil. The rattlesnake stirred slightly, adjusting itself to catch the sun, then settled back on the rock. Connolly stood frozen, feeling his muscles twitch with fear. It was the surprise of it, the unexpected lurking while they paid no attention. He had a city boy's terror of wildlife; it crept up on you, alert only to its own rules. Frantically he looked around the trail for a rock, even a stick, to defend himself. But the snake lay still, coiled motionless in the sun. Connolly felt the slightest sound would arouse it, but Emma was already drawing him away, stepping carefully from the edge. He almost jumped when he saw it move, a nearly imperceptible tremor along the markings as it began to uncoil. He watched, fascinated as prey, while it sluggishly stretched out its length and glided down off its ledge to a sunnier shelf below, unaware of anyone else in its garden. Emma continued quietly moving away and he followed her, his eyes still on the ledge, expecting the snake to spring back. He was embarrassed by his own fear, but his blood kept jumping.

"Shouldn't we kill it?" he said when they were farther down the path.

"He won't bother us now. He lives here, you know."

"But they're poisonous."

She smiled, calming him. "I know. But they don't come after you unless they're provoked. The first time I heard a rattle, I nearly died, but he was just telling me to go away. At least they give you fair warning. Not everything does. What they don't like is being surprised."

"I guess I don't either," he said, catching his breath. "I've never seen one before."

"Maybe you'll never see another. I've only seen two. The horses spot them. But they're here, you know, they come with the territory." She put her hand on his arm. "Come on, we'll go up to the Pueblo Alto. Just be careful where you walk. It's probably like speeding tickets, you never get two at once."

But the snake had unsettled him. The limitless space had been exhilarating and now made him feel exposed. What if it hadn't gone away? He saw himself holding an ankle full of poison, miles from anywhere, any cry for help muted by the wind. He had thought they had got away, that all this bright, uncomplicated space was theirs, and now he saw that he had merely intruded in it, made unsafe by what he couldn't see.

They cut across the land to the center of the mesa, where the high ruins were, on the roof of the Anasazi world. There was wind up here, constantly drying their skin and blowing their hair, and as he watched her striding ahead, the white sleeves of her blouse fluttered back like little banners. He wondered what had brought her here, coolly avoiding snakes and climbing over slickrock, so far from the rainy hedgerows of Hampshire. But it was hers now. He liked the way she delighted in the land, as if she had made it all up.

At the Pueblo Alto they could see miles in every direction, and she pointed out the faint traces of straight roads coming from the north, then going out the valley to the south.

"Of course, *why* they had roads is another mystery, since they didn't have wheels. Not even pack animals, apparently."

"You couldn't walk for miles in that," he said, pointing to the desert.

"But they did. Hundreds of miles. They've found macaw feathers that must have come from Mexico—you know, on the Gulf. And conch shells from lower California. Somebody must have brought them."

They were sitting on the wall, smoking. Connolly felt the heat of sunburn on his face, but the clouds kept moving across the sun, throwing the mesa into cool late-afternoon shadow.

"Right up that road, too," she said, pointing toward the straight track between South Mesa and West Mesa. "Can't you imagine it, though? Feathers and beads and whatnot—a whole stream of people, all coming here."

He smiled at her. "I don't believe it. Maybe a handful staggering with thirst. It's some place, though," he said, looking around again.

"Yes, it makes it all worth it."

"Makes what all worth it?"

"You know, the Hill. The life there."

"Why don't you leave?" he said quietly.

"Where would I go? I don't mind, really, as long as I can get away like this. Besides, I've come this far. I wouldn't go back now."

"I didn't mean that."

"I know." She crushed her cigarette, then stripped it, letting the bits of tobacco blow away. "But it's true just the same. I like it here."

"But it has to end sometime. The project'll be finished."

"And everyone go home? Do you think so? I don't know. I used to think that—it was all so temporary in the beginning. But now I think it'll just go on."

"It has to end when the war ends. You know what they're doing there?"

"Everybody knows. We just don't like to talk about it. It's nicer to think of it as pure science," she said, an edge in her voice, "not blowing everything up. Anyway, they'll want to make another. Something bigger, perhaps. We won't be going anywhere. You can't just build a whole city like that and walk away from it."

"They did here."

"Yes. But did they walk away?" She got up, tired of sitting, and paced idly, turning over a loose rock with her boot.

"Didn't they?"

"You like a mystery. What do you think?"

A question in school. He looked out at the landscape and shrugged. "I think they ran out of water."

"Hmm. That's the obvious answer, isn't it?"

"But you don't think so?"

"They may have. Just moved on to greener pastures. Of course, anywhere would be, wouldn't it? But then, why not pack up? They just left things, you see. Pots, *farm* tools. I mean, you'd take your tools. And valuables. Feathers, shells—the sort of thing you'd take with you if you were moving on. Like your good china. Turquoise beads."

"Turquoise?" he said. "They left turquoise behind?"

"Yes," she said, puzzled at his interest. "They had turquoise—it was their jewelry. Funny sort of refugees, leaving jewelry behind."

"Maybe they thought they'd be coming back," he said, his mind in Karl's drawer now, wandering.

"But they didn't."

"Because they were killed."

She looked at him. "What makes you say that? We don't know that."

"Nothing. I was thinking of something else." He stood up. "Maybe they were too weak. Maybe there was too much to carry."

"Jewelry?"

He smiled at her. "You're reconstructing the crime."

"They say that's what archaeology is. Reconstructing the crime."

"If there was one."

"There usually is, one way or another."

"So what *do* you think?"

She paused, looking out again across the mesa. "I think the Germans came."

"The Germans?"

"Their Germans. I think they rounded them up and took them away."

His mind, already distracted, now leaped to magazine photos, a man weeping at a cello.

"Why?"

"Well, there's never an answer to that." She shrugged, as if she could shed the thought with her skin. "This is a funny sort of conversation to be having."

"Maybe they did it to themselves."

"What? Had some Hitler who led them away?"

"Or just went mad. Blew themselves up."

She looked at him again, then crossed her arms, holding herself. "Don't let's talk about it anymore. We'll never know anyway."

"But wouldn't you like to know?"

"I suppose so. But what does it matter?

Maybe it *was* drought—everyone thinks so. I rather like its being a mystery."

"But if we knew—"

"Then this would only be a place, wouldn't it?" She turned to go. "Come on. It's getting late."

The trail down was easier, but they stopped several times to take in the view. The white light of the day was gone, replaced by the late afternoon sun with a deep yellow fire that colored the rocks. Part of the valley was in shadow and the sandstone had lost its bright reflection; it was now just harder earth, dark as dried blood. By the time they reached the bottom, even the sky had changed, its steady blue beginning to streak with color.

"My legs are going to feel this later," he said, rubbing his calf.

"Tired?"

"Not too tired."

She grinned. "That's good. We've miles to go."

"Where now?"

"We'll drive north to Nageezi, then cut across on the road to Taos."

"Can't we stop at Nageezi?"

"That's just for the maps. There isn't anything there—it's a trading post. Just a filling station. When it's open."

"Where, then?"

"Anxious? I thought we'd go to Hannah's."

"That's hours from here."

"Everything's hours. We'd have it to ourselves."

"We'll be exhausted," he said, taking her by the waist.

"You can sleep in. All day."

He smiled. "Let's go. What if we find something on the way?"

"It would be a mirage," she said, getting in the car. "There isn't anything. Don't worry—I'm worth the wait."

They said a courtesy goodbye to the ranger, then headed northwest out of the valley into the orange sky. This access road was rougher than the one to the south, and Connolly, driving now, cursed as the car bounced through deeper holes. Even on a straight stretch of dirt he was forced to slow down, dodging rocks. Emma put her head back against the seat, squinting dreamily into the light.

"Why did you ask about the turquoise?" she said, mildly curious.

"I was thinking about Karl."

"Oh," she said, opening her eyes. "Why him?"

"He left turquoise behind in his room. It just seemed an odd coincidence, hearing about it. Well, not really a coincidence. It just reminded me of it, that's all."

"What was he doing with turquoise?" she said, genuinely surprised.

"I don't know."

"Is that why he was robbed?"

"No. It was in his room."

"Oh. So it's a mystery."

"For now it is."

"But you don't like mysteries," she said.

"I don't like this one."

She laid her head back again. "Is it so important to you? He's dead, isn't he? Like my Indians. What does it matter what happened to them?"

"You don't believe that."

"I suppose not. But sometimes—oh, why not let things be? Let them be mysteries." She looked out the window, arguing with the landscape.

"This didn't happen eight hundred years ago. Whoever killed him is still around."

"I thought he was robbed in the park. Whoever did it must be long gone."

"Maybe. Maybe he's on the Hill."

She was silent. "Is that what you think?"

"It's possible."

"That's horrible. Then it wouldn't be an accident—some robbery, I mean. You think someone murdered him? *Planned* to kill him?"

He was quiet for a minute, thinking. "Planned? That's interesting. No, I don't think so. Not planned. I think it just—happened."

"How do you mean?"

"He may have provoked someone. Like the snake," he said, a sudden thought. "They only attack if they're provoked. Isn't that what you said?"

"Well, surprised. They're defending themselves, that's all."

"Yes," he said, his voice drifting off again.

"Anyway, it wasn't a snake. Murder," she said softly. "No. Why would anyone want to murder Karl?"

But he wasn't listening.

"What is it?" she said, bringing him back.

"What you said. I hadn't thought of that. What if he surprised someone?"

"Doing what?" she said. He didn't answer. "I hate all this. It scares me. You just want to believe he was murdered. It's too absurd. Things like that don't happen."

"Yes they do."

"Not here." And then, before he could contradict her, "But why not a robber? It's the obvious answer."

"I thought you didn't approve of obvious answers."

"But you're just guessing. Is that how this works? You make a guess and see if it fits?"

"No," he said, "that's how science works, or so they tell me. I need a little more than that."

She looked over at him. "Is that why you're here? It is, isn't it."

"The army just wants to know what happened."

She turned away to look out the window again. "So you'll turn over every rock in the place. I wonder what else you'll find."

"I haven't found anything yet," he said lightly. "Not even one skeleton in the closet."

She looked back at him. "Be careful you don't surprise someone too."

"That would be one way of finding out, wouldn't it?"

"I'm serious."

"So am I," he said, still light. "Don't worry, I can take care of myself."

"God, listen to you. It must be the Irish cop in you."

"Which don't you like, the Irish or the cop?"

She smiled. "The cop, I suppose."

"Good. Not much I can do about the Irish. We can retire the cop, though. Today, anyway."

She shook her head. "Maybe it's all of a piece." She laughed. "I never thought I'd end up going to bed with a cop."

"Technically speaking, we haven't actually been to bed yet," he said, smiling.

She put her hand on his knee, a promise. "No, we haven't, have we?"

"You'll make me go off the road," he said, turning to her.

It was then, his eyes off the road, that they hit the rock. There was a loud pop, as startling as gunfire, then the sudden lurch as they felt the car swerve to the right, sinking to the flapping tire.

"Christ," Connolly said, stopping the car. "Now what the hell do we do? Do you have a spare?"

"In the boot."

"Christ." He got out to look.

"Can you fix it?"

"This one's shot," he reported. "We'll have to change it." He looked around the empty landscape in the dwindling light. "Do you have a jack?"

"Whatever's back there. There's some sort of toolbox, I think." She opened the trunk.

"This? I don't know what any of it is. What's the matter—don't you?"

"I'll figure it out."

"I thought Americans knew everything about cars."

He didn't answer but instead started struggling with the jack, trying to assemble the handle, and getting down to look under the chassis.

"Can you manage it, do you think?" she said.

"Let's hope so. Unless you want to spend the night."

"Can I help?"

"You can stand out of the light." He looked up. "What's so funny?"

"You. Nothing. You should see your face. Like a cross little boy. Do you have *any* idea what you're doing?"

"I've seen it done. You have a better idea?"

"I could walk back to the ranger station and bat my eyelids and get him to fix it. He'd come like a shot."

"I'll figure it out," he said, fixing the jack in place.

She sighed. "Men. What makes you all like that, anyway?"

"Like what?" he said, only half paying attention.

"You never want to ask for help. Directions. A man will never ask directions. Just drive round and round and never ask."

"Want to hand me that?" he asked, pointing to a wrench. She jumped up, ready to help.

"Scalpel," she said, handing it to him. "Sponge."

He looked up at her. "You're having fun."

"I know. Isn't it awful? I am. I've always wondered what it would be like, stuck in the middle of nowhere. Rather exciting."

"It's going to be a lot more exciting if we don't fix this before it gets dark."

"Never mind. We can always sleep in the car."

"There's something to look forward to," he said absently, unscrewing the lugs on the wheel.

"Oh, poor Michael, still longing for bed. Jinxed, that's what it is. Still, there's always the car. I've never done it in a car, have you?"

"As a matter of fact, yes."

"Really? What's it like?"

He stared at the wheel, trying to determine the next step. "Right now, I don't know which is more annoying, you or this tire."

"All right," she said, "I'll be quiet. That's the thanks one gets for being cheerful. What *is* it like, though? In a car."

"Cramped."

She got a cigarette out of the car, then sat near him, watching him work. The heat had gone with the sun and she drew her legs up, huddling over them and smiling to herself in unexpected contentment. After a while he needed the flashlight, so she held it for him, training its beam on the tire while she studied his face in the shadow.

"I wonder what else you can't do," she said, "besides fix cars. I mean, I don't know anything about you. What do you like? What are your politics? Why aren't you in the army, for instance?"

"Eyes. I have a lazy muscle in my left."

"What's that? You mean you don't see properly?"

"No, the right compensates. It's not serious, just serious enough to keep me out of the army. They figured I'd make a lousy shot."

"Did that bother you?"

"For about ten minutes. Then I felt grateful. There, now you know something I've never told anyone."

"What else?" she said softly.

"I don't know. Hate team sports, except baseball. Not very handy fixing things around the house either. That help?"

She shook her head. "Uh-uh."

"What, then?"

"Nothing, I guess."

"That's a load off my mind," he said absently, still concentrating on the lugs. "Damn." The wrench clattered to the ground.

"Have a break," she said, handing him her cigarette. His sunburned face glistened with sweat in the narrow light. "This is jolly, isn't it?" She looked around and up at the sprinkling of early stars. "I love the desert at night. It comes alive then."

"Don't tell me with what." He took a drag on the cigarette, following her gaze upward, then settling back on her face.

"There, that's better," she said. "We may as well enjoy it."

"What, breaking down?"

"Mm. Being marooned. Can you think of a better way to get to know someone?"

"Hundreds." He handed back the cigarette. "Is that why we're here? To get to know each other?"

"It's away. I wanted to get away. From the Hill. I couldn't know you there."

"And now you do."

"A little. You always learn something out here."

"Such as?"

"All sorts of things. You're stubborn. You like to finish things."

"Don't you?"

She paused for a minute. "Not always. Sometimes I just—walk away. Go somewhere else."

"Stubborn. That's not much."

"And you're jealous."

"Of whom?"

"The ranger."

"Well, he was after you."

She smiled. "You see? That's what I mean."

"You just didn't notice."

"Oh, I noticed all right. That was just cabin fever, you know."

"Cabin fever. He couldn't take his eyes off you."

"Window shopping," she said. "There's a difference. One can tell. Like you."

"I'm that obvious."

She nodded. "Your eyes."

"When?"

"At the ranch, the music—every time. I always feel your eyes."

"Do you like that?" he said, his eyes touching her now, moving over her face.

"What do you think?" She leaned forward to kiss him. "But you are jealous."

"I can't believe everybody doesn't see you the way I do."

"Oh, that's nice," she said, kissing him again. "Tell me some more."

"Are you flirting with me?" he whispered, his breath close to her.

"No, I told you," she said, brushing his cheek, "I'm just getting to know you. Isn't it lovely here? This place? Didn't I tell you?"

Then he kissed her full on the mouth, she lay back on the packed earth, and there it was again, the quickness to his touch, as if her whole body were always waiting for even a trace of a signal. He lay over her, his elbow poking into the ground, everything dark except for a sliver of moonlight. His feet felt the rim of the tire behind them.

They heard the car before the headlights swept up the road, catching them in the beams like the surprise flash of a camera. Connolly looked up, his eyes dazzled, then rose to his knees, brushing himself off as he stood.

"You folks all right?" the ranger said, pretending he had not seen. Connolly caught the eager tremor in his voice. He got out, keeping his motor running, his lights still shining on the small screen of an unexpected blue movie.

"Flat tire," Emma said, getting up and dusting her blouse, her voice cool and matter-of-fact.

"Well, sure," the ranger said. "These roads. Let me give you a hand. Lucky I happened along."

"Yes, isn't it?" Emma said, and Connolly could hear the faint beginnings of laughter.

The ranger looked at her, not quite sure whether he should grin, then at Connolly to see what would be allowed. But neither said anything, and Connolly saw him fall into awkwardness, backing away from the silence with an embarrassed shuffle, as if he were the one who'd been caught. For a moment they stood there, listening to the hum of the idling motor, unable to move. In a second, Connolly knew, Emma would laugh, turning the scene, the ranger's own excitement, into an off-color joke. But suddenly the ranger took charge, bending down to inspect the tire, moving the spare into place. Emma watched, amused, as he twirled the lug wrench, fitting the tire with sure, swift movements in some exaggerated sexual display of competence. Connolly stood nearby, not even asked to help, frowning as he followed the performance. Then, in a minute, the ranger pumped the handle of the jack and lowered the car with an absurd sigh of climax. He stood up, wiping his hands on his pants.

"There. That ought to hold it. You want to be careful in the desert. Not a place to be at night."

Connolly glanced at him, alert to innuendo, but the ranger had lapsed into official courtesy, unaware of any effect he might have had.

"You best follow me out. I'll just go on ahead. Holler if you need anything." And then, his point made, he swung into the carryall and started down the road.

Emma looked at Connolly, her eyes laughing. "Well, there you are," she said, wiping her hands against each other as if she had done the job.

"Cabin fever, my ass," Connolly said, throwing the tools in the trunk and slamming it.

So they drove north for half an hour in the path of the ranger's red taillights, dipping and swerving while Emma coaxed Connolly into the laughter of a private joke. The stars rolled out in front of them, the darkness dissolving the horizon so that everything was sky. Connolly hunched over the wheel, watching for holes in the road, and when they finally reached the pavement of the highway and waved goodbye to the ranger, his shoulders were sore. They had the road to themselves again, the Nageezi post no more than a darkened shadow when they passed it. Emma fiddled with the radio, but in all this space even the soundwaves seemed to have been swallowed by the dark, trapped on the other side of some tall unseen mesa.

"I could use a drink," he said.

"It's Indian land. Not a drop for miles. Maybe when we get to Madrid."

284

"Will anything be open by then?"

She ignored him, leaning closer to the open window. "You can smell the sage."

"We have to eat sometime."

"Hmm," she said, but her voice was content, as if the rich night air were enough.

And after a while he didn't mind either, following the small circle of their headlights in a trance. Once he saw a rabbit bounce near the side of the road, but then it vanished, just a dreamy speck of white, and they were alone again. He forgot the time, stretched out now to match the distance so that they became interchangeable, and the car sailed lazily by itself through both. There were no signs or markers. They had driven off the map.

It was almost another hour before he saw the light, a firefly wink, and then a candle until, finally, it became shafts of light pouring out the windows of a long building. A few dusty pickup trucks were parked alongside, their hoods catching the dim neon reflection of a beer advertisement. When they got out of the car, he could hear Western music. The place was as raw and makeshift as the buildings on the Hill, and for a moment he was afraid he had imagined it. There seemed no reason for it to be here in the empty landscape, just something conjured up because they were tired and hungry.

Inside, there was a brightly lit general store and next to it a dimmer bar area filled with smoke, beer signs, a gaudy swirl of jukebox, and a few wooden booths that looked filled with slivers. At the far end of the bar several Indians in jeans and ranch shirts were drinking silently, barely talking to one another, the bar in front of them a sea of beer bottles. Nearer the door, two old ranchers in Western hats were parked on stools. Everyone looked up when they came in. The Indians quickly retreated into their quiet huddle, but the ranchers looked openly at Emma, then smiled and tipped their hats. Behind the bar was a tall Indian woman, clearly of mixed blood, her long Anglo face set off by unexpected high cheekbones and long braided hair. Her breasts, drooping from years of nursing, spilled into a white blouse decorated with beads.

"Can we get a drink?" Connolly asked.

"Sure," she said, her face as expressionless as her voice. Without asking, she set up a boilermaker of whiskey and a beer. There was no sign of anything else. Connolly handed one whiskey to Emma.

"You're like to catch your death in them shorts," one of the ranchers said to Emma, nodding toward her legs.

"Like 'em?" Emma said, stepping back to display them.

The rancher laughed, surprised at her boldness. "I guess I do."

Emma took a drink. "Thanks. Me too. That's why I keep them to myself."

The rancher laughed again. "Well, I guess so." Then, to Connolly, "I don't mean nothing by it. You don't see that every day around here."

"Oh, I don't mind a look," Emma said.

"Well, I guess not," the rancher said good-naturedly. "Where you folks coming from so late?"

"Chaco."

"Well, now, isn't that something? I thought they closed it. Not too many goes out there these days. With the gas. They say it's real nice, though." Everybody in the West, it seemed to Connolly, wanted to talk. Only the movie cowboys were silent.

"I know it's late," he said to the woman behind the bar. "Is there anything to eat?"

She hesitated.

"Come on, Louise," the rancher said, "you give these nice folks some of that stew. Ain't nobody here going home anyways."

"Anything would be fine," Connolly said to her.

"Sure," she said, pouring two more whiskeys. She pointed to a booth.

"Nice meeting you. That's a pretty wife you got there," the rancher said to both of them. "You ought to cover her up, though. Never know who you're gonna run into."

"Oh, she can usually take care of herself."

The rancher found this funny. "I'll bet she can. Yes, sir." His eyes followed them as they went over to the booth to nurse their drinks.

"Another window shopper?" Connolly said, smiling.

"Well, this one might be after a sample. Not like our Boy Scout."

"Really?"

"Oh, he's harmless. He just wants watching."

"Can you always tell?"

"Of course. Any woman can. It's what we're trained for."

"Is that so?"

"Uh-huh."

He looked at her, aware now of the drink. The booth seemed surrounded by a faint haze. He took another sip. "What do you think this stuff is?"

"Firewater." She giggled.

"You're not kidding," he said, holding his throat.

"Careful it doesn't go to your head."

"Like the song."

"What song?"

"You don't know that song?"

She shook her head.

"Just a song. You'll hear it sometime. We'll go to a club—they're always playing it. Encourages the drinking."

"Like here?" she said, cocking her head toward the jukebox, still pumping out Western music.

"They don't need encouragement here. If you can drink through that, you can drink through anything. God," he said, reacting to another sip. "I'd better slow down."

"It always hits you when you're tired."

"That was before. When we were hiking and fighting rattlesnakes and then had to watch Charles Atlas kick sand in my face."

She laughed. "Did we do all that?"

"On one lousy sandwich."

"Sounds wonderful." She put her hand over his. "Let's do it again."

He looked at her eyes, bright in the smoky light. "Whenever you say."

The Indian woman stood at the edge of the table, waiting for them to separate hands before she unloaded the tray—big heavy bowls of mutton stew with a large basket of Navajo fry bread. She set the table with surprising delicacy, placing clunky spoons down without a sound, arranging a bandanna-like napkin.

"Thank you," Emma said.

"Sure."

"And another round of drinks when you get a minute."

"Sure." She moved slowly away, pulled by an unseen tug.

Emma giggled. "Do you think she can say anything else? I haven't heard one other word. Shall we bet on it? A dollar?"

"No fair prompting."

"Okay. How's the stew?"

"Now I know why the Anasazi went away."

"That bad?"

"Not when you close your eyes."

But it was hot, and each thick gray spoonful filled him, spreading warmth through his body like a wonderful liniment.

"How do they stay in business, do you think?" he said.

"It's probably just outside Indian land. There's always a place over the border to sell liquor."

He tore off a piece of fry bread, amused at his own appetite. When he looked up again from the stew, he found her watching him, part of the slow, easy warmth that enveloped them now like steam. The beer took on flavor as he gulped it. They talked of nothing, little snippets that kept them company as they ate, then evaporated, forgotten. Before the bowl was finished he had to sit back, flushed with well-being, his head buzzing gently now with half-heard sounds from the bar. The loud, twangy music had stopped.

He got up and went over to the jukebox, hoping to find something before the ranchers could fill it with more nickels. He scanned the selection slips glowing under the yellow light, running his eye down one unfamiliar cowboy title after another, and then, unaccountably, a wealth of music in the right-hand column— Teddy Wilson, Lester Young. Where had it all come from? It was the last thing he'd expected to find here. He stood there for a minute, fixated on the puzzle. Maybe the café was so remote that no one came to change the records. Maybe they'd siphoned off some free V Discs. The music was colored; maybe the record company traveler, unable to place them on his swing south, had dumped them finally into a juke for Indians. What did it matter? He fed nickels into the machine, pressed the ivory buttons, then came back to the table, a silly grin on his face, as the room picked up the tempo of "Sweet Lorraine," the piano dancing over the steady bass. The ranchers looked at him, surprised, then turned back to mind their own business. The Indians never moved, a stocky frieze.

They sat back, listening to the music and smoking, the stew bowls pushed to the middle of the table. The Indian woman came over to fill their glasses but didn't bother to collect the dishes, as if she were still waiting for them to finish. They didn't say anything for a while, watching the smoke, smiling at their luck. *It's the mood that I'm in.* The music seemed to change the room like some slow trick of the light, the rough edges receding, so that the café took on the mellow glamour of the sounds, all wet glass rings on a bar and ashtrays and the hope of taking someone home.

"Is this what it's like?" she said quietly. "That club you're taking me to?"

He smiled. "Just like."

"And we'd sit and drink and look at each other."

"And dance."

"Yes." She looked lazily around at the ranchers and Indians. "Someday."

The record changed to the piano runs of Teddy Wilson opening "The Very Thought of You." Looking straight at her, he took her hand and stood up, the drink making him slow and fluid at the same time, an underwater movement.

"Here?" she said, a little laugh, her arm extended in his, but her legs were crossed so she was unable to move.

"Why not?" He continued to look at her,

291

willing her upward with a gentle pull until her legs righted themselves and her body rose up, leaning into his. They stood still, awkward, his hand feeling the small of her back, and then the music led them, asking nothing more than one small conscious movement to start. Billie Holiday was doing the vocal. Their feet, slow with drink, moved forward without their thinking. The room slid into the haze of peripheral vision. *I'm living in a kind of daydream.* One of the old ranchers laughed at them, and Connolly, looking over her shoulder, grinned back, joining in the joke. They must look drunk. But every inch of him felt her now. He moved slowly, lightheaded, happy. When she pulled her head back from his shoulder, they looked at each other, surprised. The dancing was supposed to have been a joke, a little parody of another life. Now it was something else, another kind of joke. He wanted to laugh out loud at the unexpectedness of it. He had held girls like this before, half-drunken nights of good times and smoky rooms and sex, but it was here, miles from anywhere, filled with mutton stew and cheap whiskey, that it finally happened, the hope of a million popular songs.

There was another record, then another, and they kept dancing, too tired to sit down. They didn't see the ranchers leave. Could he have had so many nickels? The lights went off in the general store.

"It's late," she said.

He nodded.

"I don't know where we can go."

"Doesn't matter." His words were slow, part of the music.

She touched the back of his neck. "This isn't what you had in mind at all, is it?"

"No."

"But it's all right?"

And it was. He wasn't thinking about sex; he just wanted to hold her.

"Can you drive?"

"Can you?"

"If I have some coffee."

But when they sat down, moving dreamily away from the empty floor, they found fresh drinks on the cleared table and they sipped them, the coffee forgotten. The music had stopped, but it was too late to play any more. They sat enjoying the quiet, the faint rattle of crockery in the back room, a scurrying of night sounds. He couldn't stop looking at her. When the Indians left, two of them supporting the third, he only glanced at them for a minute. Then there was a sputter outside, a roar as the pickup ignition caught and pulled away, and it was quiet again. The Indian woman didn't bother them, so they sat finishing their drinks, warm with sunburn and liquor, too drowsy to get up and go. His legs were heavy, glued to the scratchy booth.

When the woman finally came to clear the glasses, she was dressed to leave, an old army jacket covering the beaded blouse. Emma asked about coffee as Connolly got out his money, looking up at the woman for the bill. There was no check. She took a few bills, then tucked them into her jacket.

"No coffee. Back room," she said, indicating a door and leading them there. She pulled the string of an overhead light to reveal a small storage room, piles of boxes next to an old rolltop desk, and, against the wall, a daybed covered with Navajo blankets. "Don't drive," she said. "Stay here." Then, with a small smile, "Nobody bother."

She refused any money, waving off their thanks, and then turned the bar lights off and was gone.

"Our suite at the Waldorf," Emma said, smiling at the linoleum and the narrow bed.

Connolly stood under the light bulb, unbuttoning her blouse.

"I don't think I can move," she said.

"No, don't," he said, kissing her.

"The light," she said. He reached up and pulled the cord, turning the room black. In the pitch dark there was only touch, the gritty feel of dust, and the smell of sweat and liquor, and when they fell on the bed, their bare skin against the rough blanket, they finally made love, slow as dancing, as if they had already gone to sleep.

10

They found the car on May 8th, the day
the war ended in Europe. Connolly had
spent the afternoon at a motel on the Taos
road, a motor court with faded cabins that had
become their usual place, and had stayed
late. Daniel had been spending most of his time
at the test site, but he was back again this week,
so they had to steal what time they could, a
few hours of afternoon on old sheets, the sun
dimmed to evening by dusty venetian blinds.
At first Mills had been titillated by Connolly's
absences, but now, finally bored with someone else's affair, he scarcely raised an eyebrow.

"More research?" he said when Connolly
turned up. "You ought to at least check in once
in a while."

"Why? Did I miss something?"

It was a standard joke between them. For
days, weeks now, there had been nothing to
miss. Ramon Kelly had been convicted, a
one-day excitement for the *Santa Fe New
Mexican,* a longer run for the Albuquerque
papers, and the Hill had shrugged off the
news with indifference and gone back to work.
Karl Bruner, even as gossip, was gone, a few
paragraphs on the crime blotter. Corporal
Batchelor, a little nervous now at having
come forward at all, had found nothing to
report. Doc Holliday checked in regularly, but
more out of boredom than progress. The files
on Mills's desk sat undeciphered, dusted

once a week by the cleaning staff, waiting for a new key. All around them life on the Hill intensified—furloughs canceled, lights blazing at night as eighteen-hour workdays raced to some uncertain deadline—so that by contrast they seemed at a standstill, just holding their breath. Connolly, to his surprise, didn't mind. He lived in the hurried, measured hours of motel rooms. There would be time enough later for everything else.

"The car," Mills said. "They found Karl's car. One of Kisty's men."

"Down at S Site? It's been here all along?"

"No." Mills smiled. "Nothing that good. One of the box canyons off the plateau."

"I don't understand."

"Join the club. Hell of a place to stash a car."

"Wrecked?"

"I don't know. I've been waiting for you." He glanced at his watch. "For hours, in fact."

"Well, let's go." Connolly led the way out of the office.

"Relax, it's not going anywhere. We've got a guard posted."

"We ought to call Doc."

"I did. He'll wait for us at the west gate." Mills met Connolly's glance. "I told him you'd be back by five."

"Why five?"

Mills shrugged. "I'm in security, remember? I notice things. You're always back by five."

"Why is that, I wonder."

"I figure somebody's got to be home."

"A detective."

Mills smiled. "It passes the time. Quiet around here lately."

"Feeling neglected?"

"Me? I like it quiet. The Germans surrendered, by the way, in case you haven't heard."

Connolly nodded. "You'd never know it here." He looked around the Tech Area, as busy and undisturbed as ever.

"Oh, they'll pop a few corks tonight. You know the longhairs—work first."

"Unlike some of us, you mean."

"No. I figure you're pretty busy." He grinned. "Just thinking about it is what gets me through the days."

They drove past S Site, the explosives unit at the opposite end of the plateau, a new industrial plant of snaking steampipes, smokestacks, and hangars of heavy machinery. The Tech Area was the university, but S had the raw utility of a foundry, where blueprints were hammered into casings and people risked accidents.

"Who found it?"

"They were setting up a new firing range in one of the canyons off South Mesa. You know they like to keep the explosives off the Hill."

"Yes, it's comforting."

Mills grinned. "Lucky this time, anyway. We never would have found it otherwise."

At the end of a road thick with conifers, they found Holliday standing at the gate, chatting with the young sentry.

"You took your time."

The sentry, recognizing Connolly, gave an innocent half-salute.

"Funny, isn't it?" Mills said, catching the gesture. "All this time and I've never used this gate. You?" he said to Connolly.

"Once in a while," Connolly said, not looking at him.

"Well, I don't blame you," Holliday said to Mills. "My friend here says they don't get much traffic anytime. Nights they just close the road, so you'd have to drive all the way around to the front. Pretty discouraging if you didn't know that."

"But everybody does," the sentry said, his voice liquid with the South. "It's just for Hill people. Trucks go to the east gate."

"And all us folks from the outside, eh?" Holliday said.

"Ain't nobody from outside on the Hill."

"No. Well, I guess that's right. And here I was with my nose pressed against the screen, just like always."

Holliday followed their car as they skirted the plateau on winding switchbacks. The mesa was like a giant hand with a series of deep canyons between its fingers, some in turn breaking off into smaller box canyons that dipped away under the pine cover, lying as hidden as secrets. The car was in one of these, a mile or so from the entrance turnoff, at the end of an old dirt road partly overgrown with brush. An MP was posted where the car had driven off the dirt to carve its own path into the canyon floor. Mills cleared them and they moved toward the car, looking at the broken brush along the way.

"Why the road?" Connolly said.

"Probably an old logging road," Holliday said. "They used to take a fair amount of timber out around here. You notice that canyon just before this one? There's a real road there. They probably just gave up on this one."

"That's the test range," Connolly said.

"What exactly they firing there?"

"I don't know." Then, catching Holliday's look, "Honestly."

"They're measuring projectile velocity," Mills said.

They looked at each other, then at him. He laughed. "Well, I asked. That's what they told me."

"You mean like how fast an arrow goes when you shoot it?" Holliday said.

"Something like that."

"Sure are chewing up the trees to find out." He pointed toward the end of the canyon, where a series of test explosions had opened a rough clearing.

"But why come here?" Connolly said.

"Well, if they hadn't started shooting things up around here, nobody would have found it."

"You know what I mean."

Holliday looked at him. "You mean why so close to the Hill."

Connolly nodded.

"I don't know. Let's see what we got first. Maybe it's not even his."

But there had been no attempt to disguise the car; the Hill license plate, the glove compartment registration were intact. The paint in front had been scratched by the drive through the brush, but otherwise the car was as Karl might have left it. The keys were still in the ignition switch.

"That's a nice touch," Holliday said. "I've never seen that before."

"Can you have them checked for prints?"

"I could, but I've got no jurisdiction here."

"Nobody does. You're just assisting the Manhattan Project of the Army Corps of Engineers." Connolly smiled at him. "War work."

"You got a paper if I need it?"

"We've got nothing but paper."

"I think there's some blood here," Mills said, looking at the back floor.

"Yes, sir," Holliday said. "Don't touch that, now—we'll see if we can get a match."

"Try a church parking lot," Connolly said. "I guarantee it."

There was nothing unusual in the trunk. Aside from the bloodstains in the back, where Karl's head must have been laid, the car was clean.

"Let me try something," Connolly said, taking a handkerchief in his right hand. He got in and twisted the key. The motor turned over and started. He sat at the wheel for a minute, listening to the hum, running Karl's car as he had worn his boots. When he turned it off, the canyon was quiet enough to hear the birds.

"Why save the key?" he said, handing it, wrapped, to Holliday.

"Why anything?" Holliday said. "These things—they don't have to make sense."

"Yes they do. They don't have to be sensible, but they have to *make* sense."

"I'll get the boys to go over the whole thing for prints," Holliday said, ignoring him. He was searching the ground. "Too much traffic here."

"Kisty's men," Mills said. "They didn't know it was a crime scene."

"Let's check it anyway," Connolly said. "You never know. You want to square it with the guard?" he said to Mills. It was a polite dismissal and Mills took it, moving back to the road.

"What's on your mind?" Holliday said.

"I can't see the logistics of this," Connolly said, staring at the car as if there were a visible answer. "Let's say, just for the sake of argument, you kill Karl at San Isidro. You put him in the back and then you dump him in the park. Why not just dump him here?" He looked up at Holliday's stare. "Okay, you want him found, just the way you said. Like that, like it was something else. Why not find the car too? Why not just leave it in Santa Fe near the park? The blood, I guess," he said, talking to himself.

"Maybe he needed the ride."

Connolly looked up. "So where was his own car?"

Holliday shrugged. "He could have walked to the church."

"If he was already in Santa Fe. How did he get there?"

"You're assuming the guy was from here."

"Yes."

"Bus. They've got buses running from here, don't they? Saturday night. You got a few people on passes, right?"

Connolly nodded, thinking. "Then why not take a bus back? Just leave the car."

Holliday leaned against the car, staring at the ground. "Well, what did we think happened? When we found him?"

"That it had been stolen."

"Uh-huh. Which fit, right? That kind of crime. Bump him off and the next thing you know you're in Mexico. Valuable thing, a car in wartime. You leave it on the street, you've got somebody asking questions. Plus you've got the blood," he said, nodding to him.

"So you've got to get rid of it."

"Seems a shame, a nice new car, but I guess you do."

"But there are lots of ways to do that. Leave it in the desert, push it over a cliff."

"Well, the trouble is, you never know how that's going to turn out. It falls wrong or the damn thing catches fire. You don't want to attract any notice, you just want it to disappear. For good. Or a good long while, anyway. And maybe you don't have time for any of that.

Maybe you don't even have time for all the thinking we're doing about it. You just hide it."

"Here."

"Here. Like I said, maybe he needed the ride. He comes here, the gate is closed. Nobody around. Maybe he *knew* the gate was closed."

"Then he'd still have to get over to the east gate. The only way to do that—"

Holliday nodded. "That's right. If somebody else was driving his car."

Connolly stared at the ground, silent. "Two. I hadn't thought of that."

"I don't say it happened that way. Just that it could have."

"It makes sense. There had to be another car."

"Could be and had to be are two different things."

But Connolly dismissed him with a wave of his hand, still thinking. "Okay, he gets the car here and someone else gets him back on the Hill. You agree he's on the Hill?"

"I'd say it was indicated," Holliday said, a cop giving testimony.

"So why leave the keys? Why not just throw them away?"

Holliday sighed and took out a cigarette. "Yeah, why not? I've been thinking about that. Maybe just force of habit, you know? You don't throw keys away—what for? You don't want them on you, but you don't know if you're going to need them again either."

"You think he was going to use the car?"

303

"No, I was thinking of something else." He looked up, searching the canyon rim with a turn of his head. "Must have been pretty dark when he parked it here, right? So he can't tell if it's been hid real good. I mean, that time of night, you can't see anything. So I think—it's just a guess, now—that he wanted to take another look in the day, see what he could see. What if you look down from up there," he said, pointing to the rim, "and there's this shiny new car. Even just a piece of it. You'd have to move it, make sure it was really out of sight. So he might've left the keys just in case. 'Course, he never thought you boys would be shooting up the place."

"He's on the Hill," Connolly said.

"Yes, he is," Holliday said quietly. "Or was."

"He'd be taking a hell of a chance, coming back for the car."

"Mister, he took a hell of a chance when he murdered a man."

As a V-E celebration, he took Mills to dinner in Santa Fe, following Holliday's car down the back road, past Bandelier and the Rio Grande Valley and the humpy stretches of twisted piñon and red earth. The plaza was crowded, the sleepy square awake with people waving little flags and drinking openly, shouting victory with the bells of the cathedral. It was early, but La Fonda was packed, and they spent an hour at the bar before they could get a table.

"Do you really think he's FBI?" Connolly said, indicating the bartender.

"That's what they say. Makes a great martini, though," Mills said, sipping at the rim of the wide glass.

"Maybe he'll go legit after the war. A good bartender's never out of work."

"The FBI always finds something for them to do."

"What about you?"

"After? A nice house on the North Shore. Nice office with a window. Wacker Drive, I think. How does that sound?"

"Nice."

"Yeah, I know, dull as hell. Christ, it's something, isn't it, to think this might be the most exciting time of your life? And all I did was not get shot."

Dinner arrived, a broad platter of chiles rellenos, and Mills ordered another martini.

"You could catch a murderer," Connolly said. "That's exciting."

"You catch him."

"He's on the Hill," Connolly said slowly.

"I know. I figured, what with the car and all." He ate. "That what you and Holliday were talking about?"

Connolly nodded.

"You think he's still up there?"

"Yes."

"And that doesn't bother you?"

"No, why should it?"

"It scares the hell out of me. Did it ever occur

to you that if he did it once, he'd do it again?'"

"But we don't know *why* he did it."

"The motive's easier this time. You get away with murder and some guy tracks you down to nail you for it. So you nail him first. You'd have to."

"Two guys tracking you," Connolly said, looking at him.

"That's what I mean. I've never been a target before."

"Do you want to be reassigned?" Connolly asked seriously.

Mills went back to his food. "No, that's all right." He smiled. "You've got me interested now. Just watch my back, will you? Be nice to get back to old Winnetka in one piece."

"He doesn't know," Connolly said. "He doesn't know I know he's there."

Mills raised his eyes again. "He knows you're looking."

So they celebrated the end of the Third Reich with martinis and chiles rellenos, as if the war had caught them posted somewhere overseas. Afterward, pressured to give up the table, they walked out into the plaza, where people were shouting in Spanish, slightly rowdy but good-natured. It was beginning to get dark, the warm pink and coral of the adobes fading back to earth.

"Do me a favor," Connolly said. "Let's drive down to San Isidro."

"There's nothing to see there. They've been all over it a hundred times."

"I know. I just want to be able to picture it in my mind. Indulge me, okay?"

"For a change."

It was slow going over the Cerrillos bridge, with the streets still filled with pockets of celebration parties, but they thinned as the road headed south, past gas stations and quiet houses. There were a few cars in the alley next to the church and, inside, the glow of candles and the sound of voices. Mills idled the car across the street, watching Connolly study the building.

"Seen enough?"

"Let's go in for a minute. They must be saying mass. They do this every night?"

"No, we checked. Probably a celebration. For the war."

"Not very many cars."

"People walk. It's a neighborhood church. Only the tourists drive out here."

Connolly frowned, brooding, then shook the thought away and entered the church. It was crowded inside, rows of women with shawls over their heads and men holding hats. The small lights of votive candles licked against the whitewashed walls, and the reredos, intricate and dark during the day, glowed now as if it were simmering on a low flame. At the altar end of the narrow room, carved wooden saints, crude and bright with paint, looked down on the congregation like primitive Aztec gargoyles. A priest was speaking in Spanish at the lectern. Connolly felt he had literally stepped back in time. The faithful had gathered like this for centuries, fingering rosaries, praying for rain, while the rest of the world went to hell. But these were the people who had beat the Nazis too. In the room there must be Gold Star mothers. He wondered if they sent telegrams in Spanish or if the bad news was the piece of yellow paper itself, the army messenger. From the outside their lives seemed timelessly simple, hoarding squash and chiles, sticky candy on name days, but they had driven tanks and thrown grenades at scared, frozen teenagers who were trying to kill them. All those mad northern people who wanted—what? More room to breathe, or something like that. Now a victory in Europe. And they had walked here. Only the tourists drove.

Connolly stepped back out the door, feeling like an intruder. San Isidro had nothing to do with them. He asked Mills to head for the Alameda, trying to imagine that other drive as they passed the quiet streets. It was dark in the ribbon of park along the river, but a few people were out strolling, lit by passing headlights. He saw one couple kissing against a tree. Mills parked the car by the murder scene without being asked, and they sat looking at the bushes.

"There are people," Connolly said finally. "Why bring him somewhere where there are people?"

"There weren't," Mills answered. "It was late. It was raining."

"But he couldn't be sure."

"Maybe he drove around until the coast was clear."

"Maybe."

"It's a park. You mind your own business, especially at night. Look at those guys." He nodded toward a man walking unsteadily, propping up a drunk friend under his arm. "Who's to say he isn't dead? Who's going to ask?"

"You have an answer for everything," Connolly said.

"Let's go home, Mike. There's nothing here."

But Connolly, not yet satisfied, asked that they drive the back way to the canyon by the west gate.

"Retracing steps?" Mills said as they climbed the road to Bandelier.

"I can't see it. Look, we figure the car's here because the guy needed to get back to the Hill, right? Then why leave the Hill at all? You've seen the church. If you were meeting somebody, there are a hundred places on the Hill that would be better. Why go all the way to Santa Fe to a public place?"

"I thought the idea was they didn't want to be seen together. You know."

"That was the idea. It's wrong." Mills looked from the wheel, surprised. Connolly ignored him. "They could just go into the woods for that. Or for anything."

"If the other guy was already on the Hill."

"Exactly. That's what doesn't make sense. He was. He must have been. There's no other explanation for the car. So why go all the way to San Isidro to meet somebody who's just down the street?"

"I give up. Why?"

"He wasn't meeting Karl."

Mills drove in silence for a minute. "Want to run that by me again?"

"He was meeting someone else. Someone off the Hill. It's the only way it makes sense."

"But Karl's the one who's dead."

"He wasn't supposed to be there. It was—a surprise."

"You don't know any of this."

"No, I'm guessing. But follow me. Tonight I stood there in that alley next to the church and I thought, no one in his right mind would pick this place to kill someone. Open like that. A Mex neighborhood. But no one *did* pick it. It must have been an accident—an accident that it happened there, I mean. But it happens. Then what? Everything has to be done in a hurry. You have to take some risks, even. All along we've been trying to follow Karl's moves. How would Karl see it? What would he do? Like he was the criminal. But all that stops in the alley. It's the other guy we ought to be thinking about. What would he do? Tonight I was trying to imagine how he saw it."

"And?"

"I had to get rid of a body. I had to get rid of a car. And I had to get home."

"I'd say you did a pretty good job."

"I was lucky too. Nobody saw. The one

310

thing I couldn't imagine, though, was Karl. If I'd *wanted* to kill him, I would have done it somewhere else. Why go to San Isidro to see him? Answer: I didn't."

Mills thought for a minute. "But he was there anyway. Another accident?"

"No. He followed me."

"Now you're really guessing."

"Why not? He was security, wasn't he? He was used to tailing people."

"There isn't much of that. We go *with* people. Guards. We don't usually tail them. That's FBI stuff."

"But Karl might. He was capable of that, wasn't he?"

Mills hesitated. "Yes," he said finally.

Connolly looked at him. "What?"

"Nothing."

"He did tail people, didn't he?"

"I guess so. He knew things—where people went, things like that. He liked knowing things. He'd say something once in a while. How else would he know? I guess he must have been following them. I never thought about it before."

"Yes you did."

"All right, I did. But it wasn't official, so what was it? I figured it was just Karl. He liked being the sheriff. You learn not to pay too much attention to things like that."

"That's a hell of a thing for a security officer to say. You're supposed to pay attention."

"Yeah, well, how did I know he was going

311

to get himself killed, for Christ's sake? I just thought he was a nut like the rest of them."

"The rest of who?"

"Security. They're all a little nuts. Maybe you too. How do I know? Look, I didn't ask for this assignment. I don't get shot and I keep my head down. You stick it out and there's always somebody ready to chop it off. You never know what anybody's up to. For all I knew, Karl *was* FBI—he sure acted like it. So you don't look too closely. Just keep your head down and stay out of the way."

"He wasn't FBI."

"You know that for sure?"

"Groves would have told me."

"Yeah." Mills laughed. "Just like he told Lansdale about you, right? You've got the head of project security sitting there in Washington and his boss puts an outside man in and he doesn't know *what* the hell is going on. He's a little nuts already. Now how do you think he feels?"

"I don't know," Connolly said quietly. "How does he?"

Mills looked ahead at the road, saying nothing.

"He asked you to report on me, didn't he?" Connolly said, his voice low. Mills still said nothing. "Didn't he?"

"I'm sorry, Mike."

"Jesus Christ." He felt disgust mingled with irrational fear, the way he had felt the time his apartment had been burgled. There was nothing to steal. It was just the fact of someone's having been there at all. But now there was something. He imagined Emma's name sitting in a Washington file. "Tell him anything interesting?"

"No, nothing like that," Mills said. "It's just the case, Mike. He wants to know what's going on. He thinks Groves should have put him in charge."

"So your boss tells you to spy on me so he can spy on *his* boss. All in the family. Nice."

"I was ordered, Mike," he said quietly.

"What a fucking waste of time. And who's checking up on you?"

"I don't know. Maybe you. That's what it's like. Maybe Karl was."

Connolly thought for a minute. "Is that possible? Would he be asked to do something like that? Unofficially?"

"I don't think so."

"Why not?"

"I don't think they trusted him that way."

"The way they trust you. Why not?"

"He was foreign."

"Everybody here's foreign."

"That's what makes them crazy. They can't trust anyone. Mike, look, I have to ask. Anything I tell you—"

"You can trust me," Connolly said, his voice heavy with sarcasm.

They were driving around the bottom of the mesa, away from the canyon where the car had been hidden, back toward the east gate. Connolly looked out the window, again imagining the drive that night.

"I don't want any trouble," Mills said.

But Connolly was lost in his own thoughts. "You have to admit, he'd be ideal from their point of view."

"No. You don't know them. He was too smart for them."

"You weren't."

"They didn't have much choice. I'm the only one you're working with. Anyway, I'm not a Communist. Karl might have been. For a while, anyway. That makes them crazier than anything."

"I thought he was tortured by them. Or was that a lie too?"

"No, there's no question about that. He hated them. But there it was in his file. They're not going to use anybody with that in his file. I know. They had me on the clearance files the first few months I was here. Lansdale's like a maniac with that stuff. Van Drasek's worse. You met him yet? He's a real cutie. Crazy."

Connolly smiled. "Pretty high opinion of your colleagues."

"They're just following orders too. But look who's giving them. Van Drasek's specialty is Reds, so he keeps busy. You know what it's like here. Half the Berkeley crowd were parlor pinks. The unions, the Negroes—the usual. It doesn't amount to a damn thing, but try to tell old Van Drasek that. He's on a mission. He's out at Lawrence's lab again—goes through the place over and over."

"Maybe he's just trying to get away from his wife."

"We'd all be better off. He's serious, though. I've seen him deny clearance to scientists here and then call the university to get them fired. A real vindictive prick. And he's got Lawrence running in every direction, scared shitless they'll stop his funding. He's got files on everyone. I know."

"You know a lot," Connolly said, thinking of that first night, Mills's shiny head bobbing at the square dance. "Why doesn't Oppenheimer put a stop to it?"

"Are you kidding? He's the one they want most. They've all got the knives out for Oppenheimer. You should see the file they've got on him."

"I have seen it."

"Not all of it, you haven't. Every meeting. Every check for the Spanish refugees. His brother. The girlfriend—she was a party member. His wife used to be married to one. His students—any kid that's left of Roosevelt they blame on him. It just piles up. Van Drasek wouldn't even clear him until Groves told him to fuck off and just pushed it through himself."

"But why? What does he think Oppenheimer's doing, working for the Russians?"

"Why. He's crazy. He'd love it if Oppie were working for them—that would be perfect. Actually, what it is, Oppenheimer thinks it's bullshit and they know he thinks it. Which means he thinks they're bullshit. Which they are. But they can't touch him as long as he's building their damn bomb and Groves protects him. And the more he tries to get along with them, the more they hate him. They're all obsessed with him—the crazies, anyway. I think that's why Karl was following him. He was a little obsessed too."

"What?"

"Well, *if* he was. I don't know for sure. You're the one who thought he was following somebody."

"I never thought it was Oppenheimer."

"I know, it doesn't fit your story. But he's the only one I can ever remember Karl talking about. He was interested in Oppie."

"Why?"

"I think because they were. Karl was ambitious, you know? Maybe he thought if he could get something on Oppie, he'd angle himself a nice big promotion. Be one of the big boys. Of course, that's where he was crazy, because they didn't trust him either."

They had begun the steep climb up the hill. Connolly was thinking again. "So if he had anything on somebody, he'd want to make sure."

"Home at last," Mills said as they approached the gate. And, oddly, it was. Connolly looked at the high wire fence, the MPs checking passes, the rough buildings dim in the moonlight, and felt at home, somewhere to screen out the rest of the world. Was this what the killer had felt—relief at being back, the canyon and the panic at the church behind him?

"Are you going to report our conversation tonight?" Connolly said.

"I have to write something," Mills said apologetically.

"Try this. Say that I have evidence Karl was asked by Lansdale to do a check on Van Drasek. And accidentally get a copy to Van Drasek. We could have some fun with them."

Mills shook his head and smiled. "You have the fun. I just want to get back to Winnetka in one piece."

After they dropped the car at the motor pool, they walked back toward the Tech Area. The streets were quiet, the usual lights still shining in the labs. Not even victory in Europe interrupted the project.

"Just out of curiosity," Connolly said, "what will you write?"

"I don't know. Nothing much. You're puzzled about the car. Can't figure it out." He paused. "He likes to hear you're stumped. Makes Groves look like a jerk for putting you in. So I usually just say you're not getting anywhere."

"I'm not. And what if there was a genuine security breach? While I was getting nowhere and he was looking good?"

Mills shrugged. "What's more important in the scheme of things, somebody else's security or your own job? They've got a healthy sense of priorities in G-2. Nightcap?"

"No, but I'll buy you a coffee if the lodge is still open."

"Mike, about all this—I couldn't help it. You know I would never say anything—"

Connolly looked at him, the pleasant, eager

face that avoided waves. "Unless you had to."

Mills looked as if he'd been slapped.

"Never mind," Connolly said, not wanting to push him. "It's just the way things are now."

"It's the war."

"Yeah, the war."

There were still people at the lodge, smoking over leftover dishes and coffee cups, the celebration dinners finished. A few men from the office hailed them and Mills joined them with something like relief, tired of intimacy. Connolly sat with them for a while, listening to the easy jokes, ignoring the rest of the room because Emma was three tables away. She had glanced up when he came in, then turned back to her table as if he weren't there. He heard her laugh. The officers at his table were telling their own war stories—Feynman sending a letter cut into pieces to kid the censors; the physicist who sneaked out through a hole in the fence and kept coming back through the gate, a Marx Brothers trick. He looked at their faces and wondered if one of them checked on the others, an easy deceit. Was she aware of him? They were ten feet apart, no more. Did Daniel see her glance over, notice some nervous pitch to her voice? He moved restlessly in his seat, uncomfortable, afraid of giving himself away. But no one paid any attention.

He looked in the other direction, toward a large table of scientists who were laughing at something Teller was saying. Ulam, Metropolis, and a few of the others surrounded him like a court, and he was beaming with pleasure, the center of attention, the bushy eyebrows raised in arcs over the round, vain face. Oppenheimer's problem child. And of course that was why he was happy: Oppenheimer wasn't there; the table, its little world, was his. Connolly wondered for a moment what Oppenheimer meant to them, whether, like Mills's boss, they were simply waiting for their moment. But it seemed absurd. The table was genial, the room itself filled with high spirits, a bright faculty lounge on Oppenheimer's enchanted campus. How had he managed it? He listened, people said, he understood everything. He kept the army away. He defused the rivalries. Von Neumann's mathematics. Fast neutrons. Diaper service. Everything. People wanted to be with him at parties. And, according to Mills, they were out to get him.

Was Oppenheimer aware of any of it? Did he notice the jealousy and suspicion, frosted over now in the consensus of getting the job done? Did he know that Karl had been following him? Just another in a long line of checks and clearances, too familiar to bother about. A nuisance. And was Connolly any better? Another one of Groves's whims, blundering in on the scent of small scandal when there was important work to be done. Did Oppenheimer resent him too? Connolly felt suddenly like Mills, wanting to explain, to excuse himself. He meant no harm to the project, and he knew that one way or another—a crime revealed, a husband betrayed—he would do it damage. And his first impulse? He smiled to himself. Like everyone else with a problem at Los Alamos, he wanted to talk to Oppenheimer.

He wandered out to the Tech Area, nodding at Emma's table as he left, surprised by the shiver of guilty pleasure he felt at getting away with something. It was easy to look at her now; she was someone else here, another person. The lights were still on in Main Tech. He showed his badge to the sentry MP at the inner fence and climbed the few wooden steps to the building. Inside, it was quiet. He turned left, toward Oppenheimer's office, then stopped in the corridor. What, after all, had he come to say? A report on the car. A question about Karl. A complaint about Lansdale. Excuses, not worth his time. The fact was, he simply wanted to talk, like an eager graduate student working out a proof. When he saw that Oppenheimer's office was dark, he felt relieved and foolish at the same time. Why had he expected him to be here so late? Yet it was part of the myth he was helping construct. In his mind, the brightly lit door was always open.

The door next to the office, however, was open, fluorescent light pouring out into the corridor. There was no one inside. Instinctively he reached in to snap out the light, then stopped. It had been years since he had been in a classroom, and he stood there for a minute taking in the familiar smell of chalk and dust and dry radiator heat. The room was small—a desk in one corner piled with books, a conference table with chairs, a blackboard, and two narrow windows that faced Ashley Pond. The blackboard had the chalk smears of a hasty eraser, and Connolly went over to it, automatically picking up the eraser to finish. He took off his coat and looked at the blackboard. In school, it had helped to map things out, make the problem visual. He remembered writing formulas on the board, so clear when you could see them that the answer followed at the end. He took a piece of chalk and, almost without thinking, began to draw.

Near the bottom he drew the outline of an adobe church, two squat towers and a cross, with a side patch of alley with an X in it. A line followed the Cerrillos Road up the board, crossing the chalk arc of bridge and inter- secting with the Alameda. The lines came quickly, a squiggle of river, a generic puff of bush, another X. Then some of the city streets, the rectangle of the plaza, and off in the far left corner, forty miles away, the wavy ridge of canyons, another X, the chalky portico symbols of gates.

When he stepped back, he saw everything he knew about the logistics of the case, an alge- bra formula disguised as a child's map. He held the chalk in one hand, resting his elbow in the other, as if he were staring at a painting in a museum. How to connect the Xes? He was at the church. He had come to meet someone. Karl arrived. Three cars? Faintly he heard the clunky government-issue clock ticking over the board. How many to the final X? But there'd been no signs of another car in the box canyon.

The building was still, saved from eeriness by a background murmur of voices down the hall. Working late. He stared at the map. He could see Karl's car moving up the Cerrillos Road. What about the others? How many at the second X? He stared until even the background sounds faded away. Rain. Headlights. There must be a way to see.

The gasp from behind startled him. He turned around to see Friedrich Eisler put a hand to his heart, a European gesture of surprise.

"I am so sorry," he said, flustered. "I didn't mean—for a moment I thought—you looked so like Robert."

"Robert?"

"Yes. Of course, you are much bigger. But the way you stood there, with the chalk. Forgive me, I didn't mean to disturb you." He turned to go.

"No, please, come in. I shouldn't be here anyway. I was just doodling."

Eisler smiled, "Yes, doodling." He pronounced it as an exotic word. "It was very like. Of course, this was many years ago. Göttingen. He would stand there for hours, you know, just looking at the board. Thinking. But what kind of thinking? That I could never discover. Once I saw him in the morning and I came back later and he was still there. And then later. All day. Just holding the chalk, looking."

"Did he find the answer?"

Eisler shrugged and smiled. "That I don't remember."

"He was your student?"

"A colleague. I am not so old, you know."

"What was he like?"

Eisler smiled again. "So. You too. Everyone wants to know Robert. What was he like? The same. Of course, not so busy. In those days, there was more time. For thinking. Like you, with the chalk."

Connolly had moved away from the board, and Eisler looked at it, puzzled. "This is not, I take it, a mathematical formula."

"No." Connolly laughed, embarrassed. "Just a map. I was trying to figure something out. I suppose I'd better clean up," he said, taking the eraser.

But Eisler was looking thoughtfully at the map, his eyes darting from one X to the others.

"No, don't bother," he said absently. "No one comes here. Perhaps you'll find your answer, like Robert." He turned wearily from the board to face Connolly. "Then you must tell me how you did it. The process. I always wondered."

"The Oppenheimer Principle," Connolly said lightly.

"Yes. Well, I leave you to your problem."

But Connolly was reluctant to see him go. "I was thinking about something you said to me."

"Really? What is that?"

"About the Nazis giving us permission. To do what we do."

"Yes."

"Today I thought, they're gone. Who's going to give us permission now?"

Eisler looked at him, his gentle eyes suddenly approving, a teacher pleased with his pupil. "My friend, I don't know. My war is finished. That is for you to decide." He stretched his arm back toward the blackboard. "You must use the Oppenheimer Principle."

"With me, it's guesswork."

"Only the answers. The questions are real. Keep asking the questions."

"Maybe you have to be him to make it work."

Eisler sighed. "It will work for you too, I think."

"I'm not like him."

"No? Perhaps not. Robert's a very simple man, you know. He does not—" He searched for a word. "Dissemble. Yes, dissemble. He doesn't know how. There is no mystery there."

"He's a mystery to me."

Eisler moved toward the door. "Perhaps that's because you do dissemble, Mr. Connolly. Good night."

Connolly watched him go, his tired shoulders sloping as he went down the corridor. When he looked back at the blackboard, he saw nothing more than crude grade-school sketches, a child's problem. No car was driving down the road, nervous about a body. No questions. He stared at it for a few minutes, then took up the black eraser and wiped the chalk away. Tomorrow there would be grown-up numbers there.

Outside, he put on his jacket against the night chill. The moon outlined the buildings with faint white lines. He felt that he was walking in one of his blackboard maps. This road went south from the Tech Area. The box canyon was in the far distance to his right. The longer he walked, the more the map filled in, until he could see the whole plateau, fingers stretching away from the Jemez toward Santa Fe. He kept walking, awake with coffee and the bright night sky. But it had been cloudy that night, perhaps already raining when the car pulled into the canyon. Dark. And suddenly he thought of a question and started walking faster, glancing at his watch as he headed away from the building toward the far west gate.

His luck held. The same soldier was on night duty, sitting inside the lighted post with a Thermos and a comic book. He looked up, surprised, when Connolly said hello.

"Mighty late," he said, a question in his voice.

"I was just out taking a walk. It's a nice night for it."

"I guess," he said, all Piedmont twang and suspicion.

"I have a question for you. You have any more of that coffee?"

"Well, sure. Nice to have some company. What's on your mind?" He poured some coffee into the lid cup and handed it to Connolly.

"At night, when they close the entrance, what happens exactly?"

"Well, they close it. I don't know what you mean."

"They lower the crossing barrier to cars, right? But someone's still here?"

He nodded. "Me, usually. I've been pulling night shift regular."

"But if a car came by accident, you'd let him in?"

"They don't. There's two barriers. Road's closed down at the turnoff, so a car don't come up this far."

"But you're here anyway."

The soldier smiled, a sly grin. "Well, that's to keep people from going *out*. Ain't nobody coming in that late."

"But if they were—I mean, someone could walk in, couldn't he?"

"Walk?" The vowel spread into syllables.

"Just for the sake of argument. Someone could walk in, right? There's nothing to stop him."

"Well, there's me. I'd stop him."

"If you heard him."

The soldier looked at him guardedly, as if he were somehow in trouble and didn't know why. "I'd hear him."

"You didn't hear me. Right now, while we've been talking here, someone could have slipped by outside, couldn't he? Look, I'm not accusing you of anything. I'm just trying to get a picture of how it works."

"It works fine," the soldier said defiantly,

the vowel stretched again. Connolly stepped out of the box, sipping the coffee as he looked around, the soldier following him. "Ain't nobody going to walk, you know," he said, still worried. "Where they going to be walking from? Who's going to walk?"

"I don't know," Connolly said, looking at the road, the wide space at the pole, the dark on the side. "Nobody, I guess. I was just wondering." It would have been easy, no more difficult than a stroll. "You patrol out here or just stay in the post?"

"I got my rounds. If somebody's complaining, they don't know jackshit. I'm up and down here all night, even if it *is* cold." But it had been raining, a comforting drum on the post roof. "What's all this about, anyway? You got some kind of problem?"

"No. They're just looking over all the security points."

"What for?" he said, still suspicious.

"It's the army. They don't need a reason."

The soldier grinned. "Yeah, I guess."

Connolly looked up and down the dark road again. One car, not two. Hide it and walk in. A long walk, but safe enough. Worth the chance. And then home.

"How long you been on the Hill?" he asked casually.

" 'Bout a year, I guess. I ain't never had no trouble before."

"You haven't got any now. I was just curious. Like it?"

The soldier shrugged. "Ain't nothin' to

327

do. Beats combat, though, I guess. You read about them Jap dive-bombers? They're just plain crazy, those people."

Connolly nodded. "Year's a long time. You must know everybody up here."

"I just look at the passes. We don't get invited to no parties. That's only for the long-hairs."

"You know Karl Bruner?"

The soldier looked at him, his eyes squinting again in suspicion. "That's the guy who got himself killed."

There it was again—Karl's fault. "Well, somebody killed him. Know him?"

"I knew who he was. I never talked to him or nothing. I heard they got the guy," he said, a question.

"Yeah, they did. He use this gate much?"

"Off and on."

"So you'd see him then."

The soldier shrugged again. "Well, sure, if I was on duty."

"They told me he liked to drive around."

"Yeah, in that Buick of his." So he noticed.

"Did he ever have anyone with him?"

The soldier looked at him, puzzled, as if he hadn't understood the question.

"Did he?" Connolly asked, pressing.

"Sometimes. You're asking an awful lot of questions," he said, cautious again.

"Just one. Who used to go with him?"

The soldier looked away. "Is this some kind of investigation or something? What do you want to know for?"

Connolly stared at him.

"I mean, he's dead. I don't want to go making trouble for nobody. That was his business. Now it's just hers, I guess."

"Hers?"

"Well, sure. I figured they was just—scootin' off, you know? None of my business."

"You'd better make it your business. I mean it. You know who she was? What she looked like? I need to know this."

The soldier looked flustered. "Well, hell, I thought you did know. I didn't mean to start nothing."

"How would I know?"

"Well, I thought she was a friend of yours too."

Connolly stood still. When he finally spoke, his voice had the low steadiness of a threat. "Are you trying to tell me it was Mrs. Pawlowski?"

The soldier retreated a step. "Well, God Almighty, you kept askin'. Now don't go and blame me."

"How many times?" Connolly said, his voice still unnaturally steady.

"A few."

"Where were they going?"

"Where?" And now his face, no longer frightened, filled with a sly grin, as if the question were irrelevant. "I guess you'll have to ask her."

11

He didn't see her until the end of the week. He sat listlessly at his desk or lying on Karl's bed, absorbed in his own mystery. The days were hot and dry, a steady wind scratching at everyone's nerves. The talk was of drought and an outbreak of chicken pox in the school and the frequent caravans to Trinity. The scientists seemed never to appear, locked full-time in the labs. There were no parties. A fight broke out in one of the enlisted men's barracks, something to do with an insult taken, but really about the new tension of the work and the constant dry wind that made everything feel as suspended as dust.

Connolly didn't notice any of it. Something had detonated in him, like one of Kisty's tests, and he sat shuffling through the pieces, repeating her conversations in his head, wondering what had been meant, what she wanted him to believe. Mills avoided him, sensing the black mood that was smothering him, and when Connolly noticed him at all, it was only as a figure of a more cheerful betrayal. He read through Emma's file, and Daniel's, as if they were new characters on the Hill, people he'd never met. Why had she married him? He'd never asked. How many others? The mood festered in him, silently, until the surprise and hurt became pure anger, and when that happened he stopped thinking about anything else.

One day he saw her walking past Ashley Pond

and he wanted to run over and take her by the shoulders. Why did you lie to me? But he couldn't bring himself to ask her, and he realized with a sick feeling in his stomach that it was because he still wanted her. The wind blew her clothes against her and there was that rider's stride, quick and straightforward, utterly without deceit. But why lie? What had she to do with Karl, with any of it? He drew his imaginary blackboard map, but she didn't fit anywhere. Instead, she was in another map, an X at Theater-2 and the punch bowl, lines to Santa Fe, to Chaco, to—and he saw that she was everywhere on this personal map, it was about her, everything that had happened to him. Was any of it true? Where had they gone? Maybe just a lift into town. But the soldier hadn't thought so, with his stupid, sly grin. The MP at Trinity hadn't thought so either. In this hot, lazy afternoon with nothing to do but brood, no one was innocent. Not even him. He'd just been the next in line.

When they did meet, he was disarmed by her smile, easy and guileless, as bright as the day. Daniel had gone down to the test site again, and they went to the ruins at Bandelier, dodging the hot sun on the shady path along Frijoles Creek, down toward the waterfall that finally emptied into the Rio Grande. She was glad to see him, talking happily about nothing, pleased to be out. She hiked briskly along the trail in the boots and shorts she had worn at Chaco, when things were different. But in fact it all seemed the same, so clear and bright that for

331

a moment he felt the weight of the past few days was nothing but an anxious dream, one of those nights whose gloom and dread were burned off by morning. She laughed when she washed her face in the stream, splashing him. He watched her, how easily she moved through her part, and he smiled back, unwilling to let her see him watching. He wanted her to say something, a disingenuous moment, so he could begin, but she hiked back in high spirits, and he waited. They ate a picnic near the Tyuonyi kiva, again like Chaco, with the sun overhead. There were no sounds but the stirrings of lizards and the faint hot breeze that blew the cottonweed seeds like bits of snow.

"You can see why they'd come here," she said, her voice lazy and contented. "Water. Bottomland. Storage bins." She pointed toward the caves hollowed out in the soft lava tufa above them. "Nothing like Chaco."

"But they left."

"Yes," she said, facing the sun with her eyes closed. "Strange, isn't it?"

In the quiet they heard a muffled explosion from one of the distant test canyons, a wave of intrusion from the Hill. They looked toward the sound, alarmed, but then it was over and everything was still again. She leaned back, closing her eyes to blot it out.

"Did the Germans come here too?" he said, stalling.

"I suppose they must have," she said, not opening her eyes. "Or maybe it was the priests.

It's always the priests, isn't it? Some bloody archbishop leading them to the promised land. Some *idea*. The Navajos were frightened by it, when they came. Found all these ready-made cities and never moved in. Wouldn't touch them."

"Maybe they were the Germans."

"No. At least, we don't think so," she said, a seminar *we*. "No sign of fighting at all. Anyway, they're not like that. They're lovely. In the creation myth, one part of the darkness makes love to another and the one on top becomes light and rises up to be the first day. It's lovely, that," she said, her voice soft. "Think of ours. God blundering about making this and that, *busy*. Everything done in a week. No wonder we blow things up."

"What happens after they have sex, the dark and the light?"

"They make the wind, the life force. I love the Navajos for that—everything beginning in bed."

"They really say that?"

"Of course," she said lightly. "Would I lie to you?"

"I don't know. Would you?"

She opened her eyes and looked at him, but he didn't say anything more and she let it pass. "There's quite a lot of sex in the myth. The earth and the sky make love, and the moisture between them, the sweat, waters the earth and makes everything grow. Do admit, it's a lot nicer than God just waving his hand here and there, making zebras and things. It's funny, though, they don't seem sensual at all, the Indians. But I suppose they must be."

Her voice drifted away, so that in the quiet it seemed she had been talking to herself. She sat up and lit a cigarette, staring out at the swath of green near the creek, waiting for him to speak.

"A penny for your thoughts," she said finally. "What's wrong?"

"Nothing," he said. "Why should anything be wrong?"

"I don't know. You're all—*coiled*. You haven't touched me all day, so something must be wrong. You're not the Navajo type."

He said nothing, working a stick in the ground, making idle patterns. "I want to ask you something, and I'm not sure how."

He felt her stiffen beside him, an almost imperceptible movement, like one of the tiny lizards flitting behind a rock.

"Oh. Perhaps you'd better just ask, then."

"Tell me about you and Karl."

She exhaled smoke as if she had been holding her breath, and continued to look ahead. "What do you want to know?"

"Everything."

"Oh, everything."

"You told me you scarcely knew him, but that isn't true, is it? You were seen with him."

"Quite the detective." She paused. "Is it so important?" she said softly.

"Of course it's important. He was murdered."

"Well, I didn't bloody murder him," she said, facing him.

"Why did you lie to me?"

"I didn't lie to you. It's nothing to do with this. It wasn't any of your business."

"You did lie to me."

"Have it your way, then," she said, getting up. "It's still none of your business."

"Tell me," he said, standing.

"What does it matter? It was *over*."

"Tell me," he shouted, his voice breaking through the still air like the far explosion.

"Tell me," she mimicked. "All right, he was my lover. Better?"

Her words hung in the air, as if neither of them wanted to pick them up.

"Why?" he said finally.

"Why. Why. He asked me, I suppose. I'm easy. You ought to know."

They glared at each other.

"Tell me," he said quietly.

She broke the stare, looking down to rub out her cigarette. "Last year. A few times. It didn't mean anything."

"Why didn't you tell me?"

"Maybe I didn't want you to think I was that kind of girl."

"Where?"

"Where?" she said, exasperated. "Places. There are places, you know."

"Santa Fe?"

"Nowhere we've been, if that's what you want to know," she said angrily. "Someplace on the road to Albuquerque. Look, it happened. I can't

335

help that. It was over. What do the details matter? You've no right."

"Yes, I do. Did you love him?"

"Stop it."

"Did you?"

"Of course I didn't bloody love him. We had sex. I enjoyed it. I didn't enjoy it. Is that what you want to hear? Anyway, it stopped. I didn't want Daniel to know. I was afraid."

"You're not afraid of anything."

"I'm afraid of you," she said, then looked away. "You want too much. "Tell me everything. Where did you go? Did you enjoy it? Were you ashamed?' All angry and wounded, as if it had anything to do with you. I didn't even know you. It had nothing to do with anybody, really. Except him. And then later he was killed. What did you want me to do, run over and tell everybody in security that we'd been having it off in some motel down the road? I was relieved. I thought nobody would ever know."

"And it didn't matter that there was a murder investigation?"

"Why should it? I didn't know anything about that."

"Even when they said it was a homosexual murder."

She looked stunned. "What are you talking about?"

"They thought Karl was homosexual. They still do. They *convicted* a man because they thought it."

"But why?" she said, bewildered. "That's crazy. He wasn't that."

"You never told them otherwise."

She shook her head, confused and angry. "That's not fair. I never knew. *You* never told me, come to that. He was killed in the park—that's all I ever heard. A robbery. Why would anyone think—" She trailed off, still trying to digest it.

"You're sure."

"What do you want to know?" she snapped. "What we did in bed? Is that part of the investigation? It was lovely, all right? Maybe he thought I was a boy. How would I know? It didn't feel that way to me."

"Emma, whoever killed him tried to make it look like that kind of crime. Probably so we wouldn't look anywhere else. He succeeded. There was no reason to think otherwise, no—history. Until now. That's why I had to know. That's all."

"Is it? Is that what this is about? I only went to bed with him, you know. I didn't kill him."

He turned away from her, squinting into the sun, his voice toneless and quick as he questioned her. "Did you go to Santa Fe with him that night?"

"No, of course not. It was over long before that."

"Did you ever go to San Isidro?"

"No. Yes, I suppose so, when I first came here. Everybody does. Oh, what does it matter? *Stop* this."

"I can't."

"You mean you won't. You're putting *me*

337

on trial. For what? Did I hurt your feelings? Well, I'm sorry."

"This isn't about us."

She was biting her bottom lip. "Isn't it? I thought it was."

"Emma," he said patiently, "he wasn't killed, he was murdered. That means there was a reason. It's important. You've got to help me."

She looked at him, disconcerted by his tone. "What do you want me to do? Tell the police I slept with him? That they've made a mistake?"

"No. It wouldn't make any difference. They don't care."

She stared at him for a minute, taking this in. "But you do."

"I just want to know."

"No, that's when you were just a cop. Now you're judge and jury as well. I've told you— isn't that enough? I went with him. I've done it before. You weren't the first."

"Why him?"

"I don't know. He was good-looking. Maybe I was bored. It just happened. Is that so hard for you to believe?"

"Yes."

"Why? Does it disappoint you? Did you think I was better than that?"

"It wasn't like that," he said evenly, sure now. "It didn't just happen."

"How would you know? Oh, you think you know something. You don't know anything. Leave me alone."

She turned to walk away but he grabbed her arm, bringing her back and holding her. "You're lying to me again."

"Leave me alone."

"Just a casual fling? With Karl? No. Karl wasn't like that. He liked to know things, that's what he cared about. He knew something about you. So you slept with him. Because he made you. Or maybe it was your idea, to keep him quiet. That's what happened, isn't it? Was it your idea?"

"Leave me *alone*," she shouted, pulling her arm free and moving away from him.

"What was it, Emma?" he said to her back. "What was so important that you'd do that? Did you give him money too, or was the motel enough?"

But she was walking away from him. "Go to hell," she said. The low wall of the kiva stopped her and she stood against the piled stones looking down the canyon, not crying but heaving gulps of air. Connolly moved toward her slowly, afraid a quick movement would make her bolt. When he spoke his voice was gentle, soothing a startled horse.

"Emma, you've got to tell me. He was killed. You were the only one who knew him."

"I didn't know him," she said, her back still to him. "I just slept with him. They don't always go together. I thought I knew you."

"Karl was blackmailing someone," he began again. "He was getting money. If it wasn't you, it was somebody else. Don't you see what I'm saying? There's somebody *else*. I've got to find out who. You're the only one who can help me."

She turned to face him, her eyes moist. "I can't. Please."

"But I will find out. You know that, don't you? I've got to."

"Why? Why you?"

"Because there's been a crime and this isn't just anyplace. It isn't New York, it's not even Santa Fe. It's a weapons lab. That's what they're doing here. Not science. They're making weapons. Secret ones. So everything's different. Why do people get killed? Money? There isn't any money here. Sex? Maybe. That would have been convenient for everybody. But what if it's about the weapons? They can't stop until they know. So they won't. If it's not me, it'll be somebody else. Is there really anything so terrible you couldn't tell me? You've got to trust me that much."

"Do I?" she said, her face creased in a sarcastic smile. "I wonder why."

"Because I'm going to find out anyway."

She looked away, letting her shoulders slope wearily. "Yes, I suppose you will," she said coolly. "For the good of the country or something. Nothing to do with you. A patriot. That was one lovely thing about Karl, he wasn't a patriot. You can trust someone who doesn't believe in anything. The rest of you—"

She walked back to where the remains of the picnic lay and lit another cigarette.

"Where do you want me to start? My first

340

husband? He believed in everything. Mostly himself, it turned out."

"You were married before?"

"Yes. Matthew. I seem to have a run of Ms. All great believers, too. Anyway, we were young—I suppose that's no excuse, but we were—and he was a great rebel and so I adored him. He was fun. I don't think you know how *boring* England can be. Sunday roast and all the eligibles in the *Tatler* and Matthew wasn't having any of it. The people's revolution was his line. God, all those treks to Highgate to see old Marx's grave. My parents loathed him. So when he went off to Spain to fight the Fascists, naturally I went with him. My father always said I'd end up in Gretna Green— that's where the wild girls elope to—but it turned out to be Madrid instead. That dreary registrar's office. Not even a clergyman—you know how the comrades are about that. Actually, they weren't very keen on marriage either, but free love in the trenches—well, it wasn't madly me, was it? You can only take the country out of the girl so far. So there I was, Señora Matthew Lawson, International Brigade."

"You were a Communist?"

She hesitated, as if his question had interrupted a reverie. "He was," she said more seriously, drawing on her cigarette. "Party membership, the lot. You had to be, really, in the brigade. I was just—what? In love, maybe. *Away.* On my adventure. Not that I didn't admire him for it. I did, tremendously. He believed in *some*thing. No one else seemed to. You know, the world is always coming to an end at that age and no one's doing anything about it. Except then—well, it really was, wasn't it? I thought he was right. Anyone could see the Germans were up to no good, and of course all the people one despised most didn't seem to mind at all. Uncle Arthur. He actually went to the Olympics and said how in*spir*ing it all was, the fool. That was typical. But Matthew, he knew, he actually did something. And then he was wounded. Nothing serious, a flesh wound it turned out, but I didn't know that then. I thought he was going to die. You can see how romantic it was, me all weepy next to the cot in that awful field hospital and the comrades crashing around in Spanish, shooting anything that flew over, and my brave Matthew stopping the Fascists with his body while everyone back home was just out in the garden and being mean about the miners—oh, I was having my adventure. Sounds rather pathetic now, doesn't it? It wasn't, though. It was romantic. Exciting."

She stopped, looking toward the creek as if it were the past, then shook her head. "Well, never mind. You don't want to hear all that. You want to know about Karl. That was Berlin. We went to Berlin—I never knew whether it was Matthew's idea or the party's. The party's, I suppose. I don't know if he *had* any ideas by then. He liked being a soldier. It suited him. Which is odd when you think of it, since he'd never obeyed an order in his life.

But now he did. I suppose he thought they were moving him back from the front lines to some other unit. Anyway, we went. Not so romantic this time, though. It was useful to them to have an Englishman there. The Huns always gave us a wide berth—I suppose they thought we were all like Uncle Arthur. The German comrades couldn't do much. I think they were paralyzed with fear. I know I was. But Matthew—well, naturally he was up for anything. I'd no idea what he was actually doing— he kept telling me it was better my not knowing, but of course that only meant I imagined the worst. I hated it. Terrible little flats. Not that I minded that, really. I was doing a course at the university, that was our cover, and students weren't expected to live high. And God knows it was better than Spain. Berlin was pretty. If you weren't being thrown into jail, you could have a good time there. But I hadn't come for any of that. I was just—isn't it awful? I suppose I was actually a camp follower, just like those women they used to drag along. Except my soldier was never there. He was always out fighting the good fight. And of course it *was* the good fight, so you couldn't complain. I'd go to the meetings just to be with him. You can't imagine the dreariness of it, all secret and squalid and—endless. Hours of it. Matthew would natter on and I'd just drift off. I doubt he even noticed I was there. But Karl did. At least, he said he did. I don't remember him being there, but I wasn't seeing much of anything then except Matthew and how miserable

I was. But Karl remembered me. Evidently I made a striking impression. So."

She got up and began to walk, absently kicking small stones as she paced.

"So you went to bed with him because he saw you at a few meetings?"

She snorted, a pretend laugh. "I said I'd tell you what happened. I didn't say it would make sense."

His stare followed her as she paced, waiting. "When was all this?"

"Just after he got here. I was getting a pass and he recognized me. And then later he asked me about it. Wondered why it wasn't in my file."

"And why wasn't it?"

"Nobody ever asked. I was just a wife. Daniel was vetted in London. They knew I'd been in Spain. So had lots of people. It was the thing to do. Maybe no one there thought anything of it. But you know what it's like here." She turned to face him. "Look, I was scared. Is that so hard for you to understand? Being here is all Daniel ever cared about. You know what happens if they pull your security clearance. I couldn't do that to him. Just because his wife went to some silly meetings? They didn't mean anything anyway. I don't even remember what they talked about. It was all—innocent. But would your lot believe that? 'Why didn't you tell us before? Who else was there?' You know what it's like. They'd never trust him after that."

"Is that where you met him? At the meetings?"

"No," she said dismissively, "he didn't know anything about that. We met at the university."

"So it was your little secret."

"I didn't think it mattered. It *didn't*. And then later—well, then it was too late. They'd always want to know why I hadn't told them in the first place. I just wanted things to go on as they were. No one was the wiser. What did it matter?"

"But Karl was wiser."

"Yes."

"So you decided to do Daniel a real favor and make a new friend."

She stared at him. "That's right. I needed a friend."

"And was he? A friend?"

She shrugged and turned away, pacing again.

"What else?"

"Why should there be anything else?"

"Because there is. Emma, half the people on the Hill went to political meetings ten years ago. You didn't sleep with him for that."

"Maybe I wanted to. Who knows why we do things? Why do you?"

"What else?"

"Oh, leave me alone."

"What happened in Berlin? To your husband?"

"I don't know," she said. "He left."

"Just like that."

"Yes, just like that. He deserted me." She looked at him for a reaction. "I guess my

345

charms weren't enough to keep him. He must have had something more important to do."

"But where did he go?"

"I've no idea. I never heard from him. I assume he died. Given everything."

"Did you try to find him?"

"No. He left *me,* you see. He didn't want to be found."

"What did you do? Go back to London?"

"No, I stayed on."

"You stayed on. In Berlin. With a missing Communist husband."

"Nobody knew he was my husband. That was—I don't know, part of it. Look, I know it sounds silly now, but things were different then. He didn't want anybody to know. For my sake. In case something happened."

"What the hell was he doing?"

"Oh, don't get your hopes up. He wasn't the Comintern's man in place or anything like that. At least, I don't think so. Probably just leaflets and setting up those awful meetings. But he liked to pretend it was dangerous. Maybe it was. Anything was then, I suppose. Anyway, he thought so."

"So you stayed."

Emma shrugged again. "I didn't fancy running home to Daddy. I'd made my bed—I thought I'd better lie in it."

"In Berlin," he said skeptically. "Living hand to mouth with the Nazis in the street."

"That's right. Stupid, wasn't it?"

He watched her as she lit another cigarette, not meeting his eyes. "Tell me, Emma," he said quietly.

She blew out the smoke, raising her head to look at him. "I was pregnant."

He waited for a minute, but she simply continued to smoke, staring at him. "What happened?"

"I got rid of it. I killed it."

"God—"

"Well, what was I supposed to do?" she said, her voice breaking for the first time.

"I didn't mean that."

"Didn't you? Well, never mind. It doesn't make any difference. I had it—taken care of. One office visit. Easy, really. Not so easy to arrange, though. The Germans had views on that sort of thing." She snorted. "Matthew always thought he was so frightfully clandestine. Try finding a friendly doctor—that was the real secret world."

"How did you?"

"Daniel helped me," she said simply. "Surprised? No German would have touched me. But he knew the refugees. They were always open for a bit of business."

"I'm sorry."

"Don't be. It was a long time ago."

"No. For asking."

She nodded. "Yes. It makes things different, doesn't it? It's not always nice knowing things."

"And that's why you helped him get out?"

She smiled wryly. "Take one life and save

another? Maybe it was something like that, I don't know. I didn't look *into* things then, I just did them. Maybe you can sort it out for me." Her eyes were moist. "I don't know why I'm explaining all this to you. Hardly what you want for your report, is it?"

"No."

"Anything else, then? While you've got the light in my face?"

"Why did it stop?"

"Well, there's a question. Because I asked. I just couldn't anymore."

"And he agreed? He didn't insist? Threaten you?"

"Threaten me? Karl? It wasn't like that. You've become as mad as the rest of them. He didn't bloody blackmail me. I'm sorry, but he didn't. That's what *you* want to think. He never threatened me. He knew things. Ordinarily it wouldn't have mattered—not exactly the end of the world to go to a meeting, is it?—but in a place like this it was—awkward, okay? There wasn't time to sort anything out. I thought they'd send Daniel packing. So." She paused, looking away. "Anyway, it's done. Now you'll tell them anyway, so it seems I needn't have bothered."

"But he didn't care?"

She considered this for a minute, as if the idea were new to her. "You know, oddly enough, I don't think he did. Oh, he was fond of me in his way, but in the end I don't think it interested him very much. He wasn't—personal. He was afraid of it. It's hard to explain. Once he had his file complete, I think he just wanted to move on."

"You liked him."

"I felt sorry for him. It's a terrible thing, not being able to trust anyone. Prison did that, I guess. I often wondered what happened to him there—oh, I don't mean physically, the fingers and all that. But inside. It made him a little crazy, I think. Goblins everywhere." She paused, wiping sweat from her face with her handkerchief. "Anyway, he came to the right place for it. Here he got paid for not trusting anybody. I think he liked that better than sex, all the—untangling. He was excited by that. Maybe it was just prison all over again, get them before they get you. He couldn't help it anymore. He always thought somebody was out to get him."

"Somebody did."

"Yes," she said, then went over to gather up the picnic things. "I think you'd better take me home now. I've had enough time in the confessional. It's not as good for the soul as they say."

Connolly watched her pack the knapsack, gracefully picking up the cups, making room for the Thermos. What was she thinking? For a moment he thought he finally understood the pleasure Karl took in it, that tension of not knowing, of wondering what was true.

"Did he ever mention anyone else?"

"What? Any other bad security risks? No."

He followed her to the car. "Don't you think it's strange, his just letting go like that?"

349

"I didn't say he was pleased—he just didn't make a fuss, that's all. I didn't think about it, I was relieved. Maybe he was too. Maybe he found someone more interesting. When you're paranoid—isn't that the word?—there's nothing more boring than an open book. No mystery there. After all, he knew everything about me."

He stopped at the car door. "Do I?"

She hesitated. "I thought you did," she said softly. "Everything that mattered. I thought—well, never mind what I thought." She busied herself putting the pack in the car, then stood up, looking at him over the roof. "There is one more thing. I wasn't going to tell you, but you may as well know. Maybe it will make a difference to you." She hesitated again, still not sure. "Karl was—well, Karl was very good at what he did, you know. He knew things that even I didn't know. Don't ask me how." He waited. "I suppose you can find out anything if it's really what you care about," she said to him with a wry half-smile. "He knew that Matthew was still alive."

"I thought—"

"So did I. I'd no idea. You can see what that means, can't you?" she said, her voice pleading. "I was frantic. Daniel only got out because of the marriage. Now he's British."

"You thought they'd send him back?"

"No, not then," she said, her voice trembling. "We weren't exactly sending trains into Berlin. But what about now? If the marriage isn't real, what happens to him? Is he supposed to go back to Poland? I can't let that happen to him."

"They wouldn't do that."

"How do you know? I didn't. So logical. I couldn't be, don't you see? I couldn't think straight. All I knew was that Daniel would have no legal status at all and it was my fault. I had to do something."

"So you went with him."

"*Yes,* I went with him," she said, almost shouting. "It always comes back to that, doesn't it? I needed time. I thought after the war I'd sort it out—I couldn't do it here. Besides, no one knew."

"Except Karl."

"Yes, except Karl. And now you. Michael, I'm asking you—"

"Don't. Don't ask me."

She bit her lip again, her face resigned. "At least Karl—"

"You don't know what you're asking."

"I can't help it. I saved him once—I won't let anything happen to him. I thought it all died with Karl. Do I have to buy you too? Or have you already had everything you want?"

"Get in the car."

They drove up the dirt canyon road in silence, Emma looking out the side window, her face blotchy but dry. Connolly stared at the road, as if he could quiet the jumble in him with a grip on the wheel.

"You can have the marriage annulled."

"Yes," she said absently.

"How did Karl find him?"

351

"No more. Please."

"How?"

"He's here."

Connolly almost stopped the car in surprise. "Here? On the Hill?"

"No. In the States. For years. Karl used to keep tabs on aliens who were friendly to the comrades. It was his specialty, remember?"

"Where is he?"

"I don't know. New York. He was, anyway. Karl lost track of him when he left Washington and all his precious files there. It shouldn't be hard if you want to find him."

"Do you?"

"No."

"Did Karl tell him?"

"Karl didn't know him. He was just a name in a file."

"Does he know where you are?"

"Nobody knows where I am. I'm a post office number. Box 1663, Santa Fe. New name. New person." She trembled again. "I got clean away, remember? A lovely new life."

They were approaching the turnoff road for the west gate. "Let me off here. I'll walk in."

He looked at her. "Walk?"

"Yes, walk. Why not? I'm a great hiker, didn't you know? I could do with a walk now. Besides, there's my reputation to consider." He stopped the car. "Well," she said, not wanting to get out yet, "I'll see you."

"Emma, what you said before, about his not blackmailing you. There must have been someone else. There's the money."

She smiled sadly. "You never give up. What are you suggesting? That I gave him the idea? Is that my fault too? Once he saw how easy it was with me, he went on to better things? Maybe he did. You find out, Michael. I don't care." She opened the door, half getting out. "Will you put us in your report too?" When he opened his mouth, she put her fingers to his lips, barely touching them. "No, don't say anything. I don't want to hear it—it's all in your face. Do what you have to do. I'll just get out here." She kept her hand on his face, a Braille touch, keeping him still. "I seem to have made a mess of things, haven't I? You always want things to make sense. Sometimes they make sense and it's still a mess." She ran her fingers across his mouth as if she were kissing him. "It was nice for a while, though. Before it was such a mess. No, don't say anything." She dropped her hand and got out of the car, then leaned through the window. "You'd better go on first. It'll look better."

He sat there for a minute, not knowing what to say, and then it was too late. She had moved off to the side, starting to walk, and when he put the car in gear and saw her in the rearview mirror she was looking somewhere else.

He drove back to the office, random phrases darting through his mind so quickly he could not assemble them. They bounced off each other, uncontrollable, until all they lived for was their speed. Fission. He knew in some part of him that he had no reason to feel angry or betrayed or shamed at his own inability to know what to do, how he ought to feel, but the feelings bounced off each other too, like glandular surges that swept through his blood, drowning thought. He saw her with Karl, in some motel room like theirs, sweaty and half lit. She had felt sorry for him. And Karl? What had he felt? Surprise at his good luck? Or did he worry, wondering what it all meant? But he had kept quiet, cared enough to lie for her. Now she wanted him to lie, another Karl. For Daniel. Because she cared enough to protect him but not enough to be faithful.

But who was he to accuse her of that? He'd never even thought about Daniel before, betraying him again and again, because for them it had been different, as natural and carefree as a hike through the canyon. I didn't know you then. But what if she had? Would it have been any different? It always comes back to that. She had walked in through the gate. I thought it died with him. But no, this was crazy. You've become as mad as the rest of them. And suddenly he felt for the first time what it had been like for Karl, this endless noisy suspicion ricocheting so loudly inside him that he couldn't hear anything else. And when it stopped— and now it did—his mind blank—absolutely nothing. She disappeared in the rearview mirror. He felt as empty as Karl's room.

When he parked and walked through the

Tech Area fence, his mind was still cloudy and preoccupied, but it was Weber who didn't see him, bumping so hard into his shoulder that he was stopped in midflight.

"Ouf. *Pardon, pardon,*" he said in the all-purpose French used in crowds at railway terminals. He looked up at Connolly dimly through his glasses, trying to focus his memory. "Ah, Mr. Connolly. The music. Yes, I'm so sorry. I'm late again, you see."

"No, my fault. I was just thinking."

Weber smiled. "Thinking," he said, savoring the word. "For us now it's only the work. So close." He fluttered his hand in the air. "Every day a new deadline. But no matter. We're almost there." The *w* was a *v*.

"So I hear."

Weber looked up at him sharply, a pinprick of alarm, then put it aside, too absorbed to pursue it. "We all work too hard—even thinking. You look like Robert. All the troubles of the world. No time even for music. Do you play?"

Connolly smiled to himself. "No, but I like to listen."

"Good, good, come tomorrow. A small gathering. So many at Trinity now, of course."

Before Connolly could answer, Weber started off, his mind busy again with formulas. Connolly watched him go, bustling toward the gate, encased in his private bubble. He seemed the very soul of the Hill, all distraction and yeast cakes and the determined icepick at the dance.

355

But the sudden jolt to Connolly's shoulder had awakened him, like someone shaking him to get up for work. He knew that later he would sink back into his private obsession, the terrible feeling of having broken something he didn't know how to fix. But what did any of it have to do with the case? At least there was still that. He thought of Weber peering up, trying to place him. Karl had known Emma right away. All she had had to do was walk into the office.

When he got to his desk, however, he simply sat there staring, not sure where to begin.

"What's wrong?" Mills said.

"Nothing. Why?"

"I don't know. You look funny. Everything all right?"

"As rain," he said absently, then, aware of Mills watching him, picked up the phone to call Holliday.

"Howdy," Doc said when he got on. "I was just about to call you."

"Let me ask you something," Connolly said briskly. "You examined the body."

"Well, I saw it—"

"Could a woman have done it?"

"Not unless she was one hell of a strong woman. He was hit more than once, you know. Kicked too. Not many women'd do that. At least, I hope not. What's on your mind?"

"Nothing. Never mind. Just a little crazy, I guess."

"It's the altitude. You ought to watch that.

356

They say half the people up there are crazy."

Connolly said nothing, running his finger along the edge of the phone, his mind elsewhere.

"Want to know why I was going to call?" Doc said finally.

"I'm sorry. Yes. Sure."

"You're going to like this. Cheer you right up. You know those bars you told me to look into, the ones we haven't got? Turns out you were right. We got one."

Connolly said nothing but looked up from the phone, puzzled.

"Now I suppose I got to keep my eye on it. Wish I could say I was better off knowing about it, but I doubt it."

"I don't understand."

"I'm getting to it. Turns out there was a little loose talk there and one of my boys heard about it. 'Course, everybody was quiet as a mouse before, but now that they've got the guy— well, you know how it is. A few beers and—"

"Doc—"

"All right, all right. Hold on. You going to let me tell this my way? Seems one of the customers was in the park that night. Taking care of a little business. He don't want to talk about that, though. Anyway, point is he saw someone taking old Karl into the bushes. Just like you figured—thought he was drunk. Car pulls up and before you know it the two of them are heading somewhere quiet. Our boy don't think nothing of it. Tell you the truth, sounded like he was annoyed. Didn't want any company around."

"What was he doing there?"

"Said he was taking a leak." Holliday paused. "Yeah, I know, looks like I got to keep an eye on the Alameda now too. All kinds of stuff going on I didn't know about."

"Did he get a look at him?"

"Nope. Said he was tall."

"Tall."

"That's right. Now Ramon, he struck me as on the short side, wouldn't you say? So I asked him about that. But he says tall. 'Course, given what he might have been doing there, maybe anybody'd look tall."

"What else?"

"Nothing else. Next thing he knew was when he heard the car driving away. Like I said, he didn't think nothing of it. And then, when it comes out there's a body found there, well the whole thing just goes right out of his head. You know."

"He didn't see his face?"

"No. Tall, that's it. I asked."

Connolly was quiet. "So what have we got?" he said.

"Not much. He's not even what you'd call a real witness—all he saw was two guys going into the bushes, one of them drunk. Court of law, it wouldn't mean shit. But he saw what he saw. Only reason I got it out of him now is he probably thinks it was Ramon he saw and it's all over anyway. He's the nervous type. But I figured you'd like to know you weren't imagining things. Happened just like you thought."

"Yeah. Thanks, Doc. What about the car?"

In the pause, Connolly felt he could see Doc smiling.

"Oh, I almost forgot that. He did see that. Funny thing, isn't it, he didn't see the guy but he did remember the car."

"Let me guess."

"If you said a Buick, he wouldn't argue with you."

"You still holding him?"

"No, I've got no call to do that. I could charge him with something, but why would I want to go and do that and stir up everybody? He was practically pissing in his pants the way it was. Now what's all this about a woman? You on to something up there?"

"No, nothing. Just thinking out loud. Trying to figure out, you know, how strong—"

"Uh-huh."

"I'll be down in a few days. I'll fill you in."

"What's the matter? Your phone tapped?"

Suddenly he was Karl again. His hand instinctively recoiled from the black telephone, as if Doc's words had carried their own shock. Of course. Oppenheimer's phone. His. Naturally they'd do that. He looked over at Mills, blandly signing forms, paying no attention. He tried to remember everything he'd just said, imagining it typed up, one carbon for the files. Was there a phrase that drew the eye, that would have to be passed along? His mind was busy again.

"Mike?" Doc said.

But don't let them know that you know.

359

"That click you hear is me hanging up, Doc," he said easily. "I have to go. I'll call you. And thanks."

Then, the receiver back in its cradle, he looked at it again. They had every right to know. That's what they were all doing here. Karl, at least, had known that, had stayed alert.

After a while he felt Mills looking at him.

"Now what?" Mills said.

"Nothing. I've been thinking. You know those security files?" Karl had noticed her right away.

"Intimately."

"The vetting and the updates. I want to see everybody who arrived on the Hill—when was the first two hundred bucks? October? Let's say from September on. Just the new arrivals. Foreigners. How many do you think there are?"

Mills shrugged. "Some. The Tube Alloys group came through Canada about then. They'd all be foreign. But not Americans?"

"If they were naturalized. First I want the ones who were vetted abroad."

Mills raised his eyebrows. "What's up?"

"We're looking for any left-wing history— groups, contributions, Popular Front, any of it."

"Communists?"

"Not officially. What was it Karl said to you? It's what's not there. I think that's what Karl knew. A Communist who wasn't there."

Mills looked at him for a minute. "What makes you think so?"

"A hunch."

"A hunch."

"That's right," Connolly said, looking at him directly.

"Okay. I'll get started on the arrival list. You want to look at all these yourself?" It was another question.

"Both of us," Connolly said. "But no one else. No reports."

Mills stood in front of the desk, raising his palms in a kind of pleading. "It's my job, Mike."

Connolly looked up at him, just a soldier following orders, but what he heard was himself, talking to Emma, mad as the rest of them, and then the noise in his head began to clear and he felt ashamed. "Trust me a little," he said, and now the voice was hers.

He went out to Ashley Pond, shrunken now in the drought, and walked around its necklace of dried mud. The late afternoon sun burned against the windows of Gamma Building, making rows of little fires. The Hill, as always, was in motion, trucks grinding past scientists rushing to meetings and secretaries in wobbly heels heading to the PX on their break. It all went on behind him, around him, while he stood apart on this margin of water. Karl hadn't said anything. Why? Out of some improbable decency? No. Maybe he thought it wasn't really over, that he could always return when his new interest had been satisfied. Or maybe he thought there was nothing to tell, just another European story they would never understand. Questions would have to be asked, about him too, already compromised. What good would it do? He lived to protect himself, now in a world of tapped phones and secret reports and files that told everything about the past except what it meant. You had to be careful. Loyalty was a bargaining chip—you had to hoard it until you could play it to advantage. And meanwhile the Hill would go on around him too, indifferent, busy with itself. Connolly saw him standing by the same pond, outside of things, looking for a way in. Why would they trust him? The Germans hadn't, the Russians hadn't. Would his new masters be any different? Unless he had something really important to offer, something more than a sloppy vetting. So he waited.

If it was true. Connolly picked up a small rock, threw it into the pond, and watched the water rearrange itself, like thoughts. He thought of Emma at the memorial service, cool-ly walking out on Daniel's arm; saw her at Fuller Lodge, her back to him, laughing. Maybe everything was a performance, the practiced story. But he had made her do that—it had all been for him, hadn't it? He had made her lie and now he distrusted the lie. He started back toward the dormitory, looking down at the ground as he walked. Maybe Karl hadn't been sure either, waiting for something more.

He only had her word for it. What did Karl really think? He thought he was beginning to know him, but Karl didn't exist. He could only imagine him.

The dormitory was quiet, even the Ping-Pong table empty, and Connolly went straight to his room. He sat in the chair by the window with Karl's file, staring at the picture that would somehow make him real. Dark, intelligent eyes. Had he trusted her? But Karl didn't trust anyone. Goblins everywhere. He came to the right place for it. Maybe he hadn't felt like an outsider at all; maybe he had liked it, his files and his private suspicions and the adrenaline thrill of a hunt. Maybe he'd felt at home. He knew how to live here, what he was expected to do. But what did he have for it? A car, some money just in case, and now the secret of his own death. Half the people up there are crazy.

Connolly stared at the room and realized with a shock that it looked exactly the way it had on his first night. Did he live here? A shaving kit on the washbasin, a bag in the closet, a book. Otherwise, the same. Neat. Empty. He hadn't expected to stay. But the room in Washington was no different. Temporary until the war was over. He was living in other people's stories. For how long? Then the war would be over and he would be back in his own, where nothing would happen. Unless it already had. He felt a panic so intense that it swept over him like a kind of nausea. If he sat back in the chair now he would disappear into Karl's room, waiting to be sure.

He threw the folder on the floor and got up, standing so quickly that his head felt dizzy. When he hurried out of the building, blinking at the sun, his head was still light, but he felt his body coming back, filling up again. There was room now for everything—the insubstantial buildings, the clotheslines flapping white, the smell of gasoline. When he reached her building he almost laughed, remembering that other time, turning left, turning right, the neighbor with the coffee. This time he knocked without hesitation, loudly, so that when she opened the door she pushed against it as if he were a gust of wind. He looked at her face, the details of it, his own story.

"What do you want?" she said, still holding the door.

"I'm in love with you."

"Oh," she said, a sound, not a word, a reflexive whimper. Her body went soft, exhaling, shoulders easing as her eyes filled. The door seemed to open by itself, pushed by the same wind, and he was inside. For a minute they just looked, her eyes fixed on him, moist with relief but not crying, moving with his, alive with conversation. "You came back," she said.

"I'm in love with you," he said again.

She put her hands to the sides of his face and brought him down to kiss her, short drinking kisses, like gulps.

"Yes," she said into his cheek.

"Do you know what that means?"

"No. Tell me." Smiling now, teasing him.

Then she kissed him again. "No, don't. So much talking. Don't say anything else."

"I don't care about the rest. I can't lose you."

"No," she said, her head back, shaking it happily. "No. You can't. Tell me again."

"Come to bed."

And this time, she took his hand and led him into the other room.

12

The drought had brought summer early and with it one of the electrical storms that usually waited for July. Outside Weber's house, Connolly could see the giant dark anvil of a thunderhead rolling toward the mesa, the sky crackling with branches of lightning that shot through the air like X-rays, leaving an inverted image on the eye. Inside, an Indian maid was refilling the coffee urn, edging her way through the crowded living room. Despite the absentees down at the test site, the room was full, the low thunder outside barely audible over the noise of the party voices. Nothing seemed to have changed. Kitty Oppenheimer was again curled up in a corner of the sofa, while Johanna Weber scurried about, playing her hostess memory trick. The air was close, warm with bodies, and Connolly, bored and beginning to sweat, had been there only a few minutes before he began planning an escape. Weber came to his rescue, asking him to fetch Eisler from his lab.

"He's always forgetful, Friedrich. But it's the Beethoven. Without him, we can't—"

The music was outside, deep cello moans of thunder under the viola staccato of the moving clouds. For once there was no dust; even the earth was holding its breath. Eisler's lab was near the edge of the plateau, not far from X Building, where the cyclotron was, and the rain began before Connolly could reach it, so that he sprinted the last few yards. Now the noise was everywhere, and when the wind banged the door behind him it was lost in a crack of thunder. The hallways brightened for a minute with lightning, and Connolly expected the dim of a power surge, but the overhead lights were steady. When he opened the lab door and stepped in, the sounds were hidden by more thunder, so that Eisler was unaware of his coming. He was about to call out but instead stood for a moment watching, afraid to interrupt.

Eisler was bending over a table in front of a blackboard, stacking small plum-colored metal cubes in a surrounding well of what looked like soft aluminum blocks. Critical assemblies. His body was tense, his long fingers barely moving with slow precision. In the noise of the storm he seemed to stand in his own vacuum, oblivious to anything beyond the table. Connolly watched as he tentatively lowered his right hand, dropping the metal a fraction, then held it still to listen for the increased clicking sound, his whole frame rigid with concentration. So this is what it was like, this awful attention, tickling the dragon's tail. Then he straightened for a minute, staring ahead at the blackboard as if it were a mirror, and took a deep breath. When he bent over again his movements were fluid, no longer hesitant, and Connolly watched, fascinated, as he lowered another cube in a steady, deliberate push.

Suddenly the clicking erupted and a blue light flashed in the room, some terrible new lightning, and Connolly gasped. Eisler whirled around, seeing him for the first time, then swept his arm across the pile of blocks, knocking them over to the floor with a crash. Connolly instinctively froze. The blue light and the frantic clicking noise stopped. For a moment they held their positions, Connolly listening to his own ragged breath, Eisler looking at him in anguish. When Connolly moved, Eisler held his hand up in warning.

"Please stay where you are," he said calmly. "You've been exposed." Then slowly, with the inevitable movements of a dream, he went over to the blackboard. "I'll be with you in a minute, Mr. Connolly," he said distantly, absorbed. "How many meters would you say? Ten?" The blocks lay scattered at his feet, now just harmless metal. He picked up a piece of chalk and quickly sketched an outline of the room, like one of Connolly's maps, then began to fill the space to its side with the numbers and signs of a formula. Connolly stood trembling, watching him move his chalk across the board, methodical as a madman.

"What are you doing?" he said finally, his

voice hoarse, scraped by shallow breathing.

"The effect of the radiation," Eisler said, his back still to him. "It can't have been more than two or three seconds. That's something. But it's the distance that matters. It's good you stopped where you are. You have good manners, Mr. Connolly," he said dispassionately, as if it were no more than another factor to compute. "Not to walk in. They may have saved your life."

"You did," Connolly said, shaking involuntarily.

Eisler turned to face him. "Unless I have taken it." He paused. "We will have to do some tests." Then, sensing Connolly's shock, "I think you will be all right. It was a very small exposure."

"But what happened? Was that a chain reaction?"

"Oh yes." Eisler came away from the board, his shoulders drooping. "I am so very sorry, Mr. Connolly. I didn't know—"

"But what—what should I do?" Connolly said, his voice still urgent and unsteady.

"Do? There's nothing to do." Eisler looked at him, then moved over to the table. "We must go to the infirmary. But first, you will permit me? One note."

Connolly watched, hypnotized, as Eisler wrote on a sheet of paper. So fast, a simple flash. What if he died? Radiation poisoning was a grisly, painful death. Everyone knew that. But nobody knew anything. Minutes ago he had been hurrying through the rain. Just a flash, like a bullet in combat. Here, as far away from the war as anyone could get.

"May I ask," Eisler said, "why you came here?"

"Weber sent me. To remind you. The Beethoven."

"Ah, the Beethoven," he said wistfully. "He will have to wait, I'm afraid. We must get you to a doctor. Right now." As he moved forward, Connolly involuntarily stepped back. "No, don't worry, it's not contagious. I am not myself radioactive. It doesn't work that way."

Connolly flushed. "Sorry." And then, embarrassed that it had not occurred to him before, "But what about you? Are you all right?"

Eisler shook his head gravely, but his voice had the tone of a wry smile. "No, Mr. Connolly, for me it's fatal. It's in the numbers, you see," he said, pointing to the board. "The numbers don't lie."

They lay side by side on the small infirmary examination tables as nurses drew blood samples and the doctor ran tests that, incongruously, reminded him of an annual physical.

"Is there anything wrong with me?" Connolly said. "I don't feel anything."

"We'll just keep you overnight to be sure," the doctor said. Then, to Eisler, "How long did you say he was exposed?"

"A second. Two. Three. It was not significant. There have been worse cases," Eisler
replied, but he was looking at Connolly, reassuring him. "They don't know, you see," he
said gently. "They put you under observation,
but what can they observe? So now we are to
be roommates."

"Just for the night," the doctor said. "Just to
be sure." But he meant Connolly. The questions,
the light reassurances, were directed to him. Eisler,
lying quietly in his hospital smock, would not
be expected to leave. He was dying.

Connolly knew it when Oppenheimer arrived.
Eisler had busied himself sending apologies
to Weber, politely teasing the doctor, making
small jokes to Connolly about the makeshift
hospital, so that it all seemed no more unpleasant
than an interrupted seminar. Then Oppenheimer came into the room, his porkpie hat
dripping with rain, and Connolly saw his pale
face, the bright, quick eyes for once still and afraid.

"Robert," Eisler said softly.

Oppenheimer looked at him, a silent
exchange, then took off his hat.

"I came as soon as I heard," he said, his eyes
never leaving Eisler.

"I'm sorry, Robert."

"Friedrich." He came over and took Eisler's
hand. The gesture surprised Connolly. It was
something new in Oppenheimer. He had seen
frustration, even a kind of haunted wisdom.
He'd never seen simple affection. "We'll have
you moved to Albuquerque," Oppenheimer
said, falling back on authority.

Eisler smiled. "Albuquerque? And leave the project? What could they do in Albuquerque? Here is fine. I'll have it all to myself. Mr. Connolly here will be leaving tomorrow—he's quite all right."

Oppenheimer took him in for the first time. "What the devil were you doing there?" he said quickly, and it occurred to Connolly that it might have been his fault, the interruption.

"Robert, Robert," Eisler said soothingly. "You blame the messenger. It was nothing to do with him. An accident. Stupid. My own stupidity."

"Are you all right?" Oppenheimer said to Connolly, an apology.

Connolly nodded. "I guess so."

"How did it happen?" He turned back to Eisler.

"The dragon. It went critical. You can see the notes."

"I told you—"

"Yes, yes, a thousand times."

"How long was the exposure?"

"Long enough."

"My God, Friedrich." Oppenheimer took his hand again, disconcerted, and Connolly felt the impulse to turn away, his face to the wall.

"It's a risk, Robert, that's all. You don't take risks? Every day? How else can we go forward?"

"It was foolish."

"Perhaps. But now there's much to be done. We have the moment now. We need to calculate—"

But Oppenheimer had got up and was nervously lighting a cigarette, glancing toward the open door.

"Robert, a hospital—"

"It's my hospital," Oppenheimer snapped, drawing some smoke. He turned back. "It's over, Friedrich," he said quietly. "I can't allow it."

"Allow? I'm not dead. The effects aren't immediate, you know. There will be a week. Maybe two. I can still—"

"I'm asking you to stay here. Or Albuquerque."

Eisler looked up at him to protest, then, seeing his face, settled back on his pillow. "Under observation."

"Yes," Oppenheimer said reluctantly, "under observation."

Eisler was quiet for a minute. "So I am to be the guinea pig."

"Friedrich—"

"No. Of course you are right. I myself should have thought of this. Each day we observe and then, in the end, we go a little forward. But you will allow me to help organize it, the experiment?"

"Friedrich."

"No, no, please. We are not sentimentalists. It's important to know. We can observe the elements break down—how the body reacts."

Oppenheimer walked over to the sink and doused his cigarette under the faucet. "I'm not asking you to—"

"No, not you. I volunteer. It's my idea. My wish. For the project." Eisler's voice was clear, eager. "It seems fair it should be me."

Connolly looked over at him, puzzled, but there seemed no irony in his voice. He was back at the blackboard, going about his business, getting ready to keep the chart on his own death.

Oppenheimer turned away from the sink, and Connolly saw that his eyes were moist. "Is there anything I can get for you?"

Eisler thought for a minute. "You have morphine? For later? I'll need that, I think. I'm a coward when it comes to that. And there's nothing to learn then. Just the pain."

"Of course," Oppenheimer said, almost a whisper.

"Nothing to learn," Eisler repeated.

The nurse drew a screen between them at night, white cotton stretched on a wheeled frame, but Connolly couldn't sleep. He had never been in a hospital before and it unnerved him—the constant light in the hall, the discreet sound of rubber soles in the corridor, even, once, the faint smell of night-shift coffee. But Eisler was quiet behind his screen, so Connolly was forced to lie still as well, listening to occasional bursts of rain on the asphalt shingles of the roof. He would drift into a kind of half-sleep, then find himself peering at the shadows on the ceiling, his mind moving from one to the other, making pictures, until he no longer knew when he was awake.

He saw Eisler bending over the lab table, then

Emma biting her bottom lip, then, oddly, his friend Lenny Keazer, who had been killed in New Guinea. Shot down. Connolly wondered whether he'd seen anything more than a flash before the plane tipped. He had never imagined dying before. Now he saw that it was being nothing. And everything else just went on. Lenny didn't know whether they'd won or— But what was the point? It wouldn't matter if you weren't there. Karl found his secret and then it didn't matter. And Eisler, who'd said his war was over. Then Connolly was back on his street in Washington, home that afternoon, with the bay window of the little room open to the spring air. Magnolia trees. And he leaned out to see the brown army car move slowly down the street, looking for house numbers. Was anyone else looking out, holding a crack open in the curtains? A soldier got out across the street, carrying an envelope, and walked up the steps to the house, and the next thing Connolly heard was a scream, a long wail that tore the air. A sound from the ancients, a lamentation. He watched the soldier get back in the car and drive away. Then a truck drove down the street, the paper boy on his rounds, another car, and everything went on. That had been the afternoon he thought he had seen the war, the brown car going down one street after another. It would be worth anything to end that. A quick flash and it would stop, the Japanese, finally, startled out of their mad reverie. A hundred to save a thousand. A new kind of mathematics. Did Oppenheimer think of it that way?

The rain woke him, a little spurt of gunfire, and he heard Eisler breathing. The fancies of the night. The ceiling was dark, like the blackboard, and he filled it with chalk marks. So many minutes, so many meters. Eisler had saved his life, then calmly gone about his business. Connolly had been the surprise. He closed his eyes, looking at the lab again, the steady hand on the cube, the cool dispassion of science. He watched Eisler bend over, carefully inching the metal down, and suddenly he knew what was bothering him, all this fitful dreaming. There hadn't been any accident. He had been the accident, quickly corrected. The cube had been deliberate. It had done just what Eisler had wanted it to do. Not an accident. He heard him tell Oppenheimer, an easy lie. He wanted to be nothing.

Connolly turned toward the screen, his whole body awake now, and listened. The breathing was light, barely audible, not the heavy patterned rhythm of sleep.

"Professor Eisler," he said quietly.

"Mr. Connolly?" Eisler's voice was alert, politely surprised.

"When you said before that it was fair it was you, what did you mean?"

Eisler did not answer right away. When he did, his tone was interested, as if the phrase intrigued him. "Did I say that? I don't remember. You must have—what is the sound equivalent of a photographic memory?" The question, disembodied, seemed to rise in the dark. Connolly stared at the ceiling, waiting for it to float over the screen. He said nothing. "I suppose I meant that one of us should feel—what? The effect of what we're doing here. Yes, you might put it that way."

"Won't people be killed outright? Like an ordinary bomb?"

"Most, yes. But there will be others. We just don't know."

"But why you?"

Eisler was quiet for a minute. "I can't say, Mr. Connolly. Some things even I can't answer." He paused. Then, more lightly, "Maybe you will tell me. You must use your Oppenheimer Principle—your leap in the dark. On the map. How is your other problem coming along?"

Connolly felt he was being diverted. His ear searched for nuance in an idle phrase. But clearly Eisler wished to be left alone with his demons. "Not very well," he said, playing along.

"Ah," Eisler said. "But you will get there, I'm sure. The elegant solution. Yes, I think so. But now—you don't mind?—a little sleep."

Connolly said nothing, and after a while the breathing deepened and he fell in with it, so that he wondered whether they'd talked at all or whether he'd been having a conversation with the dark.

The next morning brought a flood of visitors. Weber was there early, fluttering, then a graver Fermi, then Bethe and what seemed to be all of Bathtub Row. They nodded politely to Connolly or ignored him, drawn to Eisler with an embarrassed mix of concern and prurient curiosity, like people at a highway accident. No one stayed long, and no one talked about the radiation. Once in the room, good instincts and duty satisfied, they were at a loss, talking around the incident until they could excuse themselves to work. Only Teller asked for details, precise and brisk, a consulting resident brought in for a second opinion. By the time Emma arrived, Connolly was dressed, waiting to be released. She looked at him in surprise, expecting to find him in bed, and her eyes filled with relief. She smiled at him, a broad, involuntary grin, then caught herself and turned to Eisler, the ostensible point of the visit.

"You too, Mrs. Pawlowski," Eisler said. "Has everyone heard?"

"News travels fast," she said.

"Bad news."

"Well, I don't think Johanna Weber makes the distinction."

Eisler laughed out loud. Connolly realized it was the first time he'd ever heard Eisler laugh, and for a second he was filled with an odd embarrassed pride that it was Emma who could make the joke. It flustered her, however, and she said apologetically, "How are you feeling?"

"No, don't be somber," Eisler said gently. "Everyone here plays the nurse. Tell me the gossip. What else does Frau Weber say?"

"She's baking you a cake."

"Excellent," Eisler said, smiling, and Connolly thought again how little he knew anyone. Last night he had spoken to a dead man, and now he saw the eyes were alive and playful, taking delight in a young woman. Had he been like this at Göttingen with Oppenheimer, a world ago?

They talked, making an awkward joke about angel food, but it was Connolly she had come to see and her eyes kept moving away, sliding over to where he sat on his bed, the night screen now gone. Eisler, courtly in his smock, seemed not to notice, but Mills caught it immediately. He stood in the doorway, looking at them like three points of a triangle, and Connolly could see him putting it together, a theorem proof. He raised an eyebrow at Connolly as he walked in.

"Lieutenant Mills," Eisler said. "At last, a visitor for Mr. Connolly. Or have you come to arrest me?"

"Arrest?" Mills said.

Eisler leaned forward conspiratorially to Emma. "My parking tickets. We have to give them to him and then he scolds us. What do you do with them?" he said to Mills. "Do you make the apologies?" Then, again to Emma, "But I can't help it. If the space is straight, I can do it, but to back up for those little slots? It's too difficult. My driving—" He waved his hand.

Mills smiled, a little surprised by the party atmosphere. "Parking's the least of it," he said to Emma, joining in. "He's a menace behind the wheel."

"Not only there, it seems," Eisler said smoothly, indicating his presence in the bed.

No one knew what to say. Connolly felt the air go out of the room. In the awkward silence, Mills turned to him. "You look all right," he said.

"I'm just waiting for my walking papers."

Eisler, aware that the atmosphere had changed, now looked moodily down at the bed.

"I'd better be going," Emma said, getting up. She went over to Eisler and put her hand on his arm. "You'll let me know if there's anything I can do for you."

He patted her hand. "No, nothing. Mr. Connolly here will get my few things," he said, a question to Connolly, who nodded. "It's absurd. I'm still all right, but now I'm a prisoner here. My jail," he said, with a nod to the room.

"Just walk out," Emma said, sympathetic. "They can't make you stay."

"But where will I go? No, this suits me."

"C'mon, Mike," Mills said, fidgeting, "let's go fix you up with the doc."

"Mr. Connolly," Eisler said as Emma and Mills headed for the door. "You don't mind? A few things?"

"No, of course not."

"Some clothes. I don't want to be in bed. I'm not an invalid. Not so soon."

"Do you have the key?"

"The key?" Eisler smiled. "It's not locked. We never lock things at the project. There's nothing to steal."

"Anything else? Books?"

"You pick. Do you know German? No. Well, pick anything. And—" He looked up to see if the others had gone.

"Yes?"

"If you wouldn't mind, a Bible, please." He smiled. "No, not for the angels. I'm a scientist, you know. But I like the stories. So simple. An eye for an eye. Wonderful stories."

"I'll get one."

"Of course, the angels," Eisler said wryly. "Nothing is proven, you know. Not yet."

Outside, the three of them walked together for a while. Then Mills, with a pointed glance at Connolly, spun off to head for the office.

"I'm just going to get cleaned up," Connolly said. "I'll be over in a bit."

"Take your time. I'll cover," he said, almost winking. "I'm good at that." He tipped his head, a little bow, to Emma.

"He knows," Connolly said, watching him walk off.

"I don't care. I had to come."

Connolly smiled. "The reports of my death were greatly exaggerated."

"It's not funny. I was out of my mind with worry. What if—"

"It didn't. I'm all right." He put his hand on her arm, facing her.

"No, not here."

"I thought you didn't care."

"But not like this, not in the open. Oh, I don't know what I want anymore. More time, I guess. Until I know what to do," she said, almost to herself. "But you're all right, that's the main thing. Now I feel silly. What must Eisler have thought? Charging over there. I hardly know him well enough for that."

"I don't think he noticed. He has other things on his mind."

"Poor man," she said. "He's the nicest of the lot, too. It's not fair. All your life and then one slip—"

"It wasn't an accident."

"What?" she said, stopping.

"It wasn't an accident."

She stared at him for a minute. "You mean he tried to kill himself?"

"He did kill himself. He's just waiting it out."

She shivered. "That's an awful thing to say. How do you know?"

"I was there."

"But why?"

He shrugged and continued walking. "I don't know. I don't know if he knows. It's all mixed up in his mind. Something about the gadget. He feels guilty about that. I think he sees this as a kind of penance. I don't know— is there ever a good reason? Can there be?"

"That's insane."

"Maybe. Anyway, it's his life. I doubt we'll ever know."

"Funny your saying that. You always want to know everything," she said, not looking at him.

"Not this time."

They had reached the turnoff for Connolly's building. Emma stared down at the drying mud in the road. "I wish you hadn't told me. It's so—unhappy. All alone like that. Oh, Michael," she said, looking up, "don't let's— Why shouldn't we be happy? When I heard this morning—"

"Are you happy now?" he said, taking her arm again.

She nodded.

"All right."

"And miserable. Happy. Miserable. Scared. Everything."

"All that?"

"Don't tease. Anyway, it's your fault."

"What do you want me to do?"

"Nothing. Just come tonight, that's all," she said, looking at him.

"That'll make it better?"

"No. But come anyway." Then, in broad daylight, she took his hand and put it against her face for a second before she walked off.

He showered and changed and headed for Eisler's apartment. The office, Mills's smug discretion, could wait. Eisler lived in one of the Sundt units, a modest one-bedroom that was nevertheless several steps up from Connolly's spartan room. There was a fireplace, with a Morris chair and a floor lamp to one side and Indian carpets scattered over the hardwood floor. It was clean without being really tidy—old coffee cups still in the sink, a tie flung over the edge of the couch. There were books everywhere, a pipe near the chair, another on the nightstand, and rows of shelves lining the wall, full of German books, some bound in leather, others with the yellowing paper of European books whose edges you sliced as you read. Connolly ran his finger along the shelves, recognizing a few names. Which would you take to a desert island? Goethe? Mann? He took out a title, then stopped, sliding it back. It was too long. There would never be enough time to finish it.

He went into the bedroom to get the clothes. The bed was made but lumpy. Next to it was the photograph of a young woman, her hair bobbed—presumably his wife. A girl. What had he said about how she died? You just turned down the wrong street, that's all it took.

He was in the bathroom, filling the old leather shaving kit, when he heard the door open. He looked up into the mirror, waiting for someone to appear, but the steps went to the kitchen. He heard water running. He stepped out of the bedroom and peered around the corner, surprising Johanna Weber. She was busy at the sink, washing the cups, and she jumped when she saw him. "Oh," she said, grabbing the saucers with two hands before they could rattle. "Mr. Connolly."

"I'm sorry, I didn't hear you come in. I was just getting a few things."

"You? Oh, yes, you were with him, weren't you? Terrible." But she was busy again, putting the cups on the drying rack, wiping her hands. "Such mess. A bachelor. Always the same. You found the satchel?"

He held up his palms, a helpless gesture.

"Under the bed," she said, smiling. "Here, I'll show you. You sit, and let me pack. A man can't do it. Look at this." She picked up the tie. "Clothes everywhere."

In the bedroom, she scurried around, opening drawers, rolling socks, talking to herself as she worked, drawing the air into her circle of activity like a whirl of dust. She picked up the photograph by the bed and held it for a minute before she put it in the satchel.

"His wife?" Connolly said.

She nodded. "He never forgot her. All these years. Such a long time." She shook her head and Connolly saw her at one of her parties, a frustrated matchmaker. Or had she been in love with him herself, checked by a memory? Nobody knew anything.

He retreated to the living room and ran

his eye again along the shelves. You could tell a man by his books, but the language made these meaningless. There was no visible order. All Connolly could tell was that he'd never left Germany. He thought of Karl's modest shelf, all new, the dictionary, the Westerns. But these had the depth of a culture remembered. He bent down, searching the lower shelf for a Bible. Heine. *Das Leben von Beethoven. Principia Mathematica. Historic Santa Fe.* His eye paused, intrigued by the English. He took out the book, with a glossy photograph of the cathedral on the cover, and flipped through the pages. One of the corners had been turned down and the book opened to it, a black-and-white picture of San Isidro. His heart stopped. No. The picture seemed to blur, as if Connolly had moved it out of focus, and when he stood up it swam back again. A paragraph of history, the reredos dates marked in bold-face, the church with its belltower, the smooth adobe walls, the alley parking lot to the side. No. The corner turned down, bent. To remind him? No, he would never violate a book that way. Someone else had marked the page, a message. Why hadn't he turned it back? But who would look?

Connolly stared at the book, his face growing warm. This wasn't what he'd wanted to find. Just a Bible. Why hadn't Eisler thrown it away? But he never threw books away. Look at the room. The parking lot was easy, no problem there, everything straight. Had he gone into the church at all? What had they said to each other? Connolly drew in a breath, still staring at the picture. He heard the voices in his head, crossword clues falling into place, until they came to a blue flash. An eye for an eye. But not for the gadget. Something else.

"Mr. Connolly?" He looked up. "Is something wrong? I've been calling you."

"No, nothing." He stood there, startled, holding the book in front of him.

"Are you sure? You look—"

"I'm sorry. I was thinking."

She clicked her tongue. "Just like Hans. Once he puts his head in a book—"

She glanced toward it, and for a second Connolly wanted to snap it shut, before anyone else could know. He looked down. It was absurd. A tourist guide. There could be any number of explanations. But he knew there wouldn't be. Eisler. But how? The head had been smashed in.

"You were reading?" Frau Weber said, drawing him back.

"No, just looking for something to take him. I'm afraid I don't know German."

She smiled. "I'll find something for him. I know what he likes. Go to work now—I'll take the valise. You've been very kind."

"Isn't it heavy?"

"This? A feather. Wet laundry is heavy. Don't worry, I'll take care of everything."

He started to turn away, the book still in his hand, and she looked at him strangely, as if he were stealing.

"I thought I might borrow this," he said, closing it. "I don't think Professor Eisler would mind. It's just what I've been looking for."

"Sightseeing?" Mills said when he saw the book in Connolly's hand.

"You still have those bank files?"

"Boy, you never stop, do you? Who's the suspect this time?"

"Let me see Eisler's."

"Now what? What are you going to do, cuff him in his bed?"

"Do you have the file?"

"No, but I can tell you. It's all up here." He placed a finger by his temple. "There's nothing in it."

"But he opened one?"

Mills nodded, now curious. "When he got here. One deposit, the first month. Nothing after that. Guess he kept it himself."

Karl had recognized Emma right away. "You're sure?"

"Positive."

"Let me see it anyway."

"What's all this about, Mike?" Mills said, but Connolly just looked at him until he backed away from the desk, holding up his hand. "Okay, okay. I'll get it." He went over to rifle through the stack on his desk.

Connolly sat looking at the book. Adobe Press, something local; copyrighted before the war. Glossy paper, but thin, photographs darker than they should be. He took out the

387

Santa Fe directory and when he couldn't find a listing called Holliday instead.

"Ever hear of something called the Adobe Press?"

"Sure. Now what made you think of that?"

"Where are they?"

"Well, 'they' is a he. It's just old Art Perkins. Made that guidebook. I guess that's what you mean. Not bad either. But the tourists just kinda dried up during the war, so he closed the shop. Well, shop. Garage was more like it. What's the interest?"

"Where can you buy them?"

"Anywhere. Art had a nice little business with that. I've got one myself if you need it, but they're still around in the stores."

"He do any mail business?"

"Not now. Art died about a year ago."

"Oh."

"Now you going to tell me what this is all about?"

"In a day or two, Doc. Some things I want to check out first."

Mills had slid the account sheet in front of him, an empty column with one deposit, just as he'd promised.

"Don't forget to call, now," Doc said, hanging up. "The suspense'll kill me."

Connolly pushed the sheet aside and looked at the book. You could buy it anywhere. So Eisler had walked into a store, maybe one of those near the plaza, and bought—no, it was too elaborate. How would he know where to mark? If it was a message, it had to be sent. But not by the Adobe Press.

"Mills, the mail censor's off-site, right?"

"Right. The envelope goes unsealed. They check it out, then seal it and send it on its way so no one out there's the wiser. Or it comes back here if they've got a problem with it."

"What about incoming?"

"That just goes to the post office here. Problem's in the other direction."

"But the top scientists. Somebody must look."

Mills shifted in his chair. "I wouldn't know about that," he said carefully. Again Connolly just stared at him. "Check with Bailey, two doors down," he said finally. "And don't mention my name."

Bailey had no such scruples. He was sitting in front of a pile of unread mail, glad of the interruption. "We don't keep a record," he said. "No point. But what are you looking for?"

He was small and delicate, not quite filling the neatly pressed uniform, and when he took off his glasses he looked no older than fifteen.

"Dr. Eisler."

"That's easy. He doesn't get any. No letters. Nothing."

"Ever?"

"Not since I've been here." He noticed the book in Connolly's hand. "Well, there was that," he said nervously, as if he'd been caught in a lie.

Connolly, unaware that he was still carrying it, held the book up. "You remember this?" he said skeptically.

"Well, he never got anything, so it stuck out."

"Any letter with it?"

"No."

"You're sure?"

"Of course I'm sure," he said, slightly prissy, a craftsman challenged in his work.

"When was this?"

Bailey looked at the book again, then closed his eyes, concentrating. "April," he said, opening them.

"You're wasted here," Connolly said, impressed. "And nothing with it. Just the envelope."

"Right. I figured it was something he sent for."

"What about a return address?"

Again he closed his eyes. Connolly waited.

"No. Nothing."

Connolly sighed. "Okay. Thanks," he said, turning to leave.

"But it was from Santa Fe," Bailey said, eager to help.

"How do you know?"

"The postmark. Santa Fe."

"You remember a postmark?" Connolly said, amazed. The boy nodded. "Christ. You are wasted here."

"No, I enjoy it. It's interesting."

Connolly looked at his open young face, imagining him reading Oppenheimer's correspondence, witnessing history. Another Hill

390

story. But now there wasn't time. "Thanks," he said, "I appreciate it."

When he got back to his desk he lit a cigarette and took out Eisler's security file, leaning back in his chair to read. He wasn't looking for anything specific; the trick was to look at the same information differently, like turning a prism. Wasn't the money enough? Why not, all of a sudden? The book arrived in April, a meeting notice. But Karl had been there too.

"Mike," Mills said, interrupting him. "What's going on?"

"I'm not sure yet. I'm trying to figure it out."

"But you're not going to tell me. Look, if you don't think you can trust me, you should—"

"I trust you," he said, stopping him. "I just don't trust myself. Not yet."

Mills shrugged. "Suit yourself. I'm going to get some air." He headed toward the door. "One thing." Connolly looked up. "Karl liked to work alone too."

When he was gone, Connolly didn't turn back to the file but looked at the wall instead. Karl did like to work alone. Nobody planned to kill him. A snake would attack if surprised. But the meeting was planned, and he was there. Connolly pictured the road down from the mesa. The alley. The car in the box canyon. All the lines were there, waiting to be connected. You just turned down the wrong street, that's all it took.

He didn't notice it was beginning to get

dark, and when Mills came back and flipped on the light, it startled him. He got up without a word and started for the infirmary. Lights had gone on everywhere; the hive still busy. The thin air, as always, carried gasoline fumes and coal smoke, but he was oblivious, his mind still on the blackboard. When he got to the room, he found Eisler dressed, sitting up to read. He looked over the top of his glasses when he saw Connolly standing in the door, holding the guidebook. His eyes moved from the book to Connolly's face and stayed there, calm and bold. For a minute neither of them said a word. Then, gravely, he sighed and slowly took off the glasses.

"Mr. Connolly," he said.

"I've finished my map."

13

Have you ever killed a man, Mr. Connolly? So quick. And then the responsibility, that goes on forever." Eisler paused. "Well, as long as life. Not very long."

The room was dim, the dark shadows broken only by the small reading lamp near his chair. Outside, the nurse was quiet, so that Connolly felt they wre lying side by side again, talking into the night. Eisler was rambling, as if in a fitful sleep, and Connolly let him lead, not knowing where to begin, afraid he would stop. "Have you come to arrest me?" he had said before, and Connolly hadn't known how to answer. Now that he'd got what he wanted, he was dismayed. He'd imagined the scene so many times, his list of questions as orderly as a deposition, and now suddenly he felt powerless. What threat could possibly matter? He would hear what Eisler wanted to tell him, and that gentle voice came out of a depression so profound that each statement seemed a favor, one last tentative offering before it would stop altogether and stay silent. What punishment was left? So Connolly sat in the opposite chair, waiting, afraid to interrupt, as Eisler moved from Karl to Göttingen and back again, randomly stepping between remorse and cool reflection.

"I knew when I saw you at the board," he was saying. "It was a relief. Do you understand that? But I thought I would have time—before you knew."

"How much did you get out about the bomb?" Connolly said, trying to steer the conversation back.

Eisler paused, and for a moment Connolly thought he had lost him. Then he sighed. "Yes, the bomb. That's the important thing, isn't it? Not Karl, not even now. How did you know?"

"You said there was nothing to steal on the Hill. But there was always one thing to steal here."

"Is that how you see it? Stealing?"

"Don't you?"

"Prometheus stole the fire," Eisler said quietly, "but not for himself. Scientific knowledge—do you think that belongs only to you?"

"It does for now. How much did you tell them?"

"I am familiar with all the principles involved in our work here," he said formally. "Surely you already know that."

"And now the Russians know them too."

"My friend," Eisler said, gentle again, "the Russians have known them for some time. These are not secrets. The mechanics, yes, but that is simply a matter of time. They will know them."

"And now they'll know just a little bit sooner."

"Yes. Mr. Connolly, do you expect me to apologize for sharing this knowledge? About Karl—" He hesitated. "That was a great wrong. I accept the guilt. But the fire belongs to everybody. The bomb is only the beginning, you know. All this money—" He swept his hand to indicate the entire mesa. "It took the bomb to get this money. And since America is rich, it can afford to pay. But what we will have here, when we're finished, is something new. Energy. Not just for bombs. Such a thing cannot be owned. Would you keep electricity to yourself? It's not possible, even if it were right."

"The fact remains, it wasn't yours to give. The fact is, you took classified information and passed it on. That's treason."

"So many facts. I came with the Tube Alloys group. Was it treason to work with the English?"

"We're not at war with England."

"My friend, we are not at war with Russia either. Germany is at war with Russia. More than you can know. The real war. America is a factory and she is getting rich. England—" He waved his hand. "England is a dream. The war is Russia and Germany. It has always been. *That* is the great struggle. To the death. And what have you done to help? The second front? That had to wait. Tube Alloys committees for Russia? No, not for that ally. For them, the great secret. Not my knowledge to give? To defeat the Nazis, I would give anything."

Connolly listened to his voice gathering speed, feeling the rhythm of a lecture, and looked at him in fascination: the kind face, the austere ideology. But why answer? The debate was old, and the war was over. He looked away.

"So you have," he said quietly. "The Nazis. And who will give you permission now?"

Eisler's cheek moved in a small tic, as if he'd been struck. "A good pupil, Mr. Connolly. You listen well."

"Not that well. I didn't know you were a Communist."

"You weren't supposed to know."

"But Karl knew. Did you give the same speech at the meetings?"

"Meetings?"

"Where Karl saw you."

Eisler smiled slightly. "What makes you think that?"

"Karl had a good memory. He recognized someone else from the meetings in Berlin. He recognized you too."

"You interest me. I wonder whom he saw."

Connolly didn't answer. "But for once your method has failed you. I never attended meetings. I was in a secret chapter. From the start."

"Then where did you meet Karl?"

"He was a messenger. Just once, but he remembered."

"A messenger? For you?"

"Yes, he did some work for us. A good Communist. He must have been sent to meetings to—well, to observe."

Connolly looked at him in surprise. So Karl had had his secret too. "Karl was a Communist? I thought the Nazis had made a mistake."

"The Nazis rarely made that kind of mistake, Mr. Connolly. I told you, it was always a war between us. That's why many of us had to work in secret. Otherwise, they always knew. A mistake—is that what he told your people?" He seemed almost amused.

"But later, in Russia—"

"Yes, that was unfortunate," Eisler said seriously. "A terrible time. He was foolish to go."

"As a good Communist?"

"As a Jew. Do you think it was only the Germans—" He stopped, his eyes moving away to the past. "The revolution doesn't always move in a straight line. It moves and then there are dark times. It was madness then. Shootings. Thousands of people, maybe more. Friends. People informed on their own friends. Yes. You're surprised I would tell you this?"

"Yet you did all this for them."

"The idea is right. The country is sometimes flawed. Do you not feel this about your own country?"

"You're not Russian."

"The idea lives there now. It doesn't matter where."

"So you want them to have the bomb."

"Don't you? Have you thought what it will mean to be the only one? Do you trust yourself that much?" He paused. "But, I admit, that is in the future. A philosophical point. I was thinking of this war, nothing more."

"The war's over."

"Yes," he said slowly. "So, we were wrong? That's for you to say. My work is over too."

Connolly stood up, annoyed. "Your work," he said heavily. "Murder. That's what we're talking about. My God, how can you live with yourself?"

Eisler looked up at him, not answering.

"Why?" Connolly said, his voice almost plaintive.

"Mr. Connolly," Eisler said, "may I suggest we confine our discussion to what—how, if you prefer. The why is my concern. I make no apologies. I did what was asked of me. I could not do anything else. Not now. I was—useful. I don't think you can know what that means. An obligation. No, even more than that. I would never have refused. But my motives are irrelevant now, so let's speak of something else."

His tone, soft and reasonable, seemed a reproach.

"Why tell me anything at all?" Connolly said.

"Why? Perhaps I want to explain myself. Perhaps I am curious."

"Curious?"

"Yes. To see if the Oppenheimer Principle works. To see what you know." He paused again, gathering his thoughts. "I like you, Mr. Connolly. Such a passion for truth. You want to *know* everything. But to understand? I'm not so sure. They're not the same thing. So this time maybe it's different. I'll make you understand. My last student."

Connolly looked at him, thinking of Emma at Bandelier, then turned to pace in the room, as if he had a pointer in his hand. "So let's start at the beginning, wherever that is. Your wife, I think. She didn't just walk down the street. There was fighting all right, but she was part of it. I assume she was a Communist too?"

Eisler nodded. "That is correct."

"Possibly even before you were," Connolly said, a question, but Eisler didn't answer. "Possibly not. But afterward—you were committed then. You had to carry on the fight, or anyway carry on the memory."

"Mr. Connolly, please. This is psychology, not facts. What is the point? Let us stay with what you know."

"But you want me to understand it. What was she like?"

Eisler grimaced, looking straight ahead. "She was young. She believed. In what? A better world. In me. Everything. Does that sound foolish now? Yes, to me too. But then it seemed perfectly natural to believe in things. I loved her," he said, then paused. "It's too simple, Mr. Connolly, your psychology. She may have been the beginning, yes, but she was not the cause. For that you had to be alive in Germany then, to see the Nazis come. It was bad and then worse and worse. How was it possible that no one stopped them? Did you even know about those things here? What were you, a boy? Can you remember Nuremberg? There must have been newsreels. I remember it very well. The Cathedral of Light. Even the sky was full of them. So much power. They would kill everybody, I knew it even then. And no one to stop them, no one. What would you have done?"

"We've been over this before."

"Yes," Eisler said, stopping.

"So you worked for the Communists. That must have been lucky for them. A prominent scientist."

"I was not so prominent then. But it was useful, yes. I knew many people. Heisenberg. Many."

"So your bosses knew them too. Then you had to get out. And you kept doing the same thing in England."

"In Manchester, yes."

"How did it work there?"

"Mr. Connolly. Do you really expect me to tell you that? I made reports. I met with people, I don't know who."

"And you told them about Tube Alloys."

"Yes, of course. Mr. Connolly, would you

please sit down? You're making me anxious, all this back and forth. You can smoke if you like."

"Sorry." Connolly sat down, feeling reprimanded, and lit a cigarette. "You don't mind?"

"It's Robert's hospital," Eisler said with a small smile.

"Then you came to the Hill early last fall," Connolly continued. "Karl would have known right away. He's probably the one who got your file—he took an interest in that. But there wasn't anything there. It's what isn't there," he said aloud to himself. "And Karl knew. You'd done some work together in the good old days. So he asked you about it—he couldn't resist that—but he kept it to himself. Why, I wonder. Or was Karl still a Communist too? That Russian jail just another story?"

"You are too suspicious. The mirror in a mirror? No, the jail was real. You had only to see his hands. He was never the same after that—certainly not a Communist. He renounced everything. It was not so much—" He stopped, searching. "Not so much what they did to him there, as perhaps the feeling—how can I say it?—that they had renounced *him.*"

"And the pain didn't help. A disillusioning experience all around."

Eisler glanced up at his sarcasm, then looked away again. "Yes, it must have been."

"So you made him think you felt the same way."

"Yes, that was very easily done," he said with a hint of pride. "A matter of the past. You know,

400

Mr. Connolly, when you stop loving a woman you can't imagine what anyone else might see in her."

Connolly was jarred by his tone. In the lamp's small circle he felt, absurdly, that they might be swapping stories around a fire.

"So you'd both seen the light. But nothing in the file—he wouldn't like that. That's the sort of thing that would worry Karl."

"You forget there was nothing in his file either. He could understand not making a point of it here. In a place like this. People are not so understanding—they don't know what it was like there. Would he have kept his job? It would be natural to let the sleeping dog lie. For both of us. I assure you, he was—sympathetic."

"Sympathetic enough to put the bite on you."

Eisler looked at him, puzzled.

"You gave him money, didn't you? What was that for, old times' sake?"

"Oh, I see. You think he threatened to expose me? No, no, it was not like that. Karl was an opportunist, but not a traitor. If he had really thought I was still—active, nothing would have stopped him. Certainly not a little money."

"But you gave him money. Not a little. And he kept your secret. And it wasn't blackmail."

Eisler waved his hand. "You insist on this term. It's not precise. What do you think he said to me? Thirty pieces of silver for my silence? This is a fantasy, Mr. Connolly. Be precise."

"Well, why did you give it to him? Six hundred dollars, wasn't it?"

Eisler looked up, pleased. "Very good. A little more, but that is close. How did you know?"

"What did he say it was for?" Connolly said, ignoring his question.

"He appealed to me. He had the chance to buy members of his family out. There are such cases, you know. How much for a life? And he had very little."

"His family's dead."

"Yes, of course. It was much too late for such arrangements. That was all in the past, when they were letting people out. But that is what he said. I did not contradict. I knew it was— an opportunity for him."

"Did he know you thought that?"

Eisler shrugged. "I can't say. I didn't question him. I was generous. Perhaps he felt our past was a bond between us, that he could approach me this way. Perhaps he enjoyed seeing how far he could go. A game. He could trust me not to say anything. It was very strange. I think, you know, he felt I was the only person he *could* trust."

"Maybe the first time," Connolly said, picking up the story. "But after—it was too easy. He asked for more money and you gave it to him. And then again. Why? He'd be suspicious. So he started following you—where you went. Especially off the Hill. He liked driving around. Were you aware that he was tailing you?"

"No."

"So you never saw him at any of your meetings?"

"There was only one other. He wasn't there."

"How did you set them up?"

"The first had been arranged before I came. The second you know. I already had the date; I would be contacted about the place. The book arrived and I knew."

"And this time Karl *was* there."

"Yes."

"And he saw that you were passing information. There were papers?"

"Yes."

"But he was suspicious before that. He followed you down. You probably didn't see him that time either—he'd be a good tail—but I imagine you drove around Santa Fe for a while, just to be sure. Standard procedure for meetings. Then out to San Isidro. But you wouldn't want to stop there until your man was already in place, you wouldn't want to risk being seen waiting in the alley. So you drove past, and then again, until the car was there, and by that time Karl knew something was going on. How many times did you go around?"

"Is that important?" Eisler said. "A few. It was as you say. You seem to know everything."

"Except who you were meeting."

"I don't know the name. I couldn't help you even if I wanted to."

"And you don't want to."

"No. But it's useless to pursue this. I do not know."

"What if you couldn't make it or had to postpone the meeting? How could you contact him?"

"I couldn't. Another meeting would be arranged."

"How?"

"That I don't know either. That was not my affair. But it's of no importance. I *was* there. And Karl—Karl was there too. Foolish, foolish boy," he said, shaking his head. "It was impossible. We could not allow—" He stopped. "So. He was there. And now I am here. I think I'm a little tired now, if you don't mind. Is there anything else you want to know?"

"Who killed him."

Eisler looked up. "I killed him, Mr. Connolly."

"No, you didn't."

Eisler looked at him quizzically.

"It's a popular murder," Connolly said. "Everybody wants to confess to it. We've got one guy in prison, and I don't believe him either. You bashed Karl's head in, then dumped him in the park and drove on home? I don't think so."

"You do not have any choice in the matter."

"I still want to know. Karl was killed in that alley all right. We have the blood samples to prove it. And you were there—I don't doubt it for a minute. You might even say it was all your fault. You're so eager for blame, fine, take some. But you never killed him. Your contact did that. Right there. Were you shocked? All that blood. What did it sound like when his skull cracked? That's not in your line at all. You must have had a disillusioning experience yourself. Which is why you're here. What I don't know is why you still want to protect him."

Eisler bowed his head, staring at his hands. "We were alone, Karl and I," he said quietly. "The other was only a messenger—already gone."

"No. He was there. Did you help clean up and shove Karl in the car, or did you just leave right away? That must have been some trip back. Lots of time to think." He paused. "I know he's here."

"Here?" Eisler said, looking up, confused.

"What did you do with the car?"

"The car?" he said, thrown by the question.

"Karl's car. You didn't leave it there."

"No, no. On the streets," he said, improvising. "Not far. Perhaps it was stolen."

"No. We found it. It's in a canyon, just down the road from the west gate."

Eisler fumbled, his hands nervously picking at his trousers. "I don't understand."

"Somebody drove it there. Your friend. You didn't know? You had to hightail it back here, get away from San Isidro as soon as possible. The usual way, I would guess, through the east gate. It's closer. Shall we go back to the map? Your friend has to dump the body. He was seen, it turns out. Just him, one man, not you, so I figure he was on his own. You were probably safe and sound back home by then. No risks, just in case. Then he drove Karl's car up the back way and stashed it close enough so he could walk in. Unless you waited around to give him a lift, but I don't think so. Why chance it? But you see what this means. You see why I can't let it go? He's here."

"I'm tired," Eisler said again. "It's enough."

"Who was it?"

"I don't know."

"That's not possible."

Eisler sighed wearily. "It is possible, Mr. Connolly. It's necessary. Surely you see that. To us it's just a contact, not a person. We aren't supposed to know. In case—well, of something like this."

"An interrogation, you mean."

"Yes. If you are forced. I could not tell you even if you tortured me."

"We don't go in for pliers here. That's your people," Connolly said.

Eisler looked away. "Please go now. It's not enough for you, all this? You have your answers. I compromised the project, yes—it's done. And Karl, that too. You don't believe in my guilt? It was enough for God. He has already punished me."

"You were the one playing God. I was there, remember? That's suicide, not punishment."

"So," he said quietly, "you know that too. Maybe I was just helping him."

"The way you helped the Russians."

"If you like. I make no apologies. It's done now."

Connolly stood up to go. "No apologies.

You want to be guilty for everything? That's just playing God again. Wipe the whole thing away in some—what? Sacrifice? You're right, it's not enough for me. You want me to understand. What? How everything was justified? But what was actually done? 'Compromise' the project? What is that? Betraying Oppenheimer, an old friend. Betraying your colleagues, all the work they've done. Do you know what hell this is going to make for them? Do you think it ends here with you? Prometheus, for Christ's sake. They'll have to live with all this shit, the secrecy—the war will never end for them. And Karl? A conniver, a snoop. 'So unfortunate. We couldn't allow—' So you know how they found him?" He saw Eisler wincing now, almost cringing in his chair, but he couldn't stop. "His head cracked—you knew that. Did you also see him get his face smashed in? Or did your friend do that later, a little goodbye gesture? A kick—several kicks. The poor bastard. They couldn't recognize his face. But I guess that was the point. Pulp and blood. And his pants yanked down, with his dick sticking out so that everybody would think—So that's how Karl ended. That's the way it goes down in the books, one kind of disgrace he had no right to expect. Let's not even think about the future, all the bombs and God knows what. I just want to know, did you see his face? And for what? Some cause? Your big idea? Your *wife*? All this. Was it worth it to you?"

Eisler raised his head, his tired eyes filled with tears, as if he were being beaten.

But Connolly couldn't stop. "Was it worth it?" he said, his voice hoarse. "Was it?"

"I don't know," Eisler said, a whisper.

It was the only outburst. He saw Eisler's face in the night, floating through his sleep like a plea, old and uncertain, and felt ashamed. In the morning they went on as before, a couple who'd had a spat, careful and polite, eager to put things behind them. Connolly couldn't let go. The radiation poisoning had created a deadline, firm and immediate, so that he felt himself in a race, like the men at Trinity, who worked too fast, with no time for consequences. When had he left the Hill that day. Were they alone at San Isidro before Karl arrived. Describe the contact. Had Karl mentioned anyone else from the early days. How had it been left. Was another meeting scheduled. Were there people in place at Hanford, at Oak Ridge. Describe the contact. But Eisler deteriorated with the meetings, the pain coming swiftly, knotting his face, and Connolly found himself fighting the drugs now as well as time. The lucid periods, fencing with remembered details, became a kind of martyrdom, some final struggle for Eisler's soul.

They were alone. At first Oppenheimer refused to see Eisler at all, devastated by the betrayal, but Connolly couldn't ask about the science and there was no one else. But his visits were erratic, stolen time. It was Connolly who kept the vigil. He welcomed the isolation, away from the others' questions, sealed off from the rest of the Hill. Holliday, Mills, even Emma had to be content with promissory notes. Not now, not yet. He couldn't leave. One evening, when the pain was very bad, Eisler gripped his hand, and he was startled at the touch, bony, desperate to make any contact, and he felt, oddly, that he had become Eisler's protector. In the close, sour-smelling room, he was tormentor and guardian, Eisler's last thread.

Oppenheimer had turned away. He had never quite recovered from the shock of that first day. Connolly had insisted they leave the office and walk over toward Ashley Pond. "What the devil is this all about?" Oppenheimer had protested, annoyed at the interruption, but when Connolly told him, he stopped still in the road. People, unnoticed, passed around them, and for a minute Connolly thought that something had happened—a heart attack, a stroke, as if the mind couldn't absorb the blow alone and had passed it on to the body. "You're sure?" Oppenheimer said finally, and Connolly, unnerved by his calm, was almost relieved when he noticed that Oppenheimer's hands were shaking as he lit his cigarette. He didn't know what reaction he had expected—a howl? a denial?—but when Oppenheimer began to talk, he didn't mention Eisler at all. Instead, irritated, he said, "Was it really necessary to bring me out here?"

"We have to assume your office is wired."

His eyes flashed for a moment in surprise. "Do we? Don't you know?"

"They don't tell me. I'm the one they brought in from outside, remember?"

"Vividly."

"They check on me too."

"Who? The general?" Then, as if he'd answered his own question, Oppenheimer started to walk. "My God, I suppose you'll have to tell him."

"I think it might be better coming from you. On a safe phone, if you can manage it."

"According to you, there's no such thing. Aren't you letting your imagination run away with you? Anyway, I fail to see the difference. They'll have to be told."

"Groves has to be told. Not the others, not yet. He'll want to run with it, but you'll have to persuade him to keep it to himself."

"How do you propose I do that?"

Connolly shrugged. "Call in a favor. He owes you."

"That's the city desk talking," Oppenheimer said, almost sneering. He dropped his cigarette and rubbed it out, thinking. "May I ask why?"

"Have you stopped to think what will happen the minute Army Intelligence gets this? They won't stop with Eisler."

"If I remember correctly, that's precisely what you were brought in to prevent."

"I am preventing it. Look, it's up to you. You're the boss. My advice is to get the gen-

eral to sit on it. You'll never finish otherwise."

"No," Oppenheimer said, looking now over
the pond. "The good of the project. I'm
touched. I'd no idea you were so concerned
with our work here."

"They'd close me down too. I have an idea
Eisler might talk to me. You think Lansdale
or any of his goons would let that happen if
they knew? Groves brought me in to sniff
around some queer murder. They didn't like
that much either, but what the hell? But Reds?
A spy case? They live for stuff like that."

For a moment Oppenheimer looked almost
amused. "Are you asking me to save your
job?"

"And yours."

"Ah. And mine. What a funny old world it's
become. Friedrich," he said to himself, then
turned to Connolly. "And what makes you think
Groves will agree?"

"Because the only thing he cares more
about than security is getting the damn thing
done. And it won't get done if he starts a
Red scare now. He'll believe you. He can't finish this without you. He has to trust you."

"And that's why he spies on me. You really think he's got the phone—"

"He'd have to," Connolly said quietly.
"You know that."

Oppenheimer sighed. "You forget, though.
After a while you get so used to the idea, you
aren't even aware of it anymore. I don't know
why I mind. I've never had anything to hide."

"You do now."

When Oppenheimer finally came to the infirmary, he almost broke down. He stood at the foot of Eisler's bed, holding on to the frame as a barrier between them, his thin body rigid and unyielding. Then he took in the swollen skin, splotched now by intradermal bleeding, the thinning hair, and Connolly saw him let go, nearly folding.

"Robert," Eisler said softly, the old affection, his first smile in days.

"Are you in pain?" Oppenheimer said.

"Not now. Have you seen the charts?"

Oppenheimer nodded. Connolly felt he should leave, but the silence held him, the air filled with emotion too fragile to disturb.

"It will take them years," Oppenheimer said finally.

"Perhaps."

"Years," Oppenheimer repeated. "All this—for what? Why you? My friend."

Eisler held his stare, then looked away. "Do you remember Roosevelt's funeral? The *Bhagavad Gita*? What a man's faith is, he is."

Oppenheimer continued to stare at him. "And what are you?"

Eisler's face fell, and he turned his head to the window. "I'm sorry about the boy," he said finally.

"A Jew, Friedrich. A Jew." Then he took his hands off the frame and moved away from the bed, his eyes hard again. "Were you the only one?" he said, his voice detached and composed.

But Eisler was quiet, and after a while

Oppenheimer gave up. "Very well," he said, brisk and matter-of-fact. "Shall we begin with the fuel? The purities? I assume they're not familiar with the alloying process?"

So they began their interview, the first of several, while Connolly sat on the other side of the room and listened. Explosive lenses. The initiator. Tampers. None of it meant anything to him. Instead he watched Oppenheimer, cool and efficient, run through his checklist of questions. He never wavered again. Connolly marveled at his single-mindedness. There were no more reproaches, no more attempts at any human connection. My friend. Now there was just a flow of information. How much was lost? It was the project that had been betrayed; Oppenheimer's own feelings had disappeared in some willed privacy. Perhaps he would take them out later, bruised, when the project was safe.

Eisler told him everything. Connolly felt at times that he was eavesdropping on some rarefied seminar. Question. Answer. Observation. They anticipated each other. With Connolly, Eisler sparred and evaded, but now his answers came freely, as if he were a foreigner relieved to find someone who spoke his native language. To him, science really was universal and open—it belonged to everyone who could know it. But mostly now it belonged to Oppenheimer. As Connolly watched them, he felt that Eisler's eager cooperation had become a kind of sad last request for forgiveness. He would give Oppenheimer every-

413

thing. They would talk as they always had, and Oppenheimer would feel the pleasure of it again and understand: what scientist could believe it must be secret?

But Oppenheimer was somewhere else now. Whenever he saw that Eisler, too sick to go on, needed medication, he would stop without complaint, almost relieved to go back to his real work. In the morning they would take up where they had left off, and Connolly would see Eisler's eyes, strained and cloudy, clear for a minute in anticipation. It became a question of how long he could last. Connolly would watch for the signs—a few beads of sweat, the voice suddenly dry, the small movements of his hands on the sheets—and see him struggle with it, ignoring the pain just a few minutes longer to keep Oppenheimer there. Then, after a week, they were finished, and Oppenheimer stopped coming. Eisler would look at the door in the morning and then, resigned, turn his head toward the chair and smile weakly at Connolly, who was now all there was.

"Groves wants to come," Oppenheimer told him one day, outside.

"Tell him to wait a few days. He's dying. I'm still hoping he'll talk to me."

"How much longer, do you think?"

"I don't know. A few days. It can't go on much longer. He's in pain all the time now."

"Yes," Oppenheimer said, and for a moment Connolly thought he saw something break in his eyes. Then he turned to go. "Why this way? There were a hundred easier ways to do it."

414

"I don't know. Fit the punishment to the crime. Maybe something like that."

Oppenheimer looked at him, a question.

"No, not Karl," Connolly said. "I think it's about the bomb."

But Oppenheimer didn't want to hear it. "Nonsense."

"He's a scientist," Connolly said. "Maybe for him it's the elegant solution."

Oppenheimer started at the words. "No," he said wearily. "It's an atonement. My God, what a waste. Does he think anybody's watching?"

"He asks for you."

Oppenheimer ignored him. "Groves wants to come," he said again. Then he anticipated Connolly's reaction. "I told him you were doing everything possible."

"He doesn't trust me?"

"He'll have to. We'll all have to, Mr. Connolly. Interesting how things work out, isn't it? Do you think he'll talk?"

"If he doesn't, we're at a dead end. Literally. It dies with him. Keep Groves away, will you? And no goons either."

"I'll do what I can. He has to come sometime, you know. We have to decide what to do."

"Like what? There's nothing to be done."

"You don't know G.G. There's always something to be done. In fact, I suggest you start thinking about what—he'll want ideas. I'd better go now. We've still got a gadget to build."

"You don't want to see Eisler?"

"I've seen him," he said, and walked away.

So Eisler talked to Connolly. Some days he would lie staring at the ceiling, his eyes half-closed in a daze, and then there would be a rush of talk. Hamburg. A back garden. The damp rooms after the first war, when there was no coal. He talked pictures for Connolly, gabled roofs and tramlines and a summer lake. Then, as if a cloud had passed in front of the sun in his mind, block-long factories and slate skies and his father, the hacking cough of damaged lungs. A last attempt, even now, at precision. Connolly didn't interrupt, hoping instead for a revealing moment. Sometimes he drifted into German, a secret testimony that left Connolly helpless. He had long since stopped answering questions. If Connolly drew him back to the alley at San Isidro, he would grow quiet, then speak of something else. He no longer enjoyed the verbal fencing. There wasn't time to go over it again. He was talking out his life. Now Berlin. Trude. A hiking trip in the mountains. Connolly sat in the dim room day after day, listening for clues.

He saw Emma only once, on a Saturday when they drove up to Taos Pueblo for an outing, past Hannah's ranch and along the high mountain road where the villages reminded her of Spain. After days with Eisler, the sun was too bright, glaring off the whitewashed walls, and after a while Connolly wished he hadn't come. What if Eisler said something and there was no one to hear? He missed the puzzle of the stories. Eisler had wanted him to understand, but all he had learned so far was that his life was inexplicable. It couldn't end in the alleyway. He had to leave a name, a description.

The pueblo itself was poor and dusty, filled with scratching chickens and occasional pickup trucks and quiet, resentful Indians selling blankets. The mud apartment blocks, windows outlined in bright blue, seemed like tenements, all clotheslines and old tin cans and rickety ladders leading to roofs. Maybe it had always been like this, he thought, the splendor of the Anasazi ruins no more than a leap of imagination. They sat near the fast, high stream that divided the two sides of the settlement, watching children crossing on the railless wooden bridge.

"Are you really all right?" she said.

"What do you mean?"

"People are talking. They say you've got it too. That's why you're the only one allowed. They're afraid to let anyone else in."

"No. I'm fine. I just talk to him, that's all."

"You mean you're questioning him. I thought he was dying."

"He is."

"What about? Karl? You think he killed Karl? I don't believe it."

"Neither do I. But I think he knows who did."

"Why would he?" she said, and then, when he didn't answer, "Oh, I see. Don't ask. Run along, Emma. Is it something terrible?"

"Yes."

She shivered. "Then don't tell me. I don't want to know. I like him."

"I like him too."

"Then why do this to him? What do you actually do, anyway? Give him shots to make him talk? Keep at him till he breaks down? Like the films? God, Michael. Sitting there like a vulture waiting for him to die. Everybody deserves a little peace."

Connolly was quiet for a minute. "He doesn't want peace. He wants to talk. We just—talk."

"About what?"

"His life. Germany. Everything. He's dying, Emma. He wants somebody to talk to."

"And you volunteered."

"It just worked out that way. I can't explain it now. I don't like it either, you know. It's a lousy way to die. It's not fun to watch."

Emma stood, picking up a stone and throwing it at the water. "I hate what you do."

"I didn't ask to do it."

"You didn't say no, either. And now you'll never give up. Sometimes I wonder how far you'd go. Would you do anything?"

"No."

"What's your limit, then? Do you know?" She came back from the stream.

"I'm not a cop."

"No, something else. God, I wish he *would* tell you. Put an end to all this. We could just be ourselves. What's the difference, anyway? We could go away somewhere together."

Connolly stared ahead. A dog was barking on the bridge, herding the children across.

"Is that what we're going to do?" he said.

"I don't know. Is it?"

He got up and took her arm. "If that's what you want, yes. We'll do whatever you want."

She looked up at him and nodded. "But not now."

"No. When it's finished."

Eisler got worse that night. The morphine had made him itch, and, unconscious, he had scratched himself over and over, so that in the morning his arms were covered in jagged red lines. Connolly found him tethered to the bed with narrow strips of gauze, and when he reprimanded the nurse and gently untied the arms, thin as sticks, he felt Eisler look up at him, momentarily coherent and grateful. "Robert," he said, his voice little more than a croak. "Is Robert coming?"

"Later," Connolly said.

Eisler nodded. "He's very busy," he said, then drifted off again.

Later that afternoon they talked a little, but Eisler's mind wandered. He no longer cared about his charts or his own disintegration. He lived now entirely in memory, sustained by an IV dripping into his arm. When Connolly asked once about Karl, he seemed to have forgotten who he was. He went back to Göttingen, a lecture about the instability of negative charges. Connolly fed him small pieces of ice, and when the ice began to melt it ran down his chin, his cracked lips too dry to absorb the moisture. The gold crown on one of his molars had become radioactive, causing the tongue to swell on one side. When they capped it with a piece of lead foil, a last tamper, his gums bled. Warm June air blew in through the window, but the smell, resistant, hung over everything. Connolly no longer noticed. He watched Eisler's face, waiting. When Eisler gasped, involuntarily wincing in agony, Connolly knew it was time to ask for another injection, and then he would lose him again until the pain had soaked up the drug and brought him back.

"You've got to see him," he said to Oppenheimer. "He asks for you." And when Oppenheimer didn't reply, "He won't last the week. It would be a mercy."

"A mercy," Oppenheimer said, examining the word. "Have you learned anything?"

"It's too late for that."

"Then why do you stay?"

Connolly didn't know what to answer. "It won't be much longer," he said.

Oppenheimer did come, in the morning, with the sun cutting through the slats in the blinds. He took off his hat and stood for a minute at the door, appalled, then forced himself to cross to the bed. Eisler's eyes were closed, his face immobile, stretched taut as a death mask.

"Is he awake?" he said in a low voice to Connolly.

"Try," Connolly said.

Oppenheimer took Eisler's hand. "Friedrich."

He held it, waiting, while Eisler's eyes opened.

"Yes," Eisler said, a whisper.

"Friedrich, I've come."

Eisler looked at him, his eyes confused. "Yes. Who is it, please?"

Oppenheimer's face twitched in surprise. Then, slowly, he let the hand go and stood up. "Yes?" Eisler said again vaguely, but his eyes had closed, and Oppenheimer turned away. He faced Connolly, about to speak, but instead his eyes filled with tears.

"Don't go," Connolly said.

"He doesn't know me," Oppenheimer said dully, and turned toward the door.

Connolly went over to the bed to wake Eisler, but when he looked back again Oppenheimer had gone, so he dropped his hand to his side.

"Yes?" Eisler said faintly, returning.

"It was Robert," Connolly said, but Eisler seemed not to have heard.

"Robert," Eisler said, as if the word meant nothing. Then his eyes widened a little and he felt for Connolly's hand. "Yes, Robert," he said, holding him.

There were two more days, as bad as before, and now no one else came at all. Connolly sat for hours by the bed, listening for breathing. Once Eisler came back, his voice clearer and his eyes steady, not moving as they usually did to avoid the pain.

"What is troubling you, Robert?" Eisler said, for Connolly was always Robert now.

"Nothing. Get some sleep."

"No more questions? What happened to the questions? Ask me."

"It's all right."

"Ask me. Can't I help you?"

"You remember Karl?"

"Yes," he said vaguely. "The boy."

"The man you met—he was wearing work-boots."

"Workboots? I don't understand."

"Workboots. On the Hill. It doesn't fit."

"I don't understand, Robert. Why are you asking me these things? What about the test? Trinity. Be careful of the weather. The wind—the particles. The wind will spread everything—"

"We'll be careful," Connolly said.

"Good," he said, closing his eyes again. "Good."

In a minute Connolly tried again. "Friedrich," he said. "Please. Tell me. Who was driving the car?"

Eisler lay quietly, his eyes fluttering. "They stopped at the river, Robert," he said, opening them. He looked at Connolly, troubled and confused, and Connolly leaned forward to hear him. But it was another river. "The Russians. They stopped at the river. Until the fighting was over. They wouldn't cross. They waited till everyone was dead."

Connolly knew then that the Hill had slipped away for good. He had lost. "In Warsaw," he said, giving in.

"In Warsaw, yes. They waited. Till everybody was dead."

Connolly watched his eyes fill with tears, a spontaneous sorrow. He wondered if everyone ended this way, overwhelmed with regret.

"Can you imagine such a thing?" he said. "The Russians." Then, his eyes moving irrationally, he grabbed Connolly's hand. "Don't tell Trude."

Connolly patted him soothingly. "No. I won't."

Eisler lay back, his eyes closed again, but he kept Connolly's hand. Connolly, helpless to remove it, sat there feeling Eisler's fingers pulse faintly, then clutch and relax, as if he were touching what was left of his life. Of all the strange things that had happened to him since he had come to Los Alamos, this seemed to him the strangest. The sour room. The swollen hand holding on to someone else he thought was there. The unexpected intimacy of death, confiding in an imposter. When Eisler clutched him tightly toward the end and said, "Was it so terrible what I did? Was it so terrible?" he knew he meant not this last betrayal but the ruined faith of a lifetime.

"No, not so terrible," he lied, giving comfort to the enemy.

14

Groves used the funeral service as the excuse for his trip. The entire Hill closed down for the afternoon, eerie in the sudden stillness, like a forest in the absence of birds. Connolly had never realized before how noisy the place usually was, voices and motors and the clangs of the metallurgy unit vibrating in a constant hum. Now you could actually hear the wind blow across the mesa, a character in the creation myth. It was even quiet in the crowded theater, only a few whispers and scraping chairs until Professor Weber's quartet filled the room with some mournful Bach. Afterward, Oppenheimer and Groves sat on the stage with the speakers, Groves in his tight, bullying uniform and Oppenheimer almost languid, the dark cloth of his suit hanging in folds over his gaunt frame. He had refused to speak, ceding his place to Weber as a gesture to the émigré community, and only Connolly was aware that it was a deft evasion, the maneuver of one practiced in compromise.

The speakers said the expected. Eisler's contribution to science. His contribution to the project. His concern for humanity and the arts. His generosity. His ethical standards. Connolly looked around the room at the hundreds of people in varying stages of grief; Eisler had betrayed all of them. What if they knew? Weber broke down in the middle of his speech, weakened by genuine sentiment, and some people in the audience cried. Eisler was science at its best, the pure inquiry, the search for truth. He even—here Connolly, restless, almost rose to leave—died for it. Connolly thought that the hypocrisy of eulogies was a final mercy to the survivors. If people knew the truth, would there ever be kings? Tyrants were always praised for their love of the people, politicians for their vision, artists for their selflessness. Now Los Alamos had its own martyr, the one they needed, and he did them more honor than most. He had died for science. But Oppenheimer sat on the stage, his legs crossed, and did not speak.

Afterward Connolly walked with Oppenheimer and Groves out toward S Site, an inspection team of three.

"A little hot for a walk, isn't it?" Groves said, wiping the back of his neck, his uniform already showing splotches of dampness.

"Connolly tells me people listen in my office. Bugs. I know you'd never allow that," Oppenheimer said, mischievous, "but you know what the intelligence unit is like. Better to indulge them. Interfere with a delusional and they go stark raving. Or so I'm told. Why don't you take off your jacket?"

Groves, choosing comfort over dignity, flung it over his shoulder and held it with his forefinger. Without the camouflage of the jacket, his stomach strained at his shirt buttons, spilling over his belt.

"You pick one heck of a time to make jokes. We've got a real mess on our hands here. I always said this would happen."

"Yes, you did," Oppenheimer replied.

"Foreigners and—"

"Would you feel any better if he came from Ohio?"

"All right," Groves said. "Make your point."

"These pesky foreigners are making your gad-

425

get, so don't let's start down that road again. It could have been anybody."

"Well, you would think that," he said, backing off but not mollified. "How's the timetable? Still on track?"

Oppenheimer nodded. "Just. Five minutes' leeway, give or take a minute. We can't afford any time off," he said, directly to Groves.

"That's why I'm here," Groves said. "So let's get started. First, assess the damage. How bad is it? What do they know? Can they make a bomb?"

"No," said Oppenheimer thoughtfully. "I don't think so. Eisler was a theoretical physicist. He knew the plans for the implosion bomb. That's a plus for them. But he can't build their reactor for them. He didn't know the purity requirements. He couldn't alloy plutonium. It's a complicated metallurgy— five different phases and five different densities. He had nothing to do with that. So, yes, they know, but they don't know how. They will, though, you know. Sometime."

"Not on my watch," Groves said. "How about all those coffee klatches you like to have? Wouldn't he hear about the alloy requirements there?"

"Yes." Oppenheimer sighed. "I didn't say he didn't know about them. He just wouldn't know in any meaningful detail."

"He wouldn't have to know if he just passed them plans."

"No. He only had access to theoretical. His own papers."

"He could steal them."

"He didn't. He told me. Yes," he said, responding to Groves's questioning look, "I believe him. He was a traitor, but he wasn't a thief."

"That's some difference."

"At any rate, he didn't give them that. I don't mean to minimize what's happened here. He passed valuable information. We don't know how valuable because we don't know where they were starting from. But they need more than what Eisler gave them to actually make a bomb. It's almost a certainty they don't have one yet. Of course, the point is they know *we* do."

"Wonderful," Groves said.

"Yes, it's awkward. Politically."

"Awkward," Groves said, almost snorting.

"Not telling them. Of course, if that's the main concern, we could simply tell them now."

Groves stared at him as if he had missed the point of a joke. "That's the kind of thing you say that keeps me up at night." Then he dropped it and kept walking, forcing them to flank him in a kind of brooding convoy. "What gets me is how easy it all was," he said finally. "This place is like a sieve. A man walks out, hands over some papers, and that's it. We wouldn't even know about it now if they hadn't killed someone. It shouldn't be that easy. At least we can plug up a few holes. I want you to cancel all leaves. Nobody goes out anymore."

"Isn't it a little late for that? The horse is already out of the barn."

"I think it's a good idea," Connolly said.

Oppenheimer looked at him in surprise. "You do?" he said, displeased.

"What's on your mind?" Groves said. They both stopped and turned to him.

"It doesn't end with him."

"Go on," Groves said.

"Eisler only had a piece. But what if he wasn't the only one? What if there are others? The Russians must want all this pretty badly. Why stop at Eisler?"

"How many of us do you suspect?" Oppenheimer said. "Ten? All?"

Groves, who had paled even in the sun, shook his head. "He's right. The Reds could have people planted all over the Hill. All over."

"But we don't know," Connolly said. "And we're not going to. Not this way. There's no point looking on the Hill. We have to find out who Eisler met."

"You said there was one here," Groves said.

"Well, I think there is. It still doesn't make sense, but somebody drove Karl's car up here. Eisler's contact? No. Why meet off the Hill in the first place? There *has* to be an outside guy. But somebody drove the car and then walked in through the west gate. Which means—"

"There were two," Oppenheimer said quietly.

"Exactly. I don't know how or why, but it's the only way the logistics work."

"Then find them," Groves said.

"That's not so easy. The trail really did die with Eisler. We've got to find the outside guy. If there's someone else on the Hill, he's the key."

Oppenheimer stopped to light a cigarette. "What makes you say that?" he said thoughtfully, as if he were looking at a math problem. "Why would he know anyone else? If everyone was working in isolation?"

"I'm guessing," Connolly said, "but the odds are good that the outside contact was the only mailman. The more people you have running around on the outside, the more chances you have of someone getting caught. Why spread the risk? He's not essential, like the scientists. He's just collecting the rent. You lose him, you replace him. But you don't lose him, because he's the pro. The tricky part is getting the stuff to him—you've got to rely on, well, people like Eisler. You don't know what they're going to do if they get excited. So you keep it simple and you keep them in the dark. But once you've got the information, you want someone who really knows what he's doing."

"And he's not the one on the Hill?" Groves said.

"No, he couldn't be. My guess is he's nowhere near the Hill. Maybe Santa Fe or Albuquerque, but you're always taking a chance with somebody in place. More likely he breezes into town—a businessman or a tourist, he met Eisler as a tourist—collects the rent, and then clears out till the next time."

"All the way to Moscow," Groves said.

Connolly shrugged. "Somewhere."

"Well, that's just fine," Groves said. "Now what are we supposed to do?"

"Cancel the leaves," Connolly said to Oppenheimer. "Make it difficult for him. You've got the test coming up—it's a legitimate excuse. According to Eisler, there was no procedure for a missed meeting, they just rescheduled somehow. If other meetings are planned, at least we can make him sweat for them. Put a few people on the tourist spots," he said to Groves, "if we can manage some surveillance without being obvious. I could get some of the local boys to help—Holliday's a good guy and won't ask any questions. See who turns up and whether they come back. It's a long shot, but you never know. Somebody was waiting for Eisler at San Isidro. Maybe he'll be waiting somewhere else now. The locals aren't great, but they're all we've got. We can't use anyone from up here."

"Why not?" Groves said.

"Why did you bring me here in the first place? Because we can't trust anyone here."

"I never said that."

"You thought it. Karl was security, and you didn't know whether that meant anything or not, but you sure as hell weren't going to take the chance. Now we know we can't. And we can't let anyone know we suspect. Business as usual. They'll wonder about Eisler. They'll look for anything suspicious.

But nobody bothered him. I was with him in the lab, so it made sense for me to be in the hospital too. You might want to spread the word that you're still worried about my health," he said to Oppenheimer.

"I am," Oppenheimer said dryly. "What makes you think they even know he's dead?"

"If they don't, they will. You don't need newspapers up here—it'll get out. We have to assume they know everything. Except that we know. Karl gets killed and they pull down his pants and what do you know? The army gets squeamish and falls for it," he said, shooting a glance at Groves. "And somebody else comes along and takes the rap. You don't get luckier than that. Then Eisler dies. An accident? Remorse about Karl? But he'd never talk. And he didn't. Nothing happens. No security. No sudden visits from Washington. Things just go on. They're still lucky. Except now they're missing a source. Maybe their only source, maybe not. Either way, they'll be hungry. Which is just what we want."

"And that's it?" Groves said. "Say nothing and have the police watch the churches? That's your plan of action?"

But Oppenheimer was studying Connolly, his eyes following the sequence of his thought. "What do you mean, they'll be hungry?" he said quietly. "What are you planning to do?"

"I want to offer some rent to collect."

Groves stopped and looked at him, his face squinting in appraisal. "What do you mean by that?"

431

But Oppenheimer, lighting a fresh cigarette, was already there. "I think Mr. Connolly means he wants to go into the spying business," he said, smiling.

"Forget it," Groves said quickly.

"We're already in it," Connolly said, smiling back at Oppenheimer.

But Groves had drawn in his breath, swelling his chest, so that involuntarily Connolly thought of the storybook pig, huffing and puffing.

"Hold on. Both of you," he said. "The last time I listened to you," he said to Oppenheimer, "Connolly here was going to pull the rabbit out of the hat. Leave him alone, you said. Eisler'll talk to him. Well, he didn't. And now he's dead, and so is our last chance of getting anything out of him. You're not FBI," he said to Connolly. "You're not even Army Intelligence. So it's my own fault, I guess. I don't know what I was thinking about. But I know enough not to make the same mistake twice."

"G.G.—" Oppenheimer began, but Connolly interrupted.

"General, I've just spent two weeks watching a man die. There's nothing anybody could have done to him—he'd already done it to himself. Maybe that's why he did it, who knows? You can't torture a man who's already in that kind of pain. It wasn't going to get any better. He knew that. If he didn't want to say anything, nothing on God's earth was going to make him."

"Who said anything about torture?" Groves said.

"That's right, I forgot. Only the enemy does that. Maybe Eisler couldn't see the difference."

"Mister, that's out of line."

"Let's everyone calm down, shall we?" Oppenheimer said. "General, we're all disappointed about Eisler. It's a great pity. But that's all very spilt milk now. The question is—"

"I know what the question is. We've spent billions of dollars to create a strategic advantage to end this war. Now the whole project's being undermined and Connolly here wants to play cops and robbers."

"General," Oppenheimer said soberly, "you've still got your strategic advantage, unless the war ends before we can use it. Nothing's been undermined. What exactly is your concern?"

"And afterward?"

"Well, afterward. That's a very interesting question. But it's not the question before us right now. Not yet."

"I suppose it doesn't bother you that somebody's selling us out to the Russians right under your nose. Maybe you'd like to tell the President we've been handing this stuff to the enemy. I know I'm not looking forward to it."

"You're wrong. I mind very much," Oppenheimer said slowly, almost to himself. Then he turned to Groves. "I didn't realize we thought Russia was the enemy. Or are we just planning ahead?"

"I don't know about that. And don't go putting words in my mouth. I'm just doing a job here, and so are you. You can think about policy on your own time. But I'll tell you this: whoever has this thing won't *have* any enemies."

Oppenheimer looked up at him, smoking. "That's a comforting thought."

Connolly had watched this exchange as if it were the volley of a tennis match. Now, looking at each other, they seemed stuck, or at least reluctant to press an advantage.

"Don't tell him," Connolly said, breaking the moment. Groves turned to him, puzzled.

"Who?"

"The President. Don't tell him."

They both looked at him, shocked. It was Oppenheimer, finally, who spoke. "He has to, Mr. Connolly," he said, as if he were being patient with a child.

They now stood together in front of him, and Connolly saw in that instant a couple locked in some strange union that would always supersede quarrels and irritation, married, finally, to the project.

"Why?" Connolly said.

"I'm going to forget you said that, mister," Groves said. "This is the army. Don't *you* forget that."

"I'm not suggesting anything—disloyal."

"What do you call it?"

Connolly hesitated for a minute. "A strategic advantage."

Groves glared at him, then backed down.

"You've got two minutes. And keep it simple. I'm just a soldier."

"Look," Connolly began, speaking to Oppenheimer, "you asked me to think about what we should do here. I have thought about it. And every time I come back to where we started. Karl." He turned to include Groves. "You sent me here to find out who killed Karl. Eisler didn't kill him, any more than that kid they've got locked up down in Albuquerque did. We still don't know who killed Karl. But now we know something else, something even more important, and it turns out the one leads to the other. The same guy. Get who killed Karl and we get the link outside. Agreed? Up until now, we've been looking for a murderer. Instead we found a spy. Karl led us to Eisler. And now we're stuck. So we have to turn the thing around. It's like a crossword, see? We've been doing the horizontal, and we're out of clues. So we've got to work downward instead. Fill it in that way. Look for a spy to find a murderer."

"This make any sense to you," Groves said to Oppenheimer, "or am I the only one who still doesn't know what he's talking about?"

"Let him finish," Oppenheimer said, interested.

"What exactly am I not supposed to tell the President?" Groves said.

"Well, what exactly *do* you tell him?" Connolly answered. "We can't prove anything. I made a lucky guess and Eisler confessed. Maybe he was crazy. This is a guy who kills himself with radiation, so how reliable is he? Maybe I'm crazy. You've only got my word that he said anything."

"He talked to me too," Oppenheimer said, playing devil's advocate.

"And maybe he was lying. For whatever reason. Who knows why? Maybe none of it happened. Can we prove it did?"

"He wasn't lying," Oppenheimer said.

"No. He wasn't. But we're the only ones who know that. Look around," Connolly said, sweeping his hand toward the sunny mesa. "Anything seem wrong to you? Any reason to think—any *proof*—that something's wrong? What do you believe, General? Do you believe me? Do you think I was taken in by a crazy man telling stories? Maybe *I'm* telling stories— that's what I get paid to do. All you've got is my word. Do you trust me that much?"

"You're wasting time," Groves said. "I don't have to trust you. If Dr. Oppenheimer says it's true, then it is. We have to do something."

"Then let me finish what I started. You know as well as I do that once they get hold of this, we'll have a Chinese fire drill around here. Everybody'll want to do something. I can hear them already. "Why didn't you tighten security? How could it happen?' You've got a new President. Do you know him? Is he going to back you up when everybody starts jumping up and down? He'd have to do something. Maybe he'd start at the top."

Groves frowned, not saying anything.

"The point is, we don't know. But the odds

are they won't be able to fix anything and they'll make one hell of a mess trying."

Oppenheimer looked over at Groves, waiting.

Groves stared at the ground, moving his foot in thought. "You're a good talker," he said to Connolly, "but you don't know what you're asking. I can't do it. I have to tell him."

"Maybe. But not quite yet. All I've raised is a suspicion. You'd have to investigate to find out if there's anything to it. You're not putting the project itself in danger. This isn't about sabotage. And you don't want to send out any false alarms. If there's the possibility of a security leak, you'd have to try and plug it. It's your project—you'd have to decide the best way to go about that."

"And that's you."

"It's not them. It's a chance, I know. But we'll never get it if this goes beyond the three of us. I could delay telling you," he said, looking directly at Groves. "I'm independent. Maybe I didn't want to come to you until I had more to go on. I should have, but—"

"It would be your head," Groves said.

"Yes."

"I wouldn't have any choice."

"No, you wouldn't."

"You'd do that?"

"I'm not in the army. It's easier for me. I just—wanted to close the case."

Groves looked around, glancing over toward the Jemez Mountains. "But you weren't the only one there. That leaves you, Robert."

Oppenheimer took a drag on his cigarette, then looked at Groves. "We wouldn't be here if it weren't for Connolly. We wouldn't know any of it. Under the circumstances—" He paused. "I think he might be given a little more rope."

Groves was silent. "You hang yourself with it," he said finally. "Dr. Oppenheimer's out of it. That understood?"

Connolly nodded. "You'll have everything you need for the record. If you need it. I just delayed telling you. Both of you."

"I don't like this," Oppenheimer said.

"No, he's right," Connolly said. "You can't have anything to do with this. You know, it *could* have happened this way," he said, turning to Groves. "You wouldn't know anything about it if I hadn't told you."

"Why did you?" Groves said.

"I need your help."

He had been looking at Groves, but it was Oppenheimer who said, "What do you have in mind?"

"First, some classified papers, something to hook him. Something Eisler's already handed over, so they know it's real, but that somebody else might have access to. Bait. Could you do that?"

Oppenheimer nodded.

"Wait a minute," Groves said. "You want to pass classified documents?"

"Something they already have," Connolly said. "Or Eisler said they have. If we believe him. But we do believe him, don't we?"

"I can't allow this. Do you know what it means if—"

"Yes, but I won't get caught. I'm not planning to go to jail."

"How about first telling me what in God's name is going on?" Groves said irritably, wiping his forehead. "And do we have to stand out here in the sun?"

Connolly nodded and began leading them toward the shade of the water tower. "There's only one way to do this. We have to give him another Eisler. We don't know how they put people here. Maybe there isn't anybody else. But either way, they're going to need a new source. It's late. They're hungry."

"Just who did you have in mind?" Oppenheimer said.

"I've been thinking about that. Ideally, a scientist, of course, but it's too tricky and there isn't enough time. We have to assume they've got a list of the scientists working on the project—that would be the first thing they'd ask for."

Groves groaned out loud.

"So it's too easy to check," Connolly continued. "They'd spot a marker right away, just from the list. Who's the new guy? Never heard of him. And of course if they do have somebody else up here, he'd spot it as a ghost. Then there's the background. We say our man's from Berkeley, they check Berkeley. It's a fairly small community, isn't it? It's unlikely you'd have a spare physicist up here nobody's ever heard of."

"Quite," Oppenheimer said. "Are you proposing to use a real person?"

"No. You've got four thousand people up here. Technical support comes and goes. We make up a dummy file in one of these areas. Maybe the Special Engineering Detachment. There are always new SEDs coming in. But someone who could put his hands on the papers. An idealist," he said to Groves, who was watching him with growing discomfort. "You could set up some army records, couldn't you? I'll make up a project folder—bio, clearance, the usual. Just put it in the files. If we've got a leak up here, he'll know where to go and we'll have it all ready for him." He looked up at the giant tower, crisscrossed wooden slats rising to support the broad tank, Los Alamos's Empire State Building. "Maybe we'll call him Waterman."

"There's a Waterman in metallurgy," Oppenheimer said.

"Okay, Waters, then. Steve, I think. That sounds about right. Corporal Steve Waters, SED. The rat."

"You think this is funny?" Groves said impatiently. "I fail to see anything funny about it. I don't know what we're playing at here. This isn't some petty crime anymore."

Connolly reddened at the schoolboy reprimand. "What makes a crime petty—the amount you steal?"

"Don't start with me."

"It's the same," Connolly said. "Same people who knock over a liquor store. Calling them

440

agents doesn't make them smarter. Who do you think does this, anyway? Masterminds? I'm not trying to break up the rackets, I'm just looking for a guy who got jumpy with a tire iron."

Groves snorted and looked away, his eyes following a coal delivery truck rumbling toward Boiler No. 1.

"There's only one thing I don't understand," Oppenheimer said, as if nothing had happened. "Your phantom Corporal Waters has some valuable papers to offer. How do you let them know? Put an ad in the papers?"

"I assume there's a network. Our rent collector may be only one link, but no one works alone on that end. You know, like the numbers," he said, looking at Groves. "I need to get access to the network, someone to pass on the invitation. If they're as efficient as we think they are, they'll come calling."

"You know someone like that?" Groves said. "Why don't we just haul *him* in?"

"Anyone can pass a message. I thought of your brother," he said to Oppenheimer, then turned to Groves. "But I suspect you're already having him watched. That would complicate things."

No one said a word. Groves, already red and sweating, flushed and looked away.

"Frank left the party," Oppenheimer said quietly. "Some time ago."

"And they'd probably think it was all a little too good to be true," Connolly continued. "They'd want to be very careful with anyone close to you, and we don't have time for

441

that. There's someone else. I don't know if he's involved in the party's extracurricular activities or not. I doubt it. But he'd know someone who is, or someone who knows someone. We just need to get the ball started and hope they pick it up and run with it. It may not work. It's only a chance."

"He'd be taking a chance too, your friend," Oppenheimer said thoughtfully. "He'd have to trust *you*. Would he?"

Connolly met his gaze. "Yes, he would."

"He's here?" Oppenheimer said tentatively.

"No. That's where I need your help, General," Connolly said, drawing the still sulking Groves back to the conversation. "I assume you could get a Section 1042 file without raising any eyebrows? That's alien registration."

"I know what it is."

"I need an address. Current."

"Name?"

Connolly looked at him. "Are we on with this or not?"

Groves hesitated for another minute, then sighed. "Name?"

"Matthew Lawson," Connolly said. "Brit. Here since before the war. New York, maybe. Can you get it?"

Groves nodded. "If they've got him on file, I can get it. Who is he?"

"You don't want to know that. In fact, from now on you don't want to know anything. You don't want to know what I'm doing.

You'd need to be able to say that. Honestly. I'm just—late telling you about Eisler. That's all."

Groves nodded again, then folded his arms across his chest. "One thing. If I don't know, I won't be able to say anything to Army Intelligence. If they should get the idea to put you under surveillance. I can't call them off."

"I know."

"The minute you take those papers out of here you're breaking the law."

"Let's see how good they are. It'll be a test for them."

"Test," Groves said grumpily. "I don't like any of this. Any of it. This place. It was easier building the Pentagon."

But Oppenheimer was looking at Connolly with amusement. "Mr. Connolly has a flair for the clandestine. Have you done this before?"

Connolly thought of motel rooms and glances avoided in Fuller Lodge. "Just lately."

"Are we finished here? Can we go back and cool off before I change my mind?" Groves said.

"We're finished," Connolly said. "I'm going over to the hospital to get Eisler's things. I'll go through his place one more time. You never know. When you get the address," he said to Groves, "maybe you'd better send it through the telex line. The code's safer."

"One more thing," Groves said, putting his damp jacket on. "You want me to go out on a limb for you. No questions. So just tell me one thing: what do you think the odds are this can actually work?"

443

Connolly shook his head. "The odds are always good when it's the only hand you've got."

His bravado evaporated as he walked toward the infirmary. How many times did a long shot come in? Except this time it wasn't just the bet, it was what he'd have to use to make it. Everything would depend on her. It wasn't right. But it had sat there, his only idea, and he'd had to pick it up. He wondered, in that moment, why he'd jumped at it, excited by something he knew was wrong, then caught in a tangle of inevitability, deaf now even to himself. Could he lose her? No, he'd stop if it came to that. He thought of Eisler in his lab, those desperate seconds lowering the cube before it went critical. The trick was to stop in time, before the dragon turned. But what if it took on a life of its own? What if simply starting the process demanded its only conclusion? He looked around the Hill—clothes near the McKee units flapping on lines in the bright, dry air; a repairman high up on one of the overhead transformers; soldiers in jeeps—and it seemed to him utterly ordinary. Everyone was just getting on with the day, making a bomb.

In the infirmary, someone was sitting on Eisler's bed. He took in the bruised side of the face, the bandage over the forehead cut, before he recognized Corporal Batchelor.

"What happened to you?"

"I walked into a door," Batchelor said, his voice flat. Next to the neat pile of Eisler's effects, his battered face was jarring, the disorder of violence. "How did you hear?" he asked, embarrassed.

"I didn't. I came for these. Are you all right?"

The boy nodded.

"That must have been some door," Connolly said, moving toward Eisler's things. "You going to let him get away with it?"

The soldier shrugged. "It was just a door. I'll live."

"The unfriendly kind."

The boy smiled weakly, wincing a little from the cut at the corner of his mouth. "Yeah, the big unfriendly kind. I'll have to be more careful at the PX."

"Maybe next time you should just stay away," Connolly said. Then, hearing the tone of his voice, "Sorry. I didn't mean it like that."

"It's all right," the soldier said, his face weary. "I had it coming."

"Nobody has it coming," Connolly said, suddenly angry for him, then aware that he didn't know anything about it. What was it like living this way? Was every meeting a risk? He thought again of the ordinary world outside, so bright that it made any other invisible. And then it occurred to him that it might have been a different kind of misstep, the wrong question. Connolly's fault.

"This didn't have anything to do with—I mean, I hope you weren't—"

"Snooping?" The boy shook his head. "No. Nothing like that. Just a door. I never heard a word, by the way. Since you ask."

"I know. He wasn't—we made a mistake."

The boy looked at him. "So what was it?"

"We know it wasn't that. Don't worry. Nobody's going to bother anybody."

He nodded his head again. "Good. I'm glad about that, anyway."

"So don't go banging into any more doors. Not because of that."

The soldier shrugged. "I'm just a bad judge of character, that's all. I never was good at that. How about you?"

The question caught Connolly off-guard, as if it had come from another conversation. "Not very. Sometimes." He moved to gather up Eisler's things. "I still think you've got a lot of guts, though."

The smile this time was fuller, a wry grimace. "Yeah. Thanks."

"I also think you're a damned fool to let him get away with it. You ought to turn the bastard in."

When Batchelor looked up at him, his eyes seemed almost pleading. "I can't. Don't you know that? That's the way it works. I can't."

Connolly thought about him as he walked toward Eisler's apartment, carrying the valise. It shouldn't be that easy to get hurt. He wondered what would happen to Batchelor after the war, when he would drift off the Hill to some other life, hidden from Connolly and everyone else until it showed up again on his face.

At least his mystery had its bits of visible evidence. Eisler's had receded with him. Here were the clothes, the books, the old pictures. Connolly sat smoking for a while in Eisler's living room, peering at the walls as if some idea lurked there, waiting to be found. Then he started going through the books. He took them down from the shelves, flipped through, then made piles on the floor. Nothing. He remembered that first night in Karl's room, the presence in those few neat possessions, someone who was still living there and had been delayed on his way back. But Eisler was gone, perhaps had never been here at all. All these objects, rooms full of them, pared away until finally there was only one idea. Those last weeks with Connolly had been his one brief contact. And then he had gone back into hiding. What was it like to believe so completely, to let everything go but one thing? What was it like not to care who got hurt? Standing there with a meaningless German book in his hand, Connolly felt the room go empty. An entire life for a single idea. And it had been wrong.

15

won't bloody do it," she said, sitting up. "You've got to."
"I don't."
She had gathered the crumpled sheet around

her as if she had been surprised by an intruder. The room was warm, closed against the afternoon light.

"You're the only way it can work," he said calmly.

She stared at him, then jumped out of bed and grabbed the clothes off the floor. She held them in front of her, then turned to the bathroom door, tripping in the dimness. "Bugger," she said, stumbling toward the window. When she jerked the cord of the shade, the light of the room, amber and erotic, flashed harsh white. A cheap rug and Formica table, Connolly sitting up in the messy bed. He watched her try to pull on her slip, turning it around to find the opening, anxious to be covered.

"I'll be with you. Every step," he said.

She stopped, frustrated with the slip, and stood holding it.

"You're lovely," she said. "Lovely. Waiting till we'd done it before you'd ask. What did you think? A good slap and tickle and then a bit of spying on the side? There's a good girl. You must be mad. I won't."

"Emma, please. I've explained it badly."

"Have you?" she said, struggling with the slip again. "Cheat on one husband, then go and trap another. That's roughly it, isn't it? I won't, thank you very much. He's my husband. Or was. Is. Whatever he is, I'm not sending him to jail."

"He won't go to jail. They don't want him—he's the go-between. At the worst, they'd ship him home."

"Yes? Funny, I can hear the keys rattling already."

"I don't understand you. He walked out on you."

"Well, that's not quite a prison offense yet, is it? They wouldn't have enough jails."

"It's not about him."

"It is to me. I don't *want* to see him. He's dead. And I'm not bringing him back to life. Just so you can put him away."

"Nobody's putting him away."

"Well, whatever happens, it would be my doing, wouldn't it? You wouldn't even know he existed if I hadn't told you. Before you got your marvelous idea."

"Calm down."

"I *won't* calm down," she said. "I suppose you've already offered my services. That must have caused quite a stir in the security office. Lord, what a past. Who'd have thought. I didn't know she went in for that sort of thing."

"Nobody knows. Nobody's going to."

"What made you think I'd do it?"

"I thought you'd want to," he said evenly. "We've got to find out. It's important."

"Want to? Why? For the good of the country? Don't make me laugh."

"I thought you'd do it for Karl."

"Karl?" she said, disconcerted. "Karl's dead."

"So is Eisler. Maybe somebody else, for all we know."

"Maybe the whole bloody world. Look,

you carry the sword of vengeance. You're good at it."

"Emma, I need you to help me. He'll trust you."

"What makes you think so? Old times' sake? Or am I supposed to go to bed with him? Is that it? Maybe you want to watch."

"Don't."

"Is that it? Just like Mata Hari?"

"No, of course not. If you'd let me explain—"

"Oh, you. You'd talk the birds from the trees to get your way. I suppose we'll be saving the world next. With me on my back."

"Will you listen?"

"You listen," she said, giving up on the slip and walking over to the bathroom. "Listen to yourself. You might be surprised what you hear." She slammed the door behind her.

He sat on the bed for a minute, waiting, but there was only the sound of running water. He put on his pants and went over to the window, turning the slats of the blinds halfway to look out at the dusty parking lot. Her anger had surprised him. It seemed to thrash and spurt like some well that bursts deep down, thwarted till it reaches air. He thought of that night at the square dance, when it seemed no more than high spirits, when he had first wanted her. He wondered if she was douching, washing him away. He lit a cigarette and watched the smoke catch the light. The awful thing was, she was right. He'd waited till they were finished. He'd made love to her knowing he would ask.

When she came out of the bathroom, she was

in her slip and her face was still damp with water. She brushed back her hair with her fingers and sat down, crossing her legs with a theatrical calmness. "Don't worry," she said. "I won't bite. Do you have another one of those?"

He handed her a cigarette, not saying anything, so that the silence was an apology. The air in the room settled, all the bad words seeping out the window with the smoke.

"Is it important to you?" she said finally.

"Yes."

"Yes, it would be, wouldn't it?" Her lips curled in a kind of amused resignation, as if she were laughing at herself.

"What are you thinking about?" he asked.

"About my father," she said, almost dreamily. "He got it right, didn't he? Here's the room—seedy, that would be his word for it. In the middle of some American desert. That's about nowhere, or near enough. And I'm sitting here, smoking a cigarette in my slip, like a slut."

"Emma."

"No, like a slut. Some man's sweat still all over me and a husband down the road and another somewhere else—my God. Quite a sight. And my lover. Well, my lover. All very much as he predicted."

"No it isn't."

"Isn't it?"

"I love you."

"And that makes it all different. Whatever that means."

"It means I won't ask you again. I won't ask anything. Forget it."

"Could you? No, you may as well ask, now that we've started. What, exactly?"

"You mean you'll do it?"

"I won't do him any harm. Can you promise me he won't be harmed? No, never mind. You can't promise, but you would. You'd lie. You couldn't help it."

"I won't lie to you. Nothing's going to happen to him."

"I won't whore for you."

"Do you really think I'd ask you to do that?"

"No."

"Then what's this all about?"

She turned away, facing the room. "I don't know. Not wanting to rake up the past, I suppose. Can you understand that? You never know what you're going to find. I don't want to go back."

"It's just this once. You'd have to sometime."

"To straighten things out, you mean? Oh, that's good. Darling, do let's get a friendly annulment. Meanwhile, here are some lovely secrets for your trouble. Is that the idea? My God, I don't know if I can do it. I'm not that good a liar."

"It's not a lie. The papers are real."

"*I* wouldn't be. He'd spot it in a minute. Why him, of all people?"

"You didn't have anywhere else to turn. You trust him." He met her glance.

"Why now? How did I know where to find him?"

"You've known for some time. You just didn't want to—rake up the past."

"But now I'm ready for a bit of gardening."

"This was important. You need his help. For your lover's sake."

"Well, at least that wouldn't be lying."

"Your lover, Corporal Waters. Box 1663, Santa Fe."

"What's he like, this one?"

"An idealist. Like the first one."

"What a bastard you are."

"He'll believe you. These things run to type."

"Until you," she said, stubbing out the cigarette. But she was interested now, in spite of herself. "Why not Daniel?"

"He's real. They could check."

"What am I supposed to tell *him*, by the way? I'm off to New York for some shopping?"

"I don't know yet. We'll have to come up with something. Maybe Oppie's asked you to help with some visiting Brits. It's a chance to get away. Something."

Emma got up and looked out the window. "I'll have to tell him about us sometime, you know. Maybe it's now."

"Not yet."

She turned to look at him. "Why? Out of curiosity."

"It's better to wait. We don't know how he'll react. Besides, he's busy."

"Useful, you mean. To the project. We wouldn't want to risk any complications now, would we? Of a personal nature."

"No, we wouldn't."

She looked at him for a minute, then began pacing across the room. "Right. So my new friend—I suppose you've got a whole history worked out for him?"

"We can do that on the train."

"My new friend, the latest in that long line Daddy predicted—" She put her hand up before he could speak. "You want me to get into the spirit of things, don't you? Anyway, he's all in a bother. Conscience?"

Connolly ignored the tone. "We're building a terrible weapon," he said deliberately. "So terrible it will change everything. We thought the Nazis were building one too. But now they're gone, so he doesn't understand why it's still secret. Some of the scientists don't want it used at all. They want to get the word out, but there's nothing they can do. The whole place is sealed up tight. The only hope they've got of controlling it is if everyone knows. If everyone gets scared. Otherwise the army can do anything it wants. Not just Japan. Russia, anywhere it likes. Why not tell our own allies, unless we want to keep it for ourselves? For afterward. As long as we own the secret, we're a threat to everybody. We'll be the Nazis."

Emma stared at him, her face sober and quiet. She had stopped pacing and was crossing her arms and holding herself as if she were huddling against a chill. "Is that true?"

"It's how Corporal Waters would see it."

"The scientists, I mean. Do they really want everyone to know?"

454

"They will. Right now all they can think about is getting it to work. They think it's theirs. They don't realize they're just doing piecework for the army."

"Do you believe it, though? Or is it all just part of the story?"

"It doesn't matter. But I think if you're the only guy holding a gun, a lot of people will feel like Corporal Waters. Maybe they'd be right."

"But you want to stop them. Even if they're right."

"I don't believe in handing someone else a gun either. He might shoot. People usually do."

"Like cowboys."

"No, like countries. Like show trials and wars and killing lots of people, not just one. I don't trust them with a gun. I'm not an idealist."

"Yes, you are," she said quietly. "You're the worst kind. You want to do it yourself." She dropped her arms and slowly moved toward him. "I know. I run to type."

He stood now, facing her, afraid to touch. "I won't ask. If you don't want to."

She shook her head, placing her hand on his arm. "No. Ask me. Nobody ever did before."

"You'd have to be careful. Remember Karl."

"Careful. If I were careful, I wouldn't be here at all."

"Then you will."

"You want me to, don't you?"

He nodded.

"You'll come with me?"

"I have to. You're my cover," he said.

"What do you mean?"

"I told you, nobody knows. If I leave the Hill, our friends in G-2 will follow me. They'll wonder where I'm going. They won't wonder after they see you."

"You think of everything, don't you? And what's our story? Are we supposed to be having an affair?"

"We could be," he said, smiling.

"Do you think anybody would believe that?"

"Anybody."

She was silent for a moment. "But no harm to Matthew. What if you're wrong? What if he won't do it? What if he sends me packing?"

"Then we'll have a weekend in New York. He won't, though. The stuff's real. They won't be able to resist."

"But no harm."

"No," he said, reaching for her. "You're awfully loyal to your husband."

"Mm," she said. "All of them. But think what I do for you."

He kissed her, holding her close to him now. "I just appeal to your better instincts."

"You're a bastard. You'd even use this to get your way, wouldn't you?"

"If it would work," he said, kissing her again. "Would it?"

"Ask me later."

"I thought they canceled all leaves," Mills said.

"Civilians get special privileges," Connolly

said. "It's only four days. Don't you think I'm entitled to one, listening to you all day?"

"Two leaves were arranged," Mills said, handing him the papers. "Maybe you'd better take both."

"I don't think so. I only need one," Connolly said, taking it. "Are you being cute, or is it just my imagination?"

"Anything special you want me to do while you're gone?"

"No. Check in with Holliday, though, just to be nice. See if anybody's gone to church. Tell him I still haven't got a goddamn thing. Not even an idea. Maybe I'll think of something while I'm away."

"You intend to do a lot of thinking, huh?"

"You know, in security you get to know all kinds of things. The trick's not to leap to any conclusions. Of course, I don't have to tell you—you're a professional."

"Right," Mills said, then grinned. "Have fun anyway."

Connolly smiled back. "Do me one favor, though, will you? When you talk to whoever it is you talk to, would you leave her name out of it? I wouldn't want anyone to get the wrong idea. People get upset."

"You're lucky you don't get shot. You going to leave a number? It's procedure."

"Make one up. I'd only leave a phony."

"And I'd find out. That's procedure too."

Oppenheimer had pulled strings for a Pullman, an oasis of privilege on the crowded train, but even so the trip was hot and dusty. After the high New Mexican plateau, they went down into the flat bottomland of America, where the heat was oppressive, a furnace of hot air that left grit on the skin as it blew through the car, drying sweat and scattering paper. A group of servicemen, rowdy and insistent, had taken over the club car, and their singing as they crossed the empty plains had the disruptive sound of a brawl. Chattanooga Choo-Choo, Connolly thought irritably. Maybe the musicians who had written the happy train songs had been drunk in the club car too, seeing the dingy interiors glow with a boozy shine. Dinner was chewy lamb chops and canned peas, slapped down by harried waiters with an eye to the line already forming at the door for the next sitting. They drank cold beer and went to bed, exhausted without being tired, waiting for the clicking of the rails to lull them to sleep. Instead Connolly lay on top of the hot sheets, squirming in the dark, and finally dreamed of Eisler standing at the blackboard, studying his fate.

The next day was better. Emma sat leafing through magazines, her skirt hiked up around her thighs to catch the breeze. The landscape was green now and moist, and Connolly watched it lazily, ignoring the magazine in his lap. A GI's account of Okinawa, filtered through another Connolly at OWI for the right polish. No incontinence and night fears. Wounds to the abdomen, never lower. No one was ever hit in the genitals. Corpses in photographs were whole. Connolly had heard stories of loose body parts being removed from the ground so that the picture could be shot. But that had been before, when morale had been an issue. Now there was a new brutality to the layouts. GIs stared out from the slick pages, glazed and slack-jawed, stunned by the fanaticism of the enemy. The hills were pockmarked with thousands of hand-dug caves. Even at the end, the war meant to go on and on. There was still time for the gadget. Outside the window, farms and wooded hills slipped by, sleepy and unknowing.

A quick thunderstorm sent streaks of rain along the dining car windows during lunch, blocking the view. Emma, preoccupied, picked at her chicken salad, too listless to look out.

"You all right?" Connolly said.

She nodded.

"You're not sorry you came?"

"I was sorry before I came. Now I'm curious."

"About Matthew?"

She nodded again. "What's he like, do you think? Do you know, actually? Did they tell you?"

"An address. He works in Union Square. He still does some kind of work for the party. I don't know what."

"Do you mind? About him, I mean."

"I haven't seen him yet," he said lightly. "Is he good-looking?"

"He was. Maybe he just seemed that way because the comrades were so dreary." She caught his look. "Yes, he's good-looking. Fair. Thin—he never ate. Cheese and a biscuit, that would do. He liked—You don't really want to know all this, do you?"

"No."

"No," she agreed. "Anyway, that was then. People change." She turned her fork, thinking. "If he's still working for the party, why is he allowed to stay?"

"It's not illegal."

"But they keep an eye out."

"I guess."

"Do they know about me?"

"No, you don't exist."

"I like that. Like riding on trains, isn't it? No one knows who you are. You're just a ticket. I've always liked that. Even now. I shouldn't, I know, but I'm rather enjoying this."

"You don't look as if you're enjoying it."

"I am, though. In a way. Watching you get all cross in the heat. Nobody to bother us. Not even having to talk."

"Not a care in the world."

She looked up at him. "All right, not exactly."

"We're not exactly alone, either."

"What do you mean?"

"Don't look—no, really, don't look. Why do people always turn when you say that? When you get a chance, the guy two tables behind you in the paisley tie."

460

"What am I supposed to do, drop a fork?" she said, teasing. "I haven't done that since school. Are you serious about this?"

"You might look for a waiter. If you want some more iced tea."

"You are serious." She waited for a minute, then turned to look, her eyes resting only for a moment on the other table.

"What, the man with the ice cream?" she said as she turned back. "You're joking."

"No. He's tailing us."

"How do you know?"

"Did you see his hat? They always put their hats where they can get them in a hurry. It's practically a calling card."

"Rubbish."

"He hasn't looked at you once."

"Maybe I'm not his type."

"Not that way. He hasn't looked at you at all."

"I don't believe you."

"Fine. All the better. You'll act naturally, which is what we want."

"Not now, I won't," she said, putting down her fork. "Why all the mystery, anyway? It's ridiculous. Isn't he one of yours?"

"I hope so."

"Then why—"

"Army Intelligence doesn't like me very much. Somebody comes in from the outside, they have to think something's going on. They hate being left out. So they watch. It's what they do."

"But can't you have him called off?"

"Then they'd *know* something was going on. Right now I'm just a bad boy taking advantage of some privileges they wish they had. They have no idea what we're doing."

"Except the obvious."

He smiled. "Except the obvious."

"Then why did you say you hoped it was them?"

"Well, there's another possibility. We still don't know who's on the Hill. Karl was in intelligence and he's dead. This guy may be one of ours, but I don't recognize him. So I hope it's just somebody Lansdale's brought in to play house detective. Otherwise, we could have a problem. Either way, I don't want him around when you see Matthew. That could ruin everything."

Emma thought for a minute, stirring with her long iced tea spoon. "You're right. I'm not enjoying this. Not anymore. It's not much fun, is it, everybody lying to everybody. I wish you hadn't told me. Why did you?"

"You'd have to know sometime. We have to lose him. I can't do that alone."

"Why bother? You'd just be looking for the next. At least he's the devil you know."

"We can't do this with an audience. Whoever he is. One of ours. One of theirs. Maybe both at the same time. We can't take the chance. Matthew has to believe you, or this won't work at all."

"And what if he's just a man with a hat?"

"Then he won't mind. Look, nobody knows about Matthew. It's the one chance we have of protecting him."

"Unless it works," Emma said, turning her head to the window. "The rain's stopped. Now it's just steaming."

"I said I'd do what I could," Connolly said. "Why don't we take this one step at a time?"

"Right. What do we do first? Push him off the train?"

"It's not a joke, Emma."

"Then stop enjoying it so much. It's all a game to you. Spot him, lose him. See how good they are. See how good you are. My God, I wish we were done with this."

"We're almost there," he said evenly, calming her.

"Can I ask you something? If no one knows we're doing this, that means no one's looking after us either, doesn't it? If anything happens, I mean. There won't be anyone. Not even the man with the hat."

"That's right."

"I hadn't thought about that. Should I be frightened?"

"Are you?"

"No. Oddly enough. But then I'm a well-known fool."

"Nobody knows that here," he said, smiling. "You're just a ticket, remember?"

"Your friend knows," she said, moving her head slightly toward him.

"He knows you're here. He doesn't know what you're doing."

"What am I supposed to be doing?"

"Having fun. Being bad."

He reached across the table to cover her hand.

"I'm not," she said.

"Pretend. Smile back at me. Laugh a little, if you can manage it."

"I thought we were trying to lose him, not put on a show."

"Not yet. Later. First we have to establish you."

"How do we do that?"

"Finish your tea. Then we'll go back to the compartment and hang out a DO NOT DISTURB sign and make lots of noise."

"They listen at keyholes?" she said.

"They bribe porters."

"You're serious?"

"About the noise, anyway."

"It's hot."

"Steaming. We'll take some ice."

She laughed at him now, a low murmur.

"That's it," he said. "Just like that."

"How long does all this take? Before I'm established?"

"We have all day. We can lose him in New Jersey. People are always getting lost in New Jersey."

They left the train in Newark, half hidden by a pool of servicemen greeting their families on the platform.

"Go to the ladies', then meet me at the buses," he said as they walked.

"Where?"

"Out to the right. Follow the signs."

464

"While he follows you."

"No, he'll assume we're still on the train."

"What about the porter?"

"We left the tip—he won't care. He'll think we're in the club car. Last call."

"And if he does follow you?"

"Then you won't see me at the bus station."

But he was waiting for her, fanning himself with a newspaper on one of the wooden benches. The air, heavy and sticky, smelled of cheap diesel.

"What have you got in here, anyway?" he said, pointing to her suitcase.

"My trousseau." She sat down. "So are we alone?"

"I think so."

"Now what?"

"Bus in ten minutes. Then we find a hotel."

"You didn't book?"

"Yes," he said smiling, "but if we go there, why did we bother to get off the train?"

"I told you I wasn't very good at this. I just want a bath. I don't care where it is. What do you think that man's doing now?"

"Our friend? He's running around Penn Station. Sweating."

Emma giggled. "Goodness, he must be angry. Unless you're wrong, of course. Maybe he's just a man heading for a long soak in the tub and we're the ones running around sweating."

"Either way," Connolly said.

The bus was crowded and Connolly had to

stand, resting against the arm of her seat and holding on to the luggage rack as they bounced through the New Jersey marshes. When they swept around the great curve to the tunnel, the city gleaming across the water, he felt for the first time the excitement of homecoming. Then the overbright bathroom tiles of the tunnel and they were in the crowded streets, turning down into the basement of the Hotel Dixie with its rows of storage lockers and shoeshine stands and people holding tickets on their way to somewhere. Out on the street, he felt overwhelmed, like a farm boy in the movies. Even in the heat, everything moved quickly, taxis and boys in navy whites and khaki and lights racing through neon tubes. No one had even heard of Los Alamos.

They took a taxi to a hotel on Lexington, not far from Grand Central, where he managed to wangle a room facing the side street. When he opened the window, soot blew in with the sound of the Third Avenue el, but there was a fan and water gushed from the taps, a world away from the drought on the Hill.

"Not exactly the Waldorf, is it?" Emma said.

"We wouldn't get into the Waldorf. Have a bath, you'll feel better. It's the same water."

"At half the price. Care to join me?" she said, undressing.

"You go. I have to make some calls."

"Old girlfriends?"

"No. About tomorrow."

"Oh," she said, no longer smiling, then

went to the bathroom and closed the door.

He called Tony at Costello's to arrange the next day's meeting—"Yeah, two booths, I got it. What you got going, some skirt?"— then talked to a friend on the paper about the wire. He placed a call to Mills, smoking a cigarette by the window as he waited for the long-distance connection.

"I thought you were at the Hotel Pennsylvania," Mills said.

"What makes you think I'm not?"

There was a pause. "Very funny," Mills said finally.

"I never made it. It's hot back here. I decided to cool off in the country instead."

"Which is why the operator said the call was from New York."

"Must be a mistake."

"Yeah. How'd you manage the disappearing act?"

Connolly was silent.

"Okay, so I'm just wasting the government's money. Why'd you call, anyway?"

"To hear what you just told me."

Mills paused again. "You don't want to annoy people, Mike, you really don't. Now what am I supposed to tell him?"

"Tell him there's a good band on the Pennsylvania roof. He'll enjoy it. I just want some privacy. Out here in the country."

"Yeah, privacy. Well, you've got it. Unless I can trace the call."

"Don't even bother. I'm in a booth. But you probably figured that already."

"Shit," Mills said, hanging up.

When he went into the bathroom, she was lying back with her knees sticking out of the water like islands, staring ahead at nothing.

"You going to stay in there all night?" he said, starting to undress.

"Everything's going to be all right, isn't it?" she said, still preoccupied.

"Yes."

"I mean, really all right," she said, looking up at him.

He nodded. "Come on, finish up and we'll go out somewhere."

"You're joking. I can't move."

"Okay," he said, climbing into the tub and falling on her, splashing water over the side.

"What are you doing?" she said, laughing.

"Let's stay here," he said, kissing her.

"Stop. Oh, look at the mess."

"It's water. They expect that here."

"Oh, it's that sort of hotel, is it?"

"Sure."

"No, really, we can't. Look at the floor." She sat up, water sliding off her breasts.

"I thought you couldn't move," he said, holding her by the waist. "Come on, lie down."

"You ought to cool off," she said, rolling over on top of him and pushing him under. When he pulled his head up, sputtering, she was already out of the tub, grabbing a towel. He stood up, playing a sea monster, and reached out for her.

"My God, you're not going to chase me

around the room," she said, laughing. "You look ridiculous."

He lunged for her. She darted out of the room, and ran over to the fan, but he grabbed her by the waist, pulling her toward the bed.

"We're all wet," she said, playing.

"So what?" He lowered her to the bed.

"The bed'll be sopping."

"We'll sleep in the tub," he said, moving his hand up along her leg, soapy and slick. "Anything else?"

"The curtain," she said quickly, her breath shallow.

He grinned at her, then got up and flicked off the light. He had thought she might move, but she lay still, the fan blowing over her body. He stood at the foot of the bed, looking at her white skin in the faint light that came from the bathroom, then moved his hands along her legs, passing over her belly until they rested under her breasts. When he bent over and kissed them, one after the other, she shivered.

"It's not right," she said. "This isn't supposed to be fun."

He moved his face from her breasts up to her neck, lowering his body onto hers so that their wet skins slid against each other.

"Who says? Who made that up?"

She took his head in her hands as he bent to kiss her. "Tell me you love me. Tell me it's all right."

"It's all right," he said. And then, entering

her, he felt her clutch him inside, as if her whole body were holding on to him.

Afterward they showered separately, suddenly shy with each other. She toweled her hair by the fan, rubbing it with a tropical laziness.

"Do you really want to go out?" she said. "Can't we just have room service?"

"I don't think they have room service here. Maybe a bellboy with an ice bucket. Do you want a drink?"

"I'd fall over."

"You'll feel better after some food."

"Should I call him now?" she said unexpectedly.

"No. In the morning. Don't give him any time to think," he said, a hunter's voice. "I mean—"

"I know what you mean," she said dully, and got up to dress.

They ate in a restaurant near Times Square, oysters wedged in a plate of crushed ice and tall glasses of beer whose coating of frost evaporated in the heat. Outside, the streets were crowded and steamy. Emma picked at her food, barely making conversation, and after a second beer Connolly began to wilt too, so that even the rattling noise of the restaurant became fuzzy.

"Want to go hear some music?" he said.

She smiled at him. "You always said we'd do that. And now that we're here, I'm too tired to go. Maybe tomorrow. When it's over."

"All right," he said, not wanting to talk

about it. "We could go to the top of the RCA Building. There's always a breeze there."

"You don't have to entertain me. I'd be happy with bed."

But it was too hot to go back to the hotel, so they went to an air-cooled movie instead, where the crisp refrigerated air reminded him of the Hill. The newsreel was still filled with clips of German atrocities and now the long lines of DPs shuffling sadly past the bomb sites. The feature, something called *Pillow to Post*, with Ida Lupino, was bright and shiny, oblivious to what had come before, and halfway through Connolly forgot what it was supposed to be about. Emma took his hand in the movie, holding it lightly, as if they were on a date.

The streets were as crowded as before, people pouring out of the theaters and flirting and eating ice cream cones. The lights were dazzling. Knickerbocker beer. A giant Pepsi in perpetual effervescence. Here, anyway, the war was over, but everything familiar seemed to him suspended. They had all come out to pass the time while they waited for the next thing, the feature after the newsreel. What could it be except brighter, worth the wait?

He steered away from the theaters and they walked back on quieter streets, still holding hands, easy with each other, listening to the sound of her heels on the pavement. He'd thought of a drink in the Astor Bar, or now the Biltmore, but all that seemed curiously part of the past too, nothing to do with them.

Now they were a couple, eager to get home. When she smeared her face with cold cream back in the room, it seemed to him more intimate than lovemaking, a new familiarity.

He sat at the window while she drifted off to sleep, restless, and it occurred to him then, looking at her, that the trip wasn't about tomorrow anymore. Tomorrow would take care of itself. But while he waited, his life had changed. This was what it meant to be married. Her help, so casually asked for, now bound him in some deep obligation. If they stopped now they could be as they were, idly suspended like the crowd, hidden away in this cocoon of humid air. Instead, he would compromise her, as determined and heedless as Oppenheimer to see his project through. But they weren't going to stop—it was sleep talking, the nighttime jitters. This *was* the next thing. She had understood before he did, accepted it. She turned over in bed, no longer fitful, breathing deeply. He had always loved her fearlessness. Now she was offering it to him, a secret marriage. They could have something more than peace. He thought of her leaping up the trail at Chaco, eager, lending him a hand.

16

When he woke the next morning she was already up, sitting by the window in her slip, putting on red nail polish. A coffeepot and cups sat on the table.

"At last," she said. "Come and have your coffee. They *do* have room service, you see. You just have to ask."

He put on a robe. "What are you doing?"

"You want me to look the part, don't you?" She spread her nails in front of her. "A girl has to look her best for this sort of thing."

"It's pretty red," he said, pouring the coffee.

"Meaning too red. Darling, a lot you know. On Johanna Weber it's too red. On me, it'll be smart. There, see? Now we'll just wait for it to dry. Let's hope to God this fan doesn't give out—it's been going all night."

He drank the coffee, shaking his head to wake up. "You always do that undressed?"

"Of course. Until it dries. If it streaks, it's hell to get out. How many women have you actually been with?" she said, smiling. "Or don't you usually spend the night?"

He lit a cigarette with the Zippo, then looked at her through the smoke. "Are you always this cheerful, or are you nervous?"

She gave a half-laugh. "Don't be so knowing. A little of both, I guess. Maybe a lot. I'll be all right."

"Do you want to run through it again?"

"No. I know what to say. At least roughly. It's not exactly a script, is it? I mean, a lot depends on what *he* says."

"Okay. Let's call him."

"No. Finish your coffee and go take a shower. Then I'll call. I really don't think I can do this with an audience."

473

He looked at her, surprised. She came over and took his cigarette in one of the nooks of her outstretched fingers, taking a drag, then holding it out for him to take back. "What's the matter, don't you think I can?"

"I'll be at the restaurant."

"I know. I can't think why."

"Just to be around. In case you need me."

"Hovering, I suppose. All right. But not now, please. I mean it. Hurry up and clear out."

Connolly looked at his watch. "You think he's already at work?"

"You don't know the comrades. Up with the sun, they are."

"Better watch the jokes. He may not like it."

She glanced up at him. "You know, I hate to point this out, but he *is* my husband. I already know what he likes."

Connolly looked away and put out the cigarette. "Right. I keep forgetting."

"I don't mean what you think I mean. Oh, never mind. Come on, move. I've got a hair appointment."

"Does he like that?"

"*I* like it. I don't want to go looking like a ranch hand."

He looked at her, interested. "You want to impress him, don't you?"

She nodded. "A little. Is that so naughty of me? I suppose it is."

"You want to see if he's still attracted to you."

"I just want to see if he notices."

He stood under the shower, letting the water sting his face awake, feeling apprehensive. He hadn't expected to be a bystander. But if he couldn't trust her, what was the point? When the shower stopped, he heard her talking, low and indistinct, and he had to stop himself from flinging open the door. Instead he went over to the sink and started shaving, his ears straining to make out her voice. It had to be him. What was taking so long? He stood there, his face half covered with soap, listening, then turned on the tap to rinse the razor so that he wouldn't hear any more.

When he came out of the bathroom, a towel around his waist, she was still sitting with the phone cradled in her lap, looking out the window.

"Any problems?"

"Twelve, not twelve-thirty," she said, still looking away. "That all right?"

"Sure," he said. "Why?"

She looked at him, a wry smile at the corner of her mouth. "He has to be back for a meeting."

"A meeting?"

"You overrate my charms. Still, he did manage to fit me in."

Her voice seemed light and wounded at the same time, and he didn't know how to respond. "How did he sound?"

"Surprised."

She got up and began putting on her dress. "Did he know the place?"

"He'll find it. Third and forty-fourth, right? He did wonder why we couldn't meet nearer the office, but I said since I'd come halfway

475

across the country he might manage a trip uptown. My God, do you think it's possible for someone not to change at all?"

"Did he ask why there?"

"Yes. I told him I'd always wanted to see the Thurber murals. You got that wrong, though—never heard of him. Stop worrying, it's all right."

"And you?"

"I'm all right too," she said, going over to the mirror to put on lipstick. "A little funny right now, but I'll be fine. I'm even beginning to look forward to it." She blotted her lips. "You needn't fret. This is going to be easier than I thought."

"A piece of cake."

"Well, a piece of something. Right," she said, packing her handbag. "I'm off. What do you think?" She flounced her hair. "Something off the shoulders? But not too gorgeous."

"You're beautiful," he said seriously.

She stopped by the door and looked at him, her face soft. "Thanks," she said. Then, determined to be light, she winked at him. "Next time try saying it with your clothes on. Shall I meet you back here? We've still got the morning to get through."

"No, let's go for a walk. I'll meet you at the library. Over on Fifth. Out in front, by the lions. Patience and Fortitude."

She looked at him blankly.

"That's what they're called—the lions."

"The things you know," she said.

When she was gone, the room was quiet, and he walked around nervously, at loose ends.

Everything was different from the way he had imagined it back on the Hill. The air was close, smelling of her perfume. He went over to the suitcase and took out the envelope with Oppenheimer's papers. He held it for a minute, staring at it as if the weight of what was inside would ground him, but now it seemed no more serious than a prop. It was a piece of the greatest secret of the war, and all he could think about was how she'd feel when she saw him, the first man she'd loved.

She took hours. He waited at the library, hiding from the sun under the wispy trees on the terrace, then pacing back toward the lions, afraid he would miss her. The day was hot, but not as humid as before, and occasional drafts of baked air would sweep down the avenue, blowing skirts. He stood for a long time watching the traffic, streams of buses and shiny cars and not a military vehicle in sight, shading his eyes against the glare. Everything seemed too bright and buoyant, as if the city had opened up to the sun and even furtive meetings would have to be drenched in light. He smoked, impatient, and then he saw her coming across the street and all the waiting disappeared. He knew as she stepped off the curb that it was one of those moments that becomes a photograph even as it's happening, flashed into the memory to be taken out later, still sharp. She was wearing a white dress with padded shoulders, spectator pumps, a bag clutched under her arm. Her skirt moved with her as she walked, outlining her legs. Her hair, just grazing the back of her neck, swung as she looked back and forth, eager and expectant, her red lips already parted in a smile when she caught his eye. He felt he had never seen her before.

"How do I look?" she said, bright and pleased with herself.

"A woman only asks that when she already knows the answer."

"Tell me anyway."

"Like a million dollars. How do you feel?"

"Not quite that rich. These shoes," she said, grimacing.

They went behind the library to Bryant Park and watched people, pretending not to look at the time. She sat with her legs crossed, one shoe dangling off the end of her foot.

"Hadn't you better give me the papers?" she said casually.

He reached into his breast pocket for the envelope and then unconsciously held it in front of him, reluctant to let it go.

"What's the matter? Think I'm going to run off and give it to the Russians or something?"

He handed her the envelope and watched her slip it into her bag.

"None of this seems real, does it?" he said. "I've just committed a crime and we're making jokes."

"Sorry," she said coolly. "It's just nerves."

"No, not you—everything."

"What's it supposed to be like?"

He shrugged. "I don't know. Trenchcoats

and fog, I guess. Anyway, not a nice, ordinary day in the park."

"You sound disappointed," she said, then looked up at the sky. "You might get your rain, though. Would that help?"

"It might."

"Your trouble is, you're stuck in some *Boy's Own* story. Secret drawers and lemon-juice ink and all the rest of it. But maybe it's always like this, really. Out here in the sun. Feed the birds, exchange a little information, and go about your business. Maybe they're all up to something." She nodded toward the people on the other benches.

"They don't look it."

"Well, neither do we. Neither did Professor Eisler. I still can't quite believe it."

"He didn't feel he was doing anything wrong. He was just an altar boy."

"You always feel something," she said, looking out at the park. Her voice was darker, as if a cloud had passed over it, and he was quiet for a moment, not sure how to change the subject.

"What about the woman over there, in the straw hat?" he said, a parlor game. "What's she up to?"

"Her?"

"She doesn't look like an agent."

"Perhaps she's cheating on her husband."

"Not the same thing."

"It feels like it," Emma said. "It's exciting, all the pretending. And then always something awful underneath."

He turned to face her. "I won't cheat."

"No, don't," she said, smiling a little. "I'd know." She looked down at her watch. "You'd better push off now. I think I'd like a few minutes alone. Get myself in the mood. You know. I can't concentrate with you around, mooning and getting into a state. What's it like anyway, the restaurant? Gloomy?"

"Noisy. It's a news hangout."

"So much for your atmosphere," she said, laughing. "No, don't—you'll smudge."

"Okay," he said, getting up. "You remember where it is?"

"Yes, yes. Come on. Push off."

"You're sure you'll be all right?"

She looked up at him. "I'll be fine. I've had lots of practice."

"You're not going to get me in any trouble with that, are you?" Tony said, watching Connolly string the wire between the booths.

"Would I do that to you?" He sat in the corner of his booth, cupping the earpiece in his hand so that he appeared to be merely leaning his head against the wall. "Can you see anything?"

"Trouble. That's all I see."

"How about a beer?"

"Sure. You want something to eat? You got a whole booth."

"What's cold?"

"Fried clams."

480

Connolly grinned. "Fried when? Just bring me a tuna sandwich."

"Tuna sandwich," Tony said, moving away. "For a whole booth."

The bar in front was beginning to fill up, but Connolly still had the dining room to himself. He hid the earpiece behind a sugar canister and pretended to read the paper, everything in him alert. The Thurber murals, the pride of the house, were the color of adobe, over-sized women and wary men chasing each other around the room in a plaster frieze while no one, except the dogs, paid the slightest attention. There was a burst of laughter in the bar. Connolly had forgotten the sheer energy of New York. He thought of the polite academic murmurs of meals on the Hill. Here everyone seemed to be slapping everyone else on the back.

He had begun the crossword puzzle when Emma appeared, pointed in by Tony, who gave him a look when he saw her go past to the next booth. Connolly lowered his head to the paper, so that all he saw was the streak of red nails at eye level. Her perfume stayed behind her in the thick air. He was tempted to turn around—a last reassuring look—but instead he imagined her sitting in the booth, composed, winning Tony with a smile as he brought her iced tea. She was right, there was excitement in pretending. Absurdly, he thought of her shoes being tight and the fact that no one else knew.

He glanced up as each new arrival entered the room, then walked past to the back tables.

481

Tony brought the sandwich, but Connolly let it sit there; too anxious to eat. How could Lawson be late? But they had been early.

When he did appear, five minutes later, Connolly knew it at once. He was tall, his bony frame covered in rumpled clothes that seemed just thrown on—dark cotton shirt damp at the armpits, plain tie knotted tightly, yanked down from the unbuttoned collar, jacket held by two fingers over his shoulder, a Village look. His pale hair, receding but still full on top, glistened with sweat; his face, the boyish soft face of a perennial teenager, was red, as if he had been running in the heat. He looked around nervously, then broke into a broad smile when he saw her.

"Emma," he said, coming over to the booth. "My God, you look a treat." He continued to stand for a second, and Connolly imagined him awkward, staring at her. "What do I do? Do I kiss you?"

Connolly heard no response, but she must have nodded, because there was a rustle of clothing as he bent over, then took a seat in the booth. Connolly leaned into the wall, picking up the receiver and hiding it against his ear, his crossword pencil lifted to write.

"I can't believe it," Lawson said, his voice still English and hurried, enthusiastic. "All this time. You turning up like this."

"The bad penny," Emma said.

"No, it's marvelous. But what are you doing here? How long have you been in the States? How did—where to begin? Tell me everything." His words rushed out, happily infectious, with the guileless wonder of meeting an old school friend.

"It has been a while, hasn't it?"

"My God, look at you," he said again, and Connolly felt him lean back against the booth to take her in.

"You're the same," she said, an appraisal, but he took it for a compliment.

"Well, the hair," he said, evidently brushing it back at the temple. "I expect it'll all go one day. But you—I can't get over it. How's your family?"

"My family?" she said, disconcerted. "They're fine. I haven't seen them in years. I'm living here now. I'm married."

"Married?"

"Matthew, I divorced you years ago," she said smoothly. "Surely you knew?"

"No."

"You weren't there to contest it. You wouldn't have, would you?"

He was silent for a minute. "How could I? Look, I never explained—"

"Darling, don't. Really. It was all a very long time ago, and it doesn't matter now. I haven't come for that."

"I don't understand."

"We haven't much time. I need to talk to you. We can save all those happy days *unter den linden* for another time."

"You're still angry with me."

"I'm not really," she said softly. "I was. Well, I don't know what I was—not angry. But that

483

was a lifetime ago. Before the war. We were just children, weren't we? Anyway, never mind. We'd better order."

Connolly looked up, surprised to see Tony standing at the next booth. They ordered sandwiches.

"It wasn't all bad, was it?" Matthew said when he'd gone. "We had fun. In the beginning. God, your father—"

His voice was bright again, and Connolly thought he could hear the mischief of those years, the delight in provoking. Is this what she'd liked, the way he thumbed his nose at the world?

"You were the most marvelous girl," he said.

"I'm still pretty marvelous. What about you?"

"Me?"

"Still working with the comrades?"

"Of course."

"Doing what, exactly?"

"I work on the paper. It's quite good, actually. There was a falling off after the Pact—reporters jumping ship, you know. But of course the war changed all that. Shoulders together. Now, well, we'll see."

"You mean to stay, then?"

"If I can. We're not exactly Uncle Sam's favorite publication, but we're still in business. Browder's worked miracles. Anyway, this is the place now. Politically, it's all a bit like your Uncle Arthur, but everything will change after the war. It has to. The pressures will be enormous."

He stopped as the plates were put in front of them.

"You are the same," she said, a smile in her voice. "Still on the march."

"I can't help that," he said, catching her tone. "It still needs doing. I grant you, it's not Spain," he said, reminiscent again. "It's a different sort of fight, but as you say, we're not young anymore."

"I never said that. I said I was still marvelous."

"Yes," he said, his voice lingering. "But married. Who did you marry, by the way? Someone here?"

"A scientist. No one you know. Matthew," she said, pausing, "I need you to do something for me."

"Anything."

"No, don't say that till you hear what it is. Something important."

"Is that why you looked me up?"

"Yes."

"Funny. I thought it might be—I don't know, about us."

"What, after all this time?"

He didn't answer.

"There's nothing about us. Do you understand? I want to be quite clear about that."

"Why, then?"

"I need somebody I can trust. Or maybe it's the other way around, somebody who'll trust me. Who knows me."

Connolly cupped the receiver closer to his ear, feeling literally like a fly on the wall. The approach, smooth and plausible, was all hers.

"I don't understand. Are you in some sort of trouble?"

"No, not exactly. We all are, in a way. That's the point. God, this is complicated. I'm not quite sure where to begin. It'll seem fantastic to you. It is fantastic. Sometimes I don't quite believe it myself."

"Emma, what are you talking about?"

"Right," she said, verbally sitting up. "Here goes. It won't make sense, but hear me out. Do you have a cigarette?"

"You smoke now?"

"Oh yes, I'm all grown up." Connolly heard the match strike. "That's better. My husband is a scientist."

"You said."

"A physicist. Working for the government. We're at an army base out west."

"Where?"

"I can't tell you that," she said, then caught herself with a nervous laugh. "Sorry. Force of habit. New Mexico. It's a secret base, you see. They're very strict about that. They're making weapons."

"What kind of weapons?" he said, his voice lower.

"Bombs. Do you know anything about atomic fission? No, I don't suppose you do. Nobody does. It doesn't matter. The point—"

"I know what fission is. There was talk before the war. Nothing since. Do you mean to say they've actually gone ahead? I thought it was supposed to be impossible."

"No, they've done it. At least, they think they

have. They're going to test it very soon. That's why there isn't any time."

"Do you know what you're saying? It's fantastic."

"Yes. Funny, you get so used to it, you stop thinking about it that way. But it's real. Twenty thousand tons of TNT."

"Jesus."

Connolly had told her ten. He wondered if she had simply forgotten or had begun to be swept up in her own story. Why not twenty?

"It's capable of wiping out a whole city," she said. "Berlin, even."

"Berlin's gone."

"Tokyo, then. They'll use it somewhere. And there's something new—it's not just the explosive power. They can reckon that, but no one knows about the radiation effects. They're going to use it on people and they don't even know yet what it will do. And there's no *point* now."

"Slow down."

"No, let me finish. As long as it's secret, they *will* use it. Unless someone makes a stink. The scientists can't—they're terrified. But if we don't get the word out somehow, it'll be too late. They mustn't, you see. We're talking about thousands and thousands of lives, and they've already *won*. Someone's got to stop them." Her voice slowed. "Anyway, I thought of you."

"Me? I don't understand. Do you want me to put this in the paper?"

"No, of course not. They'd arrest you. It's a military secret—no paper's going to be

487

allowed to print it. Otherwise the scientists would just leak it."

"What, then?"

"We need to get the information out of the country."

"Out of the country," he repeated slowly.

"To the Russians. They don't know."

"That's not possible."

"Yes, it is. There isn't a single Russian on the project. Brits galore, even Germans, but not one Russian. I know, I live there. Think what that means."

"What do you think it means?"

"I think they'd make one unholy fuss if they found out—maybe enough to stop all this before it's too late. They're the only ones who could now."

He was quiet for a minute. "Do you know what you're saying?"

"Yes, I know, it's an awful chance. But someone has to take it."

"You, for instance," he said skeptically. "Joan of Arc."

"No, not me. I'm just a messenger. Someone on the project."

"Your husband."

"No, someone else. I'm—I'm seeing some-one else. You needn't look that way. I'm all grown up, remember?"

"Were you all grown up in Berlin too?" he said. "I've often wondered."

"No. Were you? Look, don't let's start. It's a little late in the day for that. Will you help?"

"You can't be serious. Do you think I'm a spy?"

"Do you think I am?"

He paused. "I don't know what to think. It's all so extraordinary. You coming here like this. Bloody thirty-nine steps. What's it to do with you, anyway?"

"I told you, I'm a messenger. I want to help him. It wouldn't be the first time, would it? Surely you remember that."

"That was different. I never asked you to do anything like this. Anyway, why you?"

"Because I know you. I couldn't think of anyone else. Do you think if I had, I'd have come to you? You're the last person I'd ask for help. But as it happens, you *are* the last person. I'm not exactly on speakers with the other comrades. They'd never believe me."

"But I would."

"I thought you might," she said softly. "Maybe I was wrong. Still, it doesn't matter. You don't have to believe me. I have some papers. Here," she said. Connolly heard her take out the envelope. "Let someone else decide."

"You are serious. What is it?"

"Scientific information about the project. A part of it. People only know parts. But Steven has more. Give them to somebody who'll know what they mean. I wouldn't have the faintest, and neither would you, so don't even bother. But they'll know. And they'll know he's real. He just wants to talk to somebody, that's all. While there's time."

"What makes you think I can do this?"

"You know people—you were always good at that. Look, Matthew, I never said you were a spy, whatever that means. Maybe you are—I don't care, so much the better. All the comrades are a little bit, aren't they? They all like a bit of intrigue between meetings. Anyway, you don't have to spy on anybody. Just pass it on and there's an end to it. Nothing to do with you. Nothing to do with me. Let the comrades decide."

"You haven't changed. You always hated them."

"I hated what they did to you."

"And now you want to help them."

"Maybe I don't care what they do to you anymore."

In the silence, Connolly could hear a coffee spoon clank against the cup. *Don't quarrel,* he wanted to shout. *Not yet. You haven't got him yet.*

"I never meant to hurt you," he said.

"If I said I believed you, would it make any difference?"

He sighed. "You've become hard, Emma."

"Well, for Christ's sake," a voice boomed next to Connolly. "I thought you were in Washington. How the hell are you, anyway?"

Connolly looked up, startled and annoyed, palming the earpiece and lowering his hand. Not now. "Jerry," he said.

"Why didn't you tell me you were back? Been over to the paper yet?"

"I'm not back. Just for the day."

490

But Jerry, taking a seat, wasn't listening. "Oswald's gone, you know. Keeled over right in the city room. Broad daylight. I almost felt sorry for the bastard. But what the hell are you doing up here?"

"Jerry, I'm waiting for somebody," he said nervously. Behind him he could hear them talking.

"Oh yeah? What, some skirt? For Christ's sake, Connolly, when are you going to grow up? Hey, you're looking good, though. You know they promoted that fuck Levine. If you're smart, you'll stay in Washington."

And on. Connolly watched his mouth open and close, the eager sounds a blur of distraction from the low voices on the other side of the booth. Why didn't he go? Connolly didn't have to talk, just nod from time to time, but he couldn't hear the others either, so he sat there in an anxious limbo, trapped while Emma carried on alone. What if they were fighting, picking at old scabs while the envelope sat there, ignored? Still, what could he have done in any case? She had always been alone here. Was she even aware of him? Was she explaining the earnest Corporal Waters? What were they saying? But she didn't need him any more than Jerry did.

"Come on, Jerry, blow," he said finally. "I'm waiting for somebody." He smiled, a kind of leer. "She's the nervous type."

"All right, all right," Jerry said, getting up. "Hey, Ken's in the bar too. Come and say hello."

491

"On the way out, okay? Have one on me."

"Nah, I've got to go," he said, looking at his watch. "Looks to me like she stood you up." He grinned.

"Not a chance."

Connolly lit a cigarette, waving to Jerry at the door, and tried to calm himself. What if Jerry had seen the wire? Made a scene? He picked it up anyway and cradled it against his ear.

"There is one condition," Emma was saying. What was this? They hadn't talked about this. Had he agreed, then? "You know I wouldn't lift a finger for your friends. They're as bad as the rest."

"They're not, but go on," he said.

"This," she said, referring to the envelope. "It's not for them to keep. Not another secret. They've got to talk about it, do you understand?"

"Yes."

"People have to know what it is. Otherwise there's no point. Steven isn't—political. They have to know that. I won't have him tricked. Will you promise me that?" she asked, an impossible request.

"People do things for different reasons. We respect that," he said, oddly formal, on duty.

"No, you have to tell them. It's not some windfall for your bloody army. He won't do that."

"Then why this?" he said, fingering the envelope.

"There's not enough there to make a bomb,

492

you know. He's not completely bonkers. Just enough to go public. That's all he wants. It's not for him. He's—he's a good man."

"Unlike the rest of us."

"No," she said thoughtfully, "in some ways he's very like the way you used to be. I was always a fool for the good-of-humanity line, wasn't I? I thought you meant it."

"I did."

"Yes. It was caring for one person that was difficult."

"Emma—"

"Never mind. We haven't time. I'm supposed to be shopping or something. This is important—thousands of people, not just two. Promise me you'll explain about Steven."

"They'll want to know more, if this is really what you say it is."

"Yes, he's prepared for that. But they have to know the *why* of it. That's the bargain."

"They don't like to bargain."

"No one's ever given them something like this before. You'll see. They won't believe their luck. God knows they don't deserve it."

"Then why hand it to them?"

"Well, it's a funny old world, isn't it? They're all we've got. Anyway, it's not me. I'm just the postman. But promise me, about Steven. No tricks."

Connolly waited for his answer, the sensible evasion, the obvious impossibility of taking any kind of responsibility for what would happen.

"Yes, I promise," he said. It was as easy and

493

expedient as a vow, and it was then that Connolly knew she'd wanted him to lie to her, a personal proof.

"That's that, then," she said. "I'd better go. Do put that away now, will you? Not the sort of thing one leaves lying about. I can't tell you the relief, getting rid of it."

"Emma," he said, "is it true, all this?"

"Why?" she said, disarming him. "Don't you think I'd have the guts?"

"I don't know what you'd do anymore. You're different."

"No, still marvelous," she said, her voice bitter. "But I tell you what. If you have second thoughts, just chuck it in the bin and no one's the wiser. But I'd have someone give it a look, I really would. Who knows? There might be a promotion in it for you. Just keep my name out of the thank-you speech. Come to think of it, you don't know my name now, do you? Maybe that's best."

"You never used to be like this," he said, not really answering her. "How do I contact you?"

"You don't. I'm finished with it now. Steven's address is inside. A box number. They read the post, by the way, so tell whoever it is to be careful—well, that sounds silly, doesn't it? Of course they would. Just tell them to give him a time and a place and he'll know. Somewhere in Santa Fe—he's not allowed to travel. If he doesn't hear, well, then he'll assume the comrades aren't interested and we'll have to think of something else."

"Emma," he said, his voice low. "In Berlin, when I—I was under orders."

"I don't want to hear it."

"No, don't go. You have to know what happened when I left. I couldn't tell you. I couldn't tell anybody. They said lives might depend on it."

"Lives did," she said sharply.

Connolly heard her get up. Flustered, he turned and looked up to see her standing there, her padded shoulders pulled back, rigid with anger. He wanted to signal her, but her eyes were fixed on Matthew, oblivious to the room around them.

"I don't mean ours," Lawson was saying. "We were just kids. The others—they had a list, the whole network. I had to disappear. I couldn't tell anybody. They *ordered* me not to, do you understand? It was important. There were people involved. It wasn't my decision."

"Wasn't it?"

"No. Do you think I'd run away? Just like that? They had something for me to do. I couldn't say no. It's the discipline—every link. I had to do what they told me. Then, after—"

"Why are you telling me this?" she said, her voice cold. Connolly had dropped the wire and was staring at her.

"I don't want you to think—I couldn't help it, do you see?"

"Do you want me to forgive you? What a bastard you are."

"I just wanted you to know what happened," he said, hesitant now under her glare.

"That's not all that happened in Berlin, Matthew," she said, her voice so low and intense that the noise of the room seemed to step away from it, afraid. "You left a child. I cut it out."

Connolly stared, helpless, as her eyes filled with tears.

She leaned in. "I saw it in a pan. Like a blood clot. But they cut out all my children. Didn't mean to, but they did. You think I'm hard? I'm barren, Matthew. That's what happened in Berlin. Here," she said, picking up the envelope and throwing it at his chest. "Go save the world. Save it for your children."

For a minute, no one moved. Then Emma picked up her bag and walked quickly out of the restaurant, her shoes clacking hard on the wood floor. Connolly watched her go, expecting Lawson to follow her, but there wasn't a sound in the booth. He waited another minute, catching his own breath, then got up to go.

When he looked over the partition, he saw Lawson sitting, his face as red as if it had been slapped, staring at the brown envelope. Then suddenly he got up, bumping into Connolly.

For a split second Connolly met his eyes, wide and frantic. "Sorry," he said automatically, but Lawson was already running out of the room.

Connolly followed through the noisy bar and pushed the door out into the hot air. Lawson was halfway down the block, walking quickly. He stopped and shouted something—her name?—but it was lost in the roar of the overhead train. At the corner, he had to stop for a light, and Connolly could see Emma across Third, already far along the side street, her white dress darting in and out of the crowd. They crossed together, Connolly hanging back a little, waiting for him to sprint, but there were too many people now and he couldn't break through. Instead he sidestepped them, jumping into the street, then back again, trying to keep her in sight. When she turned right on Lexington, he quickened his pace, pushing against the crowd.

Emma hadn't noticed any of it. When she reached the hotel she went straight in, not looking around. Lawson followed her to the door, dodging a car against the light, and then, finally there, stopped unexpectedly. Connolly turned at the window of a deli, watching to his left. Lawson stood for a second, rooted in indecision, then took a step toward the entrance and stopped again. A soldier and a girl came out of the hotel, carrying suitcases. Lawson took a handkerchief to wipe his face, then, his whole body slumping in some final resignation, turned and started walking slowly away. When he passed Connolly in the deli window he was looking at the sidewalk, glum and confused, as if he had just missed a train. Then Connolly lost him in the crowd.

Emma was sitting on the bed, breathing deliberately to calm herself. She glanced up when he came in, then looked away again, obviously not wanting to talk. He touched her shoulder, then went into the bathroom and started putting things in his Dopp Kit.

"Did you hear?" she said finally from the bedroom. "I'm afraid I muffed it."

"No," he said, coming out, "it was fine. Perfect." His voice went low. "Emma, I'm sorry. I didn't know."

"No, you didn't." She shrugged, shaking the hair off her neck. "Now what?"

"Now we wait."

"Like a message in a bottle." She stood up and went over to the window. "Anyway, it's done now. Good luck to him."

"You all right?"

She nodded. "Funny how voices don't change. Everything else, but not voices. It gave me quite a turn at first. 'We respect that.' My God." She lit a cigarette, still looking out the window. "Promise me something, will you? When this is over, all this Karl business, no more, all right? You see what it's done to him. Always some war to fight, whether there is one or not. He's stuck in the trenches for good now."

"It's a promise. You can count on this one."

She turned, smiling a little. "He couldn't help himself, could he? What are you doing?" she said, noticing the Dopp Kit. "Going somewhere?"

"I thought we might change hotels. Our last night. Change of scene."

She smiled. "You don't have to do that. I'm all right, really."

"Actually, I think we'd better," he said. "He followed you."

"Followed me?"

"Not like that. I think he probably wanted to make up."

"But he didn't come in," she said quietly.

"No," he said, closing the kit. "But he knows you're here. Which means they'll know I'm here too, if anyone's interested. And they might be, once they get a look at his mail. We can't afford to take that chance."

She folded her arms, holding herself. "You think he'd have us watched?"

"It wouldn't be up to him."

She took that in. "I thought this was over."

"Almost. It's just a precaution."

"Still on the job," she said, putting out her cigarette. "Right. And here I thought you were being romantic."

"I can still be that."

"Where now?" she said brightly. "Do you think you could manage something a bit grander? The Waldorf?"

He grinned. "No. I was thinking of the Pennsylvania. It's the one place we're sure to be alone."

"Unless that man's still there."

"He won't be. Anywhere but there."

He was there, however. After dinner, a little tight, they went to the Café Rouge to hear the music, and it was Emma who spotted him, sitting not far from the band.

"It's him," she said. "He must be off duty—he's checked his hat."

"And picked up a girl," Connolly said. "What do you know."

"I don't think he's seen us."

"Come on, let's dance."

Emma giggled as Connolly maneuvered her toward the other table. "You're torturing him," she said, watching the man pretend not to recognize them. The girl, all bright lipstick, was drinking a highball.

"Just a little."

"He'll be furious."

"Because we ruined his little night on the town? I doubt he'll want to go into that. Looks bad on the report."

She giggled again. "But what will he *think*?"

"That we've been here all along and he should have kept his mouth shut. Now he's going to have to explain it."

"Who do you think she is?"

He grinned. "There's a question."

She leaned her head against his shoulder. "Now he'll be on the train."

"Paying very close attention this time. Just think of him as your personal bodyguard. Look, he's getting up to dance. I didn't think there was anybody in G-2 who could do that."

"Stop. He'll see you laughing. We shouldn't be doing this, you know. It's not supposed to be funny. Why is it?"

"He doesn't think he's funny. And he's going to write a report and it's going to sit in a file until it's useful to someone who isn't funny either. And there won't be a thing in it about his pumping his way across a dance floor and trying to get some girl into bed. That's the way it works."

"Not funny at all."

"No. How do you feel?"

"I don't know. From one minute to the next. Today—"

"Don't think about it."

"I did something I never thought I'd do. Deliberately harm someone."

"That depends on how you look at it."

"I'm not even sure it was wrong. How is that possible? Not to know what's wrong. And I didn't mind. I *wanted* it to work. And now we're laughing at that man and dancing, as if nothing had happened. What sort of person does that make me?"

He looked at her. "I don't care. Like the rest of us, I suppose. Everybody has his reasons."

"Even Matthew."

"I don't know the answer to that, Emma. Some are better than others, maybe."

"So maybe you can be wrong for the right reasons."

"I don't know that one either. We're not going to solve it here, you know. Let's take a little time out. You're still all keyed up."

She smiled weakly at him. "The wine, no doubt. At least you didn't say that. I have to sort it out sometime, though." She looked up at him, studying his face. "What about you? What were you thinking about today?"

"In the restaurant? That I wasn't helping you at all."

"But you did. You made it easy."

His eyes asked a question.

"I didn't know how I would feel. And then it was easy—I knew I could do it. It's easy when you don't love somebody anymore."

"He was a fool to let you go."

"We let each other go. Anyway, he's gone."

"Pretty quick divorce, by the way."

She smiled. "I couldn't resist. I wanted to hear what he'd say. I must say, he might have protested a little," she said lightly. "Anyway, there's our answer. Free. Aren't you pleased?"

He looked at her. "He's not the one I'm worried about."

17

Oppenheimer's voice came through the half-open door, as angry as Connolly had ever heard it. "You picked one hell of a time, Jeff," he was saying, his tone almost witheringly sharp.

"It's the right time," a voice answered, so young it seemed adolescent. "There'll never be a better one."

Connolly could see Oppenheimer standing behind his desk, holding a bulletin board notice. " 'The Gadget and the Future,' " he read disdainfully. "And just what the hell do you expect to accomplish with this little town meeting? Where do you think we are, Palo Alto?"

"We can't just ignore it, Oppie," the young man said, holding his ground. "There are issues. The scientific community has a right to a voice in this. While there's still time."

"There isn't any time. We've got people working twenty-four hours a day. We don't have time for seminars on civilization and its discontents."

"We should."

Oppenheimer, at any rate, must be working around the clock, Connolly thought. His frame, always frail, was now alarmingly thin, the eyes set deeply in their sockets, the bony fingers clutching the cigarette nearly skeletal. His voice, dry and scratchy, seemed to cry out for rest, but instead his body was in constant motion, pacing edgily, his arms jerking involuntarily to relieve the tension of being awake.

"Is Leo behind this?" he said suddenly.

"Leo?"

"Szilard. In Chicago. You know very well what Leo. Don't fence with me, Jeff."

"I don't know what you're talking about, Oppie."

Oppenheimer looked up, suddenly embarrassed. "You don't? Sorry. I thought he might be, that's all. He's circulating a petition. No doubt you'll want to sign it. Meanwhile, I'd appreciate it if you'd cancel this damn-fool meeting."

"Why?"

"Security wouldn't like it."

"So what?"

"It upsets them. This is a sensitive time, Jeff, you know that as well as anyone. Let's not make it more complicated than it is."

"Oppie, we're talking about scientists getting together to discuss the implications of what we're doing. That's all."

"I know what we're talking about," Oppenheimer snapped, taking a puff on his cigarette. "I'm talking about a test scheduled for *today* that's now two weeks late. I'm counting hours. Kisty's down at S Site fixing the explosive lenses himself. You know that. In fact, why aren't you down there helping, instead of—instead of—" His voice sputtered, caught by the look on the man's face. "What?"

"Scheduled for today? The glorious Fourth? What was the idea—the biggest fireworks ever?"

"Don't be a jerk. Not precisely the Fourth. This week. Nobody thought about *fireworks*." He stopped and smiled to himself. "In fact, nobody *did* think about that. Odd. Anyway, what's the difference? We didn't make it."

"Oppie, are you ordering me not to have this meeting?" the man said calmly.

Oppenheimer lit a fresh cigarette from the end of the other, his body visibly backing down. "No," he said finally, "I wouldn't order you to do that."

"You were the one who started the open meetings."

"Yes."

"And to hell with the security bozos, remember?"

"All right, Jeff, if the men want it—"

"So what happened? We haven't had a meeting in quite a while."

Oppenheimer looked at him, his eyes flaring in anger again. "I got busy, Jeff. I'm busy now, in fact."

"You're welcome to attend, by the way. In fact, people would really like that—to hear what you have to say. We're not trying to hurt the project."

"I know," Oppenheimer said gently.

Connolly knocked on the open door.

"Speak of the devil," Oppenheimer said. "One of your security bozos, in the flesh."

Jeff, a young scientist in horn-rimmed glasses, flushed.

"I didn't hear anything," Connolly said breezily. "We don't listen at keyholes."

"Yet," Oppenheimer said quickly.

"Sunday," Jeff said, turning to leave. "If you can make it."

Oppenheimer watched him go, then looked back. "Mr. Connolly," he said wearily. "Pleasant trip?"

"What was that all about?"

"It's beginning to dawn on them that the gadget has implications," he said, his voice still taut.

"What hath God wrought?"

"I haven't been called that yet. No, they think we might be in league with the other one.

505

Implications. Where has everyone been? The implications were there from the start. Now the hand-wringing. The Chicago lab wants to talk to the President—the President, if you please—about a *demonstration* for the Japanese. Blow up some little island somewhere and the emperor and the rest of the samurai will fall to their knees, begging for terms. And no one gets hurt."

"It's an idea."

"Don't be a fool. It's already decided." The answer, quick as whiplash, stung Connolly, as if he had been sent to the children's table. Sometime during the technical crises and the drought regulations and the personal tantrums, Oppenheimer had been to Washington and watched while someone drew a target circle around a city. Already decided.

"You don't think it would work," Connolly said tentatively.

"They're fanatics," Oppenheimer said flatly. "If it's a dud, we'd actually end up prolonging the war."

"You don't believe that—that it's a dud."

"I don't know. Nobody does. Right now all we've got are numbers on paper. Numbers on paper. Yes?" he said to his secretary, who'd appeared in the door.

"General Groves on the line for you."

Connolly made a sign question—*Do you want me to go?*—but Oppenheimer waved his hand dismissively and pointed to the chair.

"One minute," he mumbled and picked up the phone, turning his body halfway to the left, creating the privacy of an imaginary booth. "General. Yes, thanks. It's the lens castings— hairline cracks, even a few bubbles. I don't know what the hell they thought they were doing. We've got accuracy to one thirtieth and we need one three-hundredth just to be safe. We're going to need a few more days." A burst of talk from the other end. "No, it's not just a snag," Oppenheimer said waspishly. "It's a problem. I've got Kisty working on it now. He's down there himself. He might make it, he might not." Another burst. "I don't think you understand. He's working with dentist drills and tweezers and anything he can lay his hands on. Filling in the bubbles. Just to get one decent set of explosive lenses. Two more days." His face, already drawn, seemed to grow even tighter as he listened to Groves's reply. A dressing-down, Connolly guessed, or at least a frustrated sputtering. "I know we've moved it once already." And then he didn't speak again, staring out the window at the Tech Area as Groves went on. He'd clearly not expected an argument or he wouldn't have asked Connolly to stay, and now he was stuck with an audience.

Connolly stood up and walked over to study the photos on the wall. With Lawrence at the Berkeley cyclotron. A group shot of the Tech Area division heads. Eisler looked straight at the camera, his eyes dreamy and benign.

Finally Oppenheimer was giving in. "Well, that's that, then. We'll do what we can. No, I understand. It's a risk—you should know that.

507

Yes, the sixteenth. You'll be here, I assume." And then he was putting down the receiver, still looking out the window.

"The President wants to tell the Russians at the meeting in Germany," he said, partly to himself.

"But they already know."

"They don't know that we know they know," he said, toying with it, a word game. "For that matter, what *do* they know? Only that we're trying. He wants to tell them we've done it. At the meeting. Ready or not. So we'll be ready."

"Why at the meeting?"

Oppenheimer shrugged. "To give him some height at the table, I suppose."

"But if they already know—"

Oppenheimer turned to face him. "The President doesn't know that, remember? Nobody does. *You* know it, if you can prove it. Can you do that before they sit down at Potsdam?"

Connolly said nothing.

Oppenheimer smiled. "But they're sitting down anyway. So there's your deadline too."

"It's out of my hands at this point, you know."

Oppenheimer nodded. "Mine too." He turned to the papers on his desk. "And I still have a picnic to get to. They'll want a speech. What is it now, a hundred and sixty-nine years? What do you do with a number like that? We were supposed to be having the test today, not eating watermelon and making speeches.

History will have to wait a little. Today we deal with cookouts. That was the good general's thought for today—no cookouts. The whole mesa's dry as dust. A spark would do it. I suppose he's got visions of the whole project going up in flames because of one Fourth of July hot dog. I have to say, the man thinks of everything. One minute international conferences, the next lemonade and egg salad. So. Now we've got campfire patrol." He looked up, as if he'd noticed Connolly for the first time. "Anyway, what was it you wanted?"

"You wanted to see me."

Oppenheimer looked puzzled for a moment, then, remembering, frowned. "Yes, right." He lit another cigarette. "About this trip."

"Thanks for the Pullman."

Oppenheimer frowned again. "I know this is none of my business."

"You want a report? I thought we agreed to keep you in the dark till we had something."

"I don't mean that," Oppenheimer said quickly. "I thought this trip was work."

"It was."

"You didn't tell me you were taking a lady. I hear you're quite a dancer."

"You're right," Connolly said evenly, "it's none of your business."

"It is when you're carrying on with one of the scientists' wives. That's all we need right now— a jealous husband. I'm surprised at you."

"The trip was work. She was part of it."

Oppenheimer raised his eyebrows. "Is that the truth?"

509

"Yes."

"Are you trying to tell me there's nothing going on?"

"No," Connolly said, meeting his stare. "I didn't say that."

"I see." Oppenheimer put down the paper in his hand. "It wouldn't be the first time, you know. Put people together and there's always a certain amount of interest generated. You have to expect that. You have to expect trouble, too. He's a good man."

"I've met him."

"And that didn't deter you in the slightest."

Connolly paused. "No."

Oppenheimer smiled. "At least you're honest. I guess. May I ask what she's got to do with all this?"

"If you ask, I'll tell you, but I'd rather you didn't ask. Not yet."

Oppenheimer put out his cigarette. "I used to know everything that went on here. Looks like I wasn't as well informed as I thought. Murder. Adultery. A vipers' nest, it turns out. Cookouts."

"You're forgetting espionage."

"Yes," Oppenheimer said, looking at him, "how could I forget that?" He picked up the paper again. "Now what do I do with this? "Dereliction of duty. Misuse of government funds. Authorized travel for personal purposes. Sexual'—what do they call it?" He referred to the paper. " 'Sexual indiscretions with project personnel.' Indiscretions."

"Ignore it. You're a busy man."

"Not half as busy as you, it seems. I can't ignore a security request. They want you out of here."

"They're just blowing smoke. Ignore them."

"They won't let up, you know."

"You take your friends in security too seriously," Connolly said, thinking of the young scientist and his meeting.

"My friends," Oppenheimer said. "You seem to think they're a joke. Did you know they refused to give me a clearance until Groves personally vouched for me? Me. Did you know they still investigate my old associates, my family? They've put my brother through hell." He saw the look in Connolly's eyes. "But you knew that. He was a member of the party at Stanford. Given that, we both must be disloyal. They keep my file active—they never close it. So I've learned to be a little sensitive about our friends. I try not to annoy them."

Connolly got up. "The lady in question helped me make contact with someone I hope will lead to Karl's killer. The money was mine. She shared my hotel room, but I was sleeping there anyway. Our friends in security think we were off on a toot and it's just what I want them to think. You're not buying any favors with them, you know. You'll always scare them. You're everything they're not."

Oppenheimer was quiet for a minute, then smiled faintly, a tic. "Is that supposed to be a compliment?"

"A small one."

"You want me to vouch for you, then."

"Groves vouched for you."

"You forget I have a certain amount of responsibility to keep this project secure."

"So did Groves."

Oppenheimer paused. "So he did," he said, taking the paper and letting it flutter to the wastebasket. "Now will you do something for me? Keep your indiscretions discreet, will you? This particular husband is too valuable right now to be worrying about his wife."

"I don't think he knows. He's at Trinity most of the time."

Oppenheimer started and then jotted something down. "Thank you for reminding me. I almost forgot about the cables."

"Cables?"

"Coaxial cables. The rats are chewing the wires at the site. We have to patrol the whole damn desert floor now, night and day. Miles of wire. It's got everybody jumpy." He caught Connolly's look. "Sorry, what were we saying?"

"Nothing. I was going to be more discreet."

"Yes, that's right." Oppenheimer paused. "Be careful. They usually do know."

"Who?"

"Kitty was married when we met. We thought her husband didn't know, but he did."

Connolly looked up at him, surprised, then let it go. "You ought to get some sleep," he said.

"Everybody says that, but nobody tells me how."

The whole mesa seemed on edge, like some extension of Oppenheimer's nervous system. Connolly had come back west with a sense of relief—the high, dry air was the air he breathed now—but the Hill had changed. It was curiously deserted, with hundreds gone to the test site and the usual traffic at the gates slowed by travel restrictions. Los Alamos was left to bake in the arid July air. The grass had long since dried up, the little patch gardens scraggly and cracked. Children, out of school, played ball in a swirl of dust. Mothers spread blankets over bare dirt for impromptu picnics or sat in the shade of the hutments and prefab houses, fanning themselves. Without being told, they knew something was about to happen. Lab windows were bright all night. With so many gone, the summer should have been quiet and lethargic. Instead, it was anxious, wide awake, as if everyone were waiting for forest fires to break out.

Connolly checked the mail, went for walks, wandered in and out of the Tech Area looking for something to do. Eisler's books were sold to raise money for the school, his personal effects doled out by Johanna Weber to friends in the émigré community. Connolly had asked her for a picture—the theoretical team on an outing in the Jemez Mountains—and, surprised, she had given it to him with sentimental tears in her eyes. He placed it on the bureau next to the photograph of Karl, two pieces in the puzzle. He saw Emma at the movies, but they stayed away from each other, afraid to divert their attention from the waiting. Finally, after a week, claustrophobic in all the wide space of the mesa, he drove into Santa Fe to see Holliday.

"I'd just about given up on you," Holliday said pleasantly. "Coffee?"

"In this heat?"

"Old Indian trick. Just pay it no attention and after a while you don't know it's there."

"It's there," Connolly said, wiping his neck.

They sat out behind the office where a table had been set up in the shade of a giant cottonwood tree.

"Sorry I haven't been around. I just haven't had anything to tell you."

"That you can tell me, you mean. That's all right. I figure it's Hill business now. I don't ask. Looks like we'll all know pretty soon."

"What makes you say that?"

"Well, not much traffic into town these days. Real quiet. But you got these explosions going off in the canyons every night now. Folks don't even complain anymore— no point. Meantime, you got every hotel room in town booked for next week. That nice Mrs. McKibben's onto the boarding houses now, so you must have a crowd coming in. So I figure you're about to do whatever it is you're going to do up there."

Connolly smiled at him. "You're a good cop."

"That's not hard in a small town. Nothing happens. Until you came along, anyway."

"I guess you'll be relieved when I go."

Holliday sipped his coffee, looking at him. "You might be here quite a spell. One thing you learn in police work is how to wait. Now you, you hate to wait. You'd make coffee nervous."

Connolly smiled again. "So what do you do while you're waiting?"

"Mostly you turn things over in your mind."

Connolly looked at him with interest. "Such as?"

"Well, such as that car. Anybody bother it yet? No. But now you've got all these explosions going off nearby. You'd think somebody'd want to move it, wouldn't you?"

"Why should he? Nobody's found it yet. It's been months."

"True. But it's funny about that car. Easiest thing in the world to drive it somewhere else, then get a bus or something back to the Hill. That way nobody'd connect it at all."

"Nobody *has* connected it. As far as he knows, it's still hidden."

"Maybe. But that was before they started blowing those canyons all to hell. If it was me, I'd move it."

"So what are you thinking?"

"Well, the way it makes sense is if he isn't on the Hill anymore."

"No, he's there."

"You're sure."

"He has to be."

"Has to be isn't evidence."

"He's there," Connolly said firmly. "I know it."

Holliday paused. "Well, if you know it. 'Course, there's one other way it makes sense."

"What's that?"

"Well, *I'd* move it, but maybe he's not as smart as I am. That's another thing you learn in police work—they're not the brightest bunch of guys. We just like to think so 'cause it makes us look good."

Connolly smiled. "What else do you get when you turn things over?"

"Not much. The funny thing about this one is that we've got the when and the where and it sounds like you've got the why but you're not telling." He looked at Connolly, who nodded. "Well, in my experience, at least one of these ought to lead us to who. But not this time."

"We have to come at it a different way."

"That why you've got my boys watching those churches?"

Connolly nodded. "It might be a waste of time."

"Well, it won't do them any harm. Good way to get to know your own town. You take me— I've never been to the Governors' Palace. Pass it every day, but never been inside. But that's usually the way, isn't it?"

"You're leading up to something."

"No, I'm just teaching you how to wait," Holliday said, his eyes enjoying a private joke. "I've been thinking and thinking about it, and damned if I can come up with anything. 'Course, I don't know the why."

Connolly placed his coffee on the table and looked away. "Somebody was passing military secrets and Karl surprised them at the drop. At San Isidro. But you didn't hear that, okay?"

Holliday looked at him closely, then nodded. "Well, I figured that much."

"How's that?"

"Everything top secret and MPs walking around the place and people dropping in from Washington. What the hell else could it be? Still," he said, smiling, "it's nice to know. I appreciate that."

Connolly didn't say anything.

"And now you're arranging another drop?" Holliday said quietly.

Connolly got up and paced toward the tree, ignoring him. "When did you figure all this out?"

"Don't get excited. Not for a long time. See, he had me going there with that queer business. You look at that, you've got no reason to look at anything else. Smart. But there's another thing. How'd he come up with that?"

"It was in the papers."

"Yeah, but it's smart. I mean, if he's too dumb to move the car, how come he's smart enough to think up something like that?"

Connolly looked at him. "I don't know. How is he?"

"Well, maybe it's on his mind, like."

"You mean he's a homosexual after all?

517

Doc, we've been down that road, and it didn't get us anywhere. What's the difference now, anyway?"

"Maybe he just thinks about them. There has to be some way to get to the who. A trail somewhere. Everything counts in a murder. I mean, he thought of it. Now why is that?"

"I don't know, Doc. Maybe you'd better turn it over some more. I'll tell you this, though. We got the guy who was passing the secrets." Holliday looked at him in surprise. "And neither of them liked guys. Not him. Not Karl. It was a blind."

"Huh," Holliday said, a grunt of acknowledgment. He sat for a minute, thinking. "What about the one you caught?"

"He's dead."

Holliday took another sip of coffee with an almost studied casualness. "You kill him?"

"No."

"So he's not the one setting up the meeting?"

"No."

Holliday mulled this over for a minute, then stood up. "Well, I don't know. I'm in over my head now. Maybe someday you'll let me know how this works."

"I may never be able to do that, Doc," Connolly said seriously. "You understand that."

Holliday nodded, then grinned. "You may never catch him, either. Sometimes it happens that way. Even when you wait. You understand that?"

"Then my secret's safe with you."

It wasn't until the next day that, for no specific reason, Holliday's conversation made Connolly think of Corporal Batchelor.

"He transferred out," Mills said. "He's up at Oak Ridge. Why?"

"I just wanted to see how he was doing. Can we get him on the phone?"

"Are you kidding? You can't call somebody at Oak Ridge just to pass the time of day. Family emergency, maybe. Otherwise, you write."

"Let's get him anyway."

"What's going on? I've never seen you so jumpy."

"Just call him."

Mills picked up the phone with a shrug. "You're the boss. It might take some time, though."

Amazingly, it took a day. And when Connolly finally heard Batchelor's voice, wary and apprehensive, he felt foolish for having gone to the trouble. It wasn't a loose end, just a stray thought.

"The man who beat you up," he said. "Who was it?" There was no response. "You still there?"

"I don't know," Batchelor said, so quietly that Connolly thought it was the connection.

"Look, this is strictly confidential. Off the record. I mean, if you're worried about that."

"No, I really don't know."

"But someone on the Hill."

"I don't know," he repeated. "Maybe a visitor. I'd never seen him before."

"A scientist?"

"No."

Connolly frowned. "Can you describe him?"

"Dark."

"Mexican, you mean?"

"I don't know. Maybe. Spanish."

"How do you know? Did you talk to him?"

"I just thought he looked Spanish, is all. He had black eyes."

Connolly stopped, feeling embarrassed. "Would you recognize him again?"

Batchelor hesitated. "Is this an official call?"

"No, unofficial. Would you?"

"I don't want you to look for him. Nothing happened."

"I'm not looking for him. I was just curious."

"Why?"

Why indeed? "I'm not sure."

"I don't want to talk about this anymore. I'm sorry. Nothing happened."

"Okay," Connolly said. "I understand. But you'd recognize him?"

Batchelor hesitated. "Yes," he said finally. "If I had to."

Connolly stared at the receiver when they'd finished, wishing he hadn't called. Now Batchelor would worry about what he'd moved a thousand miles away to forget.

"What are you up to?" Mills said, interrupting the thought.

"Nothing. Chasing my own tail. Can't we

520

get this damn fan to work?" he said irritably.

"Crazy with the heat, huh?"

"No, stir crazy."

"Waiting for something?"

Connolly shot him a glance, then looked away. "No."

"Here," Mills said, holding out an envelope. "Post office said to give this to you. Who's Corporal Waters?"

Connolly reached up for the letter, meeting Mills's eyes as his hand touched it. For an instant he stopped breathing.

"Friend of yours?" Mills said. He held the letter suspended between them.

"One of my aliases," Connolly said, taking it. "For filthy pictures."

Mills's eyes dropped in disappointment. "Oh," he said, excluded. "Sorry I asked."

Connolly stared at the envelope in front of him. Typed. No return address. Santa Fe postmark. Now that it was finally here, he couldn't quite believe it. Why a letter? Absurdly, he realized that he had been expecting the guidebook, page turned down at the corner. Mills, mistaking his hesitation for secrecy, moved away from the desk. Connolly fingered the envelope. Not heavy. No more than a page. No, a single rectangle, like a postcard.

He slit open the envelope. An invitation. A gallery opening on Canyon Road. Sunday, from four to seven. Refreshments served. Two days from now. Connolly turned it over, looking for a message, something scrawled on the print. A public reception, not a private meeting at San Isidro. But what had he been expecting? A conversation in the alley? Had there been a pattern to the other meetings? He thought of Holliday's men, loitering at churches all over Santa Fe.

He looked up to see Mills standing by the desk.

"Are you going to tell me?" he said simply, his eyes frank and direct.

Connolly slipped the card back into the envelope. "I can't."

In fact, there was no one to tell except Emma. He walked her back from the PX, carrying grocery bags.

"You said it would work," she said. "What's the matter now?"

"They don't trust it. Why a party? There'll be people."

"They just want to see who you are, see if you're real."

"How will they know?"

"You'll be the one with me."

He looked at her. "Don't even think about it," he said. "I have to do this one alone." He stopped her before she could interrupt. "He won't know you anyway. They'd never tell the field contact about you. If anything goes wrong, the chain has to stop with him. They can't afford to have this traced back. If they believe it."

"They must. Why would they send the invitation?"

"It's worth the chance. If it's a trap, they sacrifice the one guy in the field, that's all."

"Then it really doesn't matter whether I'm there or not."

"It does to me. We don't know what might happen. Besides, they'll be looking for a man alone."

"For a uniform, you mean. Corporal Waters."

He stopped and looked at her. "A uniform. If I told you I'd completely forgotten about that, would you think I'd lost my mind?"

She grinned at him. "I was never interested in your mind. See how useful I can be?"

"But I don't want to have to worry about you," he said seriously.

"Don't, then. We'll arrive separately. I'll just be a fly on the wall. In case you need me. I don't want to have to worry about you."

He decided not to argue the point now. "What sort of crowd is it likely to be?"

"The local gentry. Hats and things. And the arts-and-crafts crowd. A few ladies in sandals and woven skirts. Loomers, I call them."

"Soldiers?"

"Enlisted men? You must be joking. Don't worry, he'll spot you straightaway."

"But I won't know who he is."

"Well, that's rather the point, isn't it?"

Mills said nothing that evening when he surprised Connolly at the office trying on the uniform, borrowed from one of the drivers. The fit was baggy, as if Connolly had lost weight. Mills looked him over, then, without a word, went to a locked drawer, fishing a key out of his pocket. Embarrassed, Connolly turned and started to change back into his clothes, so he was in his shorts when Mills handed him the gun and the cartridge of bullets.

"You'd better have these," he said.

Connolly looked at the gun, not knowing what to say.

"I never think to look in that drawer," Mills said. "I'd no idea they were gone."

"You don't have to do this. I'm not—"

"He's already killed one man," Mills said simply. "I'm on your side, you know. I always have been."

18

Later, he remembered the day as overbright, every piece of landscape sharp and hard-edged under the white sun. Emma, pretty in a pale blue dress that seemed part of the cloudless sky, drove him in her car, past the empty east gate and down the switchback road to the valley floor. With the windows down, the air smelled of juniper. The afternoon had been still and expectant, and even now, toward its end, Santa Fe seemed asleep. Connolly fidgeted in the unfamiliar uniform, shifting the gun in his pocket to arrange its outline in a shapeless bulge. His cap, folded, hung over his belt like a protective flap.

"It's not going to go away, you know," Emma said.

"Can you see it?"

"Only when I look. Shall I keep it in my bag?"

"Then I would have something to worry about."

"Actually, I'm a crack shot. I grew up in the country, you know."

"Crack shot with what?" he said skeptically.

"Well, skeet," she admitted. "You don't really think you'll need it, do you?"

"No. Should I leave it here? It's more trouble than it's worth."

"Just keep your hand in your pocket. You know, playing with change."

"Playing with change."

"Well, men do."

They were driving along the Alameda, approaching the Castillo Street bridge at the foot of Canyon Road.

"I'll walk from here," he said at the corner.

"Two blocks," she said. "Goodness, look at the crush."

The street was lined with cars, some double-parked near the gallery entrance. It seemed the only party in town.

Her voice, cool and efficient, cracked when he reached to open the door. "Michael." Her eyes were suddenly bright with panic. "You'll be careful."

"Nervous?"

"I am, actually. Funny, after all this."

"I know. This time it's real."

"It doesn't feel real." She straightened her shoulders. "Don't worry. I won't let you down."

He smiled at her. "You couldn't. Anyway, maybe it's just an audition. Maybe nothing will happen."

She looked at him, her eyes scanning his face. "That would be worse, wouldn't it?"

He nodded. "Okay, let's go. Act naturally. Look at the pictures."

"And not at you. I know."

"I've got Holliday outside. Just in case."

She looked up at him quizzically, unfamiliar with the name.

"The police."

"Oh," she said. "Is that supposed to make me feel better?"

"Take your time parking," he said, moving away.

Holliday, out of uniform, sat in a car in the next block. Connolly stopped to light a cigarette, and when he spoke it appeared he was fiddling with his lighter. "Everything all right?"

"Could've made a fortune in parking tickets here. What's wrong with these people, anyway?"

"No cops."

"What's that in your pocket?"

"My wallet," Connolly said, looking at him. "I like it in front. You can't be too careful in a crowd."

Holliday sighed. "Just watch your back."

"Spot anybody hanging around?"

"Not yet. Just you."

Connolly grinned and continued walking, glancing at both sides of the street. The gallery doors were open and people had spilled onto the side courtyard, talking in small groups, their voices like the murmur of bees. Inside the noise was louder, mixed with the tinkling of coffee spoons and ice cubes. A long table had been set up in the front room with a coffee urn and plates filled with sugary sopapillas. At the other end were bottles of wine and cheese cut into cocktail cubes. The crowd was as Emma had predicted, the women in floppy hats and long skirts cinched with silver-turquoise belts, the men in suits with bolla ties. Connolly noticed with a little relief that there were a few other uniforms, all officers, presumably local friends unconnected with the Hill.

He made his way slowly through the crowd, feeling obvious and self-conscious, but no one seemed to notice him. Busy with their friends or the paintings, they assumed he belonged to someone else. And after a while he began to feel the invisible anonymity of a large party, as if he weren't really there at all. There were fewer people in the two rooms that led from the main room in a circle around the patio, and he wandered through these, looking at paintings, aware that he'd be more easily seen. Cowboys. Pueblo landscapes. Prickly-pear cactus in flower. No one approached him.

He circled back to the main room and took a glass of wine, looking around. Suppose no one came? Or someone had already seen him and decided not to risk contact? Maybe there'd be another message, a proper one this time, with a guidebook and a quiet place. Out of the corner of his eye he saw Emma come in. He stepped back into the second room. Between the paintings were pedestals with sculptures and wide terra-cotta pots painted in geometric Indian designs. There was a painting of the park by the Alameda, the river visible behind the trees, and Connolly stood in front of it as if he'd found the prearranged meeting place. There were the bushes where they'd found Karl. He peered at the lower right-hand corner for the artist's name. Lothrop, in tiny block letters.

"Hello," a voice said. "The gentleman with the turquoise, isn't it?"

He turned slowly, prolonging the moment. For a second he couldn't place him. Then he recognized the man from the jewelry shop. Chalmers? Something like that. Sonny. Behind the wire glasses, his eyes were bright.

"Hello," Connolly said. The man seemed slighter outside the shop. Connolly tried to imagine him with his arm raised, holding a crowbar. No, it didn't seem possible. Unless the eyes had been furious, the body coiled in surprise.

"I thought it was you. I didn't realize you were in the service," Chalmers said pleasantly. "Do you like the pictures?" He glanced toward the wall to see what Connolly had been looking at. "Ah yes. The park." He turned to face him. "I often wondered, did you find what you were looking for?"

The question floated as casually as an inquiry about the weather. Connolly met his eyes. "Yes, I did."

"Good," Chalmers said. "Good. What happened to the turquoise pieces?"

"I still have them."

"Perhaps you're interested in selling them." So this was how it was done—the new meeting, a chat back at the store.

"Maybe. I don't think I ever introduced myself. My name is Steven Waters."

"A pleasure," Chalmers said easily, nodding. Just a name. "Are you"—he hesitated—"with somebody?"

Connolly, caught off-guard, had the unexpected feeling that Chalmers might be making a pass. Or was he just making sure Connolly had come alone? "No," he said. "Why do you ask?"

Chalmers fluttered, embarrassed. "Forgive me. I thought I knew everyone here, that's all. It's my gallery, you see. You're very welcome."

"I am supposed to be meeting someone here," Connolly said, another try.

"Yes, I see. Well, I hope you enjoy the pictures. If you do wish to sell the turquoise, come and see me at the shop."

"Any particular time?"

Chalmers looked at him, puzzled. "Whenever it's convenient for you."

Connolly watched him move away, turning to another group of guests like a concerned host. But was he anything more? Connolly walked out to the patio to have a cigarette, feeling oddly deflated. Had they made contact or not? Is that all that happened, the suggestion of another time and place? After all the waiting, the anxious drive down, did he turn now and go? Or had he imagined it all? Perhaps the man was simply checking his guest list or looking for a new friend. The fact was, Connolly didn't want it to be Chalmers, so unprepossessing and ordinary that he seemed hardly worth the long search. But why not him? A drive to the church, a quick meeting, a meeting afterward with someone else, and it was done. No fog and trenchcoats, just business as usual. But what had Chalmers really meant? He went over the conversation in his mind. Was it possible—almost a comic thought—that the language of espionage was no different from that of a pickup, all the words that meant something else, verbal sex, the invitation not really offered until it was accepted?

He looked around. All over the room people were making contact. He put his hand in his pocket, feeling the gun. The late afternoon sun flooded the patio. In broad daylight, he thought. Maybe this was how it was done. A nice middle-aged man, a harmless exchange that might mean anything. But there had

530

been nothing casual about the meeting at San Isidro. Except they'd already known Eisler. This was just a sighting. Connolly tried to imagine himself as the other man. What would he be looking for? An amateur. A soldier, nervous, looking around. Someone new to it, who needed to be approached with more than the vague promise of the jewelry shop. But carefully. Connolly realized then that if it was going to happen, he was already being watched.

He went into the gallery rooms, moving toward the refreshments, then back again, staring openly at people now, a soldier looking for someone. He caught Chalmers glancing furtively at him, but with no more purpose than a proprietor keeping an eye on the stock. Emma avoided him, talking to a man in a double-breasted suit who was probably asking her too whether she was with somebody. A woman jarred his elbow, brushing past toward the cheese. So where was he? Hadn't he made himself visible enough? He moved into the interior room, empty now as people, finished with the paintings, clustered on the patio with drinks. He walked slowly, pretending to study the pictures on the wall. The cathedral in the snow. A Soyer imitation of the bar at La Fonda. A heavy metal statue of a rider—where had they got the scrap?—his horse reared back, hooves sticking up. A giant cob of corn. "Do you like it?" A woman's voice, throaty.

He turned around. The bobbed hair. The eager eyes. "Hannah," he said.

531

She looked up at him, startled for a minute, then said, "Oh, it's you. Emma's friend. Forgive me, I didn't recognize—" Her voice wavered, still puzzled. "But have you joined the army?"

Hannah. He felt the hair on the back of his neck. She had approached a soldier. He stared at her, frozen, as still as the moment on the trail at Chaco. Hannah. Not a man.

"Just for the day," he said.

But only he had made the leap. "I don't understand," she said, disconcerted by his stare. Then, quickly, catching herself, "But where is Emma?"

"She's not here," he said. "I was looking for you."

Hannah. Eisler had been billeted at the ranch.

"Me?" she said, a nervous laugh, uncertain. "But I didn't know I was coming myself. It's so difficult to travel now."

Back and forth to Los Angeles. There would be people there, the next link. No need to risk another meeting in Santa Fe.

"But you sent me an invitation."

"No," she said. "I'm sorry. You're mistaken. It must have been the gallery. Of course, if I had known—" She looked away from him, turning her head as if she wanted to be rescued from the conversation. "But there she is. Emma!" she said loudly, calling her over, but Connolly had glanced up and caught her eye. He shook his head, stopping her at the door.

Hannah turned back to him, bewildered. "I thought you said—"

"She doesn't know," Connolly said evenly. "I've brought you a message from Corporal Waters."

Did her eyes widen, or was it his imagination?

"And who is that?"

"Me."

She looked at him for a moment in disbelief, not saying anything. "Is that your name?" she said finally, polite. "I'm sorry. I forgot. There must be some mistake."

"No. The invitation was for me."

Her eyes, shrewd and cautious, darted across his face, trying to see behind the words. Then she closed herself off and looked away. "You are mistaken," she said, so simply that for an instant he wondered if he was wrong. Everything was supposed to fit. Everything counts in murder. How could it be her? Another European story?

She had turned her head, searching for something, and he followed her look out onto the patio, to the tall Mexican in a denim jacket leaning against the adobe wall. Her right hand. Ajax. A classical name. No, Hector. The constant companion. As if he were taking snapshots, Connolly looked from the patio to Hannah, then again to the Mexican, his mind back at the blackboard. Connect everything. The workboots. Hector's job on the Hill. Of course he'd be with her, just in case. Strong enough to carry a man. Strong enough to kill one. Two people, one to drive the car back. A wrench, some tool. Had she watched? Had she turned away, like Eisler, or had she watched? Eisler was meeting her, the person off the Hill, but Hector had to return. He worked there now. The car. The back gate.

When he turned back to Hannah, he saw that she had been following his eyes, watching him fill in his crossword. "There's no mistake," he said. "Eisler's dead. He talked to me before he died. I know."

And then he did know. It was in her eyes. One look, one unguarded point of recognition. "Who are you?" she said softly.

He didn't answer.

" 'I know,' " she said. "What does that mean?"

"I know what information Eisler gave you. All of it, every detail. I know about the meeting at San Isidro. I know what happened to Karl." For a second her face held a question, and he realized she had never known Karl's name. "The man you killed there. You and your friend."

She looked at him closely, then shook her head. "*Phantastische,*" she said. "Poor Friedrich. A delirium. Why would he say such things? But it's often like that at the end. The fantasies, the paranoia. And you believed him? All this nonsense in his sleep."

"He was wide awake," Connolly said flatly. "I interrogated him."

"Ah," she said, her voice wry with scorn. "So

now we have the Gestapo too. Like the movies. The rubber hose. The castor oil. Some drug? Is that how he died?"

"No. He killed himself."

She looked up at him, interested. "Why?"

"Remorse, I think."

"Remorse."

"Not about you. He was loyal to the end, Eisler. A good party man. But Karl—that was something else. I don't think he'd ever seen a man killed before. That shook him. I guess he didn't know your lover was the hot-blooded type."

"My lover," she said, her voice cold with contempt, and Connolly thought of that day at the ranch. Something had happened between them. Not a lovers' quarrel. No. She'd been angry with him for putting them at risk.

"Maybe he just didn't know his own strength," Connolly said.

"Enough foolishness." She turned slightly to go.

"Don't," he said, his voice hard.

She froze, looking up at him.

"That's right. You don't want to make a scene. Not here. Not in front of the customers. We'll go somewhere else. Then we can talk some more."

"You must be crazy. You come up to me here, in this place, with these—what? Accusations? The rantings of a dead man. 'I know.' 'I know.' You don't know anything. Leave me alone."

"I have a gun," he said quietly.

She stopped. "Now the melodrama too?"

"It's over, Hannah. There was a witness at San Isidro," he said. "He's identified your friend. And you."

She looked at him again, assessing. "It's a lie."

"Is it?"

"Then why wait so long? All this—" She spread her hand toward the room.

"We wanted to see if they'd send someone else. But they didn't, did they? Your friends. What if it's a trap? Send Hannah. She's expendable. Now that Eisler's dead. They're closing you down too."

He had touched some anger. "You fool," she said, glaring at him. "Do you think that matters? There'll be someone else. Always. That's why we win. Yes, we," she said, catching his look. "Who do you think won this war? The baby GIs with their Hershey bars? We won it. Communists. Such a dirty word to you. But we *knew*. We stopped them. You think politics is about elections? No—bodies. So, one more, one less? What difference?"

"Then we'll start with you."

She tossed back her head. "Yes, start with me. Take your time. You think you have so much time? *Idiot*," she said in German. "It's already too late. What did you think? We could sit by and watch you do this? And not protect ourselves? Children—you're all children here. Do you think we would give a gun to a child?"

"Do you think we'd give one to a gangster?"

She paused, a flicker of a smile on her face. "No. He would have to take it. While the child was playing, perhaps."

"For his own good."

"Yes, for everybody's good. But very carefully. So he wouldn't know. We had to be very careful."

Connolly paused. "And yet here you are."

"For exactly one more minute. Then we are going to smile—it's very pleasant, the gallery, yes?—and people will say, 'You see, not so serious. They must have been talking about the art.' You think you know something? Where is your proof? Friedrich? I was always very careful with Friedrich. When they put him at the ranch, I thought it was a trap—I wouldn't even look at him. And he thought *I* had arranged it, so clever. But you know, there is luck in America. Not like Germany. Everything is lucky here. They thought he'd feel at home speaking German. But we never did. All that time, we were too afraid to talk. We couldn't believe our luck, you see. But afterward, that was more difficult. So I had to be careful. No paper. No strings. Nothing. Nothing to connect us at all. Now what do you want to do? Arrest me? With your gun? Over nothing at all? I don't think so. Who would believe such a thing?"

"Do you really think you're just going to walk out of here?"

"No. I have to say goodbye to some people first," she said coolly, "but then—It's getting late. You can follow me, of course. But what will you find? Friedrich's gone. So there is no Corporal Waters. Then my work—well, that's over. You see, I don't even have to be careful anymore. Unless you have something else to tell me?"

Then, smoothly, she began to turn away, and Connolly, in an instant of panic, looked around the room—Emma still lurking by the doorway, the kitschy art, people laughing outside—and felt everything slip away. Without thinking, he grabbed her arm, jerking her back toward him.

"It's not about Eisler. It's about Karl. You're not listening. I don't have to prove a thing about your 'work.' I'm arresting you for murder."

"Let me go."

"That wasn't careful, killing Karl."

"Let me *go*," she said, pulling her arm away, but Connolly held it. "What do you think you're doing? On whose authority? Whose authority?" Her voice, louder now in the empty room, caused a few people out on the patio to look up.

"The police are outside. On their authority. You can say your goodbyes later."

Her face, gone white, now twisted itself in a cold rage. "Take your hands off me," she said, so self-possessed that Connolly obeyed the order and dropped her arm. "Madman. I never killed anybody."

"Yes, you did. Technically, you might get away with being an accessory," he said. "I don't

538

think so. Either way, you'll be gone for years and years. I'll see to it."

"You," she said, almost spitting the word.

"What's the problem?" A deep voice: Hector, looming next to them.

"Come," Hannah said, another order.

Connolly looked up at him, feeling suddenly dwarfed. Black eyes. "Hannah says you killed Karl all by yourself," he said, improvising. Again the question mark. No one had known Karl's name. "The man in the alley at San Isidro. You shouldn't have done that, Hector."

Hector glanced at her, then stared at Connolly, stunned. He seemed to lean back, as if he had been struck.

"Don't listen to him. He's crazy," Hannah said.

"All by yourself. We thought she helped, but she said no, you did everything."

Hector's confusion made him jumpy. Connolly could see the tension creep into the broad, impassive face, the eyes as alert as an animal's.

"You should have thrown away those boots," Connolly said, pointing at his feet. "We matched the prints." A lie, but would Hector know? "Just like a fingerprint. All over the bushes. When you pulled his pants down."

Now the eyes, no longer confused, took on a shine of menace.

"Come," Hannah said. "Foolishness."

"You weren't trying to kill him. I know. Just knock him out, the way you do." As he said it, another blackboard leap. Someone else looking up at the tall, glowering man, black eyes flashing. "Like Batchelor. The soldier at the PX. You weren't trying to kill him. Just teach him a lesson, right?"

"Shut up," Hector said, his voice a low rumble.

"You didn't kill *him,* just roughed him up a little. I can't blame you. So why'd you kill Karl? We thought she told you to." He nodded his head toward Hannah. "But she says she wasn't there."

Hector turned and looked at her, obviously surprised.

"Don't say anything," she said coldly.

"We know you killed him," Connolly said quickly. "We didn't know you did it alone. See, the way we saw it, you knocked him out—he's just out. Messed up. But she said you had to kill him, you had to finish it. Did you even know who he was? Did she tell you? Eisler said you didn't know."

"Shut up," Hector said again, louder now.

"It was smart making it look like the murder in Albuquerque. To tell you the truth, we thought that was her idea too."

"Hector, come," she said, a pet command, and took his arm to lead him away.

Connolly glanced from one to the other, feeling he had to do something, say anything to hold him.

"But that was you. See, I didn't put two and two together until you beat up the guy at the PX. I didn't realize you were queer too."

The fist, exploding, came up and smashed into Connolly's face. He staggered back against the wall, blood spurting out of his nose in a rush.

"I'll fuckin' *kill* you," Hector said, moving toward Connolly and chopping his fist down against the side of Connolly's neck, forcing him to drop to his knees, stunned. He heard a woman scream in the other room, saw in a hazy flash of peripheral vision people turning on the patio to see what was going on. Connolly leaned forward for a second, catching himself, afraid he would black out.

"Hector, no!" Hannah shouted.

"Shut the fuck up," he said, pushing her aside, heading for Connolly.

But it gave Connolly the second he needed. He brought the gun out of his pocket and held it up before him with two hands. He saw that they were shaking, one of them smeared bright with blood. "Stop," he said, the word garbled by the blood in his mouth.

More screams. Footsteps. Hector looked down at him, hesitating for a split second, then, sneering, brought up his foot and kicked from the side, knocking the gun out of Connolly's hands. It slithered across the polished wood floor toward the corner, and Connolly lost sight of it as the workboot came up again, kicking him. He fell over, his face hitting the floor with another crack.

"Stop it!" Emma's voice. Dimly, Connolly saw her pounding Hector's back. His face raging, Hector turned away from Connolly and flung her aside as if her fists were nothing more than wasp stings. She fell against the pedestal, the scrap-metal cowboy crashing to the floor beside her.

Connolly tried to stand, but Hector's foot caught him in the stomach, and when he fell this time he put his hands around his head, curling his body into itself to protect it from the blows. "Stop it!" he heard Emma scream again. Then there was another kick to his chest. He groaned. Hector kicked him again, a machine now, uncontrollable. Connolly realized that if he didn't move, he was going to die, bludgeoned to death like Karl. Then, in some bizarre transference, he turned to look up and saw not Hector but Emma, her hand held high in the air, swinging the metal down toward him, just the way it must have happened at San Isidro. When he turned his head slightly to protect his eyes, he heard the statue connect, a crack, a thud into flesh, and heard Hector grunt, rearing his head back so that the force of the smash was strengthened and the horse's hooves pushed into his scalp. There was an explosion of blood from Hector's head, spattering in a circle around them, an oil well of blood, before he fell over, partially covering Connolly, his body twitching in one long drawn-out spasm.

Connolly heard the statue fall to the side. Now there were lots of voices, screams of surprise, and he knew it was almost over. He looked along the floor to the gun in the corner, but it was gone. Raising his head to see better, he felt the nausea that he knew meant he would black out. He stretched his fingers to grasp the statue and drew it toward him by the hooves, so that when the crowd finally arrived it was clutched in his hand, and with his breath crushed by the weight of the body on top of him and his face sticky with blood, he did pass out.

He couldn't have been out more than a minute. He felt Hector's body being lifted off him, then hands hooked under his arms, pulling him to his feet, holding him from behind. "Jesus Christ," someone said, and Connolly looked at Hector too, his head still oozing blood. Connolly weaved, dizzy, trying to draw breath through the dull pain in his chest. For a moment nobody moved, and Connolly saw the drops of blood on the painting next to him, the end of the arc. One of the guests was leaning over Hector's body, turning it so that his face, absolutely still, stared up at them. His legs, twisted, hadn't moved with the rest of him. Connolly tried to move toward him, but someone still held his arms, restraining him.

"Somebody get an ambulance," the man kneeling over Hector said, feeling the side of his neck for a pulse.

Connolly saw Holliday run into the room, people moving aside in a wave to let him through. He stopped in front of the body, taking in the scene—Connolly with his arms pinned, the statue still dangling from one of his hands, the giant body lying on the floor, blood spreading out from the head in a small lake.

"Let him go," he said to the man behind Connolly, and Connolly, his arms suddenly free, slumped against the wall. He watched Holliday bend over and examine the pupils, then close the lids of the Mexican's eyes.

"Oh my God," someone in the crowd said.

"Call my office," Holliday said to the man next to him. "Get some of the boys over here. Quick." Then, turning to Connolly, "You all right?"

Connolly, still breathing heavily, nodded, feeling another wave of nausea as he moved his head.

"This the guy?" Holliday said simply.

Connolly nodded again. The nausea was gone now, and he took a handkerchief from his back pocket to stanch the blood in his nose.

"Broken?" Holliday said. Connolly nodded. "Anything else?"

"Maybe a rib. I don't know."

"He's lucky to be alive," a woman said. "He was kicking him, *kicking* him. It was awful." Everyone seemed to be talking.

Holliday turned toward the guests. "You folks want to give me a little room here?" His voice, easy and unhurried, stopped them. "How about all of you wait outside till the boys get here. But don't anybody run away now— we'll need to make a report," he said, slipping into his small-town police manner.

"I saw everything," the woman said, beginning to cry. "It was awful. *Awful.*" Someone took her arm to lead her away. The room began to empty, some people craning their necks to get a last look.

Holliday looked at the body, then up at Connolly. "He's dead," he said simply. "You kill him?"

Connolly nodded.

"Well, that's a hell of a thing. He come after you?"

"It was him. He killed Bruner."

An ambulance siren wailed outside, rising over the voices on the patio.

"Who was the woman with him?" Holliday said calmly.

"Hannah. His boss."

But where was she? Connolly looked around the empty room, suddenly panicked. "Where's Emma?" he said, but Holliday didn't know what he was talking about. "Doc, come on." He moved away from the wall, but Holliday stood up, blocking him.

"Take it easy. I don't want two bodies on my report."

"I'm all right."

"Well, we got a killing here."

"Doc, she's got the gun."

"Who?"

"Hannah," he said impatiently. "The other one. I'll explain it later. She's got the *gun*."

Holliday stared at him as the ambulance crew rushed into the room, carrying a stretcher. Connolly could see police uniforms moving through the crowd on the patio.

"Doc, *now*," he said. "She'll kill her."

Holliday looked at him for another minute, deciding. The ambulance crew swarmed around them. Then he said, "I'll drive."

On the patio, people moved away as Connolly approached, afraid to make contact with the violence. "Ask them," he said to Holliday. "Somebody must have seen them leave." Holliday glanced at him and turned to a group standing next to one of his men, already reporting details of the fight.

But it was Chalmers, finally, who came forward, hypnotized by the blood on Connolly's face. A black Chevy, yes. Emma's car. Heading down toward the bridge. Not the Cerrillos Road, to Albuquerque. The bridge. He thought they'd been too frightened to stay. Two of them, yes. He hoped it wasn't wrong, their leaving the scene—

Connolly grabbed Holliday, moving him toward the street, so that a few people, puzzled, thought, that it was the chief who was being taken into custody.

"They're going to her ranch," Connolly said, getting in the car. "Up past Tesuque."

But when they reached the Alameda, one of Holliday's men, on traffic duty, had seen the car going west. "Hell of a way to get to Tesuque," Holliday said.

"The Hill," Connolly said.

"Now why would they do that?"

"I don't know."

Just in case, Holliday ordered the traffic cop to check the road to Albuquerque, then turned sharply onto the Alameda, wrenching the gearshift hard so that the car shuddered as they shot forward.

Connolly was wiping his face, the handkerchief stiff now with dried blood.

"How's your rib?"

"It hurts. Maybe just a bruise."

"You ought to get that taped. You could puncture a lung."

Then they were out of town, rounding one of the low hills to an open stretch of yucca and gray mesquite. "Can't you go any faster?" Connolly said, still anxious.

"If they're going that fast, somebody's likely to pick them up. Save us the trouble."

"She wouldn't be thinking that clearly. She just wants to get away."

"She capable of killing her?"

"Yes," Connolly said grimly.

"Then we better not let her see us. First rule of pursuit—the minute they see you, they'll go that much faster."

"That doesn't mean you have to slow down."

"Well, that looks to be them up ahead."

In the distance, Connolly saw the dark speck of a car heading toward the Jemez foothills. "How long have you known?" he said, looking at Holliday.

"Few miles. You ought to calm down— you'd see more. 'Course, when you do this for a living you get a feeling for it. Now look at that," he said, as Emma's car took a curve wide. "Not a very good driver, is she?"

"No."

"Someone special to you?"

547

"Yes."

"Funny thing. Someone back there thought it was a woman hit him."

"No. Me. The statue was on the floor. I grabbed it just in time."

"He was on the floor, was he?"

"Bent over. He was leaning over to pop me."

Holliday was quiet for a minute. "It could have happened that way, I guess."

"It did," Connolly said, looking at him. "I don't think anybody could've seen it clearly. He was blocking the way."

"And of course it all happened so fast."

"That's right."

"What'd you say to him, got him so excited?"

"I told him we had proof he killed Bruner."

Holliday paused. "That would do it."

The road was climbing now, out of the Rio Grande Valley, and it was more difficult to keep the car in sight.

"Sure does look like they're heading for the Hill."

"Don't lose her."

But a huge cattle truck, lumbering off a secondary road, swung onto the highway to block their view.

"Pass him," Connolly said.

"Now just where in hell do you expect me to do that?"

They crept up behind the truck, close enough to see the cattle watching them through the slats. The truck ground upward, slowing at each incline, spewing clouds of diesel exhaust. Connolly leaned over to beep the horn, but there was nowhere for the truck to go; the narrow shoulders rimmed the side of the hill. There was an agony of waiting as the truck made its way up the high grades of Highway 4, trapping Holliday's car and another behind it. Finally, a few miles before the turnoff for Frijoles Canyon, the truck slowed nearly to a stop and turned onto a dirt road that dropped precipitously to some canyon where lonely grazing land was waiting.

Holliday, in a hurry now, lurched forward, spinning around a curve so tightly that Connolly was thrown against the door. Pine trees passed in a blur. Connolly craned his neck, hoping to see the car around each turn, but they still hadn't spotted it by the time they reached the turnoff for the west gate. Improbably, a sign posted in the middle of the road announced that it was closed.

"Well, what the hell," Holliday said.

"They put it there. So nobody would follow. Just drive in." Even as he said it, he remembered the extra security, sealing the Hill before the test. But where else would they go?

Holliday drove around the sign and sped down the gate road. The same Georgia cracker was on duty at the sentry post. He came out carrying a rifle, clearly upset to see the car.

"Can't you fucking *read*?" he said, his twang turned mean. "This road's closed."

"Black Chevy come through here?" Connolly said.

"Ain't nobody come through here. Road's closed. Can't you *read*?" He took up the rifle.

Holliday flashed his badge out the car window. "Put your dick back in your pants," he said. "Now, that car come through here or not? Two ladies."

"No, sir," the soldier said sullenly.

Holliday turned to Connolly. "Now what?"

They'd been on Highway 4. He'd seen them. Had they slipped into one of the canyons? Frijoles? Those were traps, nature's dead ends. It had to be the Hill. But they didn't know the gate road would be closed. They'd have no choice but to continue on. Maybe she had even planned it that way. Anybody trailing them would come here, following the wrong scent.

"They're still on 4," Connolly said.

"They could have turned off. They could be anywhere."

"She's not hiding. She's running." All the way to the Pacific, he thought. "Come on, just a little farther."

They saw nothing for miles. They drove by the green valley of the caldera, Connolly thinking of that other drive, to Chaco, when everything had changed.

"If you're wrong, we're just going farther and farther in the wrong direction," Holliday said. "This road's a bitch." They were driving into the sun, and at this speed the curves and hills came at them like an obstacle course. There was no other traffic—Sunday.

"She's heading for 44," Connolly said. "Why else would they come this way?"

"If they did."

And then, minutes later, coming down from the caldera, the views began to open up and they saw the car below them, moving through the landscape like a figure in a child's picture book.

"Get closer," Connolly said.

"Why?"

He imagined the Chevy for a minute on a canyon road, a short detour, one shot. How long would Hannah feel she needed her? "I want to see if they're both still there."

Holliday glanced at him, then nodded quickly. "You're the boss."

The car, already going fast, speeded up, taking one dip in the road so quickly that for a moment they felt suspended. When their stomachs followed them down, Connolly groaned.

"Open the glove compartment," Holliday said.

Connolly leaned over and pushed the button. The door of the compartment flapped down. He stared at the gun, struck by its size, the bulky carved handle and long, thin barrel. A Western gun. It was like looking at a snake, threatening even when it was still. He touched it, as cold as dead flesh, and held his hand there, feeling another death. But the violence ended with Hector. Karl to Eisler to— The chain had to stop now.

"Ever use one?" Holliday said.

"No," Connolly said, taking it out. A cowboy gun. Chasing the runaway stagecoach across the screen. A prop. Heavy. One shot. "We need her alive," he said, taking his hand away. "She's the key."

"Who?"

"Both of them."

Holliday took a breath. "Leave it on the seat. Just in case."

"Could you hit one of the tires?" Connolly said.

"You don't want to do that. Not at this speed."

Connolly placed it carefully on the seat next to Holliday. It wasn't finished. Guns go off. For a second he wanted to stop the car, stop everything in time before it moved the next notch. Hannah was bound to be caught, somehow. He saw her at a train station, melting into the crowd, leaving Emma in the car. But Emma was still, slumped against the door.

When he looked up, he saw the sign for Jemez Springs. Everything now reminded him of that other drive. They were still dropping, literally putting a mountain between them and the dead man in Santa Fe.

"They see us," Holliday said.

The car in front of them jerked with a new burst of speed. Connolly imagined Hannah's panic. Her one chance was to lose herself in all the empty space, leaving the past behind the mountain. You could do that in the West. Now it was following her, a bogeyman always just over her shoulder. No time to be careful. She would have the gun on Emma, watching her steer, then looking out the window behind, trapped.

"Not too close," Connolly said. "She has to stop sometime."

"She's not going to stop," Holliday said quietly.

Connolly saw the few buildings of town, Emma's Chevy streaking through, past the wide porch of the old hotel, the gas station. Suddenly a police car pulled into the street behind her. *Our old friend the speed trap,* Connolly thought. Emma had been so annoyed. But not now. *Get out of the way,* he wanted to scream, *you don't know.* But the traffic cop, jolted from his lazy afternoon watch, kept on them, his one chance for a ticket. When they didn't stop, he turned on his siren.

The noise cracked the air like a long scream. Connolly felt his own blood pump faster, triggered by the sharp wail, and he knew that Hannah's would be racing. The siren wouldn't stop. It surrounded them, louder and closer, as if the air itself were chasing them. He imagined Hannah turning to see—not just Connolly's car now, but the lights and the siren, a whole posse. She was being run to ground.

"*Idiot.* He's got to stop," Connolly yelled to no one.

They flashed through the town and then they were back in the hills again, but the cop kept going, inching closer to the lead car. *It's not speeding,* Connolly wanted to shout. *You're ruin-*

ing everything. But that wasn't the point anymore. Now it was Emma, hands clenched on the wheel, terrified, the air shrieking around her. And his own helplessness. He'd found out everything and it didn't matter. He couldn't help her.

When they started climbing the long hill, the police car gained on them, the siren still furious and insistent. Holliday, grim, was pushing their car as fast as it could go, flashing his headlights to get the cop's attention. Nobody stopped. When Emma reached the top, the car shuddered for an instant, then banked into a sharp curve. Connolly saw it swerve. Then the squeal of tires as it slid toward the edge of the road, the crack as it hit the tree, so fast that it bounced away, fishtailing back in an uncontrollable circle until it flew off the road, plunging backward over the side. He heard the sound of metal crashing, louder even than the siren, a roar. Connolly's mind went blank. He thought for a second that he could not see, but that was only because the car was gone.

At the top, he jumped from Holliday's car even before it stopped, the momentum pitching him forward, past the traffic cop standing at the side of the road, over the rim, then down the hill in great leaps, sending up clouds of dust. The car was on its side, driver's side up, steam rising from the hood. There was glass everywhere. Running, Connolly thought he heard a new siren, but it was his own screaming, shouting her name. He was still screaming for her when he fell against the car, unable to stop his run.

Pain shot through his chest. He yanked the door handle, pulling with both hands until it finally came unstuck and popped open. The angle of the car made it snap back, hitting him on the shoulder, and he groaned, then pushed it again until it stayed open. She was flung over the steering wheel, her face covered with blood, not moving.

He reached in to pull her body out. Her head fell back. Was she breathing? He put his arm around her waist, pulling her toward him, straining with the weight. She was wedged against the steering wheel, so that finally he had to pull her out by her arms, the lower part of her body dragged along like a twisted stuffed animal. When she was halfway through the door, Holliday came to help lift her out.

"Is she dead? Is she dead?" Connolly was yelling, putting his ear against her mouth. There was a lot of blood, gashes along her arms from the windshield glass, her face almost covered with it.

Holliday quickly bent over, feeling for a pulse, checking for breathing. "She's unconscious," he said briskly. "Help me get her out of here."

"We're not supposed to move her!" Connolly shouted, out of his mind. "Don't you know that? You're not supposed to move her! You could break something."

Holliday looked up at him, using the force of his stare to calm him, bring him back. "You'd better move her. This is going to blow."

A small explosion, not deafening, then a whoosh of fire igniting. Connolly leaned over, covering her as if they were being bombed. When there was no after-explosion, he knelt back, nodding to Holliday, who grabbed her other side to carry her away from the car. They staggered uphill under the weight, finally stopping halfway up. Connolly wiped his face, thinking it was sweat, then saw that it was tears—had he been crying? hysterical?—and fresh blood.

"She's breathing," Holliday said. Then, to the traffic cop, "Here, give me a hand. We have to get her to a hospital. Connolly, out of the way. That's not doing her any good."

He was wiping some of the blood away, to see her face. Holliday touched him on the shoulder, pressing him gently backward, away from her body.

"She's not dead," Connolly said absently.

"Not yet," Holliday said. "Come on."

"What about the other one?" the cop said.

Connolly looked up, surprised. The other one. Flames were eating around the back of the car now, the air pungent with oil smoke. The one who would have killed her. Without thinking, he plunged back down the hill, stumbling, his body shaking with a fury he had never felt before.

"Get away from there!" Holliday shouted. But he had to see.

She was lying flat against the passenger door, her neck twisted, Mills's gun still in her right hand. He looked down into the car, wanting to hurt her more, and then suddenly felt nothing. Her skirt was hiked up, thrown back when the car overturned, and he felt oddly embarrassed. Had she died when the car hit the tree, snapping her neck? Or had she had a few awful moments when the car tumbled over, falling, and she knew. No more secrets. But she'd kept her last one—now she'd never tell him anything. And there was no one else. Connolly had lost them all.

There was another pop as the fire spread from the back seat. He knew he should run, but he stood there transfixed, watching it creep along until it reached her and she too began to burn, her clothes scorching and smoky. He drew his head back, away from the flames that had begun to engulf the car, and through the smoke he thought he saw her body fold into itself, curling up like a secret message burning in an ashtray.

19

The rain woke her. The blinds in Eisler's old hospital room blew in with a small gust, then flapped back against the half-open window. There had been hail earlier, the nurse had told him, but the violent clouds had passed, leaving patches of evening drizzle. She stared at him for a minute, adjusting her eyes to the dim light, to any light. Her face, wrapped in bandages, moved faintly in a dreamy smile. Sitting on the bed, looking over her, he was all she could see.

"Where am I?" she said in a whisper, trying out her voice to see if it was still there.

"On the Hill. The infirmary."

She tried to move and winced with pain. "What's wrong with me?"

"Broken ribs. Dislocated shoulder. Leg fracture. Shock. Multiple lacerations. Some internal bleeding they're watching." He paused. "You'll be all right."

She smiled at the medical report. "I must look a sight."

He felt her unbandaged hand. "Terrible."

"Am I on drugs?"

"Painkillers."

"So I'm not dreaming. This is all real." She moved her eyes again, focusing. "Why do you have your clothes off?"

He was shirtless, his lower chest wrapped in white adhesive tape. "Oh, this," he said, fingering the tape. "Hector."

Her eyes clouded. "What happened to him?"

"He's dead."

"Dead," she repeated, dismayed.

"I didn't mean to hit him so hard," he said slowly. "It must have been the angle."

"I don't understand," she said, confused.

"I hit him with the statue," he said, looking at her directly. "It was self-defense. That's the way it makes sense. There won't be any more questions. He knocked you over—do you remember that?" He waited for her nod. "He killed Karl."

She watched him as he spoke, then closed her eyes. For a second he thought she had drifted back to sleep. "You got your man," she said.

"We did."

"So it's finished?"

"Yes, finished."

She opened her eyes. "Hannah?" she said, remembering.

"She was the contact. The end of Matthew's chain."

"But she never—at the ranch."

"She didn't know. She only knew Eisler."

"All this time," Emma said vaguely, lost in her thoughts. "I thought she was my—"

"She was. She liked you."

"Then why?"

"You got in the way. Like Karl."

"Like Karl," she repeated, trembling.

"Get some sleep," he said.

But she grabbed his hand more firmly. "No, don't go. Stay. I don't want to dream about it. I want to be awake."

"You can be awake tomorrow. You're really going to be all right, you know. You're lucky."

She smiled, her eyes closing again. "Yes, lucky."

"Is there anything I can get for you?"

"Call Daniel. I want to see him."

Connolly nodded. "They're putting a call through. He's at the site."

"It's finished now," she said, not hearing him. "I can sort things out."

He looked at her nervously. "What are you going to do?"

"When I saw him hitting you," she said slowly, "I knew. So clear. Just like that. I killed him, didn't I?"

He didn't answer.

She opened her eyes. "Not the story. The truth."

"Yes."

She nodded. "I thought so. You see what that means? To kill for someone—If I felt that way, Daniel must know. Maybe all along. All those lies. Not his bed. But he knew."

"He never said anything."

"He was waiting for me. To see if it would pass. Like the others. This time he was waiting for me. It was all right, you see, until it was someone—"

He raised her hand to his lips. "I can talk to him."

"No. Me. It's time. When it's so clear. We always think we have time for everything," she said, her voice drifting.

"You're not dying."

"No. But look how fast. When did all this happen? This afternoon? One afternoon."

"We'll have lots of time."

She raised her hand to the side of his face. "We'll go dancing," she said.

"I thought you were dead. In the car."

She moved her hand along his cheek, soothing him.

"Marry me," he said softly.

560

She smiled. "A proposal. Don't you think I have enough husbands?"

"Not yet."

"Everybody always wants to marry me," she said dreamily. "Why is that, do you think?"

"You're a nice girl."

She looked at him as he kissed her hand. "Am I?"

"Hm. I'll even ask your father."

A faint smile. "He hates the Irish."

"I'll bring him around."

"You won't."

"I will."

"Promise me?" she said seriously. "No lies. Not even little ones."

He was leaning over, brushing her lips, when the nurse came in. "Telephone," she said, looking at him with disapproval. "She's supposed to sleep."

"You heard her," he said to Emma, getting up from the bed.

"Don't worry him," she said. "Tell him I'm all right."

"You are all right."

He turned to go, but she stopped him. "One thing," she said, her eyes bright now. "That place they go? Reno? Do you think they'll do two at once?"

He laughed at her. "Use two judges."

On the phone at the nurse's station he was asked to verify that the call was an emergency before he was patched through. The connection was scratchy, as if the rain were on the line with them.

"This is Michael Connolly. We met at—"

"I know who you are," the voice said coldly.

"Look, I'm sorry, but your wife has had an accident. A car accident. She's all right, but she's pretty banged up." A silence. "You still there?"

"Yes. She is all right, you said?" His inflections were still European.

"She has a serious fracture. Shock."

Another pause. "You were with her?"

"No," Connolly said, surprised. "Not in the car."

"Where is she?"

"Here on the Hill. In the infirmary. There wasn't time to get her to Santa Fe. I thought you'd better know."

"Thank you," Pawlowski said politely. "May I talk to her?"

"She can't come to the phone—she's in bed. You can see her, though. Can you leave right away?"

"Leave? Tonight? But the test—"

"Sorry," a voice interrupted. "This is the security officer. I have to remind you this is an open line."

"Listen," Connolly said, annoyed, "*I'm* security too. The man's wife is in the hospital."

"Sorry, sir. Orders. Have you finished?"

"No, we haven't finished. Pawlowski, did you hear what I said?"

"Yes. But if she's all right...," he said, his

voice drifting in the static. "It's difficult, you see. I can't leave here. Not tonight. It's not permitted," he finished stiffly.

"Permitted? It's Emma. She's in the hospital. Just tell Oppie—"

"I'm going to have to interrupt this call," the other voice said. "The use of names is—"

"No, don't. Please," Connolly said. "Pawlowski, you still there?"

"Thank you for telling me. I'll be there tomorrow. Tonight it's impossible. I'm needed here."

"That's it?" Connolly said.

"I'm sure you will look after her," Pawlowski said.

This time Connolly heard the edge. "What do you want me to tell her, then?" He paused. "Shall I give her your love?"

There was a silence, then he said, his voice cold again, "Yes, Mr. Connolly, give her my love."

He was still holding the phone, disconcerted, when Mills appeared at the door.

"Something wrong?" Mills said, noticing his expression.

Connolly shook his head. "Just a bad connection," he said, putting down the receiver.

"She going to be all right?"

Connolly nodded.

"What about you?" Mills said, indicating his taped chest.

"I'll live," he said absently. "You're up late."

For a moment neither of them spoke, then

Mills moved further into the room. "Who's Hector Ramirez?" he said finally.

"Is that his name? I didn't know." He looked up at Mills. "You've been busy."

"I mean, who is he to you?"

"He killed Karl."

Mills looked at him steadily. "Want to tell me why?"

"Later," Connolly said, turning back to the hospital room. "That can wait."

"Not for long."

Connolly stopped, his eyes raised in question.

"Lot of curious people over at the office," Mills said. "The switchboard's been lighting up. Even the boys in Washington. Seems everybody wants to talk to you all of a sudden."

Connolly paused. "I have to see Oppenheimer first."

"Why is that, I wonder? Or is that something else I'm not supposed to know?"

Connolly said nothing.

Mills shrugged. "Anyway, you're not going to see him tonight. Everybody's down at the site. Hadn't you heard? All the cats are away."

Connolly looked at him. "So all the rats got busy," he said slowly. "You playing too? They send you over here?"

Mills shifted, leaning toward the desk. "They have a right to ask questions, Mike. The guy was a project employee, and he's dead. That sets off a lot of bells. Van Drasek's in a lather—what do you expect? And he's got Lansdale jumping on *him*. You can practically hear

564

him over the wire. They want to know what the hell's going on."

"So they sent you," Connolly said. "You the advance party? What are you supposed to do, grill me? Or just keep me company till the big boys arrive? Christ. A little friendly visit. They pick on you for old times' sake, or did you volunteer for the job?"

"Fuck you."

The sharpness of it caught Connolly and he looked away, embarrassed. "Okay," he said quietly. "So you didn't volunteer. Look, I'm not ready for bedtime stories just yet. Not until I see Oppenheimer and Groves. Don't ask why. There are reasons."

Mills glanced at him, then looked toward Emma's room, trying to work out his own puzzle. "Oppie's not back until tomorrow night. I can't stall that long. Don't make this hard, okay? You're supposed to be working with us."

"Us?"

Mills hesitated. "Them."

Connolly smiled. "Okay, then let's make it easy. You got here and I was already gone. Nobody knows where."

"Mike—"

"Don't worry, I'll be back by morning," Connolly said. "Just give me one night. I need to see him. To square things."

"It's not up to me. You won't get off the mesa, Mike. They have orders to stop you at the gate."

"You're kidding."

Mills shook his head. "Remember New York? They're still pissed off about that. They think you're the slippery type."

Connolly looked away, thinking. "Then we'll use your car. You went after me. You figured I was going to the site to see my buddy Groves. Going over everybody's head again. They won't stop your car."

"And where are you going to be—in the trunk?" Mills said sarcastically.

"Just the back," Connolly said easily. "Having a rest. They're not going to search your car. Besides, you're in a hurry." He lowered his voice. "Come on, Mills. Take a chance. For once."

Mills colored, stung. "Why? More games," he said, almost sneering.

"Just one more. A little war game. Don't worry, you won't get shot. Nobody gets hurt, in fact. That's the point."

"They're not the enemy, Mike," Mills said calmly.

"They're not on your side either, you know." Connolly paused. "Just help me finish the case."

Mills stared at him. "Finish how? Another rewrite? Is that what we're talking about? You going to rewrite this too?"

"If I have to."

"For her sake?" Mills said, nodding toward Emma's room.

Connolly ignored the gesture. "Everybody's. It's better this way."

"How do you know? Just how do you decide what people ought to know?"

"I was trained in it, remember? It's how I spent the war."

"Yeah. I thought you gave all that up."

"Almost. Anyway, I won't have to do it much longer. The war's over. Everybody will rewrite it now. Pretty soon nobody will know what happened." He moved again toward the door. "Meanwhile, I could use a ride. Just a ride."

They were still staring at each other, not saying anything, when the nurse came back. She hesitated at the door, afraid of interrupting, then went over to the desk. "She's asking for you," she said to Connolly. "Two minutes. I've given her another shot."

Mills broke the stare and wearily, as if he had lost an argument with himself, turned to the nurse. "You on night duty?"

She nodded.

"No other visitors. That's G-2 orders. You understand?"

She raised her eyebrows but nodded again, a good soldier.

"Thanks," Connolly said to him.

"She doesn't talk to anyone until I get back," Mills said to the nurse, ignoring Connolly. "I mean, not anyone."

"Yes, sir."

"Her husband might show up," Connolly said.

The nurse looked at Mills. "I thought he was her husband."

"Him?" Mills smiled. "No, he's working with us."

567

When he went back into the room, she seemed to be sleeping, and he stood there for a minute watching her, the sheet barely moving with her breathing. He thought of her at Costello's, listening to the revisionist stories, somebody else's Berlin.

"Is he all right?" she said, her eyes still closed. "Did you tell him not to worry?"

For a moment, still distracted, he didn't know what she meant.

"Daniel," he said finally. "Yes."

"He's coming?"

He looked at her, hesitating. "Of course," he lied. "I have to go pick him up. There's no other transport."

"Oh, so far?" she said, looking at him now. "You shouldn't be driving."

"I'll take Mills. Don't worry," he said, leaning over. "I thought you were asleep. You should be."

"I was thinking about something. Hannah. You know she had no family?"

"No, I didn't know," he said, wondering where she was going.

"What will happen to the ranch? We could buy it. Do you have any money? I have some. Would it bother you? That it was hers?"

"Not if you get rid of the corn paintings."

The nurse came into the room. "You really will have to go now. She needs to sleep."

"Okay. You hear?" he said to Emma. "You're going to sleep whether you like it or not."

"It's an idea, don't you think? It's beautiful land."

"Beautiful," he said.

She looked up, catching his tone. "You don't like it?"

"Emma, what would I do on a ranch?"

"You could ride."

"Me? We'll talk about it tomorrow."

She smiled at him. "Have you ever proposed to anyone before?"

"No."

"No. I thought so. You don't know the form. You're supposed to agree with everything. "Whatever you say, darling.' You see? Like that. 'I'll do whatever you want.' "

He took her hand, stroking it with his. "Okay," he said softly. "I'll do whatever you want."

It was pitch dark all the way to Trinity, the night sky obscured by black clouds. After Albuquerque it rained off and on, brief shows of lightning followed by bursts of rain that puddled the road.

"They'll call it off if this keeps up," Mills said, leaning forward to see through the windshield. "The rain'll spread the radioactive particles. A good wind could blow stuff all the way to Amarillo. They won't risk that." Connolly looked at him, surprised at the technical lesson. Mills shrugged. "You hear things."

Connolly had dozed for hours, his chest aching dully, but as they neared the site he became alert, jumpy with the tension of the thunderstorms.

"What happened to the gun?" Mills asked, pretending to be casual.

"It's in the wreck. The police'll recover it. I don't know in what shape."

"You use it?"

"No. I didn't get the chance."

"So the Mex killed Karl?"

Connolly nodded. "I still don't know with what. Maybe with his hands," he said, feeling his sore neck.

"Why?" Mills said quietly.

Connolly thought for a minute. "Jealousy, near as I can make out. Karl was meeting the girlfriend. The guy went into a rage when he caught them."

"That why she ran?"

"She was hysterical. She didn't know what she was doing. Maybe she thought we'd nail her for starting the whole thing."

"Kind of a love triangle."

"I guess."

"And the business with the pants—that was just to make us look in the opposite direction, huh?"

"It did, too."

"How about the turquoise?"

Connolly hesitated. "That's still a mystery. Maybe she was generous to her friends. Older woman. I don't know. She took that one with her."

Mills was quiet for a while. He turned off the main highway onto the road to the site. "You used to be a better rewrite man than that," he said finally.

"I can't help it. That's the way it happened."

"What about all those security files I pulled? They know about that."

"The files? That was—" Connolly paused, smiling to himself. "That was just a red herring."

Mills started to respond, then stopped, seeing the roadblock ahead. MPs in jeeps and trucks were stretched across the road for what looked to be miles on either side, a human security fence. "Christ," he said, pulling up. A flashlight shone into the car.

"Sorry. You'll have to turn back. This road is closed."

"Jimmy," Mills said, recognizing the guard, "it's me, Mills. We have to get to base camp."

"Not tonight you don't. Not even a snake gets through here tonight."

"Jimmy."

"You see this ass? It's not in a sling yet."

"You have a radio?" Connolly asked suddenly.

The soldier looked at him suspiciously, then nodded.

"Radio ahead. Tell Oppenheimer that Connolly's got a message for him." The soldier hesitated, peering at him. "Do it."

He went over to his jeep, and they could see him operating the bulky field phone, then nodding. "Okay," he said, leaning into Mills's window, looking only at him. "Who the hell is he, anyway?"

Mills grinned at him, putting the car in gear. "Better watch that ass." He pulled the car around the jeep and headed into the flat waste of desert. "You sure you know what you're doing? Using his name like that?" he said to Connolly.

"We're through, aren't we?"

"I mean, this is probably the most important night of his life. He might be a little high-strung."

"We're through," Connolly said again.

In the distance they could see the camp lights and, beyond, a single tower in the middle of the desert, held in the beams of giant searchlights. The base camp at Trinity had grown. Barracks and tents had sprouted around the original buildings, and the air hummed with the sounds of makeshift generators and voices pouring out of the mess. Cars and jeeps were scattered at angles to the buildings. The rain had stopped, but small puddles from the last storm still caught the reflected light. Connolly heard what sounded like the croaking of frogs.

It was nearly four in the morning, but the mess was in full swing, dishing out powdered eggs and coffee, flat squares of French toast. Soldiers sat at tables, playing cards and reading with the studied waiting of people in a bus terminal. This time there were civilians too, men in suits and ties and wire-rimmed glasses, dressed to watch history. Connolly recognized Bush and Conant mingled with the scientists from the Hill. *The gang's all here*, he thought.

When Oppenheimer saw him, he detached himself from the crowd and walked over. In a room of nervous people, he seemed to be vibrating with tension, his cigarette hand moving to his mouth in tiny jerks. Connolly had seen him jittery before; now he seemed close to breakdown.

"What the devil is it?" he said quickly.

"I'm sorry. I had to use your name to get in. I need to see you." He glanced around the crowded room. "Alone."

"Now? You want to see me *now*?"

A hand on his shoulder interrupted him. Groves, looking even heavier than usual, a bulging mass of khaki, turned him half around, stopping him. Connolly was struck again by their odd disparity. "Meteorology says it's clearing. Another hour." Then, seeing Connolly, "What are you doing here?"

"After five-thirty there's too much light," Oppenheimer said. "The cameras—"

"They said an hour," Groves said, calming him. "Something wrong?" he said to Connolly.

"Yes, what is it?" Oppenheimer said impatiently.

Connolly looked at both of them, waiting for him. But it was impossible now. There were two stories, not one. Why had he thought Oppenheimer would be alone? "I have to see Pawlowski," he said, improvising.

Oppenheimer stared at him, amazed. "You've got a hell of a nerve coming here at a time like this. With personal problems," he said, almost spitting the *p*'s.

573

"His wife's in the hospital."

"What are you, her nurse?"

"Actually, I need to see you too, but that can wait."

"It can."

"We got the guy. It's over."

"Congratulations," Oppenheimer snapped. "Now get the hell out of here." Then, controlling himself, "Pawlowski's at S 10,000—that's the control bunker for the gadget. You can get him after the test." He looked at his watch. "*If* there's a test. We've already postponed it once. Thirty-mile-an-hour winds. Thirty. Anything more than ten and—"

"They said an hour," Groves said again, reassuring. Then, to Connolly, "I don't understand. You found—"

"Yes, Mr. Connolly's solved his case," Oppenheimer said dismissively, lighting another cigarette. "He seems to think this is a swell time to make a report." He spoke the slang word as if it were foreign. "If it's really an hour, we'd better get Kisty away from that tower. We have to clear all personnel at least an hour beforehand." Groves looked puzzled. "In case a vehicle breaks down and they have to walk. They'd need an hour. It's six miles to the bunker."

"And no one guards the gadget?" Groves said.

"No. We'll give your saboteurs a fighting chance." He checked his watch again. "They'd better hurry."

Groves glanced at him, unamused, then back at Connolly, uncomfortable with an audience. "Let's get out to S 10,000, then," he said calmly to Oppenheimer. "There's nothing more we can do here anyway. We've got the brass all taken care of." He gestured toward the Washington visitors. "You get the driver, and I'll be right along." He looked at Oppenheimer. "The weather's going to be fine."

Oppenheimer, hearing the polite dismissal, smiled. "Okay," he said, then turned to Connolly. "I'll send Pawlowski back after the test. No one leaves there now. As long as you're here, you might as well go up to Compania Hill with the rest of the visitors. Get one of the men to take you. You should be safe there—it's far enough away—in case our calculations are wrong. Of course, that's a relative thing, isn't it? If we're really off, Enrico thinks it's possible to ignite the atmosphere. A chain reaction there—"

"That kind of talk is just out of line," Groves said, annoyed. "I told him."

"Yes. He told me you told him. I think he might have been joking, you know."

"Some joke."

Oppenheimer turned to Connolly. "I'll send him back. I'm sorry if I've been rude. I still say you picked one hell of a time."

Groves watched him walk out the door. "He hasn't slept in two days," Groves said. "We're all keyed up. This rain didn't help any." He brushed his uniform, and Connolly noticed for the first time that it was covered in damp patches.

"I didn't mean to bother him."

"Well, bother me. I've got the time. This darn waiting's the worst part. Nothing to do but go over the same thing, over and over. What's this about solving the case?"

"Eisler was meeting a man called Hector Ramirez," Connolly began his new story. "Spanish. Maybe Mexican—we don't know yet. Big guy. Laborer. He even managed to get himself a job on the Hill—construction or maintenance, I guess. Anyway, not a scientist. Eisler appears to have been his only contact, so he may have been trying to scout out some new business."

"Where is he now?"

"He's dead."

"Dead?"

"I killed him." Connolly felt the bandage on his forehead. "A fight. His head got in the way of some scrap metal."

"You're sure it was him?"

"Absolutely. That's why the fight. He tried to kill me."

"He tell you anything? Who his friends were? Who he passed—"

Connolly shook his head.

"Wonderful."

"He's dead," Connolly said steadily. "It ends with him."

Groves sighed. "Now what?"

"Now I'm going to need a story to tell the papers. It was a public fight. I'd say a woman, probably. They're used to that here. Every Saturday night there's some kind of trouble like that. Police chief in Santa Fe is a friend of mine. I can fix it with him. But you'll have to call your boys off. Your friend Lansdale's already got the net out for me. So give him a call and tell him to keep his hands to himself. I'm a direct report, remember?"

Groves peered at him. "You telling me a story too?"

"General, I'm working for you."

"You're working for your country, mister."

"And both of you are going to get what you wanted all along. You had a security leak and now it's plugged and nobody ever has to know. Just you and whoever else you want to tell. If it were me, I'd keep it to myself. The guy who did it is dead, and the guy who helped him is dead. And nobody knows why they're dead. Not even their bosses. Your case is closed. Now all you have to do is seal it."

Groves looked at him, turning this over. "They'll try again."

"Maybe. Make them work for it. I'd say we've been lucky. Did you really think you could control a project like this? Thousands of people? They know something, but they don't know everything. And they don't know that you know. A poker player would kill for that. That's what they're doing in Germany right now, isn't it? Playing poker? And you're giving our guy signals."

"No, Mr. Connolly," Groves said, looking at his watch. "In about an hour, I'm going to give him the ace."

Connolly hesitated. "Then he won't need anything else."

Groves looked at him. "Such as?"

"A petty crime. That's all this turned out to be, a crime. Nothing else. Not enough to bother people about."

"Let me understand you—"

"Nothing else happened. Not Eisler. Not New York. None of it."

"Why?"

"I think it might be best. For the project."

"For the project."

"Yes," Connolly said, looking directly at him. "Nobody needs to raise any questions now. Not when they have the ace." He paused. "You won your hand." Groves stared at him. "They can turn on you too. You give them a spy case and they'll take the project away from you."

Groves stood still. "I've always played things by the book, Mr. Connolly."

Connolly looked away. "I assume you want a report?"

"What do you intend to say?"

"General, I'm writing it for you. What do you want it to say?"

Groves still didn't move, letting the crowded mess buzz around them. "Paper's a funny thing," he said finally, shifting his leg. "I'll want another briefing. Before we decide."

Connolly nodded.

"Officially, you were brought here to investigate a murder. Nothing else."

Connolly nodded again. "We had a break

there too, by the way. Our Spanish friend liked to beat up queers. We had another case, right on the Hill. The victim identified him. I can get him to testify if it's necessary, though to tell you the truth, I'd like to keep him out of it. You know how nervous it makes the guys in G-2—they start looking at everybody in the showers, just in case. Anyway, there's your link to Bruner, if you want to play that angle. Eisler doesn't have to come into it at all."

Groves took a piece of candy out of his pocket and looked at it thoughtfully as he crinkled the wrapper. "Nice and tidy, isn't it?" he said. "It's not often things end up being so neat."

"Almost never."

"But that's the way it is," he said, a question.

"And the way everybody wants it to be," Connolly said, looking at him coolly. "Isn't it what you asked for the first time we met?"

"I never thought you'd do it."

"I was lucky. Maybe we're both lucky."

Groves looked up at him. "Why do I always feel I'm making a bargain with you?"

"Because you're about to make one. I need a favor."

"What kind of favor?" he said guardedly.

"I said before that no one knows about this except you. But there is one other person. Me. In fact, I'm the only one who's public at all. I killed a man. I'm going to have to explain that. And I'm going to have to make everybody believe just what we want them to believe—what happened to Bruner, what happened to Ramirez, all of it."

"But you said—"

"And I'll do it. I'm good at it. The Manhattan Project is the best-kept secret of the war. Maybe ever. Nothing ever happened. You and Oppenheimer can take a bow. You deserve it. But the war's never going to end for you. Not now. Maybe you like it that way. But I want out."

Groves looked at him, puzzled. "Are you asking for a discharge?"

Connolly smiled. "I'm not in the army, General."

"Well?"

"But I do have a file now. I want you to close it."

"What do you mean?"

"Just that. Lose me somewhere. You've been spying on me ever since this started. You didn't think I could do it, but you couldn't trust me not to. So somebody had to watch. But then you couldn't trust them either, so you got them watching each other. You've got your own chain reaction going, and it's not going to stop now. You watching Oppenheimer too?"

"That's enough," Groves said, angry.

"Your pal. How else could it be? They'd love to get their hands on him, wouldn't they? That would be quite a catch."

"There's no reason to believe—"

"Of course there isn't. But they'll hound him

anyway. Well, that's between you and him. Just don't hound me. You close that file and I close this one. Neat and tidy, like you say." He paused. "And one other. A woman. She almost died today—yesterday. I think you owe her."

Groves raised his eyebrows.

"Don't ask why. Just close her file too. They'll be interested in her, and she doesn't need any more trouble. Erase us both."

"Like that."

"You can do it. I trust you."

"Why is that?"

"Because you're good at keeping secrets. Look at this," Connolly said, spreading his hand toward the room. "A whole city. This one's just a little secret."

"Mr. Connolly," Groves said with exaggerated patience, "this is a military project. That means there are going to be procedures—"

"Yeah, I know, you play it by the book. But the book stinks. It's going to eat you up. Not me."

Groves squinted a little. "Anybody would think you had something to hide."

Connolly looked up at him. "Don't even be tempted. You put those goons on me again, or the lady—The papers would have a field day with this story. Any way I want to tell it. Believe me. I know."

"Are you threatening me?"

"No, I'm asking you for a favor. Let us out of the war."

Groves paused, then looked at his watch again. "I don't have time to argue with you." Then, looking directly at him, "You're sure you've told me everything?"

Connolly nodded. "You can close the file."

A loudspeaker interrupted with the weather report, jolting the room into activity.

"You'd better get up to the hill if you want to see anything," Groves said. "I don't make deals, Mr. Connolly. I can't."

"Your word is good enough for me."

"I haven't given it."

Connolly nodded again. "By the way, what's S 10,000?"

"Ten thousand yards south. Of the gadget," Groves said automatically, distracted by the question. "The south bunker." He paused. "You didn't know that?"

"General," Connolly said, "I don't know anything."

By the time he got to Compania Hill, the wind had died down to the still hush before dawn. Busloads of scientists and visitors lined the sandy ridge, talking in groups around the jeeps and trucks like guests at a tailgate party. Some were looking southeast, toward the small tower in the distance, waiting for the signal flares. The rockets' red glare, Connolly thought, the bombs bursting—a macabre new version of the song. Someone handed him a piece of welding glass and he held it up, the barely visible light disappearing completely behind the tinted square. Was it really necessary? Did anyone know? Some of the scientists had smeared their faces with suntan oil, so their skins gleamed. He recognized Teller, pulling on heavy gloves like a good boy bundling up for the storm. They were twenty miles from the gadget. Could it really burn the air, like the ball of fire over Hamburg, sucking breath out of lungs? Carpet bombing? But this was supposed to be something else.

Most of the men had been there all night and were stiff with cold and waiting. Now they grew quiet, fiddling with the squares of welding glass, stamping their feet warm. There was nothing left to say. Cameras had been set up at N 10,000. Here there were only people, knotting together on a sandy grandstand, anxious and expectant, like Romans at a blood sport. Connolly thought about the first time he'd seen the Tech Area—secretaries passing through the fence, men darting in and out of lab buildings as if they were late for class, everyone too busy to stop, an endless film loop. Now, finally, they were at an end, waiting to see their work, all those meetings and calculations, go up in smoke.

Mills handed him a Thermos cup of coffee. "They say you're not supposed to look," he said. "Even this far. What's that?"

"The rocket. Five minutes."

"Jesus, this stuff goes right through you, doesn't it?" he said, agitated.

"Dark glass, everyone," someone shouted down the line.

583

"The hell with that," one of the scientists said, excited. "I'm going to see this. Even if it's the last thing I see."

"That's a possibility, Howard." A gruff Hungarian voice.

Connolly picked up his welding glass. "What's the matter?" he said to Mills, who was shaking.

"Goddamnit," he said. "I have to take a leak."

Connolly smiled. "Just turn around. I won't look."

"Now?"

"I'll tell you if you miss anything."

"Fuck," Mills said, then whirled around and took a step away. Connolly heard the tear of a zipper, then the splashing on the ground, and smiled to himself, wondering if years from now, in Winnetka, Mills would tell his children how he peed the night they exploded the gadget, or whether that story would have to be changed too.

No one else seemed to hear. They stood as still as stone, looking straight ahead. The second rocket. Connolly was aware of Mills beside him again, holding the welding glass up like a mask. There was nothing to see. Black space, the tiny light of the tower. They passed the last minute. But it didn't go off. Nothing moved.

Suddenly there was a pinprick, whiter than magnesium, a photographer's bulb, and he was blinded with light. It flashed through his body, filling all the space around them, so that

584

even the air disappeared. Just the light. He closed his eyes for a second, but it was there anyway, this amazing light, as if it didn't need sight to exist. Its center spread outward, eating air, turning everything into light. What if Fermi was right? What if it never stopped? And light was heat. Bodies would melt. Now a vast ball, still blinding, gathering up the desert at its base into a skirt that held it in place, like a mesa made entirely of light. The ball grew, glowing hotter, traces of yellow and then suddenly violet, eerie and terrifying, an unearthly violet Connolly knew instantly no one had ever seen before. Eisler's light. His heart stopped. He wanted to turn away, but the hypnotic light froze him. He felt his mouth open in a cartoon surprise. Then the light took on definition, pulling up the earth into its rolling bright cloud, a stem connecting it to the ground.

How long did it take for the sound to follow? The hours of light were only a blink of seconds and then the sound, bouncing between the mountains, roared up the valley toward them, tearing the air. He staggered, almost crying out. What was it like near the blast? A violence without limit, inescapable. No one would survive. Then he dropped the piece of welding glass, squinting, and watched the cloud climb higher, rolling over on itself, on and on, its stem widening until the cloud finally seemed too heavy and everything collapsed into the indeterminate smoke. He stared without thinking. Behind it now he could see the faint glimmer of dawn, shy behind the mountain, its old wonder reduced to background lighting.

He turned to Mills, but Mills had dropped to the ground as if he'd been knocked over by the blast, had lost whatever strength it took to stand. His eyes seemed fixed, mesmerized by their glimpse of the supernatural. Connolly heard shouts, loud whoops and spurts of spontaneous applause, and looked at the crowd. Scientists shook hands or hugged. Someone danced. But it was only a reflex, the expected thing, for then it grew quiet again, solemn, and people just stared at the cloud, wondering what they had seen. He felt an urge to swallow, to make some connection with his body. What had he thought it would be— a bigger explosion? A giant bonfire? All this time on the Hill they had talked in euphemisms. What was it but a larger version of the terrible things they already knew? A sharper spear. A better bow and arrow. But now he had seen it. Not just a weapon. He felt himself shaking. Oppenheimer must have known. Maybe nobody knew. It didn't have a name yet. Not death. People had ideas about death. Pyramids and indulgences and metaphors for journeys. Connolly saw, looking out at the cloud in the desert, that none of it was true, that all those ideas, everything we thought we knew, were nothing more than stories to rewrite insignif-icance. This was the real secret. Annihilation. Nothing else. A chemical pulse that dissolved finally in violet light. No stories. Now we would always be frightened.

He heard a retching sound and looked over toward the trucks, where one of the scientists was doubled over, throwing up on the other side of the hood. A relief from the long tension. Perhaps the first of the night terrors to follow. The men nearby turned their heads away, comforting him with privacy.

After a while people began getting into buses for the long drive back to Los Alamos. There would be a party tonight. The pulse would reassert itself. Otherwise they would have to admit to the fear. In the morning light, people looked haggard and drained, pale under the shiny lotion, their faces scratchy now with morning stubble. They shuffled unsteadily, like guests at an all-night party finally ready for bed. But Connolly couldn't move. This is what they had been doing here, all of them. The cloud was beginning to disappear. He stood watching it drift into the atmosphere, not moving until he could pretend it hadn't really been there.

Mills, still dazed and vacant, drove him back to base camp without saying a word. Here, on the outer rim of the explosion, there were twisted bits of metal and debris pulverized by the blast. Toward the center there was nothing at all. The morning, almost defiantly, was lovely. By noon Trinity would be baking again, the desert shimmering as it had that first time, but everything would be dead. Connolly looked at things without thinking, as exhausted as the scientists, and wondered why he had come back.

Everything that concerned him now seemed inconsequential. This could never be a secret, so what had it all been about? A murder solved. Would Oppenheimer care? And it was Oppenheimer he wanted to see. One last thing.

He'd forgotten about Daniel. They passed the group of soldiers outside the base, collecting sensors and measuring devices in the desert, then stood idly at the camp, not quite sure where to go next. When the man approached him, he did not, for a minute, remember who he was. The project had aged him. Connolly had thought of him as young, a gentle student. Now his face was sharp and stern, as if the blast had pulled back his skin, leaving the cheekbones and receding hairline of an older man.

"Oppie said you wanted to see me."

"Yes," Connolly said, surprised and then embarrassed. Had he really asked to see him? He seemed a figure from before, when nothing was inconsequential. "I thought you'd need a lift back. To the hospital."

"You're very solicitous," Pawlowski said stiffly.

"She thinks you're already on your way," Connolly said. "She'll be worried. You can tell her they sealed the base. It's true enough."

Pawlowski narrowed his eyes. "I thought you were there. Wasn't that enough?" he said, his voice unexpectedly arch.

"She asked for you," Connolly said. "Stop blaming her."

"I don't blame her," he said slowly. "I blame you."

Connolly shrugged. "You want to take a poke at me? It's a good time for it. I assure you, I wouldn't feel a thing."

"Is that why you came here? To fight?"

"No, I came to help."

"Help me?"

"Mills over there can drive you," Connolly said, nodding his head toward the car. "You'd never forgive yourself. What are you trying to do, get even with me? I don't matter."

Pawlowski glanced over at the car, then back again. "I wish that were true," he said, his body slumping a little, tired. "So. A car. Is that the American custom?"

"It's just a car."

"And you think I would accept this from you?"

"Just go see her. She needs to see you."

"So she can tell me everything? The guilty conscience? I already know, Mr. Connolly. I always know. You. The others. Do you think you're the first?"

"But you stay."

He paused. "Yes, I stay," he said quietly. "You wonder how I can do that."

"No. I think you're in love with her."

Pawlowski stared at him, his eyes dull with fatigue. "Why have you come here?"

Connolly said nothing.

"So it's over. Now the apologies."

"No. It's not over," Connolly said pointedly. Pawlowski moved toward the building and

589

leaned against it, deflated. "She wants to leave me?"

"She wants you to let her go."

He looked down at the ground, then up at Connolly, a last spurt of anger. "For you? And I have no feelings in the matter. Is that what you think?"

"No," Connolly said quietly.

For a minute Pawlowski said nothing, looking at the drying street. "I was right," he said finally. "You're not like the others. It's not enough for you, just to take? You want—what? A collaborator?"

"I want her to be happy. She won't be happy if she hurts you."

"So you want me to pretend?"

"Sometimes it's better."

Pawlowski looked at him, the faint trace of an ironic smile on his lips. "Than the truth? Yes," he said slowly. "Perhaps. Each time, you know, I thought, 'Why am I not enough?' Each time." He pulled himself up, moving away from the building. "You're embarrassed? To hear this? You want me to pretend to you too?"

"I'm sorry," Connolly said.

"Maybe it's a relief for me, to say it once." Pawlowski straightened himself to go. "Emma's not a prisoner. She's free to do as she likes." He looked out toward the blast area. "It seems a small point now."

"Not to her. Help her."

He looked straight at Connolly and then over toward Mills. "Ah," he said wearily, "I forgot. In America, always the happy ending. Better

590

than the truth. And so easy. Even a car and driver." He took a step, then turned. "But always there's the loose end, you know. Even here." He looked away, then pointed to a jeep farther along the road. "That needs to go back to the bunker. You'll return it?"

Connolly nodded.

"Straight out that road. You can't miss it. There's nothing else there now."

Connolly watched him walk heavily over to the car and open the back door, nodding to Mills as he got in, not turning around.

The road to S 10,000 was busy with vehicles, visitors returning from the blast area, and soldiers still collecting sensors. Connolly saw Oppenheimer's porkpie hat outside the door of the control station, bobbing in a sea of heads. Somebody was taking a picture. He parked the jeep and sat for a few minutes, not wanting to interrupt, looking out across the waste. When the group broke up, Oppenheimer spotted him and walked over, his face no longer pale, as if it had colored with excitement and was just calming down.

"How about a lift?" he said.

"Sure. Where?"

"Out there," Oppenheimer said, indicating the far edge of the blast area. "I want to get away for a bit. It's quite safe as long as we don't go near the crater. You need a lead-lined tank for that."

The paved road ended a short distance past the bunker. Out on the dead sand, Connolly looked toward the huge blast crater, the sun reflecting off what seemed to be pieces of green glass.

"The ground fused. In the heat," Oppenheimer said calmly.

There was no destination. After a while they simply stopped and got out, looking around at the empty desert. There was no sound at all in the new silence, not even the faint scratching of lizards and insects. Oppenheimer stood still, looking at nothing.

"The worst part is, I was pleased," he said suddenly, still looking away. "When it went off. It worked."

Connolly looked down to where the funhouse mirror of the morning glare stretched their shadows out along the ground. "They'll blame you," he said.

Oppenheimer turned to him slowly, surprised. "You think so? Prometheus?"

"No. Fire was a gift. This is a curse."

Oppenheimer was quiet. "It need not be. It doesn't have to be—this," he said, spreading his hand.

"Anyway, it's the end of war. They won't dare, now."

Oppenheimer looked down. "You're an optimist, Mr. Connolly. That's what Alfred Nobel said about dynamite. He was wrong."

"I'm not."

"We'll see. I hope so. That would be quite a thing—to be blamed for ending war."

"They'll honor you first. And then—"

Oppenheimer looked at him, and Connolly saw that his usual ironic glint had faded.

"Get out while you can," Connolly said.

"After this?" Oppenheimer said, looking around again. "Do you want me to leave the generals in charge?"

"No," Connolly said reluctantly. "You can't." He turned away, kicking at the sand. "Anyway, it worked. Numbers on paper. You found it. Is it what you expected?"

"It was waiting to be found, Mr. Connolly. A problem." And then, a trace of smile. "Like yours, perhaps. Waiting to be found. You said you solved it. Is it what *you* expected?"

"I didn't expect anything," Connolly said. "I just wanted to know."

"Yes," Oppenheimer said, almost to himself. "That's all I ever wanted too." He walked away, lighting a cigarette. "And how did it come out? You were going to tell me."

"Groves will fill you in. A worker on the Hill. There's one thing he doesn't know."

Oppenheimer raised his eyebrows in question.

"He was working for Hannah Beckman. She was Eisler's contact."

"Hannah," Oppenheimer said blankly, as if he had misheard.

"Your old friend."

"We used to go riding. When I first came out to the ranch. But it's impossible. Hannah? She had no politics at all."

"It's possible. It was her."

593

Oppenheimer took this in, not saying anything. "Was?"

"They're both dead. There's no need for anyone to know about her part in it."

Oppenheimer looked at him curiously. "Why?"

"Because you'd be walking into a buzz saw. They're after you as it is. And this one's too close to home. You'd be handing them a gun, you and Eisler. If it comes out that the project was being sold out by old friends of yours, they'll smell the blood all the way to Washington. The truth won't matter. They'll destroy you."

Oppenheimer held his eyes with a flicker of the old intensity. "According to you, they're going to do that anyway."

"Not with my help, they're not."

Oppenheimer smiled involuntarily, then frowned. "So I just—say nothing?"

"You don't know anything to say. You never heard a word."

"You want to rewrite history."

"Just a little. You've made plenty of it to go around. Now just change a little piece for yourself."

Oppenheimer looked at him, thinking. "Why are you doing this?"

"Because I want to keep you out of trouble. I think we're going to need you."

Oppenheimer said nothing for a minute, then nodded. "Thank you."

"Okay," Connolly said, holding his eyes and nodding back. Then, uncomfortable, he turned away. "We'd better get back. It's a great day for the project. You don't want to miss any of it."

"Yes," Oppenheimer said wearily. "I was pleased," he said again, still wondering at himself, and then pointed. "The tower was over there. It evaporated. Just—evaporated. Can you imagine that?" He looked around, now lost in his thoughts. "Everything's dead."

Connolly waited.

"We're going to use it on people."

"I know. Once."

"Twice," Oppenheimer said, correcting him. "There are two. That's what the general said to me right after it went off. 'Two of these and the war is over.' "

"Why not just one?"

"We've only tested the plutonium gadget," he said, a scientist again. "The uranium bomb needs—" And then he caught himself and shrugged. "I suppose he wants to scare them to death."

They started for the jeep.

"This is what they'll remember," Oppenheimer said, looking at the desolation. "Not the rest of it. They'll wonder what we were doing all this time. What am I going to tell them?" He paused. "My God, I was never happier in my life."

"Not just you. Everybody."

Oppenheimer glanced at him. "Yes," he said. "The time of our lives. It won't be convenient to remember that. That we enjoyed doing it." He stopped. "God help me, it's true."

For a minute Connolly thought he would break down, his thin body finally overcome by contradiction.

"People do funny things when they're scared to death. I'm worried about you," Connolly said, unable to keep the intimacy out of his voice. He looked at the frail figure beside him, the hollow cheeks and anxious eyes, and suddenly wished him back at the blackboard at Göttingen, thinking out puzzles.

"I'm worried about all of us," Oppenheimer said.

"I can't think about that many. Right now I'm just worried about you."

But Oppenheimer had recovered and had moved his chalk to the larger problem. "They won't stay scared," he said. "A little learning's a dangerous thing. A lot isn't. Maybe it's what we need—to know this much. To change."

"It won't change anything. They'll hate you for trying."

"Well—" he said, then looked over at Connolly, an almost jaunty gleam in his eyes. "You know, the trouble with you, Mike, is that you don't trust people."

Connolly flushed. It was the first time Oppenheimer had ever used his name, and it took him by surprise, the pleasure of it.

"Sometimes you have to have a little faith," Oppenheimer was saying.

And Connolly felt that he was losing him, that he was drifting away, unwilling to be distracted from his new theorem. "Not them," he said urgently, taking Oppenheimer's elbow as if he were trying to anchor him. "You don't know them. They can't stop now. You have to be careful. You have to protect yourself."

Oppenheimer's eyes wandered to the tower site. "How do you do that?" he said. Then he looked down at Connolly's hand and gently pulled his elbow away. "You know, you may be wrong."

"I'm not."

Oppenheimer looked at him, his eyes tired and knowing. "Well, we'll see," he said. "I'm going to hope for the best."

If you have enjoyed reading this large print book and you would like more information on how to order a Wheeler Large Print Book, please write to:

 Wheeler Publishing, Inc.
P.O. Box 531
Accord, MA 02018-0531